The Schooling of the Horse

*with drawings by Randy Steffen
and Claude (Skip) Johnson
and diagrams by Larry Kumferman*

THE SCHOOLING OF THE HORSE

A Completely Revised Edition of the Book Previously Known as
THE SCHOOLING OF THE WESTERN HORSE

By
John Richard Young

University of Oklahoma Press

BY JOHN RICHARD YOUNG

Arabian Cow Horse (Chicago, 1953)
The Schooling of the Western Horse (Norman,
    1954; revised edition, 1982)
Champion of the Cross 5 (Philadelphia, 1955)
Arizona Cutting Horse (Philadelphia, 1956)
Olympic Horsemen (Philadelphia, 1957)
Angst der Tapferen (Munich, 1968)
Schooling for Young Riders (Norman, 1970)

Young, John Richard.
    The schooling of the horse.

    "A completely revised edition of the book previously known as The schooling
of the Western horse."
    Includes bibliographical references and index.
    1. Horse-training.   I. Title.
SF287.Y6 1982   636.1'0888   81–11539
                                                                  AACR2

For
   Dawn
   Sheilagh
   Linda
   Séan
   and Kristen—
   with the hope that they will understand, some day,
   that this book would never have been written
   but for their Mother

Contents

Preface to the Second Edition, revised   Page xiii
Preface to the Fifth Printing   xvi
Preface to the First Edition   xvii
Acknowledgments   xix

1/ HORSEMASTERSHIP:
    THE MODERN OUTLOOK   1

I   Modern Horse Training *versus* the "Good Old Days" and Ways   3
II   What Is a Western Horse?   22
III   Breeds to Choose From   27
IV   What Makes a Good Horseman?   71
V   Training Equipment and Facilities   84

2/ SCHOOLING ON FOOT:
    BASIC ELEMENTS   95

VI   First, Think!   97
VII   "Horse Sense"   104
VIII   The Foal   116
IX   The Yearling: 1   121
X   The Yearling: 2   138
XI   Behind the Scenes   160
XII   The Two-Year-Old   166
XIII   Is He Ready?   179

3/ MAN IN THE SADDLE:
FUNDAMENTAL PRINCIPLES   183
XIV   What Is a Good Seat: Some Fundamentals   185
XV   What Is a Good Seat: Grip   199
XVI   What Is a Good Seat: Saddles   206
XVII   Tiedowns and Martingales   229
XVIII   Bits   234
XIX   What a Good Mouth Is *Not*   250
XX   The Marks of a Good Mouth   256

4/ FINISH:
COMMENCEMENT   265
XXI   The Three-Year-Old   267
XXII   The Whip   286
XXIII   The Aids   291
XXIV   Collection: The Double Bridle   317
XXV   Spoiled Horses   337
XXVI   Children and Ponies   347
XXVII   A Last Word   355
Appendix   362
Index   373

Illustrations

PLATES

1. The Appaloosa   *Page* 29
2. The Arabian   32
3. The Anglo-Arab   39
4. An Arabian Roping Horse   41
5. The Morgan   44
6. The Mustang   49
7. Registered Spanish Mustang Mares   51
8. The Peruvian Paso   53
9. The Quarter Horse   55
10. The Saddlebred   57
11. The Results of Schooling   59
12. The Thoroughbred   61
13. A Good Grade-Thoroughbred   67
14. A Well-fitted Hackamore   87
15. Types of Mouthing Bits   88
16. An Excellent Dressage Saddle   92
17. Undisciplined Two-year-old Filly   123
18. Tail Rope on Filly   123
19. Filly Leading Correctly   124
20. Weanling in Body Rope   126
21. Three-year-old Colt Fighting Body Rope   127
22. A Felt-padded Longeing Cavesson   129
23. A Heavyweight English Cavesson   130
24. Longeing   133

25. The Bitting Harness   146
26. "With Sidereins Removed . . ."   147
27. Elastic Sidereins   149
28. Ground Driving, Step One   151
29. Ground Driving, Step Two   152
30. All Is Well!   153
31. Ground Driving, Step Three   154
32. Take It Easy!   156
33. This Is Finished Driving   158
34. Relaxed and Content   162
35. The Frolickers   164
36. Tie It Up   167
37. A Well-adjusted Snaffle   168
38. Basic Work Afoot   169
39. The Dropped Noseband   177
40. The Racing Seat   191
41. The Balanced Seat at a Slow Gallop   193
42. The Balanced Seat at a Fast Gallop   194
43. The Balanced School-Seat   195
44. Effect of Saddle on Seat   208
45. A Typical Stock Saddle   210
46. The Stand-Up Seat   212
47. JRY Youth Saddle   213
48. JRY Youth Saddle Rigging   214
49. The "Forward" Seat   215
50. Another JRY Special   220
51. Author's Daughter Kristen   221
52. J. C. Collins Saddle   223
53. JRY Special Schooling Saddle   225
54. The Stargazer   240
55. The Cure   241
56. Big Surprise!   242
57. "Here I Am . . ."   243
58. Ex-Stargazer   244
59. On the Bit and Straight   258
60. Harmony   259
61. The Cavalletti, Step One   275
62. Cavalletti, Step Two   276
63. Cavalletti, Step Three   277

64. The Long Stride   278
65. Steady Hands   279
66. The Riding Whip   288
67. The Reinback   300
68. Finished Neckreining, at Speed   318
69. The Rein Effects   322
70. An Excellent Type of Child's Pony   352
71. Riding Without Stirrups   353

FIGURES

 1. Leading with a tail-rope   125
 2. Driving the colt in the figure 8 in long reins   175
 3. Center of gravity of horse   197
 4. "Kneeing" and gripping   201
 5. Ways of holding double reins   247
 6. Movements of a galloping horse   284
 7. Flexion on a circle   310
 8. Leading rein   321
 9. Rein of direct opposition   321
10. Rein of indirect opposition in front of withers   321
11. Rein of indirect opposition in rear of withers   321
12. Neckrein   321

DRAWINGS

A spirited horse . . . had to be "tamed"   5
The buster was merely a crude imitator   7
The old-time scientific tamer   11

Preface to the Second Edition Revised

MORE than a quarter of a century has passed since this book was published as *The Schooling of the Western Horse.*

During those past twenty-eight years riding in general in America has improved, by international standards, beyond the rosiest dreams of even the most optimistic observers. At the grass roots level, we probably have more skillful young riders than this country has ever known before. In world class competition, such as the Olympic Games, American horsemen have proved themselves as good as the best.

Western horsemanship in particular has advanced quite as much as, or perhaps even more than, other equestrian disciplines. Until only a few decades ago the gap that separated "Western riding" from "flat-saddle riding" was a veritable chasm. Today, among the best horsemen, it is almost negligible. Inevitably, I venture to predict, it will cease to exist. Whatever field one may choose to specialize in, good horsemastership is fundamentally the same in all fields.

These facts have not been lost on knowledgeable horsemen who read as much as they ride, and who occasionally double as book reviewers and sharpshooting critics. One such reviewer observed, "Forty years ago . . . such a book as this [*The Schooling of the Western Horse*] would have been laughed off the shelf, but now it is important and fills a need that has been increasing the past several years."

"One thing I can't understand about the work," this writer adds, "is why the title wasn't *The Schooling of the Riding Horse* instead of *"Western Horse"* because he [the author] discusses all breeds used in this country."

A Canadian reviewer, a career officer of cavalry, begins his review: "The title of this welcome book might give the impression that it deals with Western or stock horses only. In reality, it deals with all breeds of light horses and only some five pages . . . deal solely with the stock horse and the special duties required of those horses, on the ranch or in the show ring."

An English reviewer, writing in the British magazine *The Light Horse*, made the same observation, adding, "but, far from it, it deals with the schooling from foalhood to maturity of all breeds of light horses."

The editor of *The Chronicle of the Horse*, a journal devoted to all forms of equestrian sports except Western riding and gaited-horse riding, reviewed the book even though he considered it "ordinarily outside our chosen fields," because he thought it "a most exceptional book. It illustrates perfectly the fact that the methods of the world's best riders, no matter what type of horses or equipment they use or what they use them for, are basically much the same." He concluded that this book is "just as profitable reading for those who ride hunters across country and in the show ring as for those who ride stock horses on the range and in cutting classes."

Such reviews, reflecting expert opinions, gave me food for thought. Then I began to get letters from enthusiastic readers who said that they found my ideas most helpful in their riding, schooling and general horse management—even though they were *not* interested in the Western style of riding or in training stock horses. They applied my advice and suggestions to whatever forms of horsemanship they preferred, and found them effective.

Some of these readers frankly admitted that they would never have read this book at all if they had been guided only by the title. That restrictive word *Western* turned them off. But they had received the book as a gift, or had heard about it, or had chanced to glance through it just to kill time. Once into it, they were hooked, and they wanted to thank me for all the help it had given them.

Hindsight makes me wonder now why I failed to foresee all this in the first place. After all, a horse is a horse. *What* you hope to teach him is only incidental. All that really matters is how you do it.

However, what finally convinced me that this work needed a better title was my chancing on a copy of Sidney Felton's book, *Masters of Equitation.* This work is a scholarly, critical survey of horsemastership down through the ages, beginning with the first great writer on the subject, Xenophon, in the fourth century before Christ.

Since the main topic of the book is what the author refers to as "the classical school" of horsemanship, naturally almost all the great masters selected for review are, or were, Europeans. A few British horsemen are included, but Felton sees fit to comment on the works of only three native American horsemen. I was astonished to discover that I was one of them, and the book which drew Felton's attention was *The Schooling of the Western Horse.*

Commenting on "the accepted techniques of classical riding" which I advocate, Felton writes: "Obviously, Young is sponsoring methods which are not yet accepted by a majority of western horsemen. But the mere fact that this book was written is an interesting indication of the tendency to narrow the gap between the heretofore accepted standards of western riding and schooling and the methods of the classical school."

Such attention, of course, is gratifying to an author, who often must wonder whether he wrote in vain. However, I have never consciously thought of my horse training methods as being either classical or nonclassical. Usually I just want to get the job done and do it right. Nor am I under any illusion that I rank with the great masters of the past, or even come close to that honor. But I am finally and fully convinced by the consensus of my peers that this is not a book about training only stock horses or about training horses in a narrow, specialized way. This book is about training riding horses for whatever use you happen to prefer. Accordingly, I have simplified the title to *The Schooling of the Horse.* That, in essence, is what this book is all about.

JOHN RICHARD YOUNG

Leapin' Leprechaun Farm

Preface to the Fifth Printing Revised

DURING the few years since this book was first published Western horsemanship has undergone some beneficial changes. The general quality of riding today, it seems to me, particularly the riding of young people, is better than it was a decade ago, or even five years ago. Today more riders are really interested in learning to improve their own skill and the abilities of their horses—I mean interested enough to do something about it instead of merely hope or wish. They are more open-minded to new ideas because they are more aware of the need for self-improvement.

This, naturally, is a source of quiet satisfaction to those of us who, only a few years ago, met scorn and ridicule as radical crackpots or mere theorists because we advocated the ideas which have gradually changed Western riding.

These changes which have taken place are, I am convinced, only a beginning. The day is not far off, I predict, when our Western methods of schooling and riding, and the finished results they produce, will be practically identical with the methods and results of skilled horsemanship the world over. Eventually the twain must meet. There is no longer any valid excuse for equestrian provincialism.

It is gratifying to have reason to believe that this book has had some influence on the improvement of Western horsemanship. I base this belief not merely on the book's immediate and continued success, and not at all on the critic's laudatory reviews (which, in the long run, count for nothing), but on the many letters I have received from enthusiastic readers. In the words of one writer, "The ideas you set forth in this book actually *work.*"

Well, they should. For the ideas in this book have been tested on many horses over a period of many years.

JOHN RICHARD YOUNG

Preface to the First Edition

You will find it very easy to coast along agreeing with the ideas of those about you. . . . Conformity is a very comfortable state.
—*Laird Bell*

THIS is more than a book on the Western style of riding. Though it is written primarily for the horseman who is interested in the Western way of riding, it aims at more than merely telling the reader how to do things. Its fundamental purpose, beyond the imparting of practical information, is to give the reader food for thought and then induce him to *think for himself;* which is a much more difficult thing to do than most persons realize, because so few of them ever really try it.

Any horseman who cares to risk becoming unpopular among his best friends can learn some surprising things about horsemen and horsemanship simply by asking, every time he hears a dubious bit of stable lore, "*Why?*" or, even worse, "How do you know?" To about nine horsemen out of ten there is no more baffling, more exasperating a question. For it forces them to stop parroting ideas they have never really paused to ponder (regardless of whether the ideas are right or wrong) and challenges them to give sensible reasons for what they say. Too often this simple test reveals a lack of logic and sound thinking behind commonly accepted ideas. If you doubt it, try the test with a question as simple as this: Why is it considered wrong to mount and dismount a horse from the right side? Just persist in that sort of game and you will quickly learn a few disillusioning facts about human nature. You may even learn a few useful facts about horse-mastership. But by that time probably your only friends in the stable will be the horses, the dogs, and the cats.

It is long past the time when Western horsemanship should have outgrown the provincialism that has handicapped it in the past. Some of its best points have been obscured and distorted by ignorance; many of its crudities have been perpetuated by a misguided love of tradition or pseudotradition. In many ways, it has remained for too long out of touch with the principles of skilled horsemastership as generally practiced by civilized horse-men the world over. Once there were good reasons for this insularity, but modern conditions have rendered these reasons no longer valid. There is no excuse for the Western horseman of today to lag behind the times, no reason why he should not be as progressive and open-minded in his horse-handling methods as the scientific cattleman is in stockbreeding.

This book is an attempt to reconcile the old with the new. If it accomplishes nothing more than inducing the reader to think for himself, if it helps even one Western horseman to develop the priceless habit of asking himself, always and ceaselessly, "*Why?*"—that alone will make the task of having written it worth the effort.

JOHN RICHARD YOUNG

Acknowledgments

M
ANY persons shared and helped in the writing of this book; some by their active assistance, others by their interest, encouragement, advice and suggestions. A regrettably large number, who shall remain cloaked in the anonymity their deeds merit, helped unknowingly; their examples of bad horsemanship aided me in formulating standards of what to avoid.

I owe special thanks in particular to George and Eileen Baumann; Paul Brandvold; Deering Davis; Joe Dawkins; Robert M. Denhardt; Harry Dick; Myrlin Fallis; David Gaines; Joy Gioia; Don Gjermundson; Francis Haines; Dr. and Mrs. Robert W. Hansen; "Monty" and Jean Harper; George B. Hatley; Claude (Skip) Johnson; Shirley Jones; Douglas Mitchell; Tad Mizwa; Charles E. Osborne, Jr.; Benjamin F. Parker; C. D. Parks; Dr. and Mrs. E. O. Ploeger; Charles Powers; Harold M. Sorenson; Marye Ann Thompson; and Carson Whitson, whose interest and encouragement did so much to make the rough spots smoother.

Extra-special thanks for his expert editorial help and often caustic criticism are due Larry Kumferman, whose Da Vincian virtuosity as a master blivet-buster did as much as anything else, with one exception, to make this book possible—the sole exception being the extreme patience of my long-suffering family while I was writing when we should have been riding.

Part I

Horsemastership:
The Modern Outlook

A man of kindness to his horse is kind,
But brutal actions show a brutal mind.
Remember, He Who made thee made the brute;
Who gave thee speech and reason formed him mute.
He can't complain; but God's all-seeing eyes
Behold thy cruelty; He hears his cries.
He was designed thy servant, not thy drudge;
Remember, his Creator is thy Judge.

—Unknown

CHAPTER I

Modern Horse Training *versus* the "Good Old Days" and Ways

*A perfect book on riding could be written
only by a horse.*
— *Vladimir S. Littauer*

THE ideas on horse management advocated in this book are intended for modern horsemen. Modern, in the sense in which I use it here, means more than merely horsemen of today; the term refers also, and perhaps even primarily, to an individual state of mind. Too many horsemen, even though comparatively youthful in years, are anything but modern in outlook. I have known teen-agers whose ideas on horsemastership were quite typical of an era that was dead decades before their own parents were even born. On the other hand, I have known old-timers whose minds remained always eagerly receptive to new ideas. They were not convinced that they and others of their generation knew it all—or that anybody knows it all. They were much more modern in spirit and in outlook than the junior Wild West teen-agers. It is to such horsemen this book is addressed.

In spite of the nostalgia many of us may feel for the customs and ways of life of the old, historic West—or in spite of the pseudonostalgic pipedreams we may have of a fabulous Old West that never really existed, and would make better reading than living if ever it had—we might as well honestly face the fact that conditions are different now. It is wise and pleasurable to listen to old-timers' tales of the good old days on the range when riding horses were plentiful and cheap, and were "busted" and "broke" rather than trained or schooled. But to accept the ideas on horse management and training which are usually implicit in these entertaining recitals is a mistake—a mistake which young horsemen especially are prone to make. The Western riding horse of today is a quite different animal from the old-time mustang and "broomtail." Often he is half-Arab, half-Thoroughbred, half-Morgan; he may be three-quarter-bred or even purebred. Such a well-bred animal, if broken by old-fashioned rough methods, is quite likely to turn out to be as wild and "ornery" as any Mustang, and much more dangerous because he is larger and more powerful.

Bronc-busting occasionally, though rarely, still has its place in the Western horse world; but its place is not in this book. We shall avoid even thinking in terms of "busting" a horse. Fundamentally "busting" represents a fight between man and horse. Such fights are the chief things we want to avoid.

An almost equally important reason why I shall not attempt to describe the technique of bronc-fighting is that it is a dangerous art and science that cannot be learned from a book. Those who know how to handle broncs need no instruction; they learned how the hard way. Those who do not know how would be fool-hardy to undertake the task without expert, on-the-spot help and supervision. Any amateur who tries to handle a real bronc without having served an apprenticeship under an expert is risking some fancy medical bills.

Besides this, the old-fashioned method of breaking a riding horse, though it may look spectacular to the uninitiated, is quite unsuited to the average present-day horseman's needs and requirements. The days of the "forty-dollar saddle on a ten-dollar hoss" are past. Many horses today not only are well-bred animals; they are often expensive animals belonging to one-horse owners or to small stockmen who own only a few good horses in contrast to the large *remudas* found on most ranches of fifty or more years ago. Even on large ranches of today which do have big *remudas* and brood mares numbering into the hundreds, every good colt is still an expensive animal.

As a consequence, intelligent horsemen today, whether they own two animals or two hundred, want to know how to get the best out of each animal as a working ranch mount, a show horse, or simply a personal pleasure horse. They are vitally interested in getting the highest prices they can for the stock they sell; and it is no secret that an untrained or poorly trained horse will

A spirited horse that resented ill treatment had to be "tamed" like a wild animal.

not, other things being equal, bring the price of a well-trained one.

Finally, but by no means least important, we shall avoid rough-riding ideas in this book as much as possible because such methods simply do not get good results. Any roughly broken horse which turns out to be a winner in any form of equine work or sport, except that of a professional rodeo bucker, makes the grade, you may rest assured, on sheer natural ability and almost incredible willingness to learn, *in spite of* the crude manhandling he was forced to endure; and very often you will find that most of such good horses, after a bad start in life, were lucky enough to fall into the hands of an expert horseman who worked patiently to undo the damage already done. Without such fortunate expert correction, the roughly broken horse that turns out to be a winner would almost certainly have ended his days as a confirmed outlaw or as an abused, broken-spirited nag.

The plain fact of the matter is that bronc-busting, however much skill and daring it requires of a man, is about the crudest form of horsemanship. The old gag that a good buster should have "a strong back and a weak mind" has an element of truth in it. Certainly, an expert buster is, in his own way, a great athlete; but he may not be even a fair horseman, in the proper sense of the term. A twister who "can ride anything with hair on" is very unlikely to have developed good hands and legs that can make a horse light and softly responsive to the aids.

This condemnation of old-time bronc-busting methods should not be misinterpreted as advocacy of wishy-washy, sugar-feeding sentimentalism. A horse should be taught to obey, for a spoiled horse, whether outlaw or pampered pet, is a nuisance, as well as a menace. But the proper way to teach him is not by scaring him witless, bullying him, or forcing him to do something when he does not even understand what it is you want him to do.

"Next to child-training and government comes horse-training and government," reads the preface of a book on horse-training published nearly a century ago; "and which were the least understood, it were hard to say. There are eleven million horses in the United States, and not one man in a million who knows how to educate them to the highest degree of usefulness. . . . That high-spirited or slow-witted boys become good men, and high-spirited or dull colts make serviceable horses, I conceive is due to the grace of God more than to man's energy."

These statements appeared in a book on horse-training written by Dennis Magner, one of the greatest of the scientific horse-breakers who flourished in America during the nineteenth century. Magner and men like him, living in a day when the horse was the principal motive power, made scientific horse management their life work. They had complete faith in the dignity and importance of their profession, even if they all did not always live up to that dignity. Most of them, never foreseeing a future machine age, took it for granted that their profession would last forever. Yet today the average horseman never heard of most of these old "horse tamers." Most of us go through life enjoying horsemanship as a sport and a recreation in almost total ignorance of these old-timers' carefully thought-out principles of scientific horse management and their ingenious methods of subduing the most "vicious" and recalcitrant animals.

Perhaps a brief review of their basic principles and a glance at a few of their careers will prove instructive.

In spite of man's centuries of association with the horse, *scientific* horse management, logically reasoned out from careful observa-

The buster was merely a crude imitator of the scientific tamer.

tion of equine nature and based on medical evidence, is of comparatively recent origin. A rare exception to the rule was the Greek genius, Xenophon. Even the common use of the term "horse-taming" is significant of man's attitude toward the horse until very recently. In spite of the obvious fact that horses in general are naturally timid, and astonishingly long-suffering under abuse, any spirited horse that was quick to resent ill treatment had to be, men thought, "tamed" like a wild animal. Strictly, "taming" referred to that branch of horsemastership which specialized in the reformation of spoiled horses; breaking or training signified the education of colts and mature "green" animals.

The old-time horse tamers devoted most of their attention to reforming outlaws. Thus, they could best demonstrate their skill on animals which other men had given up as hopeless. The ordinary education of colts and unspoiled horses these professionals regarded as elementary, mere kindergarten stuff. They taught that to their pupils; but in order to form classes of pupils as they moved from town to town, they first had to prove their ability on the worst equine renegades anybody could bring them. Often the traveling professional would offer one hundred dollars or more to the owner of any "unmanageable" horse or mule that the tamer failed to subdue; or he would cover all bets that the local yokels would put up. Usually, though not always, the tamer agreed to cure the animal of its vice—kicking, striking, rearing, biting, balking, or an appalling combination of several such vices —within a given time, an hour or even fifteen minutes.

Thus, it can be seen, a tamer had to be good to remain solvent. He simply could not afford to lose and stay in business.

Most of the best old-time professional horse tamers were Americans. Probably the greatest of them all was Captain M. Horace Hayes, an Irishman; but he developed much of his technique from studying the methods of American professionals and from practical experience acquired abroad while touring India, Australia, and South Africa.

America produced the majority of the great horse tamers because stock-raising conditions in this country during the early nineteenth century permitted more unruly horses to develop here than anywhere else in the world. In this country, especially along the Western frontier, great numbers of horses grew to maturity with little or no training; many grew up practically wild, without ever having had a human hand laid on them. When rounded up and "busted," usually by men who knew little or nothing about scientific horse-breaking, many such horses developed into dangerous outlaws. Any man who could handle them successfully usually found horses regarded as "man-eaters" in other parts of the world comparatively simple to "tame." American experts surpassed the rest of the world as horsebreakers because they had such an abundance of material on which to experiment.

In Europe and in the British Isles, on the contrary, stock-raising conditions favored most animals being handled by, or at least accustomed to, human beings from birth. Thus, few European and British horses had much chance to develop outlaw traits. Breaking them was relatively simple, because it was a gradual process—as it should be.

While horse-raising conditions in British colonial possessions and in South America were similar in many ways to the conditions in the United States, none of these lands produced great horse masters such as North America did; for the English approach to horse-breaking, even more than the Spanish, was—and still is to a great extent—fettered by methods and traditions practiced for centuries in the mother country. In brief, what was good enough for grandfather was also good enough for everybody else, generation after generation.

Frontier conditions, however, even beyond grandfather's time, had instilled into most Americans a blithe disregard of traditional systems and methods unless they were, first of all, utterly practical; and from the Mustang-riding Plains Indians they had learned and improved upon a few ways of handling wild horses that were unknown overseas. Consequently, Americans had an advantage over foreigners right from the start. They not only had knowledge of the same traditional methods; circumstances forced them to adapt, improve, invent, combine.

It might be well to point out here that this early American class or type of professional horsebreaker was not the same man, or type of man, as the old-time Western bronc-fighter, that peerless roughrider whose memory lingers on in a haze of spurious glamour. The bronc-fighter was merely a crude imitator of the skilled breaker. With quirt, club, and spur he knocked the fight—and too often the spirit—out of a bronc by brute force. His job was finished even before the bronc's education had passed the kindergarten stage. Often a "busted" horse never progressed even that far; abuse turned him into a confirmed outlaw or a spiritless nag, forever useless. Even when this did not happen, too many Western horses, thus "busted," always retained the vices of pitching, kicking, striking. This is why some of us still labor under the moth-eaten illusion that "even the best ponies will pitch on a frosty morning." Certainly they will—when they've been taught to. Their bucking is the best proof of the wrongness of the way they were broken.

A skilled old-time horse tamer could have made the most spectacular bronc-buster look amateurish. A green bronc or a spoiled outlaw that a buster would waste weeks working over a smart professional tamer could completely deflate in twenty or thirty minutes or an hour, and accomplish the task without breaking the horse's spirit.

Tamers like Magner, Rockwell, Sample, and Hayes performed such feats as a matter of daily business, and there is no mystery about how they achieved their results, because there is no mystery about horse-breaking—no more mystery than there is about judo, trigonometry, or growing tulips. There has always been only a lack of knowledge. The entire secret is in knowing how the horse's mind works, what fears and phobias impel him to resist, how to overcome that resistance by the application of mechanical and psychological principles. Learning this is simple. Anyone can master it.

Practically applying the principles, however, is something few men are really successful in doing. Many persons simply lack the "gift" of capably handling animals. They can learn the science; they can never acquire the art. Taught what to do and how, they still lack that intuitive ability to analyze an individual animal's character and flexibly modify their methods accordingly. It was in this particular aptitude, amounting sometimes to genius, that the great horsemasters excelled.

Then why, it is logical to ask, didn't these scientific breakers put bronc-fighters as a class completely out of business?

The chief reason why these tamers did not make bronc-busters entirely superfluous was that, as highly skilled specialists, they could afford to charge fees that no ranchman would ever have paid simply to have a bunch of broncs thoroughly gentled. The tamers could afford to charge fat fees because they were not primarily interested in breaking horses wherever they traveled. Their business was teaching average horsemen how to break their own horses successfully and what to do if some day they bought a handsome animal "dirt cheap" only to discover that their prize purchase had a nosebag full of dirty tricks that made him dangerous or utterly useless.

The old-time scientific tamer could make a buster look foolish.

This was not an uncommon occurrence in the days when men used horses as much and as necessarily as they now use automobiles. The average horse owner, then as now, was quite as ignorant about his horse as the average car owner today is about his car. Yet every purchase of a mature horse was, in effect, a secondhand deal. If a man were lucky or an expert himself, he might get what he bargained for—he *might*. But the chances were not at all unlikely that in some way, or in several ways, he would get stung. He brought home a horse that turned out to be a lemon.

Even when, with luck, he got a real bargain, however, the average man through his own ignorance often let a horse develop some dangerous habit, and thus found himself with a more or less valuable animal which he could neither reform nor safely use.

It was this common situation that gave the skilled horse tamers their abundant livelihood. It was this fact also, when the horse age faded, that relegated them to limbo. When the machine took over in agriculture and industry, the old-time horsemasters' day was done.

Entirely aside from the typical horse tamer's high fees, which put his skill far beyond the ordinary rancher's financial ability to employ, there always has been—and there probably always will be to some extent—a peculiar state of mind among Western horsemen which made them prefer the spectacular inefficiency of the bronc-buster to the quiet mastery of the scientific breaker. Montague Stevens, an old-time New Mexico ranchman, relates an amusing illustration of this psychological attitude.[1]

One spring Stevens' hired bronc-fighter was injured. With no other roughrider to be hired and with about thirty colts to be broken, Stevens hit on the brilliant idea of using his old-fashioned eight-horsepower threshing machine as a means of breaking his broncs.

This machine had four long sweeps, to each of which a pair of horses could be harnessed and guided in a circle by ropes fastened to the sweep immediately ahead. Stevens reasoned that if he could hitch his broncs to this machine with gentle work horses, the broncs could not do much except pull or be pulled in circles; eventually they would tire out, calm down, and resign themselves to inevitable fate.

That was precisely what happened. The broncs, unable to buck, rear, kick, or even balk successfully, and with no man on their backs to whip, spur, or frighten them, submitted to the breaking process in a few minutes. By this horsepower ma-chine method, Stevens discovered, he could break four horses in less time than a buster could break one. With about thirty green colts on hand, the new method saved much time and expense. In less than a month every one of the thirty broncs was gentle.

"I found," Stevens writes, "that about half of the thirty broncs didn't need breaking at all. They needed intelligent handling. They never offered to pitch, and their restiveness was entirely due to timidity."

Accidentally Stevens had stumbled upon the most important principle employed by the scientific horsebreaker—quickly im-pressing upon a horse its *powerlessness* to resist man. There was really nothing new about the rancher's horsepower bronc-gentling rig. Though Stevens did not know it, his threshing machine was merely a makeshift adaptation of Dennis Magner's patented break-ing rig designed for the same purpose—and Magner probably got his idea from watching an old-time threshing crew in action.

[1] *Meet Mr. Grizzley* (Albuquerque, University of New Mexico Press, 1943).

Elated by the success of his "invention," Stevens offered to lend the horsepower and four gentle work horses to his injured buster. "You could make a good deal of money, and you wouldn't have to take any more chances of getting hurt."

But the buster regretfully refused the offer. "If I went to a man's ranch with that outfit to break his horses, he'd run me off with a shotgun."

Stevens quickly learned that the buster knew cowmen. The mechanical bronc-busting contraption became the laughingstock of the region. One of Stevens' neighbors, a ranchman for whom he had easily gentled a fine sorrel that no buster had been able to stay with, sold his favorite personal mount rather than endure ridicule for riding "a horsepower-broke horse." Finally, even Stevens' own foreman threatened to quit; other outfits were laughing at him and his men for being mounted on mechanically broken cow horses. Even though the animals were the gentlest, best-mannered ponies in the territory, absolutely free of such vices as bucking and kicking, Stevens' men preferred to put up with badly broken broncs rather than endure their peers' laughter.

Bowing to a convention based on ignorance and bigotry, which so often triumph over common sense, Stevens promised not to use his threshing rig on any more broncs and soothed his foreman by giving him permission to hire a new buster.

Montague Stevens' experience raises a question: Would it actually have been more expensive for ranchers to hire the services of a professional tamer in preference to those of an ordinary buster? In some ways it undoubtedly would have been cheaper: an expert breaker would have thoroughly gentled a string of broncs in only a fraction of the time that even the best busters required to do the job much less efficiently. However, it is very unlikely—as Montague Stevens found out—that any ranchman who tried the experiment would have found it easy to hire cowboys; when and if he did succeed in rounding up a crew, it is almost a certainty that most of the riders would have quickly spoiled the well-broken horses they were mounted on.

It is this fundamental attitude, common among horsemen, which so effectively hinders intelligent progress.

On the other hand, it was the precise opposite of this narrow-minded bigotry which helped most of the great old-time horse tamers to achieve the astonishing successes they did. Though financial success tended to make some of them, at least on the surface, act like dictatorial know-it-alls, their attitude was actually quite professional; none of them ever overlooked a chance to learn something new. Like the showman who advertises his circus as "the greatest show on earth," the old-time horse tamers were not bashful about claiming to be, each and every one of them, unique, original, the one and only world's greatest. It was all part of their act.

Most of these self-styled "professors" shared certain traits. They were a colorful blend of showman, charlatan, patent-medicine man, and the real McCoy. Possessed usually of little formal education but plenty of native shrewdness, the majority of them worked up to their "professorial" status the hard way, usually beginning as lads in small-town livery stables. They differed from the ordinary run of horsemen chiefly in their questioning curiosity, their perpetual "*Why?*"

Dennis Magner, in the opinion of J. King Ross, whose father was one of Magner's pupils, was the greatest and most scientific of them all. "His ability to evaluate the methods of his contemporaries," says Mr. Ross, "and to analyze the reasons for the responses he got made him the most important figure in the field of horse management. His methods of subjection are still accepted by the better and more scientific trainers and have never been surpassed by anyone."

Certainly Magner was superior as a horsemaster to the more widely publicized John S. Rarey, probably the most famous horse tamer of the latter part of the nineteenth century. Rarey, an Ohioan, had little success in this country. But, in England, under the clever management of R. A. Goodenough, a wealthy banker who understood more about horse-breaking than his protege did, Rarey "tamed" a notorious man-eating stallion named Cruiser. The English lionized him, and he gave a command performance before Queen Victoria. At a time when a dollar went much further than it does now, Rarey earned an estimated one hundred thousand dollars. But it was on that one feat of subduing Cruiser that most of his fame rests. His methods of subjection were quite limited, and he had learned those few from a Kentuckian named Offutt. Rarey was much more of a showman than a horseman.

Even better than the great Magner, in my opinion, was Captain M. Horace Hayes, author of that monumental classic *Points of the Horse* and other books that any serious student of horse management should not neglect to read at least once. Hayes, unlike most of his contemporaries and predecessors, was a well-educated man, a veterinarian and an officer who soldiered for more than a decade in India. Although he was a good showman, he abhorred quackery; he rejected even the imagination-stirring term "horse tamer," preferring to call himself simply a horse breaker. He knew practically everything any other professional horsemaster knew, because he made it his business to learn, and a lot more others did not know. He was as expert as Magner at reforming outlaw horses, and equally expert in training race horses, schooling hunters, and teaching horses tricks; and he achieved excellent results with astonishing speed, in less time than it would take most men to accomplish half as much. Hayes did not believe that the long way around was invariably the best; more often, he pointed out, it was merely an unnecessary waste of time. He was one of the very rare horsebreakers who understood the art of dressage and high school riding, which he studied in France and Germany. Few other horsemen, if any, have matched Captain Hayes' versatility and his breadth of scientific knowledge.

One of the most interesting personalities among the early American tamers was a friend and contemporary of Captain Hayes, "Professor" Sample. His career is a triumph of tragicomedy verging on farce. Sample was incomparably superior to Rarey, possibly as good as Magner. At a time when there was more accessible outlaw-horse territory to challenge a horsemaster's skill than ever before, Sample, like Rarey, won international acclaim. Then in midflight he rocketed downward into poverty and ridicule, not because he outlived the age of the horse, but because he, as a horseman, invented a machine, which he firmly believed to be one of the greatest mechanical wonders of the world—and in his quixotic attempts to prove that it was a godsend to humanity, he stubbornly, heedlessly, sacrificed his own career.

Sample had all the qualities of a great showman—an affable manner, a quick humorous wit, a penchant for fancy clothes and flashy jewelry, a talent for telling droll stories and an extraordinary ability to win the good will of audiences.

Once, in South Africa, according to Captain Hayes, Sample was driving in an exhibition a green colt that he had just broken to harness when the horse upset the cart on top of him. Spectators rushed into the ring to extricate the tamer from his dangerous position. "Keep outside the ring, gentlemen!" Sample yelled from under the cart. "I'm just showing you how *not* to do it."

On another occasion an excited outlaw the "Professor" was

subduing fell and broke its neck. Sample asked the owner, "How much did you value that horse at?"

"Forty dollars."

"Here's your money." Sample pulled out his wallet and paid the man on the spot. Then he addressed his silent audience: "And now, gentlemen, if you have any more vicious horses to be killed, bring 'em along and I'll settle 'em up."

Prior to Sample's tour of Australia, where he went about breaking the wildest horses anyone could bring him, another famous American horsemaster named Rockwell had won much acclaim by training a team of horses so perfectly that he could drive the pair through crowded streets, making them walk, trot, turn corners, and halt, without reins. This is an extraordinary feat of training that takes a great deal of time, patience, and skill; but by recognizing opportunity when he saw it Sample topped Rockwell's achievement.

In Australia the Professor was challenged to break a horse that for years had stubbornly resisted all attempts to make him pull between shafts. While Sample was hitching the animal to the rear of his light trap, the horse broke loose. Unable to catch the brute, Sample gave up and drove off to his hotel.

To his astonishment, the loose horse immediately cantered out ahead of the harnessed one and settled into a smooth trot, as if he were the leader of a tandem. When Sample slowed, urged on, turned, or halted his horse, the renegade did exactly the same as the "wheeler."

Telling no one of the outlaw's freak behavior, Sample bought the horse. Then with plenty of advance ballyhoo he gave public demonstrations that made Rockwell's marvelous training accomplishment pale into insignificance.

Such chicanery among the professional horse-taming gentry was considered perfectly ethical showmanship. Intensely jealous of one another's success, most of those old-time professionals took every opportunity to demonstrate their right to the title "the world's greatest horse tamer."

Greater than his showmanship, however, was Sample's uncanny insight into a horse's mind. Since no two horses are the same, a successful breaker must suit his methods to each subject. A procedure that will work well on a high-spirited, courageous horse usually fails on a stubborn, sullen "jughead." Sample seemed to be able to psychoanalyze a horse by merely glancing at it. In Australia he earned an even greater reputation than he had already won in

America. Taking the wildest, most spoiled brutes as they came, the Professor subdued horses other men had fought vainly for years. At the conclusion of one class—or so he said—his enthusiastic pupils presented him with a fifty-guinea watch.

One day, in about 1885, a well-meaning amateur advised the great man that he was wasting his talents Down Under. The really big money was waiting for him in England.

At this time Sample's troupe consisted of his chief assistant, a former printer's clerk known as Franklin, but whose real name was Sexton; an Australian roughrider named Frank; and a roustabout handyman, Joe, who had once been a sailor. Sample took this crew along to England.

In London the great horsemaster found himself completely out of his element. The English had no outlaw horses worthy of his skill. Animals that the English considered dangerous or unmanageable were, by Sample's standards, merely ill-mannered plugs, too docile to enable him to put on an interesting show.

Besides this—and it was a lesson the elderly Professor never could learn—Englishmen did not want to learn horse-taming. They attended a horse-breaking demonstration for the same purpose that lured them to a music hall or the theater. They wanted to be amused, entertained. Despite his keen sense of showmanship, Sample could not see his work in this light. To him, his great mission in life was to teach others some of his own mastery of horse-breaking.

In London, Sample discovered one of his former assistants, Sydney Osburn, putting on a successful "taming" act as "Professor Galvayne." Osburn, using crotchety English plugs, was merely imitating what he had seen Sample do expertly with genuine outlaws in Australia. But now he was advertising his phony act as his own original "Galvayne System."

When Sample's chief assistant, Sexton, *alias* Franklin, saw what his predecessor, who happened to be also his brother-in-law, was getting away with, he picked a quarrel with the Professor and quit. A few weeks later this genius himself blossomed out, complete with sombrero and boots, as "Professor Leon, the Celebrated Mexican Horse Tamer."

Sample, thoroughly exasperated, threatened to expose "Professor Galvayne" as a fraud. Osburn begged him not to; he even promised to round up the most vicious horses to be found in England for Sample's first London show. Sample relented. Osburn, however, assuming he really tried, failed to produce any real outlaws. Sample's show, widely advertised, turned out to be a complete flop. It cost him nearly five thousand dollars.

That was just the beginning of the Professor's bad luck in England. Everywhere he showed he found that "Professor Galvayne" had been there ahead of him, and even "Leon," the pseudo-Mexican. These two natural phonies, with neither skill nor talent in horse management, were experts only at faking spectacular performances; indeed, with really bad horses they could never have succeeded. Sample, on the other hand, made even difficult horses look easy. His complete mastery, utterly wasted on park-riding, fox-hunting Englishmen who hardly knew what a really bad horse was, worked against Sample. He was trying to demonstrate a great skill which almost nobody in England had the knowledge to appreciate.

Instead of leaving the foxhunters and park riders happy in their ignorance and going to some country where outlaw horses abounded, Sample stubbornly persisted in trying to sell the English the real thing in horse-taming. He wanted a "London triumph." It galled his pride to fail where mediocrities like Sexton and Osburn succeeded. And it is very likely that he wanted to stay in England so he would have at hand the mechanical facilities and craftsmen he needed to help him give material form to his new dream—the Machine.

The first conception of this new invention seems to have developed in Sample's active brain shortly after his arrival in London. It was based on his successful practice of forcing an unruly horse to chase its tail until it became dizzy—a procedure we shall discuss later in this book. The more he pondered the idea, the more enthusiastic he became. He predicted to his friend Captain Hayes that his invention would revolutionize horse-taming and "lick creation." Planning to patent the machine in all principal countries, the Professor foresaw a golden future.

The machine he had in mind was simply a horse box with movable sides that could immobilize a horse exactly as cattle on many modern ranches are immobilized in a squeeze chute or pen for branding, dehorning, etc. The box was to be mounted on a revolving base powered by a steam engine. Sample theorized that he could put the wildest outlaw into this machine, spin the animal rapidly until it was so dizzy it would hardly know its head from its tail, and thus in a few minutes have the addled horse "as tame as a mouse."

Sample entirely overlooked the fact that not one horse in a

hundred reared under civilized conditions ever would need such drastic treatment; and in colonial territories, where spoiled and untamed horses abounded, the cost of importing such an unwieldy contraption, as well as the difficulties of transporting it from place to place, would have been prohibitive.

Sample spent five years and fifteen thousand dollars building and rebuilding experimental models of his great invention. Most of the money he had to borrow, for while developing the machine he neglected all other business.

In 1891 he exhibited his masterpiece in Hengler's Circus in London. His infatuation with his invention and his absolute certainty that it would work apparently robbed the old horsemaster even of his sense of showmanship. Londoners came to his show to be entertained—and Sample, with the seriousness of a zealot, treated them to a drearily technical performance that could have interested only fellow experts. The widely advertised show fell flat. It was, in Captain Hayes' words, all machine and no show. To meet some of the expenses, Sample was forced to hock his mechanical treasure.

Ironically, the machine fulfilled every one of its inventor's claims. It took the fight out of recalcitrant horses more thoroughly, in less time, and with less effort than any other taming method ever devised. The effectiveness of the contraption so impressed the Chief Veterinary Surgeon of the British Army, a former president of the Royal College of Veterinary Surgeons, that he voluntarily wrote the Professor a flattering testimonial.

But for show purposes the machine was utterly useless. It neither amused not excited an audience.

Sample, however, with the single-mindedness of a fanatic, was convinced that he had a great thing. When his old assistant Sexton seized this opportunity to challenge him to a public horse-taming contest, a committee of experts to decide the winner, Sample borrowed money from his friend Captain Hayes to cover "Professor Leon's" bet and to get his machine out of hock.

The contest was scheduled nightly for two weeks at the Imperial Theatre in London. On the opening night, because of the down-slope of the stage, Sample's machine would function only in slow motion. The audience greeted the old man's frantic attempts to get the thing going with derisive laughter. He was finally forced to have the contraption dragged off the stage.

Then Sexton, *alias* "Professor Leon," swaggered out on the stage wearing a sombrero, a Norfolk jacket, and fishing boots—

the well-dressed Mexican horse tamer! According to Captain
Hayes, from a horseman's viewpoint his work was inept, superficial, ridiculous; but his swarthily handsome appearance, cocky
self-assurance, and faked "dangerous" way of handling a horse
went over big with the audience.

The following night Sample, still deprived of his machine, had
the good luck to face a really vicious stallion. The brute, notorious
as a "man-eater," had savaged several men and was a genuine
outlaw.

Sample, harassed by worry, debts, poor health, and public
ridicule, looked frail and old in his shabby evening clothes as
he calmly announced that he would have the savage stallion
turned loose on the stage. "Merely with a buggy whip, ladies
and gentlemen," he told the audience, "I shall, without hurting
him, make this horse so quiet that he will walk up to me to be
petted."

An assistant swung open the gate of a horse crate in the wings.
Onto the stage, as into an arena, charged a big bay stallion. Jaws
gaping, ears flattened, the stud rushed at the old man. Sample,
popping the whiplash, diverted the charge.

As though the whip were a magic wand, the old tamer controlled the stud, at once preventing him from attacking, from
rushing into the wings, from leaping over the footlights into the
audience. Each time the horse whirled to kick, Sample goaded
him into facing around with inescapable flicks of the whiplash
on the hindquarters.

Finally, powerlessness to do anything else forced the stallion
to stand still. Then step by step under the dreaded whip's exacting
guidance the horsemaster forced the animal to approach to within
arm's length.

In less than fifteen minutes Sample fulfilled his promise to the
audience. The horse stood motionless under his hand, unmoved
even by the spectators' thunderous applause.

That night at dinner Captain Hayes, Sample's backer, was
jubilant. "You can make a fool of Sexton, if you'll just forget
that infernal machine."

Sample shook his gray head. "I hope to have it running for
tommorrow night. I really don't care about winning, you know."

"Well, I do!" Hayes said. "It's my money."

"Listen, Horace, the only reason I took this challenge was to
get my machine before the public, to let people see for themselves
what a great invention it is. Don't worry about your money,

Horace. Sexton is in on this. Do you suppose that faker would actually challenge *me?* The whole idea is to advertise my machine, the greatest invention in the — —.''

"Then you're fleecing the public!" Hayes' Irish temper erupted. "I'll have nothing to do with such a scheme."

The next day Hayes withdrew his name and his backing. Somehow, the rumor leaked out that the contest was a sham. Some of the prominent judges withdrew from the committee. The public refused to be sucked in. The whole affair fell flat. Not once was the old Professor able to demonstrate his marvelous machine, the chief end and purpose of the whole fiasco.

Not long afterward, swamped in debt, tired and ill, but still indomitable, "Professor" Sample died. To the end he remained unshaken in his conviction that he had given the world a great thing and that some day the world would be forced to acclaim it—a much greater boon to humanity than that "newfangled contraption" called the horseless carriage.

CHAPTER II

What Is a Western Horse?

The only approbation a rider should
covet is that of his horse.
— *E. Beudant*

A<small>LTHOUGH</small> the principles of training advocated in this book apply equally to all riding horses, whatever particular field they may ultimately specialize in, it is well for us to have clearly in mind what type of mount we mean when we speak of "a Western horse" and why we use the term restrictively. The term has no reference to a horse's breed; he may be of almost any breed or mixture of breeds. Rather, the term denotes a general type of horse. This type is at once rather loosely, yet quite rigidly, limited by the kinds of work Western horses are commonly called on to perform. Since almost every job and riding sport which Western horsemen favor demands a rather high degree of handiness of their mounts, probably the fundamental guiding rule is that a Western horse must not be too big, too tall. A horse of 14 hands, though he may look too small under a tall rider, is big enough. If up to his rider's weight, such a small horse will almost certainly prove to be more suitable than a horse 16 hands tall. There are exceptions to all rules, but, generally speaking, a horse taller than 15.1 hands is more handicapped than helped by his size in ranch work, competitive show work, and general Western riding. The only blanket exception to this is the parade horse that is not expected to do anything more strenuous than delight spectators by his flashy appearance and animated way of going.

For years spinners of romantic fiction tales set in a West that never existed and horse authorities who had never been west of the Mississippi conveniently lumped all Western nags that could stand up under stock saddles and were lacking traceable pedigrees as "cow ponies." The Eastern experts still too often continue to do it. So do quite a few ranchmen who think entirely in terms of stock horses. This labeling, however, is as erroneous as terming every Virginia horse a hunter or every Kentucky horse a Thoroughbred. Certainly, it is far from adequate in describing the average Western horse of today.

It is a pretty safe guess that the bona fide working stock horse that truly merits the term "cow pony" is, today, a rarer animal than most people think. Even on large ranches the working cow horse whose primary purpose in life is to work cattle is less common than his prototype of several decades ago. Modern stock-handling methods require fewer horses and demand of those less real all-round cow work. As an old-time cattleman said, in answer to the criticism that Western horses of today are not as good as those of forty or fifty years ago: "They're as good or better. The trouble is there isn't enough work for them to do. Their jobs get scarcer every year."

One consequence of this state of affairs is that the term "stock horse" is now so loosely used as to be almost meaningless. Horses that have never "looked a cow in the eye," and wouldn't know what to do if faced with one, win so-called "stock horse classes" in shows. They go through all the motions without ever doing the real work. Probably this class of show stock horse is at least twice as numerous as the genuine working cow horse to be found earning its keep on ranches. Many of them are strictly show horses, as much so as gaited Saddlebreds. That they have never actually worked stock, however, does not mean that they could not do the real job. But, usually belonging to owners who live on farms or in towns, these animals have never had a chance to work cattle. Undoubtedly some of them would make excellent cow horses.

Another kind of modern show horse, similar to the cowless wonders of the tanbark ring, is the synthetic stock horse—a horse that has been trained to work cattle but has never done so under actual working conditions out on the range. The synthetic stock horse, whatever his particular specialty may be—he is often seen in cutting contests—receives practically all his specialized training within the confines of an arena or corral. Aided by level ground underfoot, he can put on a spectacular performance inside a comparatively small enclosure; but just how well he would work out in the open under normal range conditions such as genuine stock horses take in stride can be determined only by giving him a chance to try it. Some horses, adapting to the new conditions quickly, make the switch without trouble. When this does happen, your ex-synthetic stock horse of the arena usually makes the ordinary ranch horse look like an amateur; for he is likely to bring to the job a finer finish, a more smoothly working set of polished reflexes, than the average stock horse ever develops. It does not, however, always work out that way. Many flashy arena contest horses fail to make the switch to range conditions successfully; at best, they prove themselves to be only mediocre performers. Their failures point up conclusively the artificiality of the conditions under which they are trained.

Trail horses are just what their name signifies, and nothing more. They should not be termed stock horses simply because they are ridden in stock saddles.

The parade horse is the one class of Western mount that may be of any height. He is the peacock of the Western horse world; height often adds to his impressive appearance, especially when he is loaded with silver trappings. King Cortez, a California palomino well known as a winning parade horse, stood 17.2 hands tall. Many parade horses are Saddlebreds or are rich in American Saddle Horse blood.

The professional rodeo horse usually is a specialist, working only in one event. His sole purpose in life is to help his rider win money in contests. Though he works with stock, he cannot, strictly speaking, be classed as a bona fide stock horse. Instead, working under artificial conditions and often performing a task which has little relation to actual ranch work, he is more closely akin to the professional show horse. Since his value is reckoned by the amount of prize money he enables his rider to win, the rodeo specialist is generally considered to be too valuable to risk at any work other than his particular specialty. Occasionally, of course, an exceptional horse proves his outstanding ability at more than one job—for example, at both calf roping and steer roping—but such a mount is a rarity. Horses especially trained for such artificial events as pole-bending and barrel racing no more merit the title "stock horse" than would a King Cortez. A trick rider's reliable, straight-running mount need not know a cow from an elephant, yet he can be more valuable to his owner than would a dozen working stock horses.

Probably the most important riding horse on the Western scene today is none of those already mentioned. Instead, he is the personal mount of the average Western horseman who rides for recreation—the so-called "weekend rider," whom the know-it-all, born-in-the-saddle buckaroos too often scorn. This type of riding horse is much more numerous today than any of the show ring specialists or the working ranch horse. With the exception of the latter, probably this common ordinary everyday "using" horse more often has a greater claim to the title "stock horse" than do most of the fancier animals trained to compete in the ring. He might well be called the "part-time stock horse," for often he is asked to do everything his more pampered betters specialize in doing, and usually he tackles his variety of "odd jobs" with astonishing willingness. At home, he may help with handling stock, even if the job is no more than driving in the milch cows or herding a few steers from one pasture to another. On weekends this old pony is usually in his element. On Saturdays he often doubles as a trail horse. Perhaps the next day he works as a calf-roping mount, carrying his master in competition with other members of the local roping club—the jackpot may be small, but the enthusiasm is keen. He competes in local horse shows in whatever events his master fancies. At a gymkhana he may be called on to do his best in pole-bending, a quarter mile race, and a trail horse class; then he will carry Junior in a children's horsemanship class. When the Chamber of Commerce stages the town's annual rodeo you'll see him prancing in the parade—and later in the afternoon he will haze for the bulldoggers. In big-time competition he would not stand a chance against the specialists. He is seldom much for looks. No one will ever offer a four-figure price for him. But to his own family, the folks who belong to him, his value often transcends mere money. If he does not quite merit the accolade "stock horse," he is much nearer to the real thing than most professional show horses that could make him look amateurish in the ring.

The reader should realize, however, that "Western horse" and "stock horse" are really very elastic terms. This will be more evident when we discuss the Thoroughbred. In Australia and New Zealand, for example, most stock horses are of predominantly Thoroughbred blood. They do the same work our Quarter Horses do, and they do it well. In my opinion, a good working field hunter, whether Thoroughbred, grade-Thoroughbred or Irish cob or anything else, has all the inherent qualities of an excellent stock horse. On the other hand, one of the best stock-horse types I have ever owned, or have any hopes of ever owning again, was a blend of Arabian and Welsh pony blood. Another, maybe as good or better, was a mixture of Thoroughbred, Saddlebred and Arabian. Morgan horses have excelled in ranch work as well as in the show ring. If a horse, of whatever breed or size, can do the work, he qualifies as a good "Western horse."

CHAPTER III

Breeds to Choose From

*It has been stated often that some horses are
naturally vicious. There is no such thing
as a horse being born vicious. Viciousness
is simply a product of bad handling. . . .If
we bring a horse up to be a devil we cannot expect the behaviour of an angel.*
— *Colonel R. S. Timmis*

IT IS not within the province of a book on schooling
and training to dwell on the origin and history,
real or legendary, of any particular breed. Whether the Quarter
Horse is an established breed or merely a type; whether the
Arabian can be traced back in perfect purity of blood to pre-
historic times; or what was Justin Morgan's exact breeding: such
questions, though interesting in themselves, do not concern us,
except insofar as they may influence the present suitability of a
horse for our particular needs. From this latter point of view,
however, it is desirable for us to look at various light horse breeds,
or types, in an effort to determine what qualities each one has
which we want in a riding horse, as well as those characteristics
which we don't want.

Probably the most difficult part of this difficult task of critically
examining and evaluating is the vital necessity of looking at each
breed with an open mind and an unprejudiced eye. Almost all
horsemen have favorite breeds, and in a breed they prefer certain
strains and like certain horses best. As a rule, the basic reason
for their personal preference is sound: their favorite breed produces the sort of riding animals they like. Unfortunately, however,
hand-in-hand with this preference for one particular breed goes an
unreasonable antipathy for, or antagonism toward, other breeds.
Anyone who has been around horsemen for any length of time
can hardly have escaped the lamentable observation that too many

of us are narrow-minded bigots. Favoring one particular breed or
type of horse, many of us are openly scornful of some other breed
without having adequate grounds for our scorn based on genuine
knowledge. Very few of us have either the time or the means —
and too many of us might lack even the inclination — to "dabble"
in one breed after another over a period of years until, after much
testing and judging without bias, we *might* be competent to evaluate them all with reasonable accuracy. Unfortunately, hardly
one horseman in a thousand enjoys such varied experience. The
majority of us base our judgments mostly on personal prejudices.
Invariably this prejudiced attitude stems from lack of experience;
often it is an outgrowth of our own personal inadequacies as
horsemen. We cannot fairly judge a breed that we do not know,
or accurately evaluate the potentialities of a horse that we lack
the skill or the cool temperament to master.

The following remarks on leading light horse breeds are not
intended to be either interpretations or repetitions of the various
standards of judgment used in the show ring. They are intended
as general evaluations of the various breeds from the viewpoint
of Western horsemen's needs and requirements in horses they
ride. The reader is not asked to accept any of the statements
uncritically, but simply as observations meant to guide him in
the selection of a horse best suited to his own individual needs.
The reader should bear in mind, however, that the following
remarks about each breed are not the expression of just one man's
opinion. They represent a consensus formed by many horsemen
who have had much experience not only with the particular breed
of which they speak but with other breeds as well.

THE APPALOOSA (Plate 1)

As a working stock horse, the Appaloosa ranks with
the best. He has the physical toughness and the good-tempered
disposition a real cow horse needs. Most Appaloosas are of stock
horse type, for that is the kind of mount a majority of Appaloosa
fanciers prefer. Directors of the Appaloosa Horse Club have been
wise in formulating a standard that is based on the consensus of
most breeders of registered stock, the men who know what they
want and whose ideas shape the breed. Thus, for example, while
a typical Appaloosa may be as tall as 15.2 hands and weigh
1,200 pounds, most breeders prefer a horse between 14.2 and

Plate 1. THE APPALOOSA. Joker B., the Appaloosa immortal that was bred a Quarter Horse. This stallion could do it all. One of the greatest of sires, he won on the track, in the show ring, in the performance arena. A child could handle him; a novice could ride him. Joker B. was one of the truly great ones.

Courtesy Bob Gray

15 hands and weighing about 1,000 pounds. This is nearer the ideal size for a working stock horse.

Men who use him consider the Appaloosa the ideal horse for rough country. Besides possessing stamina and endurance, the Appaloosa is seldom bothered by leg trouble. One of the characteristics of the breed is that the hoofs are usually parti-colored, striped black and white vertically. Most horsemen consider black hoofs harder than white ones; Appaloosa fanciers generally regard the striped hoof as the toughest for rough going, since it is composed of alternate "hard" and "soft" layers and is therefore more "elastic."

Good disposition and willingness to learn are among the Appaloosa's most satisfactory traits. Generally, he is easy to school.

Even range-raised Appaloosas, when caught up as two- or three-year-olds, show little inclination to buck. Claude J. Thompson, founder of the Appaloosa Horse Club, in a personal letter to the author wrote of his stallion Red Eagle: "I took him up in the fall, after he had been foaled in the spring but had never had a hand laid on him. Five days later I showed him and he made a perfect showing."

Significantly perhaps, Red Eagle was sired by a registered Arabian, Ferras. "The more I study the Appaloosa horse," Mr. Thompson writes, "the more I am convinced he is rich in Arabian blood notwithstanding the fact that some Appaloosas show draft characteristics. Draft blood was infused by early settlers and missionaries who would make work horses out of the once proud war horses of the Indians."[1]

Not all Appaloosa fanciers share or welcome the idea that their spot-rumped horses are, or should be, "rich in Arabian blood," however. In a letter to the author, Francis B. Haines, president of the Appaloosa Horse Club, points out: "The Appaloosa has suffered seriously from many years of outcrossing, so it is weakened somewhat. [But] Appaloosa traits are dominant, so the colts are usually Appaloosa if one parent is. . . . Appaloosas have bred true in several important characteristics for 2,400 years. . . . Certainly this goes back farther than any other horse, *in authentic records.* It is interesting to know that horses reached Arabia about 100 A.D., and the Arabian breed was developed after that." From this viewpoint the Appaloosa horse owes the Arab nothing for his exceptionally good disposition and ability to learn.

Most Appaloosas have a natural running walk—the so-called "Indian shuffle"—an easy gait for covering long distances. According to Robert L. Peckinpah, writing in the *Appaloosa Horse Club Stud Book and Registry* (second edition), Appaloosas have "won more win, place and show monies contesting in 'open' endurance races than have all the other registered breeds combined."

Today, this rather sweeping statement, written a quarter of a century ago, might be disputed and refuted by Arabian enthusiasts, for the popularity of competitive endurance riding has greatly increased. Most successful horses in the sport now are specialists, and most of the consistent winners are of predominantly Arabian blood.

[1]Claude J. Thompson, in *Equestrian*, February, 1948, 19.

THE ARABIAN (Plate 2)

In the horse world, no more controversial breed exists than the Arab. As a general rule, the Arabian is either wonderful or worthless—depending on to whom you listen. Thoughtless admirers of the breed are prone to claim almost a monopoly of all equine virtues for their favorite, while equally thoughtless anti-Arab horsemen are inclined to damn this fountainhead of hot blood for possessing more faults than any breed could possess and still flourish.

Somewhere in the often acrimonious welter of pro and con chaff can be found some kernels of truth. The problem is not merely to recognize them but frankly to admit the recognition, acknowledging facts as facts. This, however, simple as it may sound, seems to be more easily suggested than accomplished. Apparently, it is almost impossible for many horsemen to look at the Arabian objectively.[2]

The reasons for many Western horsemen's prejudice against the Arabian are varied and sometimes rather baffling. These reasons may be summed up briefly as follows:

Arabian breeders themselves, in general, are the first to admit that the Arab horse is too expensive for the majority of horsemen; few riders can afford, or are willing, to pay the usual prices asked for good Arabians, prices which have steadily soared until now a good Arab of broodstock quality costs about as much as a good Thoroughbred racehorse. Therefore, it is natural for most of these horsemen to rationalize that the kinds of horses that they can afford, or are willing, to buy are better, anyhow. But, say Arab enthusiasts, secretly these men are jealous of and envy the Arabian horse's natural ability to excel at almost any job for which he is properly trained—an excellence based on physical and mental superiority.

Arab adherents also point out that purebred Arabians are relatively few in number compared to specimens of other breeds. Hence, the average horseman has no way of knowing, because of his unfamiliarity with the breed, whether he is looking at a good Arabian or a poor one. And too often, because of the many inferior colts that stupid breeders put to stud, it is the latter type of horse

---

[2]The author made an attempt at such an objective appraisal of the Arabian as a "using" horse in an article, "The Arab Speaks for Himself," published in two parts in the December, 1949, and the January, 1950, issues of *The Western Horseman.*

Plate 2. THE ARABIAN. This versatile young gelding, Cos, typifies the good working Arab. He is the same colt shown in Plate 21, after being straightened out. Owned by Dawn Young-Hansen, Bremerton, Washington. Author up.

Photograph by Gene A. Pearson

the stranger usually sees and by which he forms his impression of the breed.

Equally harmful to an appreciation of the Arab, fanciers of the breed point out, is the fact that the general run of horsemen who adversely criticize the Arabian do not judge him correctly. Besides having only a vague idea of true Arab conformation, these critics are prone to judge the Desert horse by special standards: they say he can't outsprint a Quarter Horse, he can't outrun a Thoroughbred, he doesn't belong in the same ring with Saddlebreds in a gaited class, etc. But this form of criticism, Arabian adherents argue, is as ridiculous as judging a Percheron by jumping ability or a jumper by how well it performs Tennessee Walking Horse gaits. For the Arabian horse, far from being a "specialist," is, on the contrary, unexcelled as the world's greatest natural *all-round* riding horse; and that is how he should be judged.

A quite common cause of prejudice, many Arabian breeders believe, is the reluctance of most Western horsemen to admit that a "foreign" exotic such as the Arabian is, or ever can be, a better horse than their own homebred product of stout heart, dubious pedigree, and plain looks. That the Arabian is just a beautiful picture-book horse, too fragilely pretty to have what it takes when the going is rugged, is a quite common idea among horsemen with little experience with the breed.[3] Even horsemen who know the Arab well admit that there is a good deal of sound reason for this widespread belief, and point out that Arabian breeders in general have nobody but themselves to blame for it. As an example, Joe Dawkins, manager of the P. K. Wrigley Rancho Escondido on Catalina Island, where fifty-seven of the sixty-five ranch horses were registered Arabians, wrote in a personal letter to the author:

I believe that the biggest drawback of the Arab today is the Arab breeders themselves. They have bred for years to get nothing but beauty

---

[3]The clearest analysis of this common prejudice that I have come across is stated by J. Frank Dobie in his admirable book *The Mustangs* (Boston, Little, Brown and Company, 1952): "The prejudice in America, shared to a less extent in England, against Arabian horses is explainable by psychology more than equine realities. It is based on an indifference to the beautiful and an at-easeness with the ugly. It expresses a distrust of the truth, as phrased by Thucidides, that 'we lovers of the beautiful cultivate the mind without loss of manliness.' A horse that is poetically beautiful, as only to the highest degree the perfect Arabian is, makes many Americans resist him as something fanciful and, therefore, impracticable. People naturally develop their horses — as they do their gods — in their own image."

and something they could show in hand, instead of picking those horses with speed and healthy brains and crossing back with the same, as the Quarter Horse men have done. The Arab people cut their percentage to where they will get only four out of ten horses that have speed to go with working ability, while the Quarter Horse men will get eight out of ten. If the percentage on the Arab were higher and the breeders would breed more for the working type of horse, the rodeo cowboy would pay the price. I have been a contestant myself and I know the prices rodeo hands will pay for a good working horse.

James R. Thompson, an Arabian breeder of Miles City, Montana, states:

Except for a few instances, the Arab has never been especially developed along stock horse lines. I am confident that with a carefully planned breeding program, with this goal in view, it would take but a few generations to produce an Arab stock horse second to none, and produce them uniformly.

The crying need in all our breeding establishments today is a functional breeding program and motive of some kind. I don't care what it is, but let's have a using horse of some type. The type can be entirely up to the individual breeder—racing, stock work, whatever he wants— but we must have a functional breeding program, try our horses, and use them for breeding only *after* they have proved themselves above average along the lines which we are trying to develop.[4]

Finally, according to an overwhelming majority of Arabian fanciers, the Arab horse is not and never will be popular with the general run of horsemen simply because training a horse as spirited as the Arab demands far more tact, patience, and sympathy in the trainer than the average horseman can bring to the job. One well-known trainer of Arabians remarked to the author that the chief handicap of the Arabian as a practical ranch horse is that a foreman finds it difficult to hire a full crew of riders "who are smarter than the horses." Average riders, though they may advertise themselves as "horse lovers," are often brutal; too many of them are, too often, deliberately rough, believing that they must show their "mastery" over a horse. Such treatment simply does not work on the Arab horse. "He is one horse," says Joe Dawkins, who has schooled many Arabians, "that doesn't work well through fear. One of the main things in training the Arab is getting his confidence; without it, you can't do much."

[4]"The Arab Speaks for Himself," *The Western Horseman*, January, 1950.

This is why many critics of the Arabian, accustomed to horses of less spirit, condemn him with such terms as "hot-headed" and "rattle-brained." They simply do not have, Arab men insist, the necessary horse sense to handle him intelligently. Rather than being "rattlebrained," Arab men say, the Arabian is too intelligent to suffer abuse meekly.

That is one side of the picture; the usual list of common reasons, according to Arabian enthusiasts, why the Arabian horse has not won the full measure of popularity that he deserves.

On the other side of the picture, many open-minded critics of the breed just do not like the Arabian's conformation and way of going. Admitting his extraordinary ability to carry weight, as well as his stamina and easy keeping qualities, these critics consider the Arabian to be too small. Especially when ridden by a big man, they say, the average Arabian looks like a weedy pony.

Stock horse fanciers in particular dislike the Arabian's action and his lofty head carriage. They consider a high head a handicap in roping. They prefer a horse that wastes no energy moving up and down when the same energy could be used to cover ground. In reply to the Arab lover's reminder that only the Quarter Horse and the Thoroughbred are faster, these men insist that they still don't want that high head up there in front of them.

Many expert judges of horseflesh criticize the Arabian for poor hindquarters, as well as a tendency to cow hocks. A well-known cutting horse trainer states flatly, "I never saw an Arab that was built right behind the saddle. I don't say there aren't any; but I never saw one, and I've looked at hundreds."

Many horsemen who are not interested in stock horses also are prejudiced against Arabians as rather useless exotics. Foxhunters don't like them as hunters. Jumping specialists dismiss the Arab as a topflight jumper, though they admit Anglo-Arabs can do the job. Even in the rarefied world of competitive dressage the anti-Arab prejudice exists. Judges as a rule do not like Arabs; they prefer larger horses—and score accordingly. Many dressage riders consider Arabians too short-backed to be sufficiently supple.

Some horsemen, preferring showy gaits, consider the Arabian's trot quite inferior; at best, only fair.

Last, but by no means least uncommon, there is a certain class of Arab critics who condemn the horse out of hand for the faults of some of those who own him. Invariably, these critics have no firsthand knowledge of the Arab breed; but they have seen and listened to Arab owners and read a few magazine articles written

by Arab admirers, and as far as they are concerned that is more
than enough.

"How could the Arabian be any good," these critics say scornfully, "if he suits the kind of persons who usually own him?
Most of these Arab nuts are a bunch of jerks. They have more
money than brains. Some of 'em can't even ride their own horses,
or any horse. All they know how to do is chatter about pedigrees.
All they care about is pretty looks. They think a horse is something just to take pictures of and admire. They brag about how
wonderful Arabians are, they point with pride to a few outstanding horses that won endurance contests or jumping competitions
or something else about forty years ago; but only about one in
a hundred Arab owners ever does anything to prove how good
his horses are *today*. The majority just enter their pretty hobby-
horses in halter classes. They dress up in fancy outfits and put
on costume classes—the worst exhibitions of riding you can see
in any show ring. If they'd spend half as much money to have
their horses well schooled as they squander on those fancy cos-
tumes, they might have something to brag about. But they don't
and they won't, because if their horses were well schooled almost
none of these fancypants Arabian fanciers would be able to ride
them. As a group, they are the poorest horsemen you can find
outside riding academies. There are too many rich hobbyists
among Arabian breeders, too many women, too many old-maid
men who do all their riding in swivel chairs. No matter how
good the Arabian was centuries ago when the tough Bedouins
had him and really *used* him, the breed can't be much good now.
For these wealthy people who dominate the breed in this country,
and like to play at being hotshot horsemen, would spoil the best
breed that ever was."

This type of anti-Arab critic is by far the most difficult to
answer. As a rule, even attempting to reason with him is hopeless
before you begin. His arguments are a disconcerting blend of
truths, half-truths, exaggeration, and error, the whole based on
shrewd yet inadequate observation, and often colored by a bellig-
erent class consciousness of which the prejudiced critic himself is
usually unaware. Add to this attitude some firmly rooted ideas of
what a horse should be—ideas based on so-called "practicality"
implicit in the term "using horse" in contradistinction to "show
horse"—and you have in this critic the human equivalent of a
stone wall against which all persuasion and argument shatter in
vain.

These then, in general and briefly stated, are the usual reasons why the Arabian is so controversial a breed, and why people who have never had an hour's experience with an Arab often hold emphatic opinions about the breed. The Arab's misfortune is that he is usually viewed through either a golden haze of glamour or a fog of stubborn prejudice. For every horseman who can give you sound reasons why he genuinely does not like the Arab, ninety-nine other critics unconsciously reveal that they are judging not the horse but the men and women who breed him and attribute the breeders' faults—or at least those traits which the critics dislike—to the animal. Probably all breeds, in various degrees, labor under this sort of critical bias, but it is doubly true of the Arabian. Whether a novice horseman becomes "an Arab fanatic" or an "Arab knocker" may well depend often on which type of "expert" he first listened to more.

It is for these reasons, and with the novice horseman in mind, that what may seem to be an undue amount of space is devoted here to the Arabian horse. The only purpose of this rather lengthy discussion is to emphasize that one of the most ardent boosters, and fervid knockers, of the Arabian breed is that eternal busybody, Ben Told.

Now let us try to look at the Arabian objectively, judging him only on his qualities as a riding horse.

To the rider of average means probably the first obstacle, mental as well as actual, to owning an Arabian is price. Good Arab colts are expensive; only the Thoroughbred averages more. One reason for these inflated prices, which have soared to ridiculous sums in recent years, is that Arabians are relatively few in number and no outcrossing is permitted; steadily increasing demand exceeds the supply. Another reason, to some extent a result of the first, is that too many breeders regard every foal they have for sale as potential brood stock. Few colts are gelded, even many that obviously should be.

Very seldom one encounters a conscientious breeder who will sell rather cheaply a stud colt that, he frankly admits, he does not consider good enough for breeding purposes. He may either offer the buyer a rebate to have such a colt altered as a yearling or exact a written promise as part of the sales contract that the colt shall never be bred to any registered Arabian mare. A buyer who enters into such a contract, whether the agreement is on paper or "a gentleman's agreement," assumes the responsibility not only of living up to his own promise but of insisting on exactly the same condition if ever he should sell the horse to a third person.

Thus, by shopping around for such a colt of this class—and by being lucky enough to find the right sort of breeder—the smart purchaser who desires primarily a "using" horse rather than a stallion can sometimes obtain an excellently serviceable Arabian mount at a reasonable price.

If he prefers a gelding for riding purposes, as most people do, the new owner can have his choice without ruining a first-class stallion. If he prefers to ride a stallion, he still has a registered blood horse of some quality that by servicing cold-blooded and grade mares can defray feed bills.

Many riders who cannot afford a purebred Arabian and others who do not want one are enthusiastic about grade-Arabs as tough, attractive, all-purpose using horses. Commonly referred to as half-Arabs, even though some individuals may be as much as 7/8 or 15/16 Arabian, these animals usually turn out to be superior and very versatile mounts. Often they are larger and sturdier than their purebred sires and sometimes more beautiful. Mares and geldings, but not stallions, may be entered in classes for half-Arabs in Arabian shows.

A horse that is half-Arab and half-Thoroughbred is called an Anglo-Arab; if both parents are registered, the colt can be registered with the Jockey Club. Anglo-Arabs are popular in France. Some have been world-class jumpers and have won in the Olympic Games. However, most Anglo-Arabs, being quite "hot," need first-class riders.

The high initial cost of a good Arabian is not really as expensive as it seems. Arabs mature slowly, live long, and usually retain their vigor and pep to a more advanced age than most other horses commonly do. In addition to this, they are "easy keepers"; they can thrive on less feed than is usually necessary to keep other horses in equally good condition. Over a long period of time— twenty years or more, which is not an exceptional Arab lifespan— this adds up. So does the relative scarcity of veterinary bills; for the Arabian, if treated sensibly, is an uncommonly healthy horse. All horse owners are well aware of the fact that, as a rule, it is not the purchase price of a horse that "pinches"; it is the upkeep, the daily, weekly, and monthly expenses piling up over a period of years. In this respect, the Arabian is an economical horse.

The tall rider's complaint that "Arabians are too small" must be admitted as just, as riding horses are measured today. An Arab

Plate 3. THE ANGLO-ARAB. Morning Dove, a mare of great substance and diverse talents, spirited but tractable. Owned by the author. Therese Hansen up.

Photograph by Robert W. Hansen

of 15 hands may be considered tall; a horse of only 14 hands may be the finest type of Arabian. Raffles, one of the greatest of modern sires, was even smaller, only 13.2 hands, though he was a "big little horse," powerfully built. Modern feeding practices and rations of good quality have increased the size of the Arabian, but the wise horseman who wants a real working Arab should beware of unusual size. Many breeders strive for increased height and bulk, sometimes catering to the market, often because they are disciples of the-bigger-the-better school of thought; but there is a limit beyond which they cannot go without sacrificing quality. Almost without exception, it can be stated, the finest Arabs are not the biggest ones. Whether judged only on true Arabian physical characteristics or on performance records emphasizing stamina, endurance, and speed, the best specimens of the breed have invariably been rather small. It is reasonable for a big man to want a horse that "fits" him, but a prospective Arab-owner who wants quality rather than quantity need waste no thought about size. His little Arabian, endowed with the weight-carrying ability of the breed, will generally do difficult jobs as easily as bigger horses and sometimes do them better, and be fresher the next day.

As a parade horse, the Arabian is a natural, one of the best. But in this rather restricted field, in which appearances count so heavily, he should not be handicapped by a rider whose size makes the horse look even smaller than he actually is. If you are big and if parade riding is your chief interest, you do not want an Arabian.

Tall riders compete under the same handicap on Arabs in saddle classes, particularly classes requiring English equipment. Your mount may be the best animal in the ring, he may carry you as effortlessly as if you were an undernourished midget; nevertheless, your very size, so disproportionate to that of your mount by modern show standards, will invariably influence the judge against your horse—whether the judge himself may realize precisely why he marks you down.

Anyone who may have lingering doubts about this can easily get rid of them: the next time you attend a horse show take particular note of the average size of riders who win ribbons in flat-saddle classes for Arabians. You will attend many shows before you see a winning rider who is of more than medium height. Usually more than half the riders will be women, and their male competitors won't be much taller.

One possible way for the fairly tall rider to get around this handicap of size is to learn to ride gracefully with rather short stirrup leathers, which will at least minimize his legginess; but there is a limit to this. If the leathers are too short, the rider will appear to be all set for a jumping class or a steeplechase.

In classes for stock horses, reined horses, cutting horses, and in such competitions as barrel racing, pole-bending, and roping, in which performance—at least, in theory—means everything and appearance nothing, the rider's size, of course, does not matter.

As a trail horse, the fast-walking, easy-gaited Arab has no superior. He has proved his exceptional endurance and stamina in many competitive distance rides.

Ranchmen generally are skeptical of the Arabian as a practical working stock horse, but those horsemen who understand the Arabian temperament and have had the opportunity to put him to use working stock are virtually unanimous in their conviction that he is as good as the best, and better than most, horses of

Plate 4. AN ARABIAN ROPING HORSE. Wardamar Alla, owned by P. K. Wrigley, Catalina Island, California. Does this stallion carry his head higher than many a Quarter Horse? He gets the job done.

Courtesy J. Dawkins

other breeds. Probably the Arabian's chief fault as a cow horse is that he is a naturally fast walker, with a quick, reaching stride that would do credit to a much larger horse. This characteristic, plus his lively intelligence that tends to make him easily bored with a monotonous job, oftens makes him impatient and fretful when forced to plod along behind fat, slow-moving cattle. If curbed too much, his long-striding walk degenerates into a nervous, jigging prance; which is bound eventually to wear down any rider's patience. When performing such dull chores, therefore, the wise rider will let his energetic Arab zigzag back and forth in long sweeps behind a herd or stride back and forth along the flanks, at least until the animal's excess energy is used up. If very rough or brushy country makes this impractical, then the horse must be trained to slow down.

As a cutting horse and as a reining horse the Arabian has proved his ability in many arenas. Farana, a registered Arabian stallion trained and ridden by Mark Smith, reached such a degree of near-perfection as a flash-reined stock horse that he was finally debarred from competition. Owners of other horses refused to let their animals compete against Farana, feeling that they had no chance to win. In cutting contests, while few Arabians have been especially trained for this event, those few have left no doubt of their breed's ability to do the job.

There is a great deal of doubt, however, that the Arabian is or ever can be worth his oats as a roping horse. Few Arab owners are interested in rodeo, except as casual spectators. Fewer still are qualified to turn out a finished roping horse capable of winning money in contests. Besides, among the horsemen most interested in contest roping, the professional contestants themselves, the vast majority completely disregard the Arabian as a mount potentially worth training because of the widely held idea that a top roping horse should work with his head low.[5] As a result of these several factors the Arabian has virtually no record to prove or disprove his potential as a rodeo roping mount.

However, on this subject Joe Dawkins is one rodeo roper who can speak with authority.

I have been a contestant myself [Dawkins says]. I have worked Quarter Horses, Thoroughbreds and Arabians. During the past two years I have worked stock and roped over two thousand head of calves off Arabians. Don't let anyone ever tell you that the Arab will not work.

I'll give you a brief outline of a working Arab, the only one I know that has worked in open competition against all types of horses. His name is Shelibe, A.H.C. 3735. We took this horse out on the circuit last year as a four-year-old, after only a little more than four months of training. Shelibe had never been off Catalina Island, yet we went on

[5] It is worthy of note that Baldy, a horse many professional ropers regard as the greatest contest roping mount of all time, was unusually high-headed, as roping horses go. Baldy's natural head and neck carriage was more similar to that of an American Saddle Horse than to the low-headed Quarter Horse ideal. This matter of a horse carrying a "low" head is almost a fetish among many Quarter Horse men. John A. Stryker, the well-known Western photographer, writing in the April, 1953, issue of *The Western Horseman*, dwells on the importance of a photographer being careful to pose Quarter Horses so that they appear to carry their heads low and thus look like "working horses," whereas Arabs, palominos, and other horses, which by implication do not or cannot "work," should be posed with their heads high to give them a "proud" look. Mr. Stryker certainly knew what his customers wanted, and their preference indicates to what an extreme this preoccupation with superficial appearance is too often carried. Why horsemen should believe that a normal horse of any breed cannot watch his footing while carrying his head in a position *natural to his conformation* is a typical example of the unrealistic prejudice referred to by Professor Dobie.

a rodeo circuit through Utah and Idaho. In two months of travel we worked seven shows. . . . Even though the little Arab had never worked under lights—in fact, had never even seen a crowd until he left the Island—and had only four months training, we placed him three times at the pay window. I think this is a very good showing for the first time out.

The little horse weighed only 840 pounds and he carried 240 pounds while roping. We roped Brahma calves that averaged about 275 pounds.

Despite the Arabian's record as an all-round riding horse, the prospective purchaser of an Arab will be wise to answer one question with certainty. That question is: *What do I want this horse for?* He should constantly bear in mind that there are poor Arabians as well as good ones, and that the good ones, to quote Carl Raswan, "appear in three distinctive types—the muscular type, the show type, the racing type."[6] Each type has its own peculiar characteristics, qualities, and limitations. For example, the classic, muscular type, best exemplified by the Kuhaylan, makes the best stock horse; but this type of Arabian "has definite drawbacks as a dressage horse," in the opinion of Carl H. Asmis, an Arab breeder who received his early training in horsemaster-ship in Europe. "One of the most important of these [drawbacks of the Kuhaylan type] is that his back is shorter than the backs of other horses, which has a tendency to make him less supple. The Seglawi, on the other hand, being slender and more supple, are quite suitable for dressage training, and several of them have made outstandingly good performers."[7]

Probably the most attractive characteristic of the Arabian horse, particularly from the amateur horseman's point of view, is his excellent disposition. More than any other breed, the Arab seems to like human company. He accepts training readily and learns quickly. If spoiled by abuse, however, no other horse will fight back more spiritedly or prove more dangerous to handle. His lightning reflexes match his dauntless spirit.

THE MORGAN (Plate 5)

Discussing and evaluating the Morgan horse of today is not so simple as, at first, it might appear. Everything depends

[6]"The Arab Speaks for Himself," *The Western Horseman,* December, 1949, and January, 1950.
[7]"Breeding Arabs for Use," *The Horse,* September–October, 1949.

Plate 5. THE MORGAN. Emerald's Aristocrat, "Corky" to his friends, an ideal type of the old-time Morgan horse. Corky was as versatile as he was beautiful. Never defeated in a halter class, he sired excellent colts, had a superb, calm temperament, and excelled at any task from work in harness to leading a parade. Owned by the author.

Photograph by the author

on one's point of view in considering the important question: Is the average horse registered as a Morgan today really a Morgan? If not, what is he? What is a true Morgan?

The first of these questions is a stickler on which even Morgan breeders themselves cannot agree. In fact, so vehement is their disagreement that a few years ago when one well-known breeder published his ideas on what constitutes a true Morgan, he was summarily relieved of his directorship in the Morgan Horse Club. So were a couple of other Morgan fanciers who dared to express their approval of his ideas.

This dictatorial attempt at "thought control" by some persons in positions of authority among Morgan breeders boomeranged with disastrous results. It precipitated a knockdown battle between adherents of the old-time general utility type of Morgan and those who favored the "improved" Saddle Horse type. One result of the fight's flaring into the open after years of smoldering under cover was the liquidation of the United States Morgan Horse Farm, at Rutland, Vermont, from the jurisdiction of the United States Department of Agriculture.

The late Colonel Joseph Battell had bequeathed the farm to the government in 1907 on condition that it be used as a means of perpetuating and improving the Morgan breed. But it was exactly this purpose, critics of the administration's breeding program pointed out, for which the farm and its facilities were no longer being used. Horses being bred on the farm by Department of Agriculture officials, these critics argued, were not true Morgans at all, had not been for years, and were becoming more un-Morganlike with each succeeding generation.

The final upshot was that Congress voted to discontinue the annual appropriation of funds needed to maintain the breeding program, and thus passed into history the only United States government agency ever established to perpetuate a specific breed of horses.

This bitter disagreement among breeders of the Morgan horse has its roots back in the nineteenth century, after Hambletonian 10, foaled in 1849, had founded the Standardbred breed. This new breed, then known as the Hambletonian, surpassed the Morgan as the world's premier trotting horse. In an effort to breed greater speed into their horses many Morgan breeders set about infusing Hambletonian blood into their stock. This crossbreeding inevitably altered Morgan type and character. Thus many so-called Morgans of an earlier day were actually only grade-Morgans. Though excellent individuals for the purpose for which they had been bred, their Morgan characteristics were diluted by those of the Standardbred.

Later, when the automobile became popular and machines began to replace horses on farms, the Morgan's well-earned reputation for all-round usefulness as a general utility horse, equally good under saddle and in harness, lost importance. Horsemen in general, using horses primarily for recreation and for show rather than of necessity, as their fathers and grandfathers had done, began to show a decided preference for showy appearance over rugged utility. This attitude is well expressed by Louis Taylor:

The Morgan horses that hammered the city streets in doctors' buggies and grocers' wagons, that carried their burdens on their backs where roads were not, these horses proved their superiority in many jobs, but the jobs are gone, along with the jobs that made our Kentucky saddlers and our trotters. . . . It is often said that the horses of today can't do what the horses of yesterday did. The answer is, why should they.[8]

As a result of these new conditions and horsemen's changed attitude many Morgan breeders tried to meet the new demand for showier "pleasure horses" by crossing with the American Saddle Horse—a breed that owed much to Morgan blood but that was now well established in its own right, with standards quite different from those of the original Morgan. Other breeders, attempting to "refine" the Morgan, turned to Thoroughbred blood. Eventually the descendants of such outcrosses, even when obviously deficient in Morgan characteristics, were accepted and registered as true Morgans. Some outstanding individuals among these pseudo-Morgans were so un-Morganlike in both appearance and performance that they consistently defeated Saddle Horses and Hackneys in the show ring.

While this steady diluting of Morgan blood was going on over a period of many years, a few breeders clung steadfastly to the old Morgan ideal as exemplified by the founder of the breed, Justin Morgan himself. These men, eschewing all foreign blood, strove to perpetuate the kind of horse Justin Morgan is said to have been, as were also his immediate descendants—a rather short, very compact horse of marked docility combined with spirited bearing, extremely hardy and powerful, able to excel at almost any task to which a horse can be put. This ideal is excellently summarized by Mr. R. Fullmer:

I am an old timer who has seen the Noble Breed in its heyday and also its decline to near disappearance.

My own experiences and observations have taught me that the old Morgan as a breed could not take anything in bloodlines from any source whatever that was in any way a real benefit to the breed itself. This is not said to belittle the many valuable families of horseflesh. If there is a horse on earth superior to the old Morgan then I am glad. But I am entirely ignorant of any such. The Morgan was never a race horse in the modern sense and yet he could get places sooner than any horse that ever lived. He was not and is not a Saddle horse and yet no horse on earth has ever been so valuable under saddle. He was not and is

---

[8]"A Tribute to the Morgan," *The Western Horseman*, June, 1949.

not a Draft horse but could kill any other horse near his size at hard farm work. He was in all ways useful to man to a degree not equalled by any other. . . . If there ever was a horse that was not a one-purpose horse it is the Morgan. When the Morgan becomes a Saddle horse in the modern sense *he ceases to be a Morgan.*[9]

The reasoning motivating these "purist" breeders who steadfastly cling to the old ideal of the Morgan horse is well explained by one of them, Dr. C. D. Parks:

Justin Morgan, was, in at least one respect, the greatest horse recorded in history. He was the only horse of which we have record that has possessed the prepotency to establish a family, type or breed which has been able to exist basically unchanged over a period of one hundred and fifty years. . . .

Other breeds . . . have been bred for a definite purpose and a standard of performance has guided their formation. . . . The type accepted has been the type of the individual most satisfactorily meeting the performance requirements. . . .

Considering the Morgan as a breed, the circumstances of its development were completely different. Justin Morgan came into being as a new type. He and his descendants were the only animals that have ever produced that type. The breed has been one of type and type alone. . . . The type was the standard. . . .

No other type is so well adapted to the need of the pleasure horse owner as the Morgan. His beauty, strength, endurance, durability and mental adaptability are not equalled by any other breed in the field of the utility pleasure horse, though many are superior for a particular purpose. . . .

In the past many deviations from the type have been attempted to make it more suitable for a particular purpose. When this is done the Morgan individuality is lost, even though the suitability for the limited purpose is improved. There are already excellent breeds capable of filling every special requirement, but the Morgan is still best qualified as a utility pleasure horse. He is capable of doing everything any other horse can do, as well as his amateur owner can himself qualify in these diversified fields.[10]

The typical Morgan is a compact horse, ranging from 14.1 to 15.1 hands in height and from nine hundred to eleven hundred pounds in hard condition. Bay with black points and no white markings is the ideal color, though many good Morgans are black,

[9]From a letter quoted in the *Morgan Horse Magazine*, February, 1946.
[10]From a paper submitted to the author.

brown, or chestnut with white leg and face markings. The Morgan's walk is fast, with short, rapid strides; the trot is low and smooth, elastic and energetic; the stride at the canter is rather short and should give an impression of great power and spirit. Morgans are noted for their tractability and "good sense." A good Morgan radiates an impression of friendly boldness, strength, and energy.

"There are only a few true type, pure Morgans in existence" today, according to Dr. Parks and other breeders who share his ideal. "The present-day registered Morgans are, in many cases, a mixture of American Saddle horse and Morgan blood." This pseudo-Morgan, according to Dr. Parks, is "a horse in practically no way resembling the real Morgan, and for the most part inferior to the American Saddle horse."[11] The prospective Morgan owner should remember this when setting out to buy a Morgan. It is much easier to buy a horse of mixed blood that is merely registered as a Morgan than it is to find a true Morgan. For the average horseman, without the help of somebody thoroughly familiar with Morgan bloodlines, it may well be a matter of almost pure luck.

The horseman who does obtain a good one, however, will quickly realize the truth of the saying that to know a Morgan is to love him, and he will learn the significance of the accolade "tough as a Morgan."

THE MUSTANG (Plate 6)

Including the Mustang among modern riding horses may be like listing a battle-axe as an item of apparel for the modern well-dressed man. For, while horses with Mustang blood in their veins are not uncommon, today the true Spanish Mustang absolutely uncontaminated by "domestic" blood is probably so rare that it is very unlikely that anyone could indisputably prove that the breed is not extinct.

However, a small minority of dedicated breeders might want to argue this. Some of them have spent years of research and a lot of effort and money in pursuit of their goal of saving the Mustang. To almost all of them it is not a business but an obsessive hobby, a glorious dream rather than a task. They are firmly

[11]C. D. Parks, "Morgans? Horses," *American Horseman-Sportologue*, as quoted in *Equestrian*, July, 1948.

Plate 6. THE MUSTANG. San Domingo, a rare "medicine hat" stallion, prized by Indians. This horse was the hero of a novel by Marguerite Henry, which was made into a movie. Owned by the late Robert Brislawn, Sr., Oshoto, Wyoming.

Courtesy Joyce Gioia

convinced that the horses they breed are genuine Mustangs, or as close to being purebred as it is possible to find today.

Unfortunately for their common cause, as well for the guidance of horsemen interested in this truly American breed, all these zealous breeders do not see eye to eye. Their basic differences appear to be even greater than those that mark the diverse ideas of other breed fanciers. Quarter Horse men, for example, do not all agree on ideal Quarter Horse type; breeders of Arabians can always start a lively argument over the purity of certain types or strains. But each group registers its horses in a common studbook. Mustang enthusiasts, on the contrary, have several different registries, each with its own standards and requirements.

As a consequence, an impartial inquirer cannot help but wonder: By what criteria is a horse to be judged as a Mustang? In the absence of reliable written records that go back far enough, who is to say that a horse is an authentic Mustang or is only of Mustang type? Why can't the various breed associations come to some agreement and clarify standards?

This is the muddle of the Mustang today, now when it is too late to rectify the errors of the past.

The fate of the Mustang presents one of the most disillusioning commentaries on the wisdom of American horsemen that it is possible to find in our history. Here was a horse that repeatedly proved its right to be placed near the top of the list of great breeds. Perhaps, as some old-timers claim, the Mustang was the toughest breed of all that ever trod grass. Only a few generations ago we had these hardy, enduring horses in abundance. But we have done our utmost, with trap, poison, and gun, deliberately to kill him off, just as we slaughtered the buffalo.

The crime might be excusable if we had succeeded in breeding a better horse than the true Mustang; but we have not even come near it. Today a proud horse owner feels justified in boasting of an exceptional mount that, after special conditioning and with plenty of grain-feeding, performs a feat of endurance which any fair Mustang—as reliable records prove—could have duplicated with ease.

Edmund C. Cleveland, a United States Customs agent, of Nogales, Arizona, had this to say of Mustang stamina and endurance:

Few horsemen today can even begin to understand how the Mustang could stand up to hard work under severe conditions. We rarely test our horses today. We think a 50 or 100 mile trail ride proves a horse's worth. All such minor tests really prove is that a winning horse, if carefully conditioned and grain-fed, *might* be able to stay with a good Mustang for a day or two, if the Mustang ate only grass.

Opinions of this sort are common among men who knew the genuine Mustang. Almost all of them can tell of examples of Mustang endurance and stamina which, by modern standards, seem extraordinary, but which the old-timers accepted as commonplace. "He was just an ordinary Spanish pony," is a typical summing up. "Nothin' special about him. I've seen plenty of better ponies."

Really outstanding Mustangs set almost incredible records for traveling amazing distances. Black Elk, a Sioux Indian, rode a Mustang stallion 120 miles in a day; the horse finished perfectly sound. Frank T. Hopkins won more than 400 long-distance riding competitions ranging from 50 to 3,000 miles. He always rode purebred Mustangs. In the 3,000-mile race he rode a spotted

Plate 7. REGISTERED SPANISH MUSTANG MARES. The roan on the left was caught wild in northern Arizona. Here we see proof that, when well fed, Mustangs are not necessarily scrawny runts. These mares thrive on good care and good grazing. Owned by Marye Ann Thompson, Willcox, Arizona.

Photograph by Marye Ann Thompson

Mustang named Hidalgo to victory over the finest horses in Arabia. Riding another Mustang in a race from Galveston, Texas, to Rutland, Vermont, a distance of 1,799 miles, Hopkins finished *two full weeks* ahead of the rider who came in second.

King Stanley, a friend of Hopkins, rode a Mustang stallion across 700 miles of rough frontier country in exactly seven days; an average of 100 miles a day. That is a mark worth shooting at by any modern trail-ride winner who may consider Mr. Cleveland's statement an exaggeration. Stanley's mount finished in good condition, in a few days was ready to go again.

A superhorse? Perhaps. But not a super-Mustang. Frank Hopkins did not consider this horse as good as two Mustangs he himself owned.

Stamina, endurance, hardiness—these have always been the true Mustang's outstanding characteristics. His weak points were his common looks and small size. These faults were not always characteristic of the breed; early Western travelers have left record that the Mustang of a century ago and earlier was often a handsome horse, especially the best specimens of the wild bands that easily proved themselves too fleet to be captured by even the best-mounted riders. Lewis and Clark, to cite just one example, likened wild Mustangs they saw to "fine English coursers," comparable in fleetness and size to "the best blooded horses of Virginia." Eventually, however, centuries of inbreeding and increasingly scanty forage as the inexorable advance of ranchers and settlers crowded the wild bands off the best ranges, as well as other factors, resulted in inevitable deterioration of the breed. The twin defects of homeliness and stunted size, increasing with the passage of time, have been the chief causes of the Mustang's decline. The same fate would have overtaken any other breed under the same circumstances.

Nonetheless, in spite of their nondescript appearance, these same ratty little ponies, if put to the test, would run most "domestic" horses into the ground over a long distance, and do it carrying weight out of all proportion to their own size. Like the camel, the Mustang might have violated most of the generally accepted principles of good conformation; but, like the camel, he could go and keep going where the going was toughest. On scanty range where other horses starved the Mustang survived; on range where other horses did poorly the little Mustang grew fat and sleek. Given the same lush pasturage and supplemental grain-feeding the average horse receives, the real Mustang exhibited a physical capacity that was truly amazing.

It is this combination of incredible stamina, endurance, and hardiness that makes a horse strong in Mustang blood probably the ideal child's pony. Few adult riders today want a horse of Mustang size, even when he clearly demonstrates that he can easily carry weight; this is especially true of pleasure riders, who fill the majority of saddles today. But for an energetic youngster who wants a pony that can stand up under a real workout the Mustang type fills the bill. Unlike many children's mounts, such as the drafty Shetland, the wiry Mustang "fits" a small child's legs; the youngster does not look and feel as if he is straddling an animated barrel.

The photographs prove that these horses when sensibly cared for and well fed need not look like ratty runts. Zebulon Pike compared Mustangs he saw to "the finest English coursers."

Many people with no experience of the breed have been led to believe that the Mustang was an ill-tempered, treacherous

Plate 8. THE PERUVIAN PASO. Several breed organizations, each with its own standards, are devoted to the Paso horse. Whatever the type, Pasos are lateral gaited; they do not trot. Horsemen experienced with the breed are enthusiastic in their praise of the Paso's smooth gaits and stamina. Western riders find Pasos to be excellent stock horses.

Courtesy Randy Steffen

"jughead." This rather widespread belief is a hangover from the old days when Western broncs were "busted" by brute force, a method that ruined the spirits of many horses and made dangerous outlaws of some. However, when handled sensibly a horse of Mustang blood is as docile as any other horse, and often a more apt and willing pupil than some. Many old-time range riders have maintained that in the possession of natural "cow sense" the genuine Mustang horse has never had an equal.

THE QUARTER HORSE (Plate 9)

There is little to be said about the Quarter Horse that the majority of riders interested in the Western style of horsemanship do not already know. Smart publicity, good performance, and the average Western rider's preference for a homegrown product have secured the Quarter Horse's position as the most popular American riding horse for many years to come. Probably two of these factors in the Quarter Horse's swift rise to widespread popularity—smart publicity and general acceptance by a majority of horsemen—may be excellent reasons why the average amateur rider who contemplates buying a Quarter Horse should first answer to his own satisfaction one important question:

Exactly what *is* a Quarter Horse?

To some fanciers a Quarter Horse is primarily a race horse, a superb sprinter at any distance up to a quarter of a mile—and often at only half that distance. They do not concern themselves with the weight-carrying capacity, the stock-working ability or even the breeding of the kind of horse they favor. He may be a registered Thoroughbred. His temperament may make him completely unsuitable for any work except racing. But to those who favor his type that is all that matters—how fast he can run under very light weight on a carefully groomed track.

To some cattlemen and professional rodeo contestants, a good Quarter Horse should be of the "bulldog" type—a chunky, heavily muscled horse, higher behind than in front, capable of speed over a short distance, and strong and heavy enough to bust a steer. He should have the stamina to carry a big man in a heavy stock saddle over rough country all day. He is primarily a stock horse. He is the offspring of horses of his own type. To men who prefer his kind, this is and always will be the only true Quarter Horse.

However, within the past couple of decades a more refined, smoothly muscled, athletic horse has supplanted the old bulldog type. This is the popular "middle-of-the-road" Quarter Horse. Horsemen who favor this kind of horse include professional contestants, many market breeders interested in a quick turnover, and amateur riders who like to show in performance and halter classes. Quarter Horses of this type usually have a good deal of Thoroughbred blood and may range up to 16 hands in height. A fancier of the bulldog type would never recognize them as Quarter Horses. Some of these horses have developed into good show jumpers; a few have done well in dressage. But whether

Plate 9. THE QUARTER HORSE. Little Peppy, registered as Peppy San Badger, excellently represents the modern athletic Quarter Horse midway between the old bulldog type and the racehorse. The King ranch owns Little Peppy. Buster Welch rides him.

Courtesy Horseman Magazine

they should be classified as Quarter Horses or as grade-Thorough-breds is debatable.

The prospective Quarter Horse buyer must consider these facts, then decide what type of Quarter Horse he prefers, before he buys. The fact that a horse is registered with the American Quarter Horse Association has long since ceased to mean anything except that he is eligible to compete in AQHA events. He might be a Thoroughbred eligible for registration with the Jockey Club or one of his ancestors might have pulled a plow. About the only thing you can be fairly sure of is that he is not an albino, an Appaloosa, or a pinto.

THE SADDLEBRED (Plate 10)

Once upon a time I wrote an article blasting the cruel mistreatment perpetrated on American Saddle Horses by those who train and show them.[12] The article was reprinted in Canada and aroused the furious antagonism of "hightail" fanciers everywhere. They bitterly branded me an enemy and an ignorant detractor of the American Saddle Horse. Actually, there is no more stanch admirer of a good Saddlebred than I am. That was why I wrote "The Shame of Saddle Horse Men." I hoped to do what I could to save the Saddle Horse from the sadistic parasites that afflict him. That I am an enemy of the usual types of Saddle Horse fanciers I frankly admit. I regard the vast majority of them as callous nincompoops who show horses only for their own egotistic glorification and who have almost no understanding of true horsemanship. I consider it a duty, a privilege, and a pleasure to condemn the cruel practices of gingering and tailsetting inflicted on the unfortunate Saddle Horse because of phony show standards. But I am not an enemy of the Saddle Horse. He represents, in fact, one of my favorite breeds.

Probably the most remarkable characteristic of the Saddle Horse is his good disposition. Even after years of abuse by men who show him—treatment that would sour almost any other horse—the Saddle Horse often retains his good temper.

Some years ago a young woman in New Orleans sent me a "problem" Saddle Horse that she wanted me to reschool for her. A grandson of the famous Wing Commander, the four-year-old

12 *Back in the Saddle*, May, 1950.

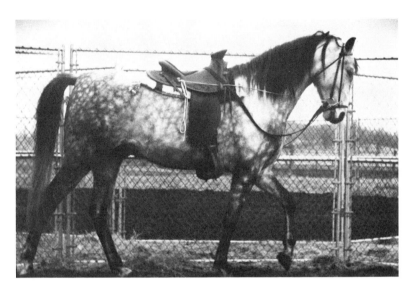

Plate 10. THE SADDLEBRED. Grand Slam, one of the kindest and unluckiest horses I ever knew, was bred to be a fine gaited show horse. He was a grandson of the immortal Wing Commander and the last foal of Beloved Belinda, a champion mare. But he suffered much mistreatment before he finally fell into understanding hands. Then he became a good jumper and cross-country horse. Owned by Mimi Stafford, New Orleans, Louisiana.

Photograph by the author

gray gelding was royally bred; he was the last foal of the great show mare Beloved Belinda. On breeding alone, Grand Slam should have developed into a great show horse himself. But unlucky fate, abetted by stupid mismanagement on the part of the colt's various owners, foiled Grand Slam's great promise. He had a spirited, sensitive temperament with which his would-be trainers could not cope. One after another they gave up on him—and, of course, it was always the horse's fault. Only his last owner, the woman who sent him to me, had any faith in Slam. Turning her back on the whole Saddlebred show racket, she wanted me to school the horse in basic dressage and start him all over as a hunter-type cross-country mount and jumper. With some misgivings, I agreed to try.

I think I might have turned down the job if I had known what was in store for me. Never have I schooled a horse that had so many faults and handicaps to overcome. From no mouth to poor feet, from poor physical condition to emotional trauma, the gray gelding was prime proof of the wrongness and stupidity of Saddle Horse training methods.

I have rarely handled a horse that proved so willing to learn. In spite of the miserable treatment he had received at human hands, Grand Slam somehow retained an innocent trust in his betrayers. The only word I can think of to describe his disposition is *sweet*. And I would say that this is the hallmark of the good American Saddle Horse—his excellent temperament.

Although he lacks extreme speed such as a good contest rope horse must have, the Saddle Horse is fast enough for all practical cow work. If properly trained, he usually turns into a good cutting horse. His conformation makes it natural for him to work well balanced and on his hindquarters. He makes an excellent parade horse.

Probably his chief fault is that he needs very little encouragement to carry his head too high without being truly collected. The trainer must watch this closely, even more so than when mouthing an Arab. Teaching a Saddlebred longitudinal flexions of the jaw and poll is easy, but the trainer should keep his hands low rather than high, and encourage full extension of head and neck.

The horse I am mounted on in Plate 11 presented a typical problem in this respect. He had acquired the habit of carrying his head in the rider's lap; he was also somewhat of a head-tosser. But by fingering the reins lightly, "playing" with his mouth vibrantly, in less than fifteen minutes I succeeded in softening his jaw somewhat and getting him to lower his head—but, of course, obtaining true lightness took time. However, after that first lesson no one rode the horse for two months; he spent all the time out at grass. Yet the next time I mounted him he went with head and neck fully extended at all gaits with light contact on the bit.

This gelding is a good example of the type of using horse many Western horsemen could buy very reasonably and would enjoy riding, if only they were not blinded by the lowdown-head bugaboo and by prejudice against all Saddlebreds aroused by seeing the show-ring peacocks that special training has turned into pathetically artificial animals which are usually of no earthly use outside of the ring. As a walk-trot or gaited show horse this gelding was worthless; God smiled on him by shaping him as a

Plate 11. THE RESULTS OF SCHOOLING. This Saddlebred gelding carried his head too high and resisted the bit the first time I mounted him. The lower picture shows the same horse after several months of schooling.

Photographs by Willadean

pleasure horse, a worker. Yet he was a good horse, sound, strong, docile; he could carry weight and jump; his gaits were smooth; he was fast enough to head any cow; he had the natural handiness and calm temperament to develop into a good cutting horse, if properly trained. His condition when these photographs were taken proved his "easy keeping" qualities, for he had subsisted solely on grass for three months previously; yet he could go all day. When fed grain he needed daily hard work to keep him from getting too "high." What more does the average rider want in a horse? His like can be found on Saddle Horse breeding farms all over the country, and because they have the good luck not to be of show-horse quality their average cost is negligible in comparison to the stout service they can give.

THE THOROUGHBRED (Plate 12)

Some years ago a Western horseman erupted in print with an article "I Want Cold Blood in My Cow Horse." The gist of the author's thesis was that purebred hotbloods, such as the Arabian and the Thoroughbred, rarely, if ever, develop into first-class working stock horses. Such horses, the author argued, are temperamentally unsuited to the hard, exacting work a top cow horse must be able to do. In moments of stress or when the going gets rough, he maintained, the hot-blooded horse is too likely to come apart at the seams, blow its top and generally mess up the work at hand by fighting the rider, instead of getting the job done. Besides this temperamental unsuitability, the author implied, the hot-blooded horse, specifically the Thoroughbred, is deficient in the physical qualifications a cow horse needs to stand up under hard work and do that work well, without coddling.

On the other hand, the horse with a liberal infusion of cold blood was held up as the ideal stock horse, equipped mentally and physically to excel at work at which, the author maintained, his better-bred brother was a complete flop.

The article precipitated a veritable deluge of readers' letters pro and con that developed into one of the liveliest controversies in the history of the magazine. If opinions on the subject were not quite equally divided, it seemed that a majority of Western riders agreed with the author of the article, and the special target of their scorn was the Thoroughbred, which many of the writers

Plate 12. THE THOROUGHBRED. Timurlane, a grandson of Man o' War, a superb type of Thoroughbred for any kind of work. Author up.

Courtesy J. D. Harper

obviously regarded as utterly useless for anything beyond the race track.

In most of the published letters written by the anti-Thoroughbred horsemen at least one, and usually several, of the following inferences stood out quite clearly:

The writers had only a brief, casual acquaintance with the Thoroughbred.

They were of the rough, heavy-fisted school of riders who relied more on forcing a horse to do something than on gradually teaching him what they wanted him to do.

Their experience and interest in horsemanship was narrow, confined almost wholly to stock horses. They evidently knew little and cared less about any other type of riding; they lacked that breadth of view and lively interest in all branches of horsemanship which would have made them better horsemen in their own special field.

Yet most of them were obviously quite cocksure that in handling stock horses they knew all the answers, had nothing more
to learn.

Finally, it was very evident that the writers had had exceedingly
bad luck in all their efforts to manage hot-blooded horses. Naturally, since horses don't write letters, the animals had to shoulder
the blame for this, and no doubt some of the blame may have
been well placed on spoiled animals and a few temperamental
misfits such as crop up in any breed; but more often the writers
left the impression that their lack of success stemmed directly
from lack of skill, equestrian tact, whatever one prefers to call
it — just lack of plain horse sense.

Undoubtedly a good number of other horsemen who followed
this spirited controversy in the magazine may disagree with my
impressions of the anti-Thoroughbred writers; but those are the
ideas the letters left with me.

Obviously my reaction must leave me open to the charge of
bias in favor of the Thoroughbred. I frankly admit that there is
no horse I like better than a good Thoroughbred of the solid,
long-winded, weight-carrying type. Bias in any form, however,
is the one thing I want to avoid throughout this book.

It seems to me, therefore, that in this discussion of the Thoroughbred as an all-round serviceable saddle mount, with special
emphasis on the breed's ability as a working stock horse, I may
be able to avoid the accusation of favoritism by keeping my
personal opinion on this subject to an absolute minimum, or
possibly even entirely eliminating it. To this end, I shall let
others speak of the Thoroughbred as they have found him to be
under practical ranch conditions of rather widely varying differences.

The reader should bear in mind that the writers quoted here
have had much experience not only with Thoroughbreds but with
other breeds and with cold-blooded horses as well. Thus they
have various standards by which to measure their ideas of excellent
performance and their individual ideals of what constitutes an
excellent working horse.

Mr. Charles Powers, of Oshkosh, Nebraska, has the floor:

I don't claim any Thoroughbred will do any more than any other
breed of horse except for running. Every Thoroughbred won't make
a good cow horse any more than every Quarter horse or Arabian or
Morgan or any other breed. I've seen a pretty well-bred Percheron or

two that were top cow horses except they weren't too fast, but that sure don't make them all cow horses.

You can get a good sensible horse of any breed, give him proper training and he will do the job for you. What I like about the Thoroughbred is that if you give him a chance to learn the job he will put all he's got into doing it.

The reason most people cuss the Thoroughbred is because they haven't got as much sense as the horse and don't know what patience is. Most Thoroughbreds can't be broken by a bronc fighter, because if you get mean and try to knock them around they have too much spirit to take it. The results are a spoiled horse and another guy who thinks he is a horseman proclaims that "you can't learn a Thoroughbred anything."

I've rode a lot of Thoroughbreds—some sorry ones and many good ones—and I broke quite a few before I found out I had something to learn.

I've had less trouble breaking and training Thoroughbreds than I have had with any other breed, because they are so much more willing to learn and so alert to what goes on.

I've raised a Thoroughbred mare that I'm training to cut cattle now. We handled and halter-broke her as a weanling, but didn't get to start her at two. So the spring the filly was three my daughter wanted to break her—and she's no expert, just raised on a ranch and has ridden a lot. She got the filly in, saddled her up, put a snaffle bit on her, took her out in the corral, got on and went to riding her. And this with no horse-training experience at all, just an easy, quiet way with horses.

By riding about two hours a day, with a little coaching from me on reining and stopping, in about 30 days she had the filly reining pretty good, setting down to a pretty good stop, and loping in a figure 8 and changing leads properly.

This filly's dam, while she had been made high-headed by kids and poor riders, had been broke and trained by a good man. As a two-year-old she was raced, ran a quarter in 22, was trained as a calf-roping horse and was a mighty good cow horse at anything except working in a small corral. She seemed to think if cattle had a fence around them she had nothing more to do and lost interest.

This mare was very level-headed and sensible, never saw anything to get scared of and never hesitated to go any place you headed her. Our kids rode her to school. She was big-boned and a little on the rough-built order for a Thoroughbred, had wonderful feet and legs, and after all the running, calf-roping and abuse a horse can get from inexperienced riders—we got her when she was 14 years old—she was sound and without a blemish on her, and showed no signs of breaking down when she died at 23 years of age.

I never rode a Thoroughbred that couldn't give you a pleasant ride, smooth and easy. They get over the ground with little effort, and their stamina and ground-covering ability has always been a big point with me here in the Sand Hills.

I've rode some mighty good coldbloods that had nerve and could get you places, but never enjoyed a step of it. You can always tell a cold-blood has a leg on each corner by the time you've rode for 10 or 12 hours steady. And a straight-shouldered horse gets stiff in front pretty fast.

I have never babied my Thoroughbreds or stabled them in winter — and we have some pretty rough winters here in Nebraska. As far as I can see, Thoroughbreds will stand anything that other horses do.

I've seen some good Quarter horses, but about 99% of the real good ones under the stock saddle or on the track carry half or more than half Thoroughbred blood.

We work cattle with our Thoroughbred horses, the whole family rides them and at county fair time we have a little fun running them; and they aren't crazy-headed. We can race them one day and work cattle the next and you couldn't tell, watching them work, that they had ever seen a track.

At county fairs we generally have a relay race team and when we are training my wife and the kids hold the horses. In a race we just stand and hold them by the bit when the rider comes in to change. Just as soon as the race is over my ten-year-old boy, or anyone that knows how to handle a horse, can get on and ride them around bare-back with only a halter.

I have a registered brown Thoroughbred, War Dictator out of Bertha Skillfull by War Instigator, now 14 years old. He was trained and schooled as a hunter, jumped at Colorado Springs as a three-year-old and, I believe, won a blue ribbon. I got hold of him as a four-year-old when horses were cheap. He didn't even know how to neckrein good, but I taught him calf-roping even though I didn't know for sure how to do it, either. Sixty days after I started this horse, just working on him evenings after supper and Sundays, I roped off him at a local rodeo. I've used him for both roping and cutting and he can sure make you hang on and you can throw his head away while he is working, too. He stands about 16 hands and weighs about 1000 pounds. At fair time we race him at the quarter and half-mile and use him in the relay string.

This horse has practically raised my youngest son. The boy started learning to ride when he was three. We have done about everything on this old pony that you can do on horseback and he never lets us down. He is one of the smoothest horses in a herd you ever saw, never fusses around or stirs up the cattle.

I've cut cattle half a day at a time on this horse and have done heavy ranch roping a day at a time on yearlings and twos, and I weigh 180 to 195 pounds. So he knows what hard work is. Yet no matter how many times I've asked him to turn and catch a critter he always puts me there.

A lot of these Quarter horse men say that it takes a 1200-pound Quarter horse to bed down a little old roping steer such as they use in contests. Now, I don't think my brown horse, Corky, ever weighed over 1000 or 1050 plumb fat. But I can produce three witnesses that I caught this horse up in February out of the winter pasture and roped 22 head of yearling and two-year-old bulls and laid them down with him alone. On one especially big bull we used two horses; the critter was so big I felt ashamed to ask Corky to tackle him alone. But had it been necessary, I'm sure Corky could have done it.

He shows no signs of breaking down.

I've pulled the bridle off this horse and roped calves out of a chute and he worked just the same as he did in a bridle.

I'm not claiming the Thoroughbred is the best horse there is, but I think he is a long ways from the poorest. I prefer Thoroughbreds for their quickness in learning and their will to do. A Thoroughbred will go farther on nerve alone than a plug will on his strength. I can get more enjoyment out of riding a good Thoroughbred than any other horse I ever rode.

Of one thing I'm sure: you can teach a Thoroughbred anything any other horse can learn and generally teach him quicker.

Thoroughbreds don't need to be pampered or babied. This is a pretty rough climate, but our horeses winter out on the range without getting any hay and come through looking as good as anybody's horses should. My wife's old Thoroughbred mare wintered every year on the meadow until she died at 23 and she always came through looking good for an old horse.

As for conformation, of course there are points we all like to see in a horse, such as a good back—which most Thoroughbreds have—and a long underline and good hindquarters. But it makes no difference what he looks like, if a horse has what it takes between the ears. If he can carry your weight and go all day and do his job, he's big enough. If he can move and put his feet in the right place at the right time, no matter how big or tall he may be, he isn't too big. Personally, being big myself, for all-round ranch work I prefer a horse that stands from 16 to 17 hands and weighs 1000 to 1200 pounds. But the really important points are a horse's natural action and what he has between the ears.

Whether one likes or can afford a horse registered with the Jockey Club, there is no disputing the great value of Thoroughbred blood in almost any kind of riding horse. Hot blood runs in the veins of almost all the top using horses that have proved their ability in the various fields of competition which claim the interest of almost all horsemen.

An excellent example of a grade-Thoroughbred that has made a good record in a type of competition quite different from the everyday ranch work that Mr. Powers' animals perform is the palomino parade horse Cobb's King Gold (Plate 13). This handsome stallion, owned by Mr. Lyle H. Cobb, of Beaverton, Oregon, was sired by Sun Down, a palomino half-bred by the registered Thoroughbred Remount stallion My Son. Cobb's King Gold's dam was Rushaway, a sorrel Thoroughbred. Lyle Cobb has this to say of his three-quarter-bred stallion:

King stands 16 hands, weighs 1200 pounds. He is a horse that has a world of stamina; he just doesn't seem to wear out. He used to love to work cattle and is really surefooted. I have never seen him stumble and he is as quick as a cat in maneuvering around. King has so much fire that when we want to show him in a Palomino Pleasure class, we have to ride him hard the day we show him in order to quiet him down for a pleasure horse. He has never been shown out of the ribbons in either Palomino or Parade classes.

Down in Sonoma, California, Mr. and Mrs. K. W. Jones used to manage the Millerick Circle M Ranch. The Circle M specialized in rodeo rough stock—bucking horses and Brahma bulls. Handling such animals is quite different in some ways from handling ordinary ranch stock. The jobs done often require saddle mounts combining extreme coolness, courage, speed, agility, and physical ruggedness. The favorite horse for all jobs on the Circle M, according to Mrs. Jones, has always been the Thoroughbred:

The Millerick Ranch has always raised and used Thoroughbreds in every conceivable use. At one time the ranch had a racing stable and when a horse proved unsuitable for racing it was often broken over for ranch work. In later years, as the racing stable was more or less given up in favor of the producing of rodeos, more of the Thoroughbred colts raised were trained specifically for ranch and rodeo work, while at the same time it was not uncommon to see these same horses used in rodeo relay and short races as well as for roping and bulldogging.

I believe one of the acid tests of a horse's disposition is whether you can chase other horses on him without having him get "crazy-headed." The work on the Circle M regularly required that a herd of perhaps forty or fifty bucking horses be rounded up and driven down the state highway a matter of three miles to the railroad corrals for shipping. It was always a source of wonder to the horsemen lookers-on that our

Plate 13. A GOOD GRADE-THOROUGHBRED. Cobb's King Gold, a well-known palomino parade horse, exemplifies the versatility of Thoroughbred blood. Owned and ridden by L. H. Cobb, Beaverton, Oregon.

Photograph by M. F. Brewstar

saddle horses would scarcely have worked up a sweat by the time the corrals were reached. Some refused to believe they were Thoroughbreds, since they were accustomed to thinking of this breed only as a racehorse unfit for any other purpose. We once had an owner of a show-ring blue-ribbon winner, a coldblood, ask to join in this trip. By the time the corrals were reached the coldblood was dripping with white lather. And our friend was well on the way to changing his views about the Thoroughbred.

The characteristic we most admire about the Thoroughbred is his intelligence. He learns rapidly to pace himself to the work at hand; he is quick at learning to handle the various phases of a job. My husband's personal mount, Post Exchange, a registered gelding, is a good example. Post Exchange was originally purchased by my husband to train as a bulldogging horse; in this event PX showed great promise. But when not rodeoing my husband used him in all the general work on the Circle M, especially in cutting work and it was working the Brahmas that PX developed into his speciality. The little horse really "knows his bulls." He can be made to move up on one a step at a time, so quietly that even the scrappiest bull will respond, without getting on the prod. Yet, when the necessity arises, PX can move mighty fast; sometimes he will even nip a bull with his teeth. I think his "sleepiness" around cattle is all an act; he really seems to get a big kick out of outwitting them. He so loves to work stock that he cannot be turned in a field with cattle; given a cow in a five-acre lot, he will work her to death, all by himself. But he is at his best when handling Brahma bulls and is uncanny at being able to handle them so quietly and slowly as not to get them on the prod.

We like the Thoroughbred for his courage, his "bottom" and his toughness. And we like his friendly disposition; as a rule, a Thoroughbred actually likes people, when he has not been abused.

I know that many people will disagree with these ideas, but it will not be men who have owned and used Thoroughbreds, as a rule. Rather, it will be folks who know the Thoroughbred only from hearsay, or those who do not understand how to get along with one (there are regrettably many of these). We do think it is true that not many persons are suited to riding Thoroughbreds, but we question that this is the fault of the horse. A high-tempered, nervous rider never made a quiet horse, and the Thoroughbred has too much heart to take injustices without a protest. He does as he is done by.

Like all breeds, he has his faults. If he gets a wrong start he will go about doing wrong with the same enthusiasm he shows when doing right, and it requires patience—and sometimes a smart spanking—to set him right. Contrary to the opinion held by many people that you "can't lick a Thoroughbred without ruining him," the trick is to know when and how to lick him, and once you've done it don't heckle him further that day.

The Millerick Ranch—to the amazement of many people—has always used its Thoroughbreds for anything and everything. A horse might be worked casually around the place for years, doing all sorts of "rough" work, only to have you discover that it was a "papered" horse that had once won a handicap, perhaps. This is not to imply ignorance or callousness; far from it. But on the Circle M the Thoroughbred was regarded as a using horse, and they used him. Last year, on a pack trip, one of the pack-horses was my Thoroughbred mare.

Sky Tot (J. C. 383697), a great little bulldogging horse, by Cherry Tree out of Wee Tot, now owned by Mack Valenti, of Petaluma, California, was used on the Circle M for all types of ranch work and in rodeos as a bulldogging horse and in short races. The first month Mack Valenti had him Sky Tot carried his new owner to the rodeo pay windows often enough to half-pay for himself.

Battlewagon, another Millerick Thoroughbred, was used for years as a roping horse.

And there was Glad Polly (Polly Timber–Glad Alice), probably one of the most versatile horses the Circle M ever owned. In her day "Old Ma," as she was nicknamed, was used for racing, roping, bulldogging, general ranch work and in show-ring reining classes, in the last of which she won many ribbons, one of them in a lightweight stake. Polly was really a using horse.

Many good Circle M horses were raced before being broken over to ranch work and completely refute the theory that, once raced, a Thoroughbred is good for nothing else. My husband's first bulldogging horse, years ago, was a registered Thoroughbred mare, Sally Russell, that had been raced for two years before he got her. The man we sold her to used her for steer roping. One of the pleasantest saddle horses I ever owned was a Thoroughbred gelding, Pat W., that was eleven years old when I got him and had been raced all his life until then. He had never had anything but a racing snaffle in his mouth, but soon developed a passable rein and was one of the nicest mannered horses I ever rode. He would lope along smoothly even when other horses galloped past him, which is more than can be said for many a so-called "well-broke" horse.

The majority of Circle M Thoroughbreds have been of the small, short-coupled type; but—odd as it may sound to people unacquainted with our casual way of doing things—no one on the ranch ever gave much thought as to whether a horse was suited or not suited, conformationally speaking, for a specified type of work. If a horse didn't pan out for one thing, someone usually found some other job for him. The supreme test was not whether a horse looked to be the type but could he get the job done and did he have any aptitude for it? If he did and could, that settled the question, whether he was sixteen hands or pony-sized.

In the main, however, we think the short-coupled horse of about fifteen hands is most adaptable for stock work. Such a horse seems capable of greater early speed than a rangier horse. Therefore, in selecting a horse for work requiring a fast getaway, such as roping, bulldogging, etc., our choice would usually be the short type. But for general ranch work, all other things being equal, we would not place too much importance upon this factor.

Neither have we ever given a great deal of thought to Thoroughbreds as weightcarriers. It has been our experience—in spite of the general consensus of opinion—that Thoroughbreds are tough as mules. Most of the pick-up men we employed were big men and the Thoroughbreds they rode packed them all day long, much of it at a gallop, and got jerked around by bucking horses into the bargain.

We regard the Thoroughbred as good at any job a saddle horse can do.

This chapter is not intended to imply that only a purebred horse is worth owning. Many cold-blooded mongrels make splendid mounts. This chapter is intended merely as a guide for those whose limited experience too often leaves them easily confused by conflicting—and often prejudiced and inaccurate—advice and information. All breeds produce good horses, and poor ones.

A horse that perfectly suits one person may be most unsatisfactory to another rider of a different temperament and degree of skill. The wise rider before buying a horse asks himself, "What do I want this horse for?" Knowing the answer to that question, knowing it positively and with perfect clarity, can save one not only money and time but often a great deal of avoidable trouble and disillusionment.

CHAPTER IV

What Makes a Good Horseman?

*I am convinced the first requisite of a
successful trainer is a complete realization
that he is not infallible.*

— *E. Beudant*

"I DON'T mean to brag," says the proud father, bragging, "but my ten-year-old boy is a born horseman. He just took to riding naturally."

"And how about his sister?"

"Well, Suzy is only eight, but, even if I do say it myself, the
kid's a born rider—a natural. She just seems to have a gift for
handling horses. Understand now, I'm not saying this just because
they're my kids. Ask anybody around here. They'll all tell you
the same."

Well, don't believe a word of it. You'll be hearing one of the
commonest and most harmful bits of equestrian mythology that
has been floating about for generations—the myth that good
horsemen are "born," endowed by nature with a special sixth, or
maybe seventh, sense which lesser mortals lack and never can
develop; and it is chiefly this "inborn gift," according to the
fable, that enables these geniuses to succeed where others fail.

The fallacy of this superstition becomes clear, however, if you
bother to dig into the records. Few of these "natural riders" ever
achieve successes commensurate with their opportunities. The
overwhelming majority soon find their own level of mediocrity;
a level which many of them could have progressed far beyond,
if only they never had learned how naturally "gifted" they were
supposed to be.

This belief in the myth of "natural horsemen" is most harmful
because so many people accept it unthinkingly. As a result it has

71

discouraged thousands of young riders whose natural modesty prevents them from considering themselves to be among the chosen few; while, on the other hand, it has ruined many promising beginners whose youthful cockiness, inflated by flattering friends and proud relatives, convinces them that they are among the chosen few.

The effect on many modest riders is to burden them with a secret feeling of inferiority that discourages them from trying their utmost to learn all they can and to develop their abilities to the maximum. Often unconsciously, they acquire a what's-the-use attitude and become satisfied with indifferent standards, content to leave higher standards to "the professionals."

The misguided egotists, on the contrary, once convinced of their own "genius," become incapable of learning for quite a different reason. Their minds close up; nobody can tell them anything. They know it all. Sometimes sad experience knocks them down off their high horses with a jar that makes them realize they still have something to learn; but, unfortunately, this does not happen often enough and soon enough. Most of these "born horsemen," once convinced of their great talent, become mental mummies.

Certainly, some persons have more talent or "knack" for learning certain skills than others do; but the true "natural" in any field is a rarity, a freak. In horsemanship, a diversified field with many ramifications, I have never known, or heard of, such a natural genius. I do not believe that there ever has been any. Even the greatest horsemasters, such as Xenophon, who have been the nearest things to true "naturals" that it may be possible to be, have never depended for success only on their inherent ability. Every one of them *worked* for success. Whether right or wrong in their conclusions, they all not only practiced horsemanship; they pondered it. They made a lifelong habit of diligent, concentrated thinking. Almost invariably, their individual skill as horsemen, aside from physical limitations, was commensurate with their ability *and their willingness* to think—to reflect on and analyze what they observed and to draw therefrom logical conclusions.

This ability to think logically and willingness to consider facts as they are rather than as we should like them to be is the first requisite of a good horseman. Without this, one can never really progress. By practice, even the wrong kind of practice, one may become a good rider, able to sit firmly on any kind of horse under all sorts of conditions—professional bronc riders are good examples of this. But to be a real horseman a rider must use his brain as well as his hands and legs. He must have ceaseless curiosity, always seeking answers to the eternal question, *Why?* He must be open-minded, always receptive to new ideas, never convinced that he has no more to learn. One who cultivates this attitude can become a far better horseman than even the most gifted "natural" rider who is cocksure that he knows all the answers.

Skilled horsemanship requires tact. Equestrian tact is the ability to understand each horse one rides as an individual, knowing when to be "easy" and, if necessary, when to be firm to the point of stubbornness. No two horses are exactly alike; even the same horse may react in different ways at different times. Horses, like people, have different moods. These often depend on such apparently trivial factors as the weather, their rider's mood at the moment, even how the wind is blowing—most horses are inclined to be a bit skittish on blustery days. A horseman proves his tact by flexibly adjusting his methods to suit the individual horse's temperament and mood under various circumstances.

It has often been said that equestrian tact is a gift of God; you have it or you don't. However, we may safely relegate this quaint belief to the limbo of "natural horsemen," together with such fallacies as the God-given "gift" of good hands, the superiority of spade bit horses and similar superstitions. Equestrian tact is a natural result of intelligent thinking plus plenty of practical experience. If you practice the former and acquire the latter you simply cannot avoid developing tact.

Almost without exception, it seems, those who claim that tact is a natural "gift" which many people can never acquire plainly imply that *they* are among the favored minority. Naturally! But invariably these same gifted experts are the persons whose ideas in general clearly prove that they fall down when it comes to clear thinking. It's so much easier to regard tact as a kind of mysterious "sixth sense."

To be a good horseman one needs much practical experience —the more, the better—but this matter of experience can be misleading. Experience can be bad as well as good. Being "born in the saddle," as some horsemen like to brag of themselves, can be a real handicap. Practice *doesn't* make perfect if one practices the wrong thing; such practice only confirms bad habits until eventually the victim often finds it almost impossible to change his methods. Many men who like to boast that they "have grown up with horses" have not had a new idea about horsemastership since they were youths. They persist in doing things in the same old one-track ways they first learned; what was good enough for Grampa is good enough for them. The lifelong experience they like to boast of is of little real value. An intelligent novice can learn more in a few years than such mental lame ducks, though "born in the saddle," ever will know.

An amusing example of how misleading this matter of experience can be is well illustrated by a professional "expert" who liked to boast that he was practically born on a horse, had spent a lifetime riding "remote" Western ranges and then proceeded to prove his claim that he had intensively studied horses and horsemanship by describing the sequence of a canter on the right lead as follows: (1) the left forefoot hits the ground, marking the first beat of the stride; (2) the right forefoot and left hindfoot touch the ground simultaneously, marking the second beat; (3) the right hindfoot marks the last beat of the stride.

To one who has even casually studied the action of a horse nothing could be more ridiculous than this. One keen student of riding has accurately placed this scrambled canter in the same category with the famous purple cow—something he never saw and never hopes to see. Yet this fabulous gait was an outgrowth of lifelong experience and "intensive" study.

Experience must be intelligently sifted, weighed, and analyzed. Otherwise it is of little or no value. Mere time is not an accurate measure of experience. One man can learn more in a year than another can in a decade. A single illuminating experience may open a whole vista of new ideas to an alert horseman, while a hundred similar experiences pass completely over the head of a dullard, making no impression whatever.

Experience can be deceiving by its very narrowness. I once—fortunately, only once—knew an alleged horseman of more than fifty years' experience who judged the horsemanship of others by whether they did things the way *he* was accustomed to having them done. If they did things differently, he dismissed them as ignoramuses. Yet he himself, with all his more than fifty years of experience, was utterly incapable of schooling a horse beyond the most elementary stage. He could not even ride a horse in a double bridle. But how expertly he knew all the right answers—in theory!

Many riders make the mistake of believing that they have considerable experience behind them simply because they have owned their own horse for a good many years, beginning perhaps with a pony when they were small. They will tell you, "I've been riding horses since I was a kid"; but in fifteen or twenty years they may have owned just one pony and one horse, and their riding has been almost entirely confined to just those two personal mounts. Wide experience, however, is the result of handling many horses of various types and temperaments, and not only riding them but schooling them. As a general rule, it is precisely this that separates the average amateur rider from the exceptional amateur and the professional. The latter two have handled a wide variety of mounts, and have schooled the animals, not merely ridden them for pleasure.

The average rider can vastly increase his stock of experience and knowledge by seizing every opportunity to ride as many strange mounts as he can. If one belongs to a riding club, he can arrange to swap horses occasionally with fellow members. Though most horse owners are inclined to look down their noses at so-called "riding academies," renting a hireling will often teach a "one-horse rider" more than he might expect to learn, provided he sets out with the idea of riding whatever nag he is given as well as the animal can be ridden. The average one-horse rider will not enjoy such an outing; let him remember, however, that he is not seeking enjoyment but increased knowledge. Every hireling is not a nag—many would make excellent mounts if given proper schooling—but often the "naggier" a horse is, the more skill the rider needs to make the animal go well.

The celebrated British horseman, the late Lieutenant Colonel M. F. McTaggart, was a superb rider on almost any sort of horse. A critic once said of him that McTaggart "could go as well on a bad horse as on a good one." One day the Colonel proved this before a whole regiment of witnesses. The regiment was his own, the Fifth Royal Irish Lancers. On marches the Colonel often saw fit to urge his troopers to use their legs more vigorously so as to make their mounts walk faster. He himself, out in front, usually kept his own mare striding along so fast that the rest of the regiment had to jog their horses to keep pace with him.

One day an officer informed Colonel McTaggart that the men were complaining about this; they considered it unfair of him to make them jog along on their common troop mounts in an uncomfortable effort to keep up with his long-striding, well-bred mare. McTaggart, who was popular with his men because he was always fair and had their welfare at heart, responded typically:

"Tomorrow give me the worst horse in the regiment. Let the men themselves choose for me the slowest crock we have. We'll see about this."

The following morning the Colonel found his saddle on a hammerheaded hayburner that was obviously so lazy it would hardly put one foot in front of another. With a grin, McTaggart mounted and rode slowly to the head of the regiment while the troopers watched with covert glee. But their glee quickly changed to amazement as the march got under way. For Colonel McTaggart easily urged his sluggish nag into a five-mile-an-hour walk and maintained the pace while the troopers had to jog along as usual to keep up with him. During the entire day's march McTaggart forced his lazy nag to stride along faster than it probably ever had walked before, and he achieved the feat simply by firmly using his legs.

McTaggart was equally good on flighty, high-strung horses that needed calming down. In fact, the finest mare he ever owned was given him as a joke after she had been cast from the army as utterly unmanageable, an incorrigible outlaw. But this great horseman denied having any special natural talent. On the contrary, McTaggart said that anyone could do anything he did if they would take the same trouble he did. His skill, and the skill of all good horsemen, was based on wide experience with a variety of horses.

That there is no substitute for experience has been reiterated often, but it is seldom added that experience cannot be accurately measured by mere time. If two novices take up riding at the same time and one rides only the same horse over and over while the other rides a strange horse every week for a year, the second rider will have gained so much more experience than the first one that the two will no longer be in the same class. By comparison, the one-horse rider will still be a green beginner. He may give an appearance of some skill on his own docile mount, for he and the horse have become used to each other; but mount him on a strange horse, particularly one of a markedly different temperament from his own horse's, and he will feel utterly lost.

This aspect of experience applies not only to novices but to many persons who are generally regarded as experienced because they have owned and ridden their own mounts for decades. Many of these cannot qualify as skilled horsemen or even as good riders, for their mounts have been, in effect, hand-picked—carefully selected, good-tempered animals that were easy to break in or that already had been taught fairly good manners by some professional before their present owners bought them. Such "experienced" horse owners, if mounted on a completely green colt or on a horse of "difficult" temperament, would be quite as helpless as any young novice. Such horse owners are the mainstays of the professional horseman's livelihood. To hear many of them talk, they know it all. But when they have a horse that needs ordinary schooling or special corrective training they have to hire a professional to do the job for them.

The average amateur who seeks more experience in the shortest possible time should ride as many different horses—good, bad, and mediocre—as he can throw a leg over. Let him not look down his nose scornfully, simply because he owns his own mount, on the lowly "riding academy" nag—or on his friends' and neighbors' personal mounts that he secretly regards as mere nags compared to his own Pegasus. If a man is alert to his opportunities, even the sorriest old crock can teach him something of value.

One great obstacle most beginners run into in their efforts to gain experience and increase their knowledge is the closemouthed attitude they encounter in experienced horsemen who could so easily help them. Let's be quite frank about this. Horsemen generally are a clannish lot; even *snobbish* might, in many instances, be a more appropriate word, for the attitude traces back to an era when only aristocrats were cavaliers. We still see vestiges of this snobbery, although—particularly among Western horsemen —it is no longer based mainly on social caste consciousness. Instead, now, it stems largely from the professionalism that taints most of our competitions in spirit if not always in fact.

This clannishness that the greenhorn in the horse world often runs into is also, to some extent, an expression of horsemen's pride in possessing a rather specialized knowledge which has become far from common in a machine age; a rather juvenile egotism quite obvious in the cant and jargon consciously "horsy" people like to talk in an effort to show off their assumed knowledge.

Of course, for a professional horseman to keep his own hard-earned knowledge to himself is natural. His knowledge, the foundation of his skill, is his stock in trade. However, many experienced amateurs, particularly those who compete in the show ring

a great deal, have exactly the same attitude. Except to a few of
their own personal friends—and not always even then—they are
no more helpful to eager novices than the sharp professionals are.
In fact, it is not stretching truth to say that a good number of
veteran horsemen, the amateurs even more so than the professionals, take a grim, rather sadistic delight in watching greenhorns
blunder. When a few words of advice from them would be in-
valuable, these sharpies will deliberately remain silent and let a
novice "cut his own throat."

Fortunately, there are a few sterling exceptions to this general
rule—men and women of experience who are above pettiness,
enjoy sharing their knowledge, and would rather lose a championship than be mean—but, make no mistake about it, they *are* exceptions.

Generally, the beginner has to acquire what knowledge he can
the hard way—by his own efforts, by trial and error—or by paying
for it in hard cash. Not everyone, of course, can afford to pay
a competent professional for help and instruction. Some horse
owners who could afford it will not even consider doing so. Some
doubt that the results would warrant the expense; others—usually
the know-it-alls—feel that placing one's self on the level of a paying
pupil is an embarrassing confession of ignorance. On the contrary,
it is an honest admission that one does not know it all and is
eager to learn more. This, certainly, is nothing to be ashamed of.

If one can afford to pay a competent professional for personal
coaching, he will usually find it a good investment. At the least,
it will probably save him many mistakes and therefore much time.
The catch in this plan, however, is that a novice is not qualified
to judge a teacher's competence, at least not until a trial has cost
him some money, perhaps more than he can afford to squander.
If he were qualified to judge a professional's competence, he
would not be a novice.

To the experienced it may seem that I dwell on this topic at
unnecessary length. Actually, however, I am hardly scratching the
surface. This problem of gaining practical experience is, today, a
far greater obstacle to many young horse enthusiasts than veterans
usually realize. Particularly blind to the problem are those elderly
and often influential horsemen whose own early training commenced in the "horse and buggy" era when people commonly
had more opportunities to learn about horses from daily contact
with them than youngsters have now.

Today, when even the smallest hamlet usually boasts at least one garage and a couple or more service stations, it is easier to become a skilled mechanic than to become even a fair horseman. Just by loitering about a garage and watching and asking questions anyone can learn a good deal about engines and general auto maintenance; but even the lowliest jobs in stables today are relatively scarce because stables are relatively few and far apart — so far apart in some sections of the country that a youngster simply cannot find one within a convenient distance where he could stand about and watch how things are done. Plenty of keen youngsters, eager for knowledge and experience, would be willing to start at the bottom as stable lads (or girls) at little or no salary, just for the opportunity to learn. But the necessary number of jobs simply does not exist.

Even if they did, the average horse owner would not have much sympathy with such a plan. He does not want to bother or "waste time" training and teaching a novice. He wants experienced help who will get the work done, usually for the lowest wages for which he can hire them. Yet it is exactly this class of owner who is first to lament loudly the scarcity of experienced help.

A kindred spirit to this type of owner, and often the same fellow, is the employer who, when he is badly in need of help, almost any kind of help, deliberately misrepresents a job to suit his own convenience and to get himself out of a temporary jam. He hires a man to do a certain type of job, the conditions and duties of which are specifically stated and understood. It makes no difference what the job is, whether it is that of a skilled trainer or that of a barnman. But no sooner does the new employe settle down on the farm or ranch than the boss begins to renege on the bargain. The new employe finds his "regular" duties increased, expanded, and diversified day by day to suit the boss's convenience and whims. Thus, a man hired as a skilled trainer finds himself expected to spend half or more of his time doing a stable boy's chores, mowing the boss's lawn, taking down storm windows and putting up screens for the boss's wife, and even running errands for members of the family when he should be working horses. The more the new employe puts himself out in an effort to be co-operative, the less thanks he gets and the more additional chores are pushed onto him, until finally he has little time for the job he was hired to do. If he doesn't first quit in sheer disgust, sooner or later — usually sooner — his employer finds an excuse to fire him for incompetence to do the work which, *in theory*, he was hired to do; for by that time the boss has located some other victim willing to work for less pay. This type of horse owner is given to moaning loudly about the difficulty of getting and keeping "good help," precisely the kind of help that he lacks the honesty and integrity ever to be able to appreciate or understand. This sort of chiseler can ruin the enthusiasm of honest workers the way Herod murdered children.

I confess with some shame that I myself never gave the problems that almost all novices have to face any thought until the editor of a magazine asked me to join his staff, to answer readers' questions about horses and horsemanship. I accepted the invitation casually, but have never ceased to be thankful that I did. The task taught me, I like to think, at least as much as my replies may have enlightened those who bombarded me with questions. Certainly it added to my understanding of, and sympathy for, the problems of novice horsemen.

Some of the questions that were fired at me would make an encyclopedia editor rack his brains and dig into his files. Others were so elementary that, for a while at first, I suspected the writers of trying to kid me. It was only gradually that I came to understand that every one of the writers was earnestly in search of information — information which almost any horseman could have given them but which, to these novices, was part of an esoteric lore veiled in mystery.

One question turned up repeatedly. It came from writers in all sections of the country. Its frequency indicates how many young horsemanship enthusiasts have their keenness badly dented by a common problem that seems to baffle them all. This problem may be summed up in one sentence: "Where can we *learn?*"

In other words, if employers want only experienced professional help who will double as handymen, how do you *get* experience? If you can and are willing to pay for personal coaching, where can you be sure of getting the right kind of coaching?

I always regretted that I could not give a pat answer, or often even an encouraging one. The problem is much more complicated than merely choosing a suitable school or finding a sympathetic instructor. In America genuine riding schools worthy of the name are rare. The general run of so-called "riding academies"—a misnomer if ever there was one!—are hardly more than just livery barns offering horses for hire. Even those establishments that merit the term school usually teach only one type of horsemanship and that in very limited form. Individual instructors vary even more widely. A few are excellent; some are good; a great many are ignorant nincompoops. Whatever their degree of knowledge and skill, each usually teaches, as fundamental principles, ideas and practices which the beginner has no way whatever of judging as either right or wrong; for there is no central authority—such as the Institute of the Horse, in England—that passes on the qualifications of instructors in the light of recognized standards, an authority to which the beginner could look for guidance.[1]

A central authority, however, is not the whole answer. Bureaucracy has many blind spots. In England and elsewhere abroad it is easier to find more poor schools than good ones. Advertisements based on snob appeal and full of false claims can be woefully misleading. A young woman of my acquaintance enrolled at considerable expense in a well-known British riding school, and she still regrets the wasted time and money. The head of the school, a charming retired colonel, spent most of his time comfortably seated in a chair with a glass in his hand. None of the pupils ever saw him on a horse, though he talked a great ride. His wife and daughter ran the school as petty tyrants. The pupils did all the dirty work, and were often cautioned not to eat so much. When a student asked why a thing was done in a certain way, the usual reply was: "Because that's the way it should be done." Any pupil who persisted in asking was bluntly told to shut up and do as he was told. Naturally, all the pupils had paid full tuition in advance. They were all delighted, if not much wiser in horsemanship, when the term ended.

One way that horsemen who can afford to own only one horse at a time can increase and broaden their experience is to maintain as rapid a turnover of personal mounts as they find practical or convenient. In other words, use a horse until you feel that you have learned all you can from him, have mastered his particular temperament and peculiarities, and have made a better mount of him as well as a better horseman of yourself. Then, stifling whatever sentimental attachment you may have developed for the animal, sell him to somebody who will appreciate him and buy yourself another horse, preferably one of a markedly different

---

[1]Since the above paragraphs were written, a splendid organization has come into being which is doing much to overcome the handicaps that beset inexperienced youngsters who aspire to skilled horsemastership. This is the United States Pony Clubs, Inc., with regional branch clubs throughout the country. The chief purpose of Pony Clubs is to develop young riders who will become worthy of the name *horsemen*.

temperament. School the new horse until again you feel that you have mastered him and that both of you have benefited from the experience. Then let him go the way of his predecessor, being choosy about to whom you sell him, and repeat the process with another new mount.

In a few years, following this system, you can teach yourself much more about horses and horsemanship than you could learn by riding the same horse for a lifetime. If lucky, you might even make a little money while learning. At worst, you shouldn't lose anything, barring accidents. If you consistently fail to sell your horses for at least as much as you bought them for, either you are paying the wrong prices or you are spoiling the horses you ride.

Many novices find this plan distasteful in practice. They fall in love with a horse and, losing sight of their original goal—the acquiring of more and broader experience—put aside all thought of selling him. Sentiment is rarely a helpful teacher.

Patience and perseverance, qualities all really good horsemen have in abundance, are often the most difficult for some beginners to learn and develop. We Americans want to speed up everything, get results in a hurry. We lack patience with "slow" methods, often even the patience to determine by actual test whether some of those methods we scorn will achieve superior results well worth the extra time spent. Certainly the most time-consuming methods are not always the best just because they are slowest, but "short cuts" should never be based on impatience, a desire to hurry. "What's worth doing is worth doing well"—but what's worth doing well usually takes time.

Finally, a good horseman has enthusiasm. Some call this en-thusiasm "a love for horses," but love implies sentiment or, worse, sentimentality. Few good trainers, however, are the least bit senti-mental, at least while training; but all have enthusiasm for their work. The bald truth is that very few persons truly "love horses." The majority of so-called "horse lovers," including those who apply the term to themselves, actually like *doing* things with horses or on horseback. If they never could ride or drive or show or race, or do whatever it is that gives them their chief satisfaction in keeping horses, they would sell their animals and never bother about horses again. The true horse lover is a genuine rarity. Occa-sionally you will find him in the form of an old stableman or groom; he may never mount a horse or drive one, and in his youth he could have carved a more comfortable niche in life for himself by following some other line of work; but he has spent his life working with horses, doing the lowliest stable chores, content to get along on little money and to put up, often, with "shacky" living quarters, not to mention employers whom he frequently despises. He is not interested in what he can get out of horses or what they can do for his ego. He has spent his life with horses because he loves them, would never want to be separated from them—and his humble life is such as the usual self-styled "horse lover" would never endure. The true horse lover is a breed apart. Being a horse lover and having enthusiasm for horsemanship are quite different things.

One of the most enthusiastic exhibitors of American Saddle Horses I ever knew was likewise one of the phoniest of self-styled "horse lovers." His favorite breed was the Thoroughbred; but since he had no success trying to breed racers and lacked both the skill and the dash to enjoy hunters and jumpers, he bred and exhibited Saddlebreds, despite the fact that he did not really like them and frankly admitted that the way they were trained for the show ring was inhumane and the finished product was artificial.

Then why, I asked, did he breed and show "high tails"?

"So that people will *know*," he replied, "that I'm a *horseman*."

A horseman, indeed! A self-styled "horse lover" whose only interest in horses was in surrounding his own name with a cloud of phony prestige and tinsel glory.

CHAPTER V

Training Equipment and Facilities

*In fact it is an admission of failure on your
part if you have trained a horse from
the start and have to resort to a severe bit.*
— *Maj. Gen. Geoffrey Brooke*

SINCE I am not writing this book for professional
horsemen, I take it for granted that very few of
my readers own or have access to all the training equipment
and facilities usually to be found in large stables; nor do I consider it either necessary or desirable that they should have. On
the other hand, since they can, I assume, afford to keep a horse,
perhaps several horses, I likewise take it for granted that they
have, or are willing to get, a minimum of good equipment, and
enjoy the use of certain facilities which, I think, are almost essential to intelligent horsekeeping. With these ideas in mind, I shall
list what I consider suitable facilities and equipment, together
with suggested substitutes for the economy-minded.

A circular corral or pen, from forty to seventy feet in diameter,
with walls about six feet high or higher, makes an ideal "school"
for colts or green horses. The walls should be high, as well as
solid, so that when a young horse is being worked he will not
have his attention distracted from the lesson he is supposed to
be learning by being able to see other horses, or things or people,
outside the corral. The sight of other horses especially, regardless
of what they may be doing, is always distracting. Not all horsemen
realize this. But if you have access to such a high-walled circular
schooling pen or can afford to build one, you will find that the
quick results you can get in educating colts will be more than
worth the trouble and expense.

However, if you must do without it, you can; don't worry about

84

it. A circular enclosure is ideal for the first lessons on the longe line; in it the horse cannot get away from you and it is easy to start and keep him moving in a circle.

If circumstances make it necessary for you to school a horse within sight of others, try to have the other horses doing something so as to fool your young pupil into thinking that they, too, are working. The average colt particularly resents being forced to work while his companions are obviously just loafing—and perhaps razzing him with horselaughs over the fence. You might liken his reaction to that of a youngster forced to stay after school. If the rest of the class has gone home and the schoolyard is deserted, the errant scholar will patiently settle down to his stint of writing, "I must not shoot spitballs," five hundred times and get it over with as quickly as possible; but if he can see and hear his classmates laughing and playing outside, his task becomes sheer drudgery, time lags, he frets and squirms, and his mind wanders. So it is with horses. Their power of concentration is very limited. The wise trainer as much as possible avoids anything that will hinder it.

A large corral or paddock with square corners is very useful and is a facility almost all horse owners have available. During the early training period we'll spend a lot of time in this training "ring," most of it on horseback. As the lessons progress, the pace of the work will be speeded up. Therefore, the most important feature of this corral that will serve as our training ring is that it should have soft, nearly level footing, the ground should be free of stones, ruts, or anything else that might cause a horse to go lame. If the surface of your corral is free of such obstructions but the ground is very hard, you will be wise to do whatever you can to soften it for your horse. Drag it, harrow it; surface it with sand, shavings, sawdust, or a mixture of all three. Using common sense, do whatever you can to prevent strain or injury to your horse's legs.

Some one-horse owners, unfortunately, do not have such a corral or paddock large enough to work a horse in. Well, with luck, you can get along without it. You may even achieve better results than others who "have everything." Actually, a training ring's chief value is its psychological effect on the horse. If he thinks he is confined to a certain limited area, he will not, ordinarily, try to get out of it. Narrow boards set on edge between stakes pounded into the ground, such as the boards that mark the boundaries of a polo field, make an excellent "ring." Even whitewashed lines, as on a tennis court, will serve our purposes. The whole idea of a training ring is not to fence in the horse but to enable the rider to work within certain bounds and to ride precisely from one specific point to another, making the horse go exactly where the rider wants him to go.

Remember, however, that our training ring, whether it is a high corral or an area in an open field marked off by lines, should allow schooling out of sight of other horses. That is important. Basically, all you really need in this horse-training business are brains and a horse.

To follow the training methods advocated in this book you should have a hackamore or a cavesson for the basic training on the longe line.

I speak here, of course, of the genuine handmade *jáquima.* All varieties of patented hackamores designed to be used with chin straps or chains as a means of controlling a horse by choking off his wind are abominations. Even when used "humanely," they upset a horse, ruining those requisites to intelligent training— relaxation and calmness.

The cavesson is a form of sturdy halter which can be adjusted snugly so that a pull on the longe line will not cause it to slide about on the horse's head, as an ordinary halter will. The noseband of the cavesson may be padded with felt or reinforced and stiffened by strips of metal. On each side of the noseband are metal rings to which side reins and long driving reins can be snapped. On the front-center of the noseband is another ring, or a D, to which the longe line should be attached. Thus, with the cavesson, by the use of side reins running back to a surcingle or bellyband or to the cinch rings of a saddle we can, to some extent, "set" a horse's head while longeing or long-reining him (though side reins should rarely, almost never, be necessary); and with the longe line attached to the ring at the front of the noseband we have the advantage of "leading" the horse as he moves in a circle around us, whereas a line snapped to the ring of an ordinary halter beneath the animal's jaw, or to one of the side D's of the halter, tends to exert rearward or sidewise pressure on the nose, which opposes and contradicts the free-going forward movement we want to encourage.

You will, of course, need a longe line. The standard longe is made of cotton webbing from one to two inches wide, is rein- forced with leather at the end which is snapped to the cavesson, and has a hand-loop at the other end. It is lighter than rope of

Plate 14. THE HACKAMORE. With the reins slack, the heel-knot should drop away freely beneath the horse's jaw. The bosal should not be tight around the horse's muzzle. If it is too snug, the horse gains no reward for obeying the reins. He will soon become sore and eventually cold-jawed.

Photograph by J. D. Harper

equal strength and is easier to handle. However, a rope with a snap at one end and a knot for a handgrip at the other end will serve the purpose. It should be at least twenty feet long.

Whatever kind of whip you prefer to use, it should be long enough to enable you to touch the horse with the tip of the lash when he is out at the full length of the line. At least, this will be necessary in the beginning, until the horse has learned to obey spoken commands such as "Walk," "Trot," "Whoa."

If you have a training surcingle, that's fine. If you haven't, you can improvise one: use an extra cinch and a latigo strap—and don't forget to include a crupper to hold the rig in place. Or you can use your saddle.

For ground driving you don't need real reins. Your longe line, with a curb strap or a snap fastened to the hand-loop end and attached, like the opposite end, to the cavesson or snaffle, will suffice. If you substitute a rope for a longe line, double the rope to make a pair of reins. Or "borrow" a length of the family clothesline.

When working a green colt, particularly a youngster with a tendency to awkwardness because of poor natural balance, it is a good idea to protect his legs with boots or bandages. Personally, I have never used either and have never had a colt strain, cut, or otherwise injure himself—and now that I've said it, I'll probably have a mess of trouble the next time I work one. All experienced authorities, however, agree that boots or bandages are wise precautions to avoid injuries, so if you have an accident don't say I didn't warn you.

Our bit requirements are simple. We'll use no odd or freak bits guaranteed to be universal cure-alls. For long-rein driving we shall use a fairly thick, jointed snaffle or a straight bar bit of the kinds shown in Plate 15. For mounted training all of the bits shown are suitable, but I consider the jointed snaffles, *A* and *B*, preferable. Bit *D*, though mild, is rather a mouthful; it is

Plate 15. TYPES OF MOUTHING BITS. *A.* Jointed snaffle with keys, or danglers, tied to the bit. The keys encourage a colt to play with the bit. This helps to keep his lower jaw mobile and soft. *B.* Racing snaffle with swivel D's. *C.* Straight bar-bit with keys. *D.* Leather-covered bar-bit with leather guards to protect a colt's lips. The strap, fastened under the colt's chin, serves to hold the bit in place better.

Drawings by Larry Kumferman

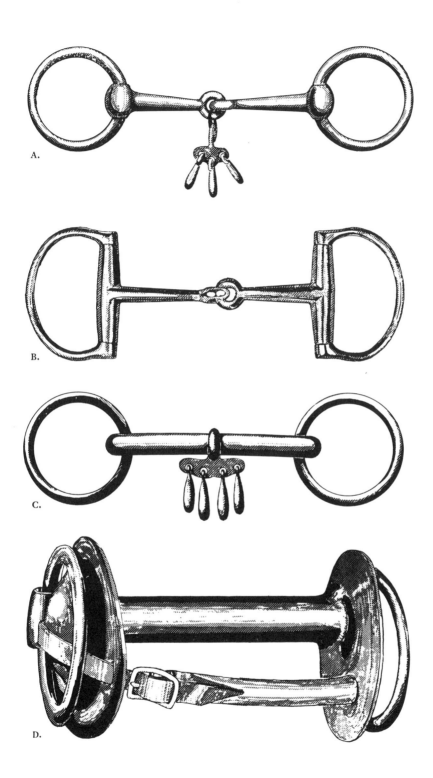

A.

B.

C.

D.

better for driving than for riding. The mouthing bits should have danglers or "keys."

A twisted wire snaffle, designed to "hold" headstrong horses, should never be used. Unless handled with extreme delicacy, it is apt to cut or abrade the mouth. Such wire snaffles are excellent for making fretful, tough-mouthed horses.

The bit I recommend for more advanced schooling will, I know, cause many a raised eyebrow and not a few loud snorts from the amateur cowboy clique. This is the Weymouth bridle—the double bridle—consisting of curb and bridoon. To the cowboy-struck dreamers any bridle having four reins is "English" and therefore anathema. (It also, though they never mention this, requires a rider to use his hands more skillfully.) But in the system of schooling advocated in this book the double bridle is almost indispensable for producing a really finished horse. It makes little difference what kind of bit the rider uses *after* the horse is thoroughly schooled.

The reins of a double bridle or of a Western curb bit should be as light as practicable. Good quality reins half an inch wide are strong enough for all purposes. Three-quarter-inch wide reins should be as heavy as anyone would want. Reins should be soaped frequently to keep them soft and pliable. New reins should always have the stiffness soaped out of them before being used. For conditioning leather, mink oil is better than pure neat's-foot oil, which in turn is superior to neat's-foot–oil compound.

Rein chains are to be avoided. They are an unnecessary weight on the horse's mouth and dull the delicacy of feeling that should exist between the mouth and the rider's fingers. Chains are suitable only for such heavy bits as the spade; then the weight of the chains and reins counterbalances the weight of the bit.

Saddles I'll discuss in more detail when considering the balanced seat. All I need to say now is that the average stock saddle is poorly suited for schooling purposes. Even when it does not have a built-up seat, the heavy fenders and stirrup leathers make delicacy of the leg aids difficult.

Another fault of stock saddles is that they prevent a rider from riding "close" to his mount. This is why few habitual stock saddle riders ever develop a really good "feel" of a horse's movements. There is simply too much saddle between the rider and the horse —too much leather and too much wood. Most habitual stock saddle riders will, of course, scoff at this, but only because they do not know any better; few truly understand what riding really close to a horse means. Exceptions to this general rule are those who have developed a good feel by having done considerable bareback riding.[1]

For all-round schooling purposes I consider those "flat" saddles designed for dressage riding and those that are popularly known as forward-seat saddles to be most suitable. This does *not* include the "cut-back" saddles used by Saddlebred and Walking Horse riders for the optimistic purpose of making a horse appear to have a better front than he does have.

There are several variations of this basic type of saddle. All are designed to enable the rider to place himself over his mount's center of gravity. They differ only in details. Probably the most widely known is the Italian saddle. The French Saumur saddle, the Phillips training saddle, the McTaggart saddle, and others are similar. The Oliveira saddle, made in Portugal, is an excellent schooling saddle. Perhaps a majority of horsemen would find the German jumping saddle most comfortable; it is designed to let the rider sit "deep" with rather long stirrups and yet remain forward and balanced with his mount.

Aside from the "flat" saddles, two other types of saddles are suitable for schooling—the Mexican saddle and the McClellan saddle. Both enable the rider to place himself where he should sit, almost directly over his stirrups when the leathers are vertical.

I'll discuss saddles in more detail in Chapter XVI.

I hesitate to recommend the use of any sort of whip in mounted schooling: intelligent use of the whip is too greatly misunderstood. The very word *whip* connotes punishment, but a horse sensibly schooled so rarely merits punishment that, as a general rule, we can safely forget about it. About the only use we shall have for a whip is as an "extra leg," a means of enabling us more easily to control the horse's forehand or hindquarters. With that clearly understood, provide yourself with a rather stiff whip or switch about three feet long, and bear in mind constantly that it is *not* for punishment.

I am opposed to the wearing of spurs while schooling a green horse; and a trained horse rarely needs spurs. On this question there are two opposite views. The commoner one is that the spur is merely an extension of the rider's leg; it enables him to get

---

[1] A good way to test one's feel of a horse is to shut one's eyes and try to tell which foot or feet one's mount has on the ground at a given moment. A rider with well-developed feel knows this almost instinctively at any gait or pace. He doesn't even have to think about it.

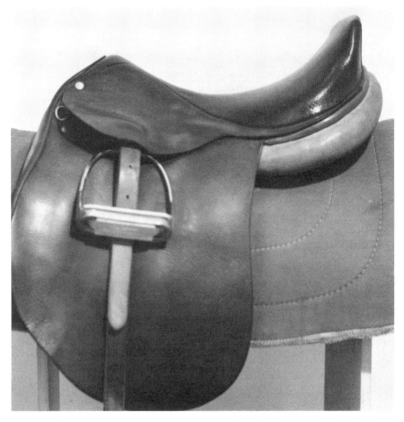

Plate 16. AN EXCELLENT DRESSAGE SADDLE. Designed by Nuno Oliveira of Portugal. Note the built-up rear and the "flat" seat that is really an arc. The stirrups are located only 4½ inches ahead of the lowest point of the seat.

Photograph by Charles E. Osborne, Jr.

certain results with less muscular effort than without spurs. Hand in hand with this view is another idea, clearly expressed, though rather exaggerated, by the late General Harry D. Chamberlin: "A properly schooled mount should be more afraid of energetic attacks by the rider's legs [armed with spurs] than anything else in the world." This fear of the rider's legs, or spurs, "as a matter of course, involves several unforgettable attacks with the spurs, at well-chosen, psychological moments during any horse's training."[2]

[2]*Riding and Schooling Horses* (London, Hurst and Blackett, Ltd., 1947), 70.

Though his vast experience certainly entitled General Chamberlin to speak authoritatively, nevertheless I object to such ideas as unsound vestiges of the old make-'em-obey-or-kill-'em theory of strong-armed "mastery"—a way of thinking that has spoiled more horses and ruined more promising horsemen than any other single factor that I can call to mind. I disagree with these ideas for the following reasons:

Reliance on spurs hinders a rider of only limited experience in learning to use his legs efficiently. If he keeps his lower legs in close against his mount's sides, as he should, he will often prick the horse with the spurs unintentionally, sometimes confusing the horse by accidentally giving directly contradictory signals with hands and legs at the same moment. No horse can be expected to remain calm and to understand what the rider really wants him to do under such circumstances. If the rider, conscientiously trying to avoid such an accident, makes special efforts to keep his spurs well away from the horse's sides, he cannot give his whole attention—as he always should—to proper execution of the movement being performed. He is, in short, worrying about something about which he would not have to worry if he had left his spurs off. He is also incidentally developing a habit which he should try to avoid because it weakens his seat—the habit of holding the lower legs away from the horse's sides and depending on knee and thigh grip.

Certainly an experienced skillful rider can wear spurs and avoid accidentally jabbing his horse—most of the time. Everybody agrees that only such experienced riders should wear spurs, those who know how to use them. But how do you *become* experienced in the use of the spur? When are you qualified to begin wearing them, and how do you know you're qualified? In my opinion, when a rider has attained sufficient skill to be qualified to wear spurs he is good enough to do without them. Just as the trained horse rarely needs spurs, neither does the skilled horseman.

Horses, I am convinced, learn more rapidly and respond more willingly when ridden without spurs. In general, spurs either irritate and upset a horse, disrupting his calmness and distracting his attention from the lesson on which he should be concentrating; or he gradually becomes callous and indifferent to them, so that the rider might as well leave them off.

Certainly a horse can be taught to dread the spur, as Chamberlin and many others have advocated, though they are always careful to avoid using such words as *dread* and *fear*. (General Chamberlin, for example, with a true cavalier's talent for euphemism, wrote of "inspiring" a horse with spurs and recommended that the rider, after having attacked the horse with spurs, allow the animal to relax at an easy walk in order "restfully to reflect" on the "punishment" he has just received—as if any horse would feel rested or in a mood to "reflect" after such treatment.) But it is sheer folly either to desire such fear in one's horse or to believe that the fear can be stronger "than anything else in the world." I say unequivocally that neither spurring nor whipping has ever made any horse do anything which he was determined *not* to do. Any rider who believes the contrary might profitably try a simple experiment: mount a horse that has absolutely no experience of jumping and try to spur him over a wide ditch filled with water; or try jumping him over a blazing fire or a fresh raw cowhide or bearskin spread out on the ground. Such a trial will quickly convince you, I am sure, of the futility of spurs when a horse is really determined to disagree with you.

At least, I hope, it will convince you of the desirability of winning your mount's willing co-operation instead of instilling him with fear.

I would be the last to minimize the importance of a riding horse's prompt obedience to the legs; but this obedience must be taught, it cannot be forced. A few skilled riders can use spurs tactfully and without doing any harm; but they do not really need them. They would get better results, in the long run, without spurs. A rider who really needs spurs should frankly admit that he does not know how to use his legs. His legs are so weak or his seat is so awkward that merely to handle his horse passably well he needs artificial aids.

Part 2

Schooling on Foot:
Basic Elements

CHAPTER VI

First, Think!

> *It often strikes me, when I am watching*
> *a horse being schooled, how very little*
> *intelligence the trainer is displaying and*
> *how very good-natured is the animal he*
> *is trying to teach.*
>
> —*M. F. McTaggart*

Almost all troubles that one is likely to encounter in schooling a horse stem from four principal errors commonly committed by a majority of horsemen. These errors are:

1. Lack of a definite plan, method, or system of procedure, with a clearly conceived objective in view, *before* the training is begun.
2. Confusing inconsistency by the trainer in applying cues or aids.
3. Demanding too much of a horse at one time.
4. "Rushing" a young horse's progress, demanding not only too much but demanding it too soon.

Let us consider these points one by one.

In schooling we must have not only a definite method of procedure but a clearly defined end in view. Our method may be—indeed, should be—flexible, allowing us to vary details of each lesson so as best to take advantage of each horse's individual peculiarities and even his temporary moods; but we must know before we begin exactly what we wish to achieve and why. Merely knowing how to teach a horse to do something is not enough. We must be absolutely clear in our own minds exactly how and why a specific lesson will benefit the horse and precisely how that lesson is to be related to the next lesson which will follow it. Each lesson should be a link in the chain of schooling: it should follow logically from the preceding lesson while at the

97

same time mentally and physically conditioning the horse for the task of mastering the next lesson.

It is in this way especially that so many would-be trainers unknowingly plant the seed of their own failure to achieve the standards they hope to attain.

Again and again I have had novice riders appeal to me for a "cure" for some specific problem they have run up against in handling their own horses. "My horse neckreins fine at a walk and trot," a rider wrote me recently, "but it's absolutely useless to try to turn him at a gallop. How can I cure him of this?" In the same mail came a letter from a woman who complained: "When I ride with others, my horse always wants to race. He just will not let another horse get ahead of him. I've pulled at him until my arms ached, but nothing I've tried does any good. I come in from every ride more tired than the horse and completely exasperated. If you can't tell me how to break him of this habit, I intend to get rid of him."

Of course, breaking a horse of such annoying habits is easy enough; yet even as I explained how to effect the "cures" they desired I have more than once realized that, in the long run, I was helping these persons very little. I had learned from previous experience that it is almost useless to tell them that their horses need, not just a quick "cure" for one bad habit, but a systematic course of schooling that would eradicate from the animals' minds any *desire* to persist in such habits. The whole purpose of schooling is to develop the horse's ability and willingness to go with maximum ease and efficiency at all paces exactly as the rider wishes him to go. This cannot be achieved by merely curing him of any one particular bad habit. Schooling must instill in the horse's mind a whole set of new habits, evidenced by the animal's prompt responses to the rider's demands. This necessitates that the successful trainer must know before he takes a horse in hand not only how to teach his pupil but what to teach and why.

A trainer who is inconsistent in his demands will ruin the best horse ever foaled. No sensible person would expect a child to obey a command uttered in a language he did not understand; yet too many people expect exactly that of their horses. They fail to make known their demands always in the same way, whether issuing a verbal order or cuing their horse to trot or halt. Inevitably the horse becomes confused; eventually he ceases to obey. Many a horse apparently disobeys when actually he is doing what his rider ordered him to do—even though the rider remains unaware of his mistakes.

When demanding anything of a horse in training, above all be decisive. Never give the horse a hint of whatever uncertainty or hesitancy you may, even momentarily, feel. Indecision by the trainer is almost instantly communicated to the horse, even a young colt. It confuses him and very often tempts him to flout the trainer's authority and "see what he can get away with." If you are uncertain about your job, do not expect the horse to puzzle out what you want him to do. Be quiet and calm, but be firm and positive.

Demanding too much of a horse at one time is a sure way to failure. Be content with little; reward generously. Never try to teach more than one thing at a time. Know when to quit for the day. Two or three ten-minute sessions a day will usually get better results and get them more quickly than one daily session of thirty minutes or more. This is especially true when you are handling colts; the younger they are, the more quickly they tire mentally as well as physically.

Forget the moth-eaten fable that once you demand something of your horse you must make him obey then and there or you will lose your authority over him forever. On the contrary, you are likely to lose your authority over him only if you take this old husbands' tale seriously and goad the horse into open rebellion. Horses disobey for reasons that, to them, are perfectly sound. It is the trainer's job to figure out what those reasons may be and intelligently to get around them.

The wise trainer, when he encounters real resistance, quickly concludes that he himself, not the horse, is probably at fault; he must be doing something wrong, something that confuses or upsets the animal. The smart thing to do then is to divert the horse's attention to something else; for example, by rehearsing some simpler lesson already learned, then letting the horse relax for a few minutes, giving him a chance to settle down. Then quietly, patiently, as if nothing had happened to interrupt the schooling, try the "difficult" lesson again—or forget about it until tomorrow.

By such gentle, patient, intelligent means you will get results to which the strong-armed, weak-headed horsebreaker—no matter how sharp his spurs are—can never aspire.

Recently a self-styled trainer in Texas offered for sale a two-

year-old colt which he described in his advertisement as a "finished" roping and cutting horse. A photograph of the colt showed
him doing a sliding quick stop, or some contorted effort that was
supposed to be a sliding stop. As I read the advertisement I
reflected that if I had a colt to be farmed out for training, I'd
avoid that Texan as carefully as I'd steer clear of someone with
smallpox.

Another self-styled "horseman" told me that he had been riding
a two-year-old filly "for six months." In other words, he had
started riding—and with a heavy stock saddle—when the filly
was only 18 months old.

Yet these are not isolated or uncommon examples of "rushed"
training. The practice is almost as prevalent among certain types
of stock horse fanciers overeager to win ribbons, profit, and
personal publicity as is the contemptible practice of racing two-
year-olds among running horse men.

As long as horse breeding is a commercial proposition and it
is easy to keep colts cooped up in barns while stuffing them with
oats, too many horse owners—I don't call them horsemen—will
insist on "quick results." No amount of argument to the contrary
will change their minds.

Considered superficially, their demand for quick results seems
sensible. Keeping horses costs money. The sooner a horse can
begin doing the work for which he is intended, or the sooner he
can return a profit on the investment he represents, the better.
If he is a big husky colt, because he has always been well fed,
or too well fed, and so was his dam while she was carrying him,
isn't it logical to believe that he can stand a lot of work, perhaps
as much as a four- or five-year-old that has not been so well
fed?

It is not, although that is exactly how many horse owners
reason, until experience and gradually acquired horse sense convince them of their error. Even the army experts who managed
the United States Remount Service in its heyday had to learn
this lesson the hard way.

A colt can be a mountain of bulging muscle—or a mass of sleek
tallow—but he is still only a youngster with a youngster's soft
bones, fragile tendons, and delicate joints. The fact that he is
overfed and probably underexercised and hence seems "full of go"
does not mean that he is up to hard work. His muscles may be
capable of it, but his young joints and tendons are not. In fact,
the more heavily muscled a young colt is, or the more "lardy" he

is, the more liable to injury are his overburdened joints and tendons. Colts that prove to be exceptions to the rule are usually small, wiry animals rather than large ones.

The wise owner will see to it that every colt is brought along slowly. In the long run, rushing does not pay. Too many horses needlessly break down. If they are purebred, they give their breed a bad name. Most horsemen consider the Thoroughbred too "fragile" for practical purposes chiefly because no other breed can show such a high percentage of physical breakdowns—in spite of the fact that the Thoroughbred generally is the best-fed and most carefully pampered horse in the world. What is the basic reason? Simply that too many Thoroughbreds are worked too hard while still too young, sacrificed to the twin demons Speed and Greed.

If a horse has an average life expectancy of, say, twenty years, aren't the fifteen or sixteen years of good service he can give more than worth the time spent carefully schooling him during his first four, or even five, years?

This book is based on the conviction that it is; that a colt should be taken in hand as early as practicable, carefully conditioned mentally and physically for the schooling he is to undergo, and gently but firmly educated step by step until he reaches maturity in his fifth year. This basic schooling is not intended to turn out a finished specialist; its purpose is to produce an excellent all-round riding horse, perfectly obedient to hand and leg, at an age when the horse will be physically and mentally ready easily and quickly to learn almost any specialized work to which the trainer has decided to put him. Usually a horse thus trained will prove to be a good performer in more than one specialized field— a versatile, all-round mount.

Let no one get the idea, however, that the system of training advocated in this book will miraculously enable him to fit a horse that is a square peg into a round hole. No system ever conceived can accomplish that. A top horse in any field must have natural talent for his specialty as well as training. The intelligent trainer watches for this special talent, spots it early, then does his utmost to develop it; he works with nature and wastes no time struggling against it. That's how top horses are made. That is the only way they can be made. Genius may be an infinite capacity for taking pains; but the infinite capacity for taking pains must be an integral part of one's nature.

In horse-training generally there are two basic schools of thought. One maintains that in all riding the horse is and must be the dominant factor. Whatever the job to be done, the horse has to do it; the rider is, so to speak, merely a passenger. Therefore, he should interfere with the horse as little as possible, letting him move "naturally." The horse, according to this view, can balance himself better and move more efficiently if left alone than any rider can hope to teach him. Among flat-saddle men this is the essence of the famous "Italian system." Among stock horse riders it might be called the "Texas way," with great emphasis on the long, loose rein. It is best exemplified in cutting horse contests, in which a horse should work without any help whatever from the rider.

The opposite school of thought develops its reasoning from the premise that the rider is the dominant factor. The man has the intelligence; the horse has the muscles. It is for the man to direct and for the horse only to obey. The horse is trained gradually to surrender his own natural initiative to the will of the rider until eventually he completely relies on the man always for guidance. A horse skillfully trained in this way, according to horsemen who favor this system, will be greatly superior and incomparably more "brilliant" than one trained any other way; for the rider can put him through any maneuver horses trained otherwise are capable of performing, as well as a number of more difficult feats which they have never learned to do and which—without the same advanced training—they are incapable of doing. This system of training, when properly carried out, reaches its apogee in high school riding. Among stock horse men the method, though in considerably modified or debased form, might, for want of a better term, be called the "California system," which aims at producing a finished "flash-reined" horse.

Speaking generally, the first system undoubtedly is best for most horses, because most riders are not and never become finished horsemen. I don't mean that they couldn't become excellent; I mean simply that they do not really try. Only a very small minority of horsemen truly want to learn to ride really well. The vast majority lack the patience and perseverance which excellent horsemanship demands. They can see no "practical" use in "fancy, high-minded stuff" which does not immediately pay off in the form of show ribbons or winning the envious admiration of their fellow members in the local riding club. For horses handled by such riders, therefore, the "natural" system is best. At least, it saves the horses from the torture of being "schooled" to do things unnaturally and wrongly by riders who themselves do not know how the movements should be done. Generally, each horse will eventually attain its own degree of mediocrity, matching that of the rider, and both horse and rider will be satisfied and reasonably happy.

The chief drawback of this system is that it encourages mediocrity. The rider never really tries to improve himself and hence the horse has no incentive to do so.

The second system of training does get superior results, but it has its drawbacks. For one thing, it absolutely requires either a finished horseman, one who knows just what he is doing and how to do it, or an intelligent novice horseman who has what it takes to become skillful, who is willing to study, observe, ponder, and reflect, and can learn at least as rapidly as his horse. For horses trained this second way, once they are trained, can be easily ruined; taught to depend always on the rider, they work as well or as badly as the man in the saddle is capable of riding them. A horse excellently schooled in this way will, if consistently ridden by a poor rider, quickly deteriorate and perhaps become unmanageable. This fact has a significance we should always bear in mind if we might ever sell such a horse: not everybody will be able to ride him; unless we can pick our buyer carefully, we are likely to end up with a dissatisfied customer and a lost friend. This idea was neatly expressed by the late Lieutenant Colonel M. F. McTaggart in a chance remark to a friend: "I can guarantee that a horse is perfectly schooled; I cannot guarantee that anyone else can ride him."

Another disadvantage of this system is that, if it is followed strictly, it tends eventually to deprive a horse of all initiative under saddle. Taught to be completely submissive to the rider, he loses to some degree the faculty of being able to "look out for himself" in moments of emergency. It would, for example, be quite dangerous to gallop such a horse over rough ground on a loose rein. Unless already accustomed to such going, he would hardly look where he was putting his feet; he would depend on the rider to guide him. But this, of course, is about the last thing we want in a horse used for cross-country riding or for working stock.

The methods advocated in this book constitute a combination of the two basic systems described. I do not claim it to be the "quickest" way to train a horse. I am convinced that it is most effective with most horses and for most riders.

CHAPTER VII

"Horse Sense"

Of all our relations with the dumb creation,
there is none in which man has so entirely
the best of it as the one-sided partnership
that exists between the horse and his rider.
— Whyte Melville

WHAT rider has not been, at some time or other, exasperated by the "contrariness" of some horse? At such times "the noble animal" we bestride becomes "that jug-headed brute," and our inclination is to brain him if he hasn't already convinced us that he was born with a vacuum where his brain should have been.

However, horses always have good reasons for whatever they do. Their reasons may be utterly nonsensical from our point of view, as when a horse shies from a harmless scrap of paper fluttering in the wind or balks at a puddle of water that a dachshund could wade through; but from the horse's viewpoint his absurd action is sensible.

For this reason it is important for us to try to understand how a horse thinks and why he acts as he does.

All horses have certain common instincts and traits. A trainer who has a good understanding of horses can use these characteristics to his own advantage. An ignorant trainer is almost certain to misuse or abuse them in his efforts to "master" the horse and "show him who's boss." When this happens—and it happens every day—invariably the result is a fight between man and horse that is worse than no attempted training at all, for the horse as a rule ends up badly trained and perhaps completely spoiled.

I readily admit that with a spoiled horse undergoing the process of being reformed a showdown is sometimes inevitable; but with the ordinary horse, and particularly with a green colt, almost the only excuse for a showdown "battle," and it's a poor excuse, is the trainer's lack of intelligence and knowledge. A ruckus is one thing an intelligent trainer makes special efforts to avoid, for it means that the horse has questioned and is rebelling against the trainer's authority. When this happens you're in trouble up to your neck, and ninety-nine times out of a hundred it's your own fault.

In training, we should make every effort to bring a colt along so that he never even gets the idea that he *can* question our authority over him. With green horses this is relatively easy; but when we take in hand a horse that someone else has spoiled it is more difficult, sometimes very difficult. Then we have need of all the knowledge and know-how at our command. So let us consider the nature of the animal we hope to educate.

All horses have to some degree, which varies with the individual animal, the following basic traits:

> Extreme timidity
> Strong gregariousness
> Excellent memory
> Love of routine
> Docility
> Cunning
> Greediness
> Laziness
> "Courage"
> Sense of justice
> Intelligence

In addition, the horse's senses of sight, hearing, and touch are very acute; much more so than his sense of smell.

Let's consider how these characteristics influence a horse's behavior under ordinary circumstances and how we can use them advantageously in our training, or at least not violate them and thus arouse the animal's resistance.

Unlike the dog, a natural fighter, the horse, despite his size and strength, is a timid animal. A creature of flight, always he has depended chiefly on his speed to escape dangers. Strange objects, sudden movements, loud noises easily frighten him; his natural reaction is to "spook" and run. Few experiences terrify a horse more than being pulled off his feet and held down. That is why most horses are suspicious of strange bridges, boggy ground, even small puddles. Anything that appears to threaten their ability to flee is a potential danger. Kickers usually develop their vice, not because they were naturally vicious to begin with, but be-cause—perhaps startled by somebody coming up behind them unexpectedly—they lashed out in sudden fear, an instinctive de-fensive action when they were unable to run, and discovered that kicking was effective against those who supposedly threatened them. A horse that bucks the first time he is saddled does so for essentially the same reason: he is afraid; fear, not viciousness, impels him to try to rid himself of the "menace" on his back. This is why it is senseless to "punish" a spooky colt, even if he leaves hoof marks all over you; your roughness only adds to his fear. Try, instead, to calm him and sooth him. About the only thing a frightened horse can learn is that, if you are the cause of his fright, then you are his enemy.

The gregariousness of horses is well known. Their herd instinct is so strong that unschooled horses will often determinedly resist a rider's efforts to make them leave a group, or even leave their stable, unless accompanied by another horse. Not all horsemen, however, realize that this herd instinct, undesirable as it is at times, can often be used to good advantage in schooling a green horse or colt. For example, the average horse will go more wil-lingly when headed toward his stable or toward other horses than he will go away from them. Conversely, when ridden in the oppo-site direction he will more readily stop and turn, in order to get back to his companions. A trainer who uses his head will know when to take advantage of this. On the other hand, it is precisely because of this strong herd instinct that we should, under ordinary circumstances, school a horse alone. The presence of other horses will only distract him from his work, and it is an essential part of every horse's education that he must learn to go alone as wil-lingly as he does in company, to go at whatever gait or pace the rider demands regardless of what other horses are doing, and to leave a group at any time his rider wishes him to do so.

A paramount characteristic of the horse is his excellent mem-ory. No elephant has a longer memory than a horse. It is almost literally true that a horse never forgets. He particularly remembers unpleasant experiences, things which hurt or frighten him. Since he is naturally timid, such experiences make especially strong impressions on his mind. One frightening or painful experience can undo weeks or months of patient, gentle training, for a horse learns as much by intensity of impression as by repetition. This is why it is so important in training that we strive to keep a horse calm and relaxed, eschew undue roughness, and avoid provoking determined resistance that might lead to an unnecessary showdown "fight." At the same time, under exceptional circumstances, as when we must break a spoiled horse of some obnoxious or dangerous habit, we can utilize this susceptibility to strong impressions by enforcing and emphasizing our authority in such a way as to convince the horse that he will make himself more uncomfortable by persisting in his bad habit than by doing things our way.

Perhaps a specific example of this sensibly gentle way of handling horses, concealing a willingness and ability to get tough if necessary, will help to make my meaning here clearer.

A horsewoman of my acquaintance acquired a young stallion that had two dangerous habits: he would kick at anyone who tried to handle his hind feet, and when led out to pasture he would try to stampede the moment the pasture gate was opened — without waiting for the formality of having his halter or lead-rope removed. Hanging onto this rambunctious young stud long enough to get his halter off or even to unsnap his lead was a job for a husky man. My friend cured him of the kicking habit simply by tying a heavy, knotted rope to his tail so that it would bump against his hocks, then letting him kick futilely until he was tired. Just one lesson was enough to convince the horse that he was wasting his time and energy.

The cure for his habit of bolting at the pasture gate, on the other hand, was drastic. Having no one to help her in handling the horse, my friend decided that if she had to choose between her own neck and the stallion's she would save her own even if it meant risking his. She looped a half-inch lariat around the trunk of a tree that grew near the pasture gate, fastened a strong metal snap to the other end of the rope and placed that end of the lariat atop the gate where she could easily reach it. Then she led her prancing stud out to pasture. Just before opening the gate she snapped the rope to the horse's halter. The instant the gate swung open His Nibs took off. He was galloping full tilt when he hit the end of the rope and "busted" himself in a flying somersault that almost knocked him cold. When he finally staggered to his feet that horse seemed uncertain whether he'd been coming or going, and he was too astounded to care. From then on he could be led to pasture on a silk thread; he was completely cured of any desire to bolt.

Certainly it would be wrong to adopt such drastic treatment as a rule under ordinary circumstances; I cite the example only to illustrate the extreme impression such an experience can make on a horse.

In this instance, the moral effect, because it eradicated a dangerous habit (and the horse was lucky enough to escape injury), was good. Under different circumstances, however, a similar crude attempt at coercion or correction might turn out disastrously. For it is the easiest thing in the world to make the mistake of trying to force a horse to do something which he is not in physical condition to do or which he does not understand, and then chastising him for "disobedience" without his having the slightest understanding of *why* he is being "punished" (actually, abused).

The usual consequence of such mistreatment is that the next time we ask the horse to do the same thing, he connects the order, not with our ability to overcome any attempted disobedience on his part (for he still does not understand what he is supposed to do), but only with the experience of pain or fright. Therefore, he immediately and automatically resists our efforts, for now he has developed fear.

Just one intense impression can make a deeper mark on a horse's mind than weeks and even months of gradual, routine schooling. One ill-timed "fight" can undo many hours of patient work.

Therefore, it is of utmost importance that a trainer should consciously strive for inexhaustible patience, imperturbable calmness, and never-failing good temper, without at any time being lax or "soft."

If you cannot or will not control your temper at all times, then let someone else school your horses, before you spoil them.

Mental laziness and a love of routine are dominant characteristics of the horse. A creature of strong habit, he tends to dislike change and to look with suspicion on anything new. But get him accustomed to a regular schedule and he will follow it as unquestioningly as a circus horse follows a regular routine. A trainer can use this liking for routine to make many lessons easier for a green horse to catch onto, as well as easily to win the horse's co-operation.

If, for example, we are teaching a colt to stop when we feel the reins, he will get the idea more quickly if we give him the signal each time he reaches the same spot in the training ring. The same idea can be applied in teaching turns, offsets, changing from one gait to another, etc. After a few trials, as he approaches that certain spot the colt will anticipate the signal; all we need do is give it and he will respond almost automatically.

Later, of course, after we know that he understands and can execute the order, we'll have to check his anticipation, not permitting him to stop or turn or change gaits, or whatever the lesson is, when reaching that certain spot; but while the colt is learning we can make good use of routine in all our schooling.

A horse intelligently handled soon acquires the *habit* of obedience. Hence, the sooner, within reason, a colt's education is begun and the more systematically it is carried on, the less trouble we are likely to have overcoming natural habits and instincts which might be termed "bad" because they are contrary to the ideal at which we aim.

This naturally leads us to one of the horse's outstanding traits —his docility. It is indeed fortunate for us that the horse is so amenable to discipline, or there would be very few men who would care to undertake the task of mastering him.

This virtue of docility, however, varies greatly with individuals, as well as to some extent with breeds. Generally speaking, a horse of a breed that has been domesticated for hundreds of years is more naturally docile than a "wild" horse. Likewise, a horse that has been raised in civilized surroundings, looking to man for his comfort and well-being, is more likely to be docile than another horse of exactly the same breeding that has run practically wild on the range since birth. The range-raised horse develops and retains to a greater degree the suspicious alertness, those instincts and habits of self-preservation, so pronounced in the true wild horse.

Individual heredity also has great influence on this trait. The Arabian and the Lipizzaner, for example, are particularly noted for their trainability—which is simply a combination of intelligence and good disposition plus amenability to discipline, often termed willingness to serve. The Lipizzaner in particular has been carefully bred for good disposition as well as physical beauty, for docility is an absolute essential in a potential high school horse. The Thoroughbred, on the other hand, has always been used primarily for racing; no serious attempts have ever been made to improve temperament or to breed for "brains." Significantly, the Thoroughbred has produced probably a higher percentage of "families" notorious for their bad temper, intractability, and general all-round cussedness than almost any other breed—which explains why so many horsemen dismiss the Thoroughbred offhand with the unqualified assertion, "All he can do is run."

Generally, the average horse is by nature a docile animal. Our chief task in training him is to *make him understand.* Once he understands what we want him to do, he is as a rule, if physically able, willing to do it. A trainer who, lacking intelligence and resourcefulness, customarily resorts to rough methods, then tries to justify his roughness by claiming that that is the only way to train a horse, or that all the horses he gets are spoiled and naturally stubborn, is invariably a poor trainer. Few really stubborn horses are born. Most are made.

Many horses, without being really stubborn, show a good deal of cunning in avoiding tasks which for some reason they dislike doing. To divert the trainer's attention from their evasions or in an optimistic effort to fool him, they will often shy, or stop abruptly and stare in false alarm at some imaginary spook far away, or pull some other bit of fakery which they think will let them out of the job to be done. Horses are especially prone to pull these tricks on riders they size up as easy marks, though with a rider who is on to their nonsense and ignores it they won't even try it. If you are alert for these displays of cunning you will often find your training sessions most amusing, for the horse is a true optimist who will try almost any "gag" once—and if it works once, he'll try it again and again. The best way to cope with these tricks is, not to blow up and belt the hide off him, but to outwit him in his trickery. Eventually he will give up and do things your way.

Most horses are greedy and some are so to the point of gluttony—their hearts overflow with "cupboard love." With such animals a judiciously awarded carrot or apple or a few oats will often work wonders. As a rule, however, tidbitting is not a good idea. If it is overdone, the horse's peremptory demands for rewards, which he soon learns to regard as his just due, become a nuisance and can, if not sternly checked, develop into a positive menace. A better way of rewarding a horse for work well done is to give him a brief recess from schooling, letting him relax for a minute or two on a loose rein. Save the oats or the carrot or the apple until you have dismounted and the schooling period is over.

Anyone who has observed horses closely will realize that even the meek drudges among them have a sense of justice. A horse may suffer abuse patiently, but his meekness does not mean that he feels no resentment. High-spirited horses, abused under the guise of "punishment," can be transformed into fiends of stubbornness, their resentful anger fanned to hatred of their abuser. Stallions in particular, when thus abused, will often craftily watch for a chance for revenge. When you feel tempted to take the hide off a horse that is getting the better of you, remember that man-haters are made, not born. Think of this before you decide to hit a colt.

One of the chief, but rarely admitted, reasons for the unpopularity of stallions as riding mounts, I believe, is that they have more spirit than the average rider understands how to curb. Stallions are usually quicker to resent abuse and to fight back than mares or geldings—and a great majority of riders abuse their mounts consistently, often when they are not even aware of doing so. So the general opinion is that stallions are "troublesome." Most really skilled horsemen, however, prefer stallions, even though they bow to popular prejudice and ride mares or geldings.

This brings us to the matter of "courage" in a horse. Courage is supposed to be an outstanding attribute of a good horse. Since the Book of Job, this courage has been celebrated in song and story. Knowing from experience, however, that the horse ordinarily is a timid animal, we might well ask: How can he be courageous too? What exactly is this "courage"?

In a race horse, "courage" is the will-to-win, the inbred urge to overtake and pass a rival. Courage, as horsemen generally use the term, is that quality of "gameness" which impels him to "go until he drops," jump or try to jump a bigger or more dangerous obstacle than perhaps he wisely should, and keep on giving his best efforts even when physically disabled or nearly exhausted if a heartless rider urges him on.

Now when we consider this objectively, is it difficult to realize that an animal that will show this form of "courage," not out of love for a particular master but for anyone who rides him (as, for example, a professional jockey), is not very bright? Isn't it obvious that a really intelligent horse—as intelligent, for instance, as a smart mule—would never run himself to death or otherwise "give his all" for a rider he did not, and had no reason to (but often plenty of reasons not to), love? How can we escape the conclusion that this marvelous "courage" which horsemen so much admire is, really, a euphemism for stupidity?

Recently I was talking with a man who earns his living furnishing bucking horses to rodeo promoters. Whenever he spoke of his rodeo broncs he usually referred to them with respect as "the bucking stock"; but the mounts his employees rode when handling these outlaws he invariably called, not saddle or riding horses, but "the slave horses." To him, there was a world of difference between a horse that would submit to a life of "slavery" and a crafty outlaw that would not. He had no understanding whatever of the sentiments expressed in the verse quoted at the beginning of this book—"he was designed thy servant, not thy drudge." But this stock contractor was, certainly, a realist. For what else is the life of the average horse if not that of a slave?

When I asked this stock contractor which of the two types of horses, in his opinion, had more "courage," he answered instantly: "There's no comparison. Most outlaws are outlaws *because* they have courage. They have the intelligence to understand that docility leads only to a life of slavery and too much courage to submit to it."

Though that term "slave horse" has a most disagreeable ring, we shall understand our horses better if we rid our minds of any romantic illusions about this matter of "courage." The average horse really has very little of it; it is strictly a relative term: some horses have more spunk than others. If, however, we except pathological mentalities—equine idiots and half-wits, the hopeless "jug-heads," on whose warped minds no intelligible impression can be made with any lasting results—it is safe to say that the spirit of the most "courageous" horse can be broken if the breaker is not only extremely brutal but has a thorough knowledge of methods which will enable him to be *scientifically* brutal, able to inflict his abuse in such ways that the strongest, most spirited horse becomes powerless to resist.

The pitiful results of such maltreatment of a horse were clearly demonstrated not long ago to a horsewoman acquaintance of mine who had a beautiful high-spirited horse of a hot-blooded breed famous for its extraordinary "courage." This stallion was most atrociously abused by a professional trainer who had been granted permission by the horse's deluded owner to accustom the animal to a spade bit and incidentally to teach him "a polite little bow." This self-styled *charro* outdid even himself. When after five weeks of "training" the stallion's owner visited him she found the horse a maimed, bloody, crippled, miserable wreck, hardly able to walk. Yet when the Mexican put him through his newly learned "tricks," the tortured horse, swaying painfully on his crippled legs, obeyed every command. He was completely submissive, "trained."

The point I stress in citing this disgusting example of brutish barbarism is that this *charro*, knowing how most effectively to inflict his savage abuse on a helpless horse, completely cowed this once spirited stallion. Yet, according to the starry-eyed romantics and sentimental theorists, this should have been impossible; it was not at all according to the books, which state that an Arab stallion cannot be forced to obey, if abused he will "fight to the death," and so on—very interesting theory, like the myth of the noble Bedouin's kindness to his beloved steed. Instead of submitting to the brutal methods employed, the courageous stallion— according to the standard scenario—should have battled the man every step of the way, should never have yielded but should have done everything possible to kill the sadistic brute who was maltreating him. That would have been according to the books.

It is of interest here to note a statement by Captain M. Horace Hayes, who spent a long lifetime, in the days before the riding and driving of horses were relegated to the realm of sports and hobbies, traveling over much of the world as a professional horse-breaker. Of "man-eating" horses Captain Hayes has written:

I have had a great number of so-called man-eating East-Indian and Arab stallions pass through my hands, as well as horses of all degrees both at home and abroad; but have never known a single instance of a horse, outside his own stall, actually attacking with his teeth a man who faced him; although many animals will make a feint of doing so. I will go farther and say that I do not believe that there is a horse in the world which, in any open place, would try his best to "savage" a man who guarded himself with a stick held in a direction across the animal's face. Although this statement may be received with incredulity by many; I not only adhere to it, but am prepared at any time to prove it practically. . . . I made a rule in all cases of reputed man-eaters who were brought to me, to turn them loose in the ring and then to catch and halter them unaided by anyone; a process which occupied only a few minutes. . . . Wherever I went, I left behind pupils who, after having been taught by me, were quite as capable of successfully handling vicious horses as I am. The whole question is one of knowledge and experience.[1]

[1] M. Horace Hayes, *Among Men and Horses* (New York, Dodd, 1894).

I think the point is clear. Some horses are bolder than others, but real courage is not to be expected of an animal whose chief instinctive defense in the presence of danger is flight. So let us not abuse our mounts' willingness to learn, and run the risk of compounding our own training difficulties, by attributing to the horse virtues or qualities that he does not really have.

Most persons like to believe that their horses, at least their special favorites, return their affection. Many a sensible adult, and almost any child, stands ever ready to offer evidence of his firm belief that horses often do become really attached to kind masters. The sort of "proof" thus offered can usually be classified in a few general types:

1. The faithful war horse—who hasn't read about him?—that stood patiently amid shot and shell beside his wounded or dead master;

2. The horse that nickers a greeting to his beloved master, though he never so greets anybody else, even at feeding time;

3. The horse that steadfastly carried his beloved master through a raging blizzard to safety;

4. The horse that won't let anyone except his master safely handle or mount him;

5. The jealous horse that throws a tantrum if he sees his master or mistress caress another horse or a dog or even a human being, the display of jealousy being "proof" of the horse's love.

I prefer to leave it to the reader himself to decide whether any of these typical examples can stand as proof of a horse's affection for any human being. I shall content myself with just one suggestion: If you hope to train a horse by depending even partially on his affection for you, you might as well stop reading right here.

One other attribute of the horse which most of us are prone to overestimate is his degree of intelligence. Horses differ greatly in their individual "braininess," but it is doubtful if even the smartest horse can compete in the same class with an average mule. This is no discredit to the horse, for, like all of us, he is as Nature made him. However, our crediting him with more intelligence than he really possesses too often has a most harmful effect: it misleads us into "punishing" a horse for errors which are due either to his lack of understanding of what he is supposed to do or to his instinctive reactions to errors which we make in handling him. Whichever of these two may be the cause of a horse's undesirable actions, if we proceed to "punish" him in the belief that he knows he did wrong but did it deliberately anyhow, then the "punishment" we inflict is actually abuse. If we face the fact that the horse is a relatively stupid animal, as well as a timid one full of instinctive fears, we shall think twice before resorting to punishment and hence achieve immeasurably better results in all our training.

Skillful training should and can develop a horse's mind as well as his muscles. Wise stable management can help tremendously in this development—a topic I'll reserve for a later chapter. Too often, however, the good effects of a daily short training session are more than offset by the bad effects of poor stable management. Even those of us who like to believe that the horse is more intelligent than he is are usually guilty of so treating him that he turns out to be duller than Nature meant him to be.

These, then, are the important characteristics of the animal we hope to train. If we keep them in mind at all times, our task will be easy. If we forget or ignore them, we are headed for failure, and shall have nobody but ourselves to blame—certainly not the horse.

CHAPTER VIII

The Foal

*The understanding of a horseman comes
from the heart, not from mathematical
calculations.*
— E. Beudant

Halterbreaking is probably the simplest of elementary lessons in a horse's life; yet it can be taught wrongly, even to the extent of lasting ill effect. A certain type of inept horseman thinks that a stallion must be led with the leadstrap chain looped around his lower jaw or over his nose or drawn through his mouth so that it acts as an abrasive bit; but whenever you see a horse so led you can be sure that you are looking at one that was improperly halterbroken as a foal or was allowed later to develop bad habits, or the man who is leading him lacks confidence in his own authority. A properly handled horse will lead almost anywhere on a slack line.

The simplest way to teach a nursing foal to lead willingly is to use its dam as a lure or decoy; the youngster will naturally follow its mother. Let's assume that you are alone in a corral, without a helper to lead the mare while you lead the foal. We'll say the foal is near the mare's right flank and you, holding both lead-ropes, are near her left shoulder in the usual position for leading. Pass the foal's lead-rope under the mare's neck, allowing the youngster about four feet of rope. Hold the mare's rope short, close to the halter. Grasping both ropes firmly in your right hand, walk out straight ahead, leading the mare. The foal will follow beside her, perhaps even before it feels the tug of the rope.

When it does feel the strange tug of the rope the foal is likely to toss its head and perhaps momentarily balk; but if you keep the mare moving the foal will come along. Next, the youngster might try to rush ahead; if it does, make a sharp turn to the left, drawing the mare with you. This will check the foal's rush forward, forcing it to turn after mama. Proceed back and forth across the corral, always at first turning to the left, accustoming the foal to follow in response to the pull of the rope.

After a few minutes of this the foal should be leading quietly, without attempting to rush ahead. Now practice making some right turns. As you push the mare away from you and follow around beside her in a right turn, the foal will have to turn, too, for the mare's forehand will block any progress straight ahead. It might be necessary to shorten the foal's lead-rope.

It is a common error to accustom a horse to being led from only one side, the left; but a horse should lead equally well, as well as stand to be mounted, from either side. Therefore, the next step is to change sides with the foal; place it on the mare's left while you lead from the right (if your mare isn't already used to this, it's your fault). Now proceed making right and left turns as before. Every time the foal tries to rush ahead, pull the mare around in a sharp turn toward yourself.

If you have someone to help you, let him lead the mare while you lead the foal close beside her. Try to avoid "hanging on" the halter rope; as much as possible, keep the rope slack. Pull on the rope only when you want to change directions or check the foal. Do not apply a long steady pull; pull sharply, then quickly slack the rope. Keep that rule in mind all the time: pull and slack. For our ideal is to have the foal quickly acquire the habit of leading on a slack line. A quick pull or jerk signifies a correction. A steady pull means nothing.

Let your helper leading the mare gradually get farther ahead of you and the foal. When mare and foal are about ten yards apart do some left and right turns. Do not let the foal rush ahead in an effort to catch up with its dam. Keep a short hold on the rope and gently check every such attempt to rush, if necessary halting the foal, forcing it to stand, while your helper halts the mare at the same time. When you do halt, command, "Whoa!" and *make that order stick* until you are ready to proceed. You will use this command frequently in all future training and it is an order which must carry authority. A horse should learn to obey the command, "Whoa!" instantly and at any time; the sooner he begins learning it, the better.

This should be sufficient for the first lesson.

Since two brief lessons a day are better than one longer one, if you have time repeat the whole lesson later in the day.

The following day repeat everything done the first day, but now add something new. Lead the foal ahead of the mare. Naturally, at first the youngster is likely to try to hang back, but if you let it see that mama is coming along right behind, it will soon settle down to going ahead quietly.

When the youngster will lead calmly beside, behind, or ahead of its dam, have your helper hold the mare near the center of the corral—or, if you are working alone, tie the mare to a corner post —and lead the foal back and forth about the enclosure alone. Once it understands that mama is not going to desert it, the young one will quickly settle down.

In two or three days—at the very most, at the end of the week —all this should be routine.

Under ordinary circumstances,we need not bother to make the foal lead out of its dam's presence. When the two are separated at weaning time that will come as a matter of course.

It is important to remember always that, if you expect your colt to learn to lead on a slack line, you must avoid "hanging" heavily on the haltershank or lead-rope. In leading, be as careful about maintaining "light hands" as when riding a horse in a bit.

Besides halterbreaking and learning to lead well, there are other aspects of a colt's education that should be begun as soon as practicable, for there is no good reason to put them off until later, as is so often done.

Once accustomed to the halter, the foal should be taught that it has nothing to fear in letting itself be handled all over. It should be groomed daily, less with the idea of glossing it up than with the idea of developing its trust and confidence in those who handle it. Pay particular attention to gently touching the youngster's head, ears, tail, and feet, for any roughness in handling these parts can start the exasperating habits of head-shyness and a tendency to kicking, vices it is easier to prevent than later to cure.

Before the foal is weaned it is a good idea to get it used to entering a trailer or a van. Eventually it will have to learn this lesson; the best time to teach it is while the youngster is small and easy to handle and willing to go anywhere its dam leads. The procedure is simple. Park your trailer near the center of a corral, or at whatever convenient location you prefer; and have some friend lead the mare up into it while you, leading the foal, encourage it to follow up the ramp.

Another way of teaching this lesson is to leave the trailer parked for several days in the corral until the foal has become thoroughly used to its presence. Then put some grain or hay in the trailer and lead the mare in to feed, but don't tie her. Leave the foal loose in the corral, free to do as it pleases. Eventually, after a day or two, it is almost certain to follow the mare up into the trailer.

If you don't happen to have a trailer of your own, it is easy to build a wheelless dummy of rough lumber. Just be sure to build it solidly. If it wobbles or seems to be insecure when the foal first puts foot on it, you will find yourself up against the task of having to overcome one of the most deeply rooted fears a horse has—the fear of losing its footing and hence being deprived of its power to flee from possible danger.

Steadiness is a mark of a well-trained horse—and extreme timidity, as we have seen, is perhaps the horse's most salient characteristic. Hence, obviously, this natural timidity can be, if not always completely overcome, at least considerably lessened. The chief cause of most manifestations of fright is strangeness; the horse's inexperience of an object leads him, his nature being what it is, to regard it with timid suspicion. The remedy, therefore, is familiarity, which will breed indifference. The sooner this process of familiarizing the young horse with a wide variety of sights and sounds is begun and the more thoroughly it is carried out, the better.

Once the foal leads well, take the youngster, with its dam, on an exploratory tour of the ranch or farm. Show it "the sights." Let it see, hear, and smell all that's going on; and the more that there is going on, the better. Start the engine of your car, blow the horn, turn the radio on full blast; let the foal look and listen, and gradually lead it closer to the strange machine. Introduce it to the tractor and start the engine. Leading the young one, ride the mare down to the highway and watch a few cars and trucks go by. Let the foal learn early in life that the world is a big place full of strange sights, sounds, and smells, but that none of them is worth getting overexcited about.

Perhaps some day you will want to ride this promising foal on a hunting trip. Then you won't want a gun-shy horse. Even if you never hunt, some day when you are mounted on this youngster a near-by car may backfire or blow out a tire. You'll be safer then if the old pony is blasé enough merely to cock his ears and forget it instead of jumping out from under you. So now is as good a time as any to let the foal hear gunfire. Begin by firing a .22 from a distance of, say, fifty or sixty yards from the youngster. Don't rush things; give the foal plenty of time to get used to the reports before you move in a little closer. You can spread this part of the training over a period of weeks or months, for there is no special reason to hurry it. When the foal will stand steady without any signs of alarm as you fire a .22 while standing only a few feet away, then you are ready to repeat the whole procedure with a gun of larger caliber, or with a shotgun. Remember the cardinal rule: *Easy does it.* Decrease distance very gradually. Eventually the young horse should casually tolerate the blast of a shotgun or the report of a .45 fired close by.

Some of my readers may consider this accustoming a colt to new sights and sounds superfluous. "I've never bothered with that kind of thing, but my horses are perfectly steady before any kind of racket." If you can say this, both you and your horses are to be congratulated, for their surroundings have been such as to let them become accustomed to many sights and sounds without any special effort on your part or theirs. However, everybody does not have this advantage — and more than one horseman has abruptly realized that this part of his horse's training has been neglected the first time he has taken his mount to a show, or the first time some passing motorist has honked a horn at him. In my opinion, it is wiser to pay some attention to this phase of training right from the start than to wait for a possible accident.

CHAPTER IX

The Yearling: I

*A perfect horseman knows neither
fear nor anger.*
                                    —*Anon.*

By the time your colt is a year old, assuming that you have had the entire handling of him, he should be perfectly quiet to handle under all ordinary circumstances. This means that he should not object to having any one of his feet picked up and held for examination or trimming; he should tolerate reasonable handling of any part of his body, including ears and tail, without flinching or attempting to kick; he should show no signs of head-shyness when you halter him. He should tolerate all ordinary noises, including gunfire, casually, and lead almost anywhere you wish to take him on a slack line, obedient to the lighest pull on the halter.[1]

Here let me anticipate a logical question that more than one reader will now be pondering. Every horseman isn't a breeder; more of us buy colts than have the good fortune to be able to rear them from birth. Hence, most of us have to start with a colt that somebody else has handled first; he may be completely green or he may already have acquired a few bad habits because of the way his previous owner handled him, or neglected to handle him. How does our system of elementary handling apply to such a youngster—say, a husky yearling or a colt of two or three years of age?

---

[1] The reader will note that we pay no special attention to teaching a colt to stand tied. A colt halter-trained as suggested here will stand tied without any fuss, as a matter of course.

Such an older colt must learn exactly the same basic lessons as our little weanling; the chief difference is that the progress of the yearling or the two- or three-year-old can be speeded up. He can be taught more in less time, for you don't have to wait for him to "grow up to" his lessons. He is physically ready for more advanced training as soon as he has mastered the kindergarten fundamentals. Therefore, you can push him right along, teaching him in a very short time all that you would teach a younger colt at a more leisurely pace.

As an illustration, let us consider the basic lesson of leading on a slack line. In the previous chapter I stated that this can be taught to a suckling foal in a few days; at most, it shouldn't take more than a week. The same lesson can be taught to a yearling or to an older colt, however, in a matter of minutes. Therefore, we need only confirm the lesson by daily repetition. Plates 17, 18, and 19 illustrate this point.

In handling a husky two- or three-year-old we must be ready to cope with a possibility which we need hardly waste a moment's thought on when handling a small foal. This is the possibility that the colt might suddenly pull back, deliberately resisting the pressure of the lead rope. When a big husky colt unexpectedly does this, catching us off guard and perhaps off balance, he can make us look pretty silly before we can dig in and get him stopped. Worse, the experience might give him a hint of his own strength compared to ours, and plant in his mind the seed of the idea that he really has the power to flout our authority if he wants to.

To avoid this chance, or quickly to rid the colt of any cocky notions he might get if he has succeeded in jerking us off balance, we can substitute a tail rope for the rump rope. A tail rope should be of soft cotton or woven nylon and less than half an inch thick. If you must use a manila lariat, first wrap some soft rags around the section of rope that will be placed under the colt's tail, for otherwise the hard rope has too much "bite" and might abrade the tender dock. A light pull on the rope will start the most reluctant or sluggish colt moving forward. Only a confirmed "bad actor" will try to resist the tail rope—but seldom more than once.

It seems hardly necessary to add the caution not to attempt to lead a colt or a horse from the rear of a truck or a car, as the drawing illustrates, unless the animal is accustomed to machines and has lost its fear of them. Otherwise, when the motor is started and the exhaust pipe belches, the startled horse might try to go into reverse, with unnecessarily painful consequences to its tail.

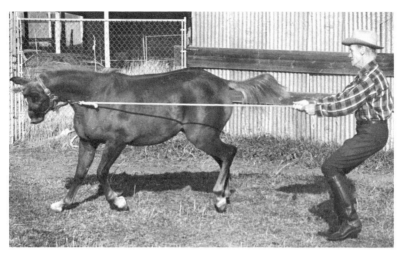

Plate 17. This two-year-old filly's basic education had been sadly neglected when I first handled her. She had never been properly halterbroken. Her notion of being led was to be the leader, dragging her handler along willy-nilly. At other times she would refuse to budge; if coerced, she would rear. This filly was not mean or stubborn, but simply had not learned discipline.

Photograph by Gene A. Pearson

Plate 18. A tail rope convinced the filly that her hoyden days were over. The tail rope is a nonslip loop of ¼-inch nylon cord. A lead, run back through the halter, is hooked to the loop. A few quick, sharp tugs on the tail rope made Heather forget her rambunctious ways.

Photograph by Gene A. Pearson

Plate 19. Less than 15 minutes after the first picture was taken Heather would lead as briskly and quietly as an old show horse. During the next few weeks she got plenty of practise doing it. For a lesson not only is taught; it must be confirmed.

Photograph by Gene A. Pearson

Another method of teaching a big colt or a green horse to come along is by means of a body rope. Loop the rope around the colt's body about where the front cinch of a saddle would be, using a slipknot or honda so that the loop will tighten when the end of the rope is pulled and will immediately loosen when the rope is slacked. Run the end of the rope out between the colt's forelegs and thread it through the ring of the halter.

To start the colt moving give the rope a sharp, quick jerk—do not use a slow, steady pull. Be careful when you do this to have a firm grip on the lead-rope and to stand a little to one side of the colt, never directly in front of him; for when that loop un-expectedly tightens around his barrel, squeezing him with an effect similar to the pressure of a rider's legs, the colt is likely to bound forward quite suddenly. If you're in the way, he'll prob-ably knock you down and sashay right over you. Should this hap-

Fig. 1. —Leading with a tail rope. *(Drawing by Randy Steffen.)*

pen, it will have a worse effect on the colt than his feet will
have on you: it will give him an exaggerated idea of his own importance and convince him, at least temporarily, that you're a
pushover. Sooner or later, usually when you will least expect it,
he will try to bowl you over again. An ounce of prevention is
worth a pound of liniment, so be prepared for this; don't let it
happen the first time.

Once our big colt has learned to lead quietly, we proceed to
gentle him for handling and to accustom him to a variety of sights
and noises exactly as recommended for foals.

We are now ready to begin real work with our yearling. Our
first step is carefully to fit him with the training cavesson, or put
a snug-fitting hackamore on him if we don't have a cavesson, and
take him into the circular breaking pen or a small corral for his
first lesson on the longe.

Before this book was published, longeing (often miscalled
lungeing) was practically unheard of among most Western horsemen. They knew nothing about it, had never even thought of it.
Today, however, a large majority of progressive Western trainers
practice longeing (as well as ground driving) as a matter of course.
They have found that it not only works but greatly simplifies basic
training. Unfortunately, few of them yet understand how to do it
correctly so as to gain full advantage from its employment. Too
many of them still think of longeing as a way of merely exercising a horse when for some reason or other we cannot or do

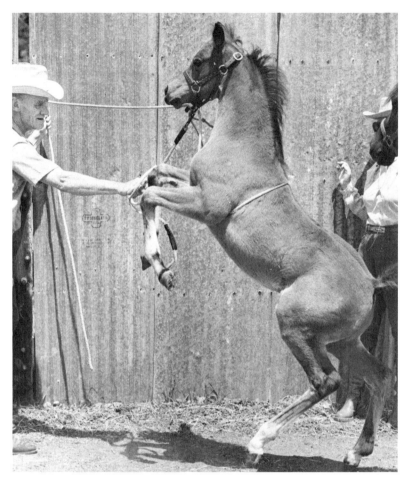

Plate 20. This frisky weanling reacts quite naturally to being tied up for the first time. However, securely restrained by a body rope, she soon calmed down. Such basic lessons are best taught when a colt is small and easy to handle.

Photograph by Gene A. Pearson

Plate 21. This husky three-year-old had a rough time learning the same basic lesson, to stand tied, that the weanling filly learned easily. Lax handling, when he should have been firmly disciplined, gave him three years to learn his own strength. Misdirected "kindness" let him develop into a spoiled brat. This is the same horse shown in Plate 2.

Photograph by Gene A. Pearson

not care to ride him. Longeing, however, can be much more than this, so let's consider it in some detail.

Longeing properly done is much more than merely a way of exercising a horse by shooing him around in circles on the end of a line. Longeing is a basic step in a logical system of horse training initiated at a time when so many colts begin to go wrong. On the longe line a trainer can nip potential faults in a colt before they have a chance to take root, as well as correct faults in a mature horse. Systematic work on the longe develops a colt's muscles and his gaits even before he is physically mature enough to be ridden. It makes teaching prompt obedience to oral commands easy, thereby giving the trainer more control. On the ground, we can see the results we are getting instead of having to rely on horseman's "feel," which must be developed gradually by experience.

First let's consider the technique of longeing, some of the problems involved, and the equipment.

The first common mistake of a novice undertaking longe work without experienced help is to assume that a green horse can be worked efficiently in a halter. His second mistake commonly is to use too short a line—because his next error is to use too short a whip; he thinks anything he can brandish at the horse will do— and in a pinch, he can throw a rock. These three initial errors do much to explain why so many novice trainers quickly get the idea that longeing is pretty much a waste of time, except to give a stabled horse needed exercise.

With green horses, and especially with big, lively colts, a halter is no good for longeing. It fits too loosely to permit good control, thus teaching a colt to pull on the line. The harder he pulls the more uncomfortable he becomes. Eventually he will resent the work; instead of getting better he will get worse. And there is always danger of the buckle or metal dees, as the loose halter shifts about, injuring his eye.

The longeing cavesson was designed for the job and it pays to get one. Given the ordinary good care any leather gear deserves, a well-made cavesson will last a lifetime.

In this country there are two types of cavessons commonly available: the English style, a strong, heavyweight cavesson with metal plates covered by leather inside the noseband; and a lighter, milder cavesson with a more flexible noseband padded on the inside with felt.

A third type of cavesson available, though usually more ex-

Plate 22. A FELT-PADDED LONGEING CAVESSON. This is a mild cavesson, very suitable for young colts and light-headed horses such as Arabians. Used by the U.S. cavalry, this type of cavesson is hard to find now, but similar models are available.

Photograph by Gene A. Pearson

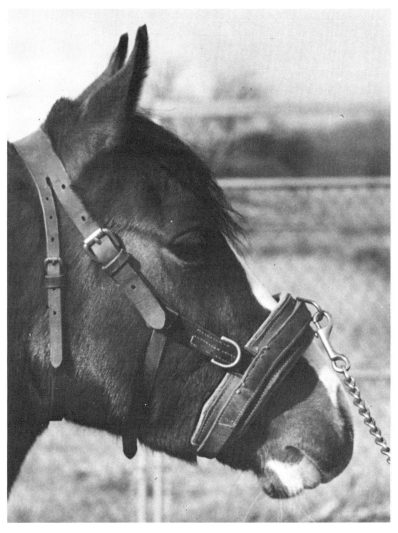

Plate 23. A HEAVYWEIGHT ENGLISH CAVESSON. The noseband is reinforced by metal plates. An unruly horse soon learns to respect its authority. It is usually too big for young colts and should be used with care on light-headed horses.

Photograph by the author

pensive, is a lightweight German model with a chamois-covered noseband stiffened by hinged steel plates.

I would not say that any one of these three is "best." Much depends on the horse and on the handler's skill. For a strong, rambunctious colt inclined to be hardheaded, or for a horse with habits that make him a bit difficult to handle, the heavy English cavesson might help to bring him into line more quickly.

Any style of cavesson, properly adjusted, should fit snugly. Never adjust it loosely, as you would a halter. A cavesson must stay put without slipping or shifting about no matter how hard the horse may pull on the line.

If you understand how a hackamore should be used—never with a dead, steady pull—you can get good results with one in place of a cavesson. But that "*if*" is a big one. The hackamore's chief drawback is that it can so easily be overused. A rough or clumsy trainer can take skin off a colt's lower jaw with a rawhide hackamore. One hard pull too many can make a horse dread longe work. The trainer must have good hands. A cavesson is more forgiving than a hackamore.

Novices who undertake to longe a horse for the first time almost always assume that the horse should fear the whip—otherwise, how do you "make him go"? But this assumption is one of the first links in a chain of errors. *The horse never should fear the whip.* The whip is not an instrument of punishment. It is merely an extension of the trainer's arm, a baton with which he gives the horse cues. The horse must learn to respect the whip, just as later he will learn to obey the aids; but he must work unhampered by fear, for a frightened, worried horse cannot learn.

An efficient longeing whip has a shaft from six to eight feet long, with a lash of about the same length or a bit longer. One of the most important benefits of longeing is to develop smooth, free, relaxed gaits. Too often, however, this beneficial effect of longe work is lost by working a colt in too tight a circle—because the handler is using too short a whip, often an ordinary buggy whip. He tries to compensate for his too-short whip by bringing the horse within reach. Unfortunately, small circles demand more balance and suppleness than a green colt has acquired. Therefore, your longe line should be at least twenty feet long, permitting the colt to follow a forty-foot circle, and your whip should be long enough to let you touch him with the tip of the lash. Later, when he has learned what it's all about, you won't have to flick

him with the lash. Merely a slight movement of the whip, with
or without an oral command, will be sufficient.

Let us assume that we shall begin by first longeing our colt
in a circle to the left. Keep in mind the following points of longeing technique:

The trainer, near the center of the circle, does not, at first,
stand still, simply pivoting to face the colt moving around him.
He moves along with the colt in a small circle concentric with the
colt's course. Only later, when the colt is well trained to the longe
and obedient to spoken commands, may the trainer confidently
pivot in place.

Moving in a small circle with the colt out on the end of the
line, the trainer stays approximately abreast of the colt's hindquarters. In this position he is best able to keep the green youngster
moving—which in the beginning is more important, because it is
usually more frequently necessary, than stopping him. When the
colt is to be halted the trainer moves quickly toward the colt's
head by taking one or two long steps to the left (or to the right
when circling right).

The trainer holds the line in his "leading" hand—the hand
toward the direction in which the colt is circling—with the un-
needed balance of the longe folded, not coiled, in the palm of his
other hand, which also holds the whip.

The whip may be held in the usual driving position with the
shaft coming out of the hand between thumb and forefinger, or
reversed with the butt toward the thumb-side of the hand and
with the shaft coming out near the little finger. Held thus, the
whip is pointed down toward the ground so that the lash drags
behind the trainer as he turns and does not unnecessarily distract
or unsettle the colt. When it is necessary to urge the colt on, the
trainer need not raise the whip; he merely flicks the lash at the
colt's hocks by quickly rotating his hand and forearm. Since the
whip is not to be used for punishment, this arm rotation will provide all the force necessary to use the lash effectively. The lash
need never touch the colt below the hocks. Very often even light
contact will be unnecessary, for when the colt catches a glimpse of
the lash snaking toward him from behind he will instinctively
quicken his pace. Eventually, when the colt is responsive to
spoken commands, we can work him without the whip.

In the Spanish Riding School, the whiplash is flicked only
against the horse's flank, about where a rider's leg would apply
an aid. The horse is thus prepared for leg aids even before

Plate 24. LONGEING. The colt is bent on the arc of the circle, facing the way he is going. The slight sag in the line proves that he is not pulling but is nicely under control.

Photograph by Gene A. Pearson

mounted schooling begins. I have no doubt that this reasoning is probably correct, but I think that this way of handling the whip is too exacting for the average amateur. Just flicking the lash toward the horse's hocks gets the job done with fewer possible mistakes.

If you have had the misfortune to acquire a whipbroken colt, one that has been taught to face a man and either stand still or walk up to him at sight of a whip, you will need all the patience at your command in order to work him on the longe. For the instant he catches sight of the whip the colt will halt in his tracks and face you. If you pretend to threaten him with the whip to start him circling, he will face you with fear-filled eyes but he won't budge—unless it is to step toward you. If you should hit him with the whip in an effort to make him keep his distance or to start circling, even that will do no good. He will either freeze in his tracks or come right in to you quickly, as he has been so painfully taught to do in order to escape the lash of the whip.

If you have a colt like this there is only one thing to do. You must "unteach" him what he has already learned. You must teach him to move out in a circle at the full length of the line instead of facing you or coming in to you, and make him understand that he will not be whipped for doing so. Your first step is to discard the whip. Don't just drop it on the ground. Get it out of the corral; put it out of sight. If the colt seems upset, give him time to calm down. Lead him around the corral, gradually letting the longe line slip through your hand so that you and the colt are walking farther apart. If you have someone to help you, let him lead the colt around in a circle from the outer side while you, holding the line, stand at the center. If you don't have a helper and if the colt persists in turning in to face you, then your only recourse is the crude one of "shooing" him around at the end of the line while you follow in a smaller circle. If you find this necessary, don't worry about the colt's pace or gait; just try to keep him from galloping. Pace and gait can be corrected and controlled once he finally understands what you want him to do. The main thing is to get him circling freely without any fear that you are suddenly going to hit him with a whip to make him stop and face you.

Let us begin, then, with our yearling, a stranger to the whip. We'll start by longeing him in a circle to the left.

If you have a round pen in which to work, making the colt understand that you want him to move around you in a circle could hardly be simpler. Simply allow him enough line to move out from you as far as the fence permits and start him moving with a few clucks or, if necessary, a light flick of the whiplash on the hocks. If he tries to veer in toward you instead of staying close to the fence, make him keep his distance by "snapping" the longe line at him with a quick vertical motion of your hand and wrist.

If, however, you have to work in a square or a rectangular enclosure, with the long distances between your position near the center and the end fences greater than the full length of your line, while the distances to the side fences are considerably shorter, the colt will tend to travel not in a circle but in an ellipse; and when he comes down the long side of the corral your line will sag. Be careful of this. Try to keep the degree of sag to a minimum by raising your leading (left) arm as high as possible to keep the line off the ground and to avoid any chance of the colt either getting a foreleg over it or stepping on it. Gradually, as the colt settles down to the job, you can take in the line until he is moving in an approximate circle instead of an ellipse.

Most well-bred colts when first longed are inclined to travel at a high trot, faster than we want them to go. After a few circuits they usually slow down, with the idea of stopping. When urged to keep moving, they are likely to extend to a canter or even a gallop. During the first half dozen lessons don't worry about this sort of ragged performance. Keep in mind that the whole thing is new and strange to the colt and that he is at least trying to do what he thinks you want him to do.

However, we must never forget that the youngster is in very soft condition and that he is only a baby, and that—particularly in warm weather—a little trotting and cantering go a very long way. Therefore, we should try at all times to hold the colt to a walk or, at most, a slow jog-trot and avoid letting him become hot. If he does become overheated or even shows signs of getting hot, we should stop the lesson at once, no matter how little we may have accomplished. We should strive above all else to keep the colt calm, which is impossible if we let him overwork.

The first lesson should be very brief—no more than ten minutes if all goes well and less than that if the colt shows signs of getting hot or overexcited.

Work the colt in circles to both sides. If he appears to move more awkwardly or more reluctantly to one side than to the other, work him a couple of minutes longer to that side. Most horses are one-sided, usually favoring the left; the only cure is work that supples the muscles on the stiffer side.

This first time on the line the colt is likely to pull a little bit, especially when moving across the width of a rectangular enclosure. In other words, you will probably have to hold him to a circle, gripping the line firmly. However, thanks to the time you have spent teaching him to lead on a slack line, he will soon get over this—it's mostly due to awkwardness in turning—and will give to the weight of the longe, circling around you without pulling the line taut. You should encourage and co-operate in achieving this as quickly as possible by handling the longe delicately.

When the colt tries to stop before you want him to, take a step forward directly toward his hip—not sidewise toward his head—and flick the whiplash at his hocks. Keep moving concentric with his course, staying approximately abreast of his hindquarters.

When you want him to stop call out sharply, "Whoa!" and take a long step sidewise in the direction of his head as you give a smooth, firm pull on the longe line, drawing his head toward you. Nine colts out of ten will come to a quick stop. The tenth colt will probably "spook" slightly, perhaps breaking into a gallop.

If he does, repeat your command as you quickly move sidewise to head him off and pull again on the line. If he has broken into a canter or gallop, try to time your pull when his forefeet are off the ground; this will swing his forehand around toward you and his hindquarters out, forcing him to face you.

Some horsemen do not approve of this method of teaching a green colt to halt. They believe, or fear, that the lateral pull might dislocate some vertebrae. Instead, they prefer to bring the whip around, pointing it toward the colt's head or shoulder to halt him. By this method they try to discourage the colt from facing inward so that he will not either walk in to the trainer at the center of the circle or turn about and start off in the opposite direction. I have never found, however, that pulling on the line has ever caused either of these things to happen with colts I have longed. In my opinion, it makes little, if any, difference which method is used to teach a colt to halt; after a few trials he will learn to obey the spoken command, anyhow. I prefer pulling on the line to pointing with the whip for three reasons: having the whip pointed toward their heads often upsets nervous colts; pulling is more quickly effective; it serves to "soften up" a green colt's stiff neck muscles to a small degree and prepares him to respond more readily to the direct rein and the leading rein effects, which will be used considerably as the training progresses. I concede that *jerking* the line might possibly dislocate one of a weak-necked colt's vertebrae; but a jerk and a smooth pull on the line are quite different.

Do not now make the mistake of letting the colt come to you. If he tries it, say, "Whoa!" and flip the line in his face to stop him. Make him stand. Never let him come in to you. If you do, he'll soon get into the habit of walking all over your toes every time you halt him, and is very likely to develop the trick of interrupting a lesson by gradually veering in toward you and suddenly stopping, his manner suggesting plainly that it's time to knock off for lunch.

That, however, is not the only reason why he must learn to stand and wait for you to walk up to him. A second reason is that you gave the command, "Whoa." You must make the colt understand that you mean it, that every time you say that word he is to stop instantly and stay stopped until you give him a cue to move again. If he has developed the habit of instant obedience to this order before you ever mount him, he will be practically trained to stand for mounting when the time comes. Finally, a third and very important reason why he should learn to obey this command is that some day you may urgently need it as an emergency brake to avoid an accident.

After you have made him stand for a few moments, walk up to the colt, keeping the whip pointed groundward behind you and gathering up the slack line as you approach. Speak to him approvingly and pat him to let him know that he has done well. Give him a minute's rest, or longer if he feels too warm; then, shifting the whip to your other hand, start him circling in the opposite direction. Repeat everything. Then call it a day.

Again I wish to emphasize that during this first lesson, as well as subsequent lessons, we should strive to keep the colt calm and normally relaxed. That is the only state in which he will be really receptive to learning. Remember that there is no hurry. He is only a yearling. Think of progress in terms of not days or weeks but months and even years. Be satisfied with a little at a time. The golden rule in training is: Easy does it.

CHAPTER X

The Yearling: 2

So, to be masters of our horses,
we must be masters of ourselves.
— M. F. McTaggart

UNTIL you have longed your yearling about half a dozen times his actions on the longe line are bound to be a bit erratic. Don't fret about this. Give him time to settle down. Concentrate on encouraging him to move at a free, fast walk and at a slow trot. Discourage his attempts to canter or gallop by commanding, "Whoa!" and pulling his head in toward you to halt him each time he starts going too fast. Just how long it will take the colt to settle down depends on his individual temperament and on how well you handle him. As a general rule of thumb, I don't think it should take more than a week at the rate of one lesson a day. If at the end of this time your colt is still overeager to go too fast, you should carefully consider three probable reasons:

1. The colt is unusually highstrung and nervous.
2. He is too fresh from insufficient exercise and too generous a ration of grain.
3. You are doing something wrong, unintentionally spooking him up.

The first of these probabilities is the most difficult to cope with, for it cannot be eradicated. A nervous colt will be a nervous horse; his inherent temperament cannot be changed. We can only hope to lessen his degree of natural jitteriness by sympathetic treatment and by taking extra precautions to calm him down.

138

Fortunately, however, inbred nervousness is uncommon; but many horses are made nervous by uncertain handlers, people who lack self-confidence and should never even attempt to school a horse.

The remedy for the second probability is obvious: cut down on the colt's grain and let him run out more. This overfreshness from lack of exercise and too much feed is common among horses kept in stables. When we are schooling a colt we can often avoid it simply by turning the colt out to pasture for several hours in the morning and then bringing him in for his daily workout after he has run off some of his surplus energy, or by working him in the afternoon. If we have time, we can work the colt briefly twice a day instead of once.

Another way of slowing him down is to work him, if we can, in very deep going such as loose sand or a freshly plowed field. This is also a splendid way of legging up a young horse, for the deep going not only slows him down but gives him a real lung-stretching workout, forcing him to burn up energy and really use his muscles. It is particularly good too in helping a clumsy colt improve his action and balance; in loose sand or deep plowland the colt just has to learn to pick up his feet and move in better balance. Be careful, however, not to overdo this. Remember that it is very hard work even for a mature horse, much less a soft colt. Begin very gradually and watch the colt for signs of getting too hot.

If you have been unintentionally spooking the colt, make it your business to figure out what you've been doing wrong; then quit it. Perhaps you have been handling the whip wrongly, unconsciously flourishing it at the colt—if he was a whipbroken colt, you shouldn't be using the whip at all. Maybe once or twice you accidentally stung him with the lash instead of merely flicking his hocks lightly. Maybe you have a nervous way of handling the longe line that makes him think you want him to go faster. Only God and the colt may know; it's your business to find out.

We shall assume that at the end of a week of one or two daily workouts on the longe your colt has settled down. He moves calmly at a walk and trot, rarely pulls on the line so that you have to grip hard to hold him to a circle, and will halt when you command, "Whoa!"—perhaps even before you have to pull on the line.

It is now time that we should begin in an elementary way to control his paces. To the familiar "Whoa," we now add another command, "Walk!" One trainer of my acquaintance prefers to use the command, "Step along"; he believes that "walk" and "whoa" sound too much alike and might at times confuse a colt. If you agree with him, use "step along" or "hopalong" or "get up" or any other words you prefer. Whatever you use, your aim right now should be to teach the colt to walk on command, and only to walk—not trot or jog or canter—and to keep on walking until you say, "Whoa," or urge him into a trot.

This is really quite simple. It demands only patience on our part and constant repetition with almost no use of the whip until when we give the command, "Walk," the colt obeys automatically. If he tries to trot, stop him immediately with a sharp, "Whoa!" Make him stand for a moment; then say, "Walk," and give the longe line a little shake, if necessary stepping toward the colt's hindquarters to start him.

It should hardly be necessary to point out that this lesson should not be attempted at first until after we have exercised the colt for a while and let him work off his first keen edge of energy. Neither do I mean to imply that during an entire lesson we should try to hold the colt only to a walk. The important object of the lesson is that when we do say, "Walk," the colt is to understand that that is exactly what he must do and that he must hold the gait until we permit him to change, not until he himself feels like changing.

Some readers may wonder why, if the lesson is so simple, and obviously any horse can walk, we should bother with it at all. Does it seem to be a waste of time? It isn't. Every step in these elementary basic lessons has just one end in view—the making of a finished riding horse, accomplished in what I believe is the surest and easiest way, easy on the horse as well as on the trainer. A finished riding horse should promptly take the gait and pace his rider demands, and maintain that same gait and pace even on a completely loose rein until the rider signals for a change. It is this idea that we wish to instill into our colt's mind before we ever mount him. When he does become old enough for us to ride, he will be practically a made horse. All he'll need thereafter will be practice in carrying weight and some advanced work to acquire finish.

If at times these elementary details seem unnecessarily "fussy" to you, remember this. Our goal is always the making of a finished riding horse.

After the colt has learned to respond to the command, "Walk," begin teaching him to obey the order, "Trot."

Every time you start him circling use one or the other of these commands. Do not make the mistake of just starting him and letting him decide whether he should walk or trot. Tell him which gait to take and make the order stick.

Work on these two gait commands and on "Whoa" for at least three months. Insist on obedience. Once you are certain that the colt understands what you want, insist on prompt obedience. Be patient, but be firm.

During this period the time of each lesson can gradually be increased from about ten minutes to about twenty. No hard and fast rule about this can be given. Too much depends on the individual colt; some can stand twice as much work as others. Use common sense. Just be sure not to overwork him.

Since the walk and trot are the best gaits for schooling not only at this stage of the colt's development but later when we shall begin riding as well, do not bother yet about teaching the command, "Lope," or "Canter." There will be plenty of time for that later.

At this time we can teach the colt to change directions without our always walking up to him. Let's assume that we have been circling the colt to the left. Halt him with the usual command, "Whoa." As he stops and faces you, transfer the whip and the extra folds of the longe line from your right to your left hand. With your right hand, which now becomes your "leading" hand, take hold of the line leading directly to the colt's head. Move a step or two to the left so that when the colt now starts circling to the right you will be in your usual position approximately abreast of his hindquarters. Command, "Walk," and if he hesitates—as he might, since this maneuver is new to him—flick the lash gently at his hocks to let him understand that he is to move off to the right.

After a few repetitions of this the colt will get the idea that every time you halt him you are not going to walk up to him and tell him what a good boy he is. Then he will change directions without hesitation. With practice, you can do it so smoothly that the colt's halt is hardly more than a pause to turn around.

However, no matter how smoothly you execute this change of directions you should make it a point to see that the colt does not start off in the new direction before you give him the order to do so. If you neglect this, then you will begin teaching him that the command, "Whoa," does not mean what, up to now, you have taken pains to make him understand it means—which is, "Stop and *stay there*."

One of the primary benefits of work on the longe is that of improving the green colt's natural balance. Moving around in a circle develops "handiness" as work on straight lines never can. The trainer can greatly increase this valuable aspect of the work by often changing the diameters of the circles, for every change necessitates that the colt adjust his balance accordingly. As the colt moves around at the end of the line, therefore, gradually take in the line inch by inch. Do it so gradually that the colt remains almost unaware of the change. Then let the line slip slowly through your hand, paying it out to enlarge the circle. This taking in and paying out should not be done constantly so that the colt never has a chance to complete a true circle, but it should be done frequently so that the colt never becomes accustomed to moving in a circle of the same size all the time. By taking in or paying out more line, in effect the trainer gently unbalances the colt, then leaves it to him to readjust his balance. If the colt seems to pull too hard on the line, it is a sign that he is unbalanced: he is traveling in too small a circle or his pace is too fast, or both. The trainer should watch for this and use judgment.

By this time you have been longeing your yearling almost daily for at least three months. He rarely, if ever, pulls on the line now, but moves around you calmly with the web or rope slightly slack. He accepts the presence of the whip as a matter of course, regarding it merely as an extension of your arm with which you give him clues. He responds to the spoken commands to halt, walk, and trot. Once in a while when feeling frisky he may still like to kick up his heels in a canter or gallop, but when you check him he obeys.

No doubt you will already have noticed that the colt's discipline and general good manners, off the longe line as well as on it, have improved notably. Some of your friends may already have remarked that your youngster shows better manners and more calm good sense than many a mature horse—or if they have refrained from remarking about it, maybe you have observed that they are aware of it, though they may not be too eager to admit it.

Another thing you will notice about this time, I think, is that these easy, almost daily workouts on the longe have improved your colt physically. His muscles stand out better; he has lost a great deal of the coltish awkwardness that was so noticeable the first few weeks you worked him. He can now undergo a workout that lasts approximately twice as long as when you first began longeing him and finish the lesson without any signs of undue exertion. In all ways he handles himself better than he did three months ago. This is not just because he is now three months older; it is chiefly the result of the regular, gradually increased exercise which you have been giving him. If you doubt this, try giving the same sort of workout your yearling is now accustomed to to an older colt that has not been regularly exercised. The older colt simply will not be able to take the same work without quickly getting hot and beginning to heave.

I mention this now only to remind you once more not to become impatient; do not think, even if your colt obeys perfectly now, that you will be wasting time in continuing the same course of exercising and schooling. Whether or not you can already see evidence of your yearling's improved physical condition, you are developing his wind and muscles for the day when you will be ready to ride him. When that day comes your colt will be far more advanced physically and mentally than if he had spent the first couple of years of his life in undisciplined idleness or semi-idleness, as so many colts do while their owners wait for them to grow up to saddle work.

Therefore, I urge you to continue with these longeing lessons — if not daily, then about three times a week—for another three months. Continue gradually to improve his physical fitness to the point where you can work him steadily at a walk and a trot for about half an hour at each lesson. Train him in obedience to the commands, "Whoa," "Walk," and "Trot," until he responds to each order promptly and almost automatically, even when you have laid aside the whip.

During this phase of the schooling you can begin to teach him the command, "Lope," or "Canter" (use whichever you prefer). Do it exactly as you taught him to walk and trot on command, always beginning each gait from a halt. You need not worry about making him take the correct lead. Since he has never had a rider on his back to mess him up with superfluous "help," he will take the correct lead quite naturally, just as he does when galloping with other yearlings out at pasture. All you need to do is watch that he doesn't go too fast. Don't let him become too exhilarated and start galloping; try to hold him to an easy lope. If he persists in going too fast, stop him, turn him around and start him circling in the opposite direction. Do this promptly each time he appears to be getting out of hand. He will soon get the idea that you will tolerate no racing.

Only three or four circuits of the corral in each direction at a canter is enough to begin with. Remember that this gait is harder work for the colt than a trot, so let him work into it gradually. A good rule of thumb to go by is this: Let the colt canter one additional circuit of the corral each day up to a maximum of ten. In other words, suppose on the first day you ask him to lope you let him go around the corral three times to the left, then three times to the right. The next day let him lope four complete circuits in each direction and the day after that five, and so on gradually until he is doing ten circuits in each direction at a lope in addition to his usual work at a walk and a trot. Do not, however, let him do more than ten, even if you feel sure that he could easily take it. It is far wiser to keep the colt a bit too fresh than to risk even a slight amount of overwork. At the risk of wearying you with my emphasis on this point, I repeat: There is no good reason for hurry. We have a long way to go and plenty of time. Barring accidents, this colt has a life expectancy of at least twenty years—plenty of good horses have lived and worked longer. So it's worth while to avoid risking any accidents that might result in blemishing or injuring this youngster before his real usefulness has even begun. *Easy does it.*

After these six months of almost daily work on the longe your colt should be almost perfect in doing everything you have been teaching him. If he isn't, very likely there is something wrong with him, or, even more likely, with you; for nothing that you have tried to teach him is the least bit difficult: it's all as elementary as "Whoa" and "Giddap." I think it is more likely that your colt learned everything so far with surprising quickness and that you have been wondering, "What next?"

Our next step is to get the colt used to carrying something on his back in preparation for the day when he will have to carry a rider. Since a man-sized stock saddle is a pretty cumbersome contraption for a yearling to become accustomed to without ever having had anything else on his back, let's try to find a substitute that will serve the same purpose. A racing saddle, an English-type training saddle, a McClellan saddle, or a child's small stock saddle will do excellently; all can be placed on the colt's back by one man without a helper more easily and neatly than a heavy stock saddle. However, if your stock saddle is the only one you have on hand, it will do; but you will be wise to tie the stirrups to the horn with a thong or a cord so that you won't have to worry about their bumping against the colt's sides. If you use a racing, a training, or a McClellan saddle, take off the stirrup leathers.

Since our colt is already accustomed to being handled all over, this first saddling should prove to be a simple matter. Whether you prefer to do it in his stall or cross-tie him in the aisle of the barn or take him outside to a corral is immaterial. Suit yourself, taking the colt wherever you think he will accept the introduction most casually. (With a greedy colt it is a good idea to lay the saddle on his back for the first time when he has his nose buried in a bucket of oats.)

As a preliminary step to saddling, it is wise first to place the saddle blanket or pad on the colt's back several times without the saddle. Lay it gently on his back. Slide it off. Put it on. Take it off. Do this as often as necessary until the colt is completely relaxed. Then, leaving the pad or blanket on his back, introduce the saddle.

The main thing is to make the colt understand that there is no cause for alarm, that this thing you are putting on his back is not a mountain lion. Let him look at and smell the saddle. Ease it gently against his shoulder to give him the feel of it. Standing close to him, facing toward his rump, raise the saddle slowly and lower it as gently as possible onto his back. Hold it there for a few seconds while you talk to him soothingly. If he acts spooky, keep on talking; then remove the saddle. Avoid making any quick or unexpected motion.

Do this several times or as many times as necessary until you see the colt relax. Then leave the saddle on his back for a minute or two, holding it so that, if he should move suddenly, there will be no chance of its falling off and frightening him. If you have handled your colt from the beginning according to the step-by-step system set forth in this book, you should be able to cinch up the saddle less than ten minutes after you have first laid it on his back; quite possibly you can do it in much less than that time.

When you do pull up the girth, be careful not to pull it tight. It should be just snug enough to hold the saddle in place.

If you have done this with the colt in his stall or cross-tied in the barn, now lead him outside and over to the training corral,

Plate 25. THE BITTING HARNESS. Precise adjustment of the overhead checkreins and of the sidereins is critical, or the use of this gear can do more harm than good. The reins must be of a length suitable to the horse's degree of training. Tight checking destroys impulsion and free movement; the horse is discouraged from reaching for the bit. A colt should be able to lower his head and relax his neck muscles. Correct headset is attained only very gradually.

Photograph by E. O. Ploeger

and longe him with the saddle on. If he acts a bit jittery—as he is likely to do, if you have put a large stock saddle on him— overlook his nervousness. Treat him this time almost as leniently as you did the first time you worked him on the longe. With all the gentle handling you have given him since he was a small foal or since you first got him, he will soon get over his nervousness about having that saddle on his back.

After he has made a few circuits of the corral, stop him and check the cinch for looseness. Probably you will have to tighten it a little. After you have done this, lay your hand on the pommel or on the horn and give the saddle a shake or two; slap your

Plate 26. With the sidereins removed, the cramping effect of too-short overhead checkreins here is obvious. Though the trainer maintains only light contact, the horse cannot fully extend his neck, as he would if not checked up. His "free walk" is not really free at all. This is a vitally important point not only in ground driving but also in riding.

Photograph by E. O. Ploeger

hand on the seat. If the colt starts, say, "Whoa!" sharply, stroke his neck; then repeat the shaking and the slapping.

Thereafter for about a week put the saddle on each time you longe him. Put it on him in his stall just before feeding time and leave it on while he eats. Gradually you will be able to pull up the cinch more and more to a normal degree of tightness.

Once the colt has learned to take the saddle for granted you can let down the stirrups or, if you have removed them, replace them. He will soon become used to them flopping against his sides while you longe him.

What is our purpose in putting a saddle on the colt now, at least a year and possibly two years before we shall be ready to ride him? The chief purpose is to accustom him to the pressure of the girth before we begin driving him in long reins. This is the next step in the colt's education and he is ready for it now.

What are the advantages of driving a colt in long reins? Ground driving may be termed the first grade in a horse's elementary schooling. Gentling, halterbreaking, longeing—these are the simple basics of kindergarten. But with ground driving we begin the elements of reining and developing a good mouth. Ground driving is the easiest way for an amateur handler of limited experience to teach—and the easiest way for almost all horses to learn—the fundamentals of reining. It enables us to gain more control over the colt before we mount him. When we do mount and take up the reins, he will know what to expect. From the ground we can begin developing the colt's gaits and natural balance without putting weight on his back, and if necessary correct any pronounced faultiness of his head carriage.

Certainly, we can do all these things in mounted schooling, but if we put it off until then instead of making use of the time we have now, we would quite unnecessarily be putting the colt's training just that much further back.[1]

I have known professional horsemen who would keep a colt in the ground driving stage for as long as a year. When mounted, the colt had little more to learn than how to handle himself under weight and at speed.

I have known other trainers who regard ground driving as mostly a waste of time. Occasionally they will use it as a last resort in reforming a spoiled horse, but as a general rule they reason that since eventually you will have to do everything from the saddle, why not do it that way from the start?

Some believe that ground driving makes it too easy to damage a colt's mouth by unintentionally hanging on the lines. However, in my opinion, many more colts have had their mouths spoiled by unskilled riders than by handlers with both feet firmly on the ground. I have often observed that those who hang on a horse's mouth when ground driving are the same ones who "tight rein" when mounted. Such persons seem to understand only the heavy, pulling hand. Whether they are afoot or mounted, they appear to be psychologically incapable of using a fixed or a yielding hand on the reins. They are naturally crude and always remain so. They lack empathy and sympathy with horses.

During the first phase of this ground driving we shall not put

---

[1] I have no doubt that more than one professional trainer who reads this book will be ready to charge me with taking an unnecessarily long time to school a colt. Actually, the one thing I can justly be charged with is not wasting time; for what I am advocating here is beginning a colt's training at an age when most horsemen are satisfied to let a youngster merely run out at grass and then take him in hand, completely ignorant, at the age of three or four. Sometimes circumstances make this latter course necessary; but when it is not really necessary it is the most foolish waste of time of which any horseman can be guilty. Look again at Plates 17 and 21, perfect examples of what I am talking about.

Plate 27. ELASTIC SIDEREINS. These reins are merely strips about an inch wide cut from an automobile tire inner tube. I have found them more useful in teaching a green horse to accept the bit than the most expensive harnesses on the market. The horse cannot avoid contact with the bit, but without being cramped. If necessary, the firmness of the contact can be increased simply by tying knots in the rubber reins.

Photograph by Gene A. Pearson

anything into the colt's mouth. We'll attach the lines to a cavesson or a hackamore, whichever we wish to use.

If you use a saddle for this work, tie the stirrups together to keep them from flopping about. If you use a bitting rig, a training surcingle or a driving harness, do not adjust the crupper too tightly. You should be able to slip your fist between the strap and the colt's back without causing him to fidget or clamp his tail. If your rig has an overhead check and side-reins, either remove them or adjust them so loosely that they can have no effect on the colt's natural head carriage. This is not the time to think about headsetting. Above everything else, we want free, relaxed forward movement.

Before you begin driving, decide which way you want the colt to circle first, whether left or right. For the sake of clarity we'll assume that you will circle him first to the right. This will make your right rein the inside or leading rein. For these first few lessons this inner rein should *not* be run through the side ring of the surcingle. Instead it should come directly from the colt's head to your right hand. The left rein, however, should be run through the ring on the left side of the surcingle; the ring will keep this outside rein from slipping up over the colt's back. This outside rein should be kept low, coming around just above the colt's hocks, for it is your chief means of controlling the hindquarters if the colt should take a notion to swing around to the right in an effort to face you. As long as you keep that outside rein low you can prevent him from swinging around or from shortening the circle by cutting toward the center.

If you are using a saddle instead of a surcingle, run this outside rein through the left stirrup. If you use a driving harness, run the outside rein through the tug on that side before bringing it around the quarters. It is possible, of course, to keep that outside rein low even though it hangs free, but it is wiser to utilize whatever safeguards you have and play safe during these first lessons than to wind up in a tangle and be sorry.

For the same reason, at least during the first ten minutes of this first ground driving lesson, you should handle the colt almost exactly the same way as you would when longeing him. Staying close to the center of the pen, you control the colt with the inside rein. The outside rein should pass up from the stirrup across the seat of the saddle or over the colt's back. Later, you will drop it around his hindquarters, but not yet; give him a little time to get used to those two lines. For sometimes a spirited colt, feeling that outside line unexpectedly pressing against his hind legs, will suddenly spook. Reacting instinctively, he just panics and explodes into a run. Not many colts will do this, though most will break into at least a lively trot; but unless you feel absolutely sure that your colt has been handled enough all over, or is lethargic enough, to accept this new experience calmly, start with that outside line across the seat of the saddle instead of around his hindquarters.

The inner rein should run directly from the colt's head to the trainer's hand because thus it functions most effectively as a leading rein, inducing the colt to face in the direction in which he is circling. The longe line had this same effect; even when we exerted no pressure on it, the mere weight of the line tended to induce the colt to bend in the direction he was moving. This is

Plate 28. GROUND DRIVING, STEP ONE. Here I have the colt ready to be driven on a circle to the left. With a short grip on the inside (left) rein, I have him under control. The outside rein passes through the stirrup, which is tied down to its mate, and across the saddle seat to my right hand. When the colt starts moving, I'll take the same position near the center just as if I were longeing him.

Photograph by Gene A. Pearson

a more important point than most horsemen realize, for a colt schooled in this way will never have to have his head canted to the left when put into a lope or gallop on the right lead or bent to the right when asked to take the left lead, as so many trainers seem to think is necessary, though in fact it is completely contrary to nature.

Since after six months of work on the longe the colt responds to spoken commands, we shall have no use for the whip now.

When he has settled, halt the colt and make him stand. Carefully gather up the lines as you walk up to him. Be sure not to

Plate 29. GROUND DRIVING, STEP TWO. With a highstrung or spooky colt, this can be a critical moment. After driving in both directions with the outside rein across the saddle, it's time to lift that rein over the croup and lower it around the hindquarters. Note that the colt is "listening" to what goes on behind him and is nervously sidestepping away from me. If the trainer bungles now or makes an abrupt movement, most colts are almost sure to spook and run. Maintain control with a short hold on the inside rein.

Photograph by Gene A. Pearson

let them drag underfoot so that they could entangle you if the colt should move suddenly.

Now lift the outside line off the saddle. Holding it high enough to clear the colt's croup, step to the rear and gently lower the line behind his haunches. Do not let it fall below the hocks.

Holding a rein in each hand, with the outside rein low around the colt's hindquarters, stand a few yards behind the colt and to the right of him so that you are near the center of the circle almost where you would stand if you were about to longe him. Give the command, "Walk," and let the reins sag slightly. As the colt moves off, move concentrically with him, as when longeing.

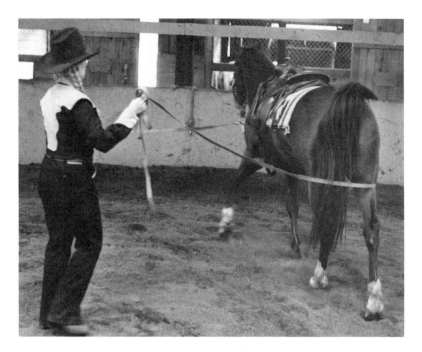

Plate 30. ALL IS WELL! This colt has accepted the pressure of the outside line around his hindquarters and moves calmly at a free walk. Trainer is in longeing position, with inside rein leading directly to her hand.

Photograph by Robert W. Hansen

Keep only a very light feel of the inner rein, just as if it were a longe line, while leaving the outer rein slightly slack. Be alert now. Concentrate on what you are doing. Be ready to anticipate and instantly correct any unexpected movement by the colt when he realizes that this is not quite the same as being longed and perhaps suddenly wonders what that strange thing touching his left hind leg is.

Generally, most colts brought along gradually and gently as our yearling has been will take to this first drive in long reins quite casually, without the least fuss. But horses are unpredictable at times, and there are two reactions for which we should be prepared: the colt, feeling that left rein against his thigh or gaskin, might spook slightly and try to run, or at least trot; or he might try to move his hindquarters away from the rein, sidling in toward the center, and turning his head outward to the left.

Plate 31. GROUND DRIVING, STEP THREE. The trainer has moved from the longeing position to follow directly behind the horse. Both reins now pass through the tied-down stirrups. By merely fixing her left hand while giving with the outside rein as the horse's inside hind leg reaches forward, the trainer gets a smooth turn with the horse perfectly flexed.
Photograph by Robert W. Hansen

The remedy for the first reaction is, of course, to prevent him from running. While still moving along with him, take a firm hold of the reins, with a bit more tension on the inner rein to keep him circling. Do not try to halt him; just don't let him run or trot. If he does stop, start him walking again at once.

The remedy for the second reaction is to slacken the left rein that passes around his hindquarters and to exert strong tension on the inner rein, forcing the colt to head in toward the center of the circle and preventing him from turning out. This will probably result in decreasing the diameter of the circle much more than you desire, but once the colt is circling properly that can be easily corrected. We need only straighten him out a bit to enlarge the circle.

As the colt settles down to a walk, gradually veer in closer to him until you are walking almost but not quite directly behind him. The first time you do this, moving in almost directly behind him, the colt might try to go faster or take a notion to turn outward, to the left. Don't let him; if necessary, move back nearer the center of the corral until he settles down.

After about five minutes of steady circling at a walk, say, "Whoa," as you apply light tension on the lines, not by pulling but simply by slowing your pace. When he halts, slack the lines immediately. Do not let him turn to face you, as he did when on the longe. Make him stand. Walk up to the colt and pat him. Now prepare to drive him in the opposite direction. Unsnap the right rein, run it through the side ring of the surcingle (or through the stirrup of the saddle or the tug of the harness), and refasten the left rein so that it will come directly from the colt's head to your hand when you turn him around.

Now repeat the whole lesson, driving the colt to the left.

During this first lesson and for the next two or three driving lessons do not let the colt trot or canter. Work him only at a walk. Since he is in fairly hard condition now and walking is easy, we can make each lesson of about an hour's duration. To avoid monotony we should frequently practice the colt in stopping and starting, being careful not to halt him always at or near the same spot. We should also set about teaching him to turn in response to tension on the inner rein. About every five minutes we should change directions, always remembering to alter the positions of the reins to suite the new direction.

It is important to remember that one of the chief purposes of this ground driving is to teach the colt obedience to a direct rein signal. This is the first step in teaching neckreining, or obedience to the indirect rein, and we shall use it a great deal before we ever switch to neckreining. Therefore, even though we are not yet driving from a bit in the colt's mouth, we should make a point of handling the reins as delicately as possible, as if we were already using a bit. Even without a bit, a heavy feel on the reins tends to discourage the colt from moving forward freely with extended head and neck. Too much tension on the reins now can give the colt the idea that moving ahead is the wrong thing to do, even though if he halts we immediately urge him on. This can result in the beginning of the habit of boring or hanging on the hands, which is about the last habit we should want to develop or encourage. So do not apply the reins with any more force than

Plate 32. TAKE IT EASY! Ground driving at a trot is necessary, but it can be strenuous work for the trainer. Unless you enjoy jogging, don't try to follow directly behind the horse. Cheat. Veer in toward the center and let the horse do most of the work. Above all, do not hang on the lines.

Photograph by Robert W. Hansen

is necessary. As soon as you do apply them, call out, "Whoa!" and relax the reins. After a few trials, the colt should learn to halt even before you give the oral command.

After three or four days of this driving at a walk, with plenty of stopping and starting, and turning in response to a pull on the inner rein, the colt should be as calm in the long reins as he was on the longe. Now we may begin driving him with both reins run through the side rings of the surcingle (or through the stirrups of the saddle or the tugs of the harness). With the reins in this position we shall begin turning the colt in either direction, regardless of which way he is circling, and driving him in figure 8's and serpentines, first at a walk, later at a trot.

Now there is a right way and a wrong way to turn the colt, and the wrong way can, at first, result in quite a mix-up so that we'll end up with the confused colt facing us. We want to avoid that kind of mix-up, because it bewilders and unsettles the colt, so let's be careful to do it right the first time.

With both reins coming back to us through the side rings or the stirrups, start the colt walking in a circle to the right. Move in almost but not quite directly behind the colt, keeping a distance of about six feet at least away from his heels. Hold both reins low, at least below the points of his hips, for when he turns we don't want either rein to slip up over his back. Just before you are ready to turn him, transfer your left rein into your right hand —and be sure to keep that right hand low, at least no higher than your waist. Reach out a full arm's length and grasp the left rein in your left hand; command, "Gee!" (or "Left," or any other word you prefer) and with a firm, steady tension on the left rein turn the colt's head in toward the fence. As you swing him around, take a couple of steps to the right in order to stay near his hind-quarters. Keep that left rein taut until the colt has done a complete about-face, and be certain that you keep the right rein absolutely slack so that it does not contradict the pull of the opposite rein or slide up over his back.

Now the colt should be parallel to the fence, facing toward your left, as you stand approximately opposite his left hip. Don't pause now; don't hesitate. Tell him immediately, "Walk!" and relax both reins and start him moving in a circle to the left. If he should try to veer away from the fence, cutting in toward the center, straighten him out with the right rein. Keep him moving until he has made a few circuits of the corral; then turn him again, this time to the right, using the oral command, "Haw!" (or, "Right," or whatever you prefer to say). To turn him right you simply reverse the movements you executed when turning left.

It is not, of course, necessary to use spoken commands when turning, but it is better to do so because the spoken order fore-warns the colt that you are about to turn him and gives him a moment or two to *prepare* to obey. Thus, he is all set to respond promptly when you do apply the aid. If you are consistent in this, eventually he will respond to the spoken command alone. The sooner he learns to do this, just as he learned to obey "Whoa," the better; for it means that after we shall have bitted him, we can virtually leave his mouth alone, thus keeping it fresh.

Work the colt on this phase of elementary reining for several weeks or a couple of months, even after you are convinced that he is "perfect." Work him entirely at a walk; stifle the temptation to see how well he will go at a trot or a lope—an especially strong temptation when you have a chance to show off to your friends.

Plate 33. THIS IS FINISHED DRIVING. To demonstrate the feasibility and importance of handling a horse without pulling on his mouth the author drives this colt with ordinary white strings in place of leather or web reins, doing turns, figure 8's, halts, and rein-backs. Fixed and yielding, but never pulling, hands guide the colt, who simply follows his bit.

Photograph by Dawn Young-Hansen

If on some days he appears to be feeling his oats too much, put him back on the longe line and let him work off his energy trotting and loping that way. But when you put the long reins on him now, drive him only at a walk. Concentrate on teaching him to turn neatly and smoothly in response to the lightest possible rein signal.

For at least the first month of this elementary reining practice always turn him into the fence; that is, when he is circling to the right, turn him left, and vice versa. This will help to get him into the habit of turning on his hocks, or at least on his center. Always be sure, however, to give him sufficient room to turn; do not drive him too close to the fence so that in order to avoid bumping his nose he has to elevate his head beyond normal height. This is a bad habit, very easily developed, and much too commonly seen in so-called "finished" horses. Allow the colt enough room to turn into the fence with head slightly lowered or at least no higher than he naturally carries it.

When the colt has learned to turn into the fence neatly and smoothly, you can begin driving him in large figure 8's the length of the corral, using absolutely no more rein tension than necessary. When he does this well, introduce him to the serpentine, driving him from side to side the width of the corral down its entire length, then working back up to the opposite end.

In this ground work, just as in riding, the position of the horse's feet at the moment he reacts to an aid influences how easily he can perform a required movement. In a turn, the inside hind leg is the pivot leg; it must be on the ground as the horse starts the turn. Therefore, we should apply the rein signaling for a turn a moment *before* that pivot leg will touch the ground. A safe rule to ensure that our timing is correct is to give the signal for the turn as the inside hind leg leaves the ground and starts forward. This will give the horse time to react. That pivot leg will be firmly under him when he obeys the rein.

Never follow a set routine or course. Vary the program as much as you can. The colt should obey the rein *when you apply it*, not when he thinks you are going to turn him or when he feels like turning. When first beginning a new lesson it is quite all right to let the colt anticipate our wishes; it encourages him to do the right thing, makes the lesson easier and even, I have sometimes suspected, flatters him into thinking that he is a very smart lad. But once he understands the lesson we must check this anticipation promptly. The colt must learn that he is to obey an order only when we give it, not when he thinks we ought to give it. For this reason vary your routine every day as much as possible.

Strive for prompt obedience and neatness and exactness of execution.

CHAPTER XI

Behind the Scenes

I know of few horsemen, grooms, or
trainers, who would not willingly put
in an extra hour's work in order to
make a horse a little more comfortable;
and I cannot say as much for many
owners.
— *Earl R. Farshler*

I THINK it wise here to interrupt our preoccupation with schooling to discuss a subject which is more closely connected with successful training of a horse than a great many horse owners realize. I refer to stable management. This is a most varied subject, and within the scope of this book I can only hope to touch on a few aspects of it; but that it has an important influence on the success or failure of our primary purpose — the making of a good riding horse — admits of no doubt. For most horses nowadays spend approximately half their lives in the stable, and some spend considerably more than that cooped up in stalls or boxes. What happens to them during these many hours when we are not using them has as much influence on how they react to schooling as does, for example, the home environment of a child on his class work. It is astonishing how many horse owners fail to grasp this simple truth and how many others never even think of it.

Men will do their utmost to acquire or breed the best horses they can; they will squander small fortunes on uselessly fancy gear which it tickles their childish vanity to show off in public, and they will spend slightly less on ornate, luxurious stable fittings. But they will devote only superficial attention to the simplest, everyday fundamentals of intelligent horse management. This is true not only of training but of ordinary care of the horse as well. Common sense certainly is uncommon, if we are to judge by many of our popular ideas on horse management.

Some of the standard stable practices we blindly accept are merely harmless hand-me-downs from grandpa's day. Others are anything but harmless, yet we rarely pause to ask ourselves what sensible reasons, if any, lie behind them. No matter how well-intentioned we may be, some of these practices result in real cruelty to a horse. Even when they aren't cruel, they prevent us from getting the best results in our schooling and riding.

Consider, for example, the loose box stall. Everybody agrees that a horse is better off in a roomy box in which he can move about and stretch out at full length than in a tie-stall. But in many stables the loose box is little better than a cell for solitary confinement. The walls are built up, or nearly up, to the ceiling, while the door is built in one section or the upper half is usually kept closed. A horse confined in such a box has only the walls to look at, with perhaps a very restricted view through the small grill in the door. Even if the entire upper half of the door consists of bars, though he can see out through them he cannot put his head out over the lower half of the door and see all that's going on in the barn and gossip with his next-stall neighbors. To a gregarious animal like the horse such isolation is real cruelty.

Is it any wonder that a horse so stabled seems to be full of spooks when you take him outside? Even if he has been given the special training herein suggested for colts to accustom them to a variety of sights and sounds, he will never be as reliably steady a mount as a horse used to thrusting his head out over the lower half of a dutch door and watching all the activities in and about a stable whenever he wants to see what's going on. I will say even that giving such training to a horse so isolated most of the time in an all-but-airtight box stall is largely a waste of time. Certainly he will not derive as much benefit from the training as a properly stabled horse will.

This isolation has an especially bad effect on the dispositions of stallions, who are the chief victims of the practice simply because they are stallions; or perhaps it would be correct to say: because their owners don't know how to handle stallions.

Sheer boredom with his own company often leads a horse to develop such vices as cribbing and wind-sucking.

Very often tie-stalls, in which horses face their mangers and blank walls twenty or twenty-two hours out of every twenty-four, are little better than high-walled boxes.

If you must keep your horse in a tie-stall, especially if the side walls are too high to let him see his immediate neighbors, I recom-

Plate 34. RELAXED AND CONTENT. This filly spent the first two years of her life in a palatial horse prison. She knew next to nothing about the world outside her high-walled boxstall. A sparrow flying overhead would make her spook. I put her in a stall she could look out of and see all that was going on in the stable and in the yard. In a few days she had so settled down that her whole personality seemed to have changed.

Photograph by Gene A. Pearson

mend that you alter the stall so that the horse can face the open end. Tear out the entire manger. Close the entrance to the stall with a low door; at most, it should not be higher than the horse's back, for he should be able to put his head out over it. If your prefer, or if a door would be impractical, you can hook a web guard across the opening. Hang the feed bucket inside the door near the hinges. If you use a web guard, fasten the bucket to a corner post so that it is easily removable for cleaning. If you find the bucket in the way when you put the horse into the stall or take him out, hook it in place only at feeding times, after which you can remove it. Eliminate the manger entirely; feed hay on the floor—eating from the ground is the natural way for a horse to eat.

Now when you put your horse away back him into the stall so that his tail is to the wall where the manger used to be. This way, able to look out, the horse can get his fill of current events and keep abreast of the latest barn gossip. He will be a happier horse, and I think that you will soon notice an improvement in his manners and in his work.[1]

If more horse owners spent as much money remodeling and modernizing their stables for their horses' real benefit as some of them squander on flashy equipment and fancy tackrooms, there would be more better horsemen and more happier horses, and both would enjoy their association together a lot more.

Blistering and firing are twin abominations practiced in the best of stables, particularly racing and show stables where nothing is too good for the inmates and expense is of minor importance—as long as the horses keep on winning. These practices are nothing better than relics of barbarism, first cousins to witchcraft and alchemy. Neither has ever done any horse a bit of good. Neither has ever speeded up the healing of a lame leg by a single minute or strengthened a weak tendon. As scientific veterinary practice they verge on sheer quackery.

I am sure that any competent veterinarian, if pressed, will honestly admit that he blisters or fires a horse only when the animal's owner expects or demands it. The average horse owner wants something to show for the fee he pays the vet. He is not likely to show much confidence in, or call again, a man who seems to insult his intelligence by telling him, "All your horse needs is a long rest and daily massage"—an obvious fact that anyone who can count to twenty without taking his boots off should be able to realize. Instead, the owner expects the vet to

---

[1]Undoubtedly some horsemen will object that keeping a horse in a tie stall with his head toward the open end, as here suggested, would make the task of cleaning the stall more "difficult," not only because of the floor slope which provides drainage but also because frequent removal of the droppings—which should be done several times each day—would necessitate either taking the horse out of the stall for a few minutes or forcing the stableman to remove the litter while working very close to the animal's heels. Obviously, it would be foolhardy to work in cramped quarters behind a kicker; but the animal should be cured of its vice without delay. Drainage can be easily changed. The "bother" of removing a horse from the stall in order to pick up the droppings is a weak objection. Essentially, the problem it conceals is simply this: Is the owner's convenience, or the stableman's laziness, of greater importance than the well-being of the horse? Far too often the answer to this basic question is: *Yes!*

Plate 35. THE FROLICKERS. These colts express their joy at being turned out to romp in the snow. Horses are hardy outdoor animals. They need plenty of exercise and enjoy companionship. Don't keep them cooped up under artificial conditions more than necessary.

Photograph by Gene A. Pearson

earn his fee by doing something about the condition. So the vet, even though reluctantly, goes through the motions: he blisters or fires the horse. This at least insures that the animal will get the rest it needs, and that is usually the only cure it needs.

Consider this matter of blistering and firing in the light of human experience. If the vet himself severely sprained an arm or leg, would he blister himself? Would the horse's owner, having a badly sprained ankle or wrist, let his family physician fire him? If the physician suggested such an idea as a means of speeding recovery, would any intelligent patient in his right mind listen to him?

Hardly one horse owner in a hundred uses or will use this sort of simple, logical reasoning in his stable management.

Spoiled horses are often the result of an indulgent owner's mis-directed kindness. The little colt that nudges for tidbits grows up to be a husky, arrogant three-year-old that is dangerous to approach when he is feeding. I take a dim view of bribing horses to obey by feeding them tidbits. I wholly disapprove of pampering them in the stable with frequent handouts. It is all right after a schooling period is ended to give your horse a carrot or an apple or a chew of tobacco or whatever he fancies, just as you would give him a drink of water and a chance to roll; but a horse that is led to expect handouts will soon, as a rule, begin to demand them, and if they are not immediately forthconing he is apt to show his displeasure in ways that can be not only nasty but dangerous. Such a spoiled horse should have his ego slapped down *pronto* so hard that it bounces.

Invariably, once a horse has become spoiled in this way, that is what eventually has to be done. Either he has to be taught manners, which he should have been taught as a foal, or he becomes a nuisance and even a menace fit only to be embalmed in a tin can. Yet it is almost impossible to convince one of these overindulgent, sugar-feeding horse-spoilers that he is being not kind but cruel to his horse. They usually have to learn the hard way, often when it's too late, that they themselves have made their horse a nasty brute that they will either have to get rid of or get tough with.

We almost all have our horses' welfare in mind, but too often we are guilty of unintentional cruelty simply by neglecting that rare commodity—horse sense.

CHAPTER XII

The Two-Year-Old

*In training there is always the tendency to
proceed too rapidly. To arrive quickly, go
slowly with careful, cautious steps. Make
frequent demands; be content with little;
be lavish in rewards.*
— *General Faverot de Kerbrech*

YOUR colt is now between a year and two years
old. He will lead on a slack line, without either
hanging back or lunging ahead. He is quiet to handle, has confidence in you, and will go practically anywhere you wish to lead
him. He is accustomed to a wide variety of sights and sounds. He
is used to the feel of a saddle and a snug girth. He will obey
your spoken commands to walk, trot, and lope; will hold each
gait; will halt when you say, "Whoa." When driven, he obeys
the reins. At slow paces he handles himself well, stopping and
turning quite smoothly for a colt. The work you have given him
has developed and hardened him so that he is in better condition
than he would have been if you had let him merely run out at
grass. In short, he is much more advanced, mentally as well as
physically, than most colts of his age are.

He is now ready to be bitted.

Two types of bits are commonly used for "mouthing" a colt—
a smooth, jointed snaffle or, less frequently, a straight bar bit
having a thick vulcanite mouthpiece. I prefer the snaffle because
it is less of a mouthful for the green colt at first; however, once
we begin driving with reins attached to the bit the bar bit is
perfectly suitable, even milder than the snaffle. Whichever type
you use, the mouthing bit should have "keys" attached to it.
These are metal danglers which encourage the colt to play with
the bit, thus tending to keep his lower jaw mobile and soft.

Plate 36. A WELL-ADJUSTED SNAFFLE. The bit is neither too snug nor too loose against the corners of the mouth.

Photograph by the author

These "keys" can be improvised from strips of copper about two inches long, tied to the mouthpiece with string. Be sure that they have no sharp edges or corners.

Since we shall not do any driving from the bit until the colt is used to carrying it in his mouth, the bridle used for holding the bit in place may be as light as you have. You can even hold the bit in the colt's mouth with a makeshift split-ear type of bridle made of slender thongs or of strong cord. At present the only purpose of the bridle is to hold the bit in place; the less bulky it is under the cavesson or hackamore, the better.

Plate 36 shows a well-fitted snaffle bridle. Note that the snaffle just barely wrinkles the corner of the lips. If the bit is hung too low in the mouth, it won't do this; if it is too high, it will exert too much pressure on the corners and cause the colt discomfort.

As a general rule, it is best to put this mouthing bit on the colt in his stall or box just before feeding him his grain. Let him wear the bit while he eats. After a few days he will forget all about the bit. He will also become easy to bridle. He will associate being bitted with being fed.

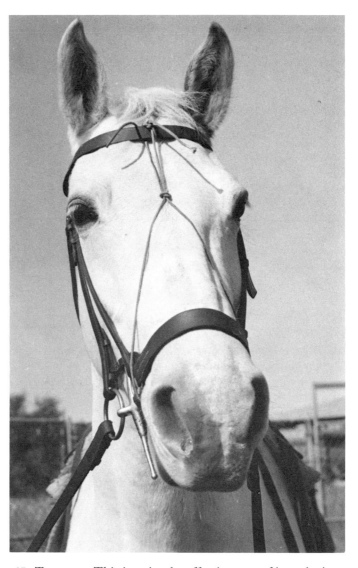

Plate 37. TIE IT UP. This is a simple, effective way of introducing a colt to the bit so that he will never learn to put his tongue over it or— much worse—ball his tongue under it. Run a cord or a leather thong through the jointed center of the snaffle and out each side of the horse's mouth. Tie a knot about midway up the horse's face and tie the ends around the browband or crownpiece, pulling the snaffle slightly higher in the mouth than it would be for schooling.

Photograph by Gene A. Pearson

Plate 38. BASIC WORK AFOOT. With a green horse, or an unbacked colt, it is usually easy to get quick response to leg aids by tapping with the whip about where the rider's lower leg would press. Here the horse is starting a turn on the forehand.

Photograph by Gene A. Pearson

Leave the bit on for about an hour. Do this for several days until the colt has become accustomed to it. Thereafter each time you take the colt out for a driving lesson, put the bit on first, under the cavesson or hackamore.

Many horsemen become greatly concerned if they discover a colt putting his tongue over the bit—even though they can make the discovery only by looking. In my opinion, this is a cause of needless worry. Practically, whether a horse puts his tongue under or over the bit is of no consequence. All that matters is that he should learn to yield to the reins. The tongue over the bit does not prevent the bit from acting on the bars of the mouth, as it should. I doubt whether any horseman can tell, with his eyes shut and simply by feeling the reins, whether a horse has its tongue under or over the bit.

It is far more important to see that a colt does not form the habit of balling his tongue under the bit, thus lessening and interfering with the bit's action on the bars, or form the unsightly habit of sticking his tongue out one side of his mouth. Both habits can be very simply prevented by correct placement of the snaffle in the mouth and holding it in position by anchoring it snugly—not tightly—to the crown or browband of the bridle with a cord or thong, as shown in Plate 37.

Another lesson that should be added to the schooling program about this time is preparing the colt to respond to leg aids before the day when we shall mount him. For the present, this means simply that he should learn to move his hindquarters sidewise in response to pressure applied against either of his flanks at a spot approximately where the rider's lower leg normally would hang. Teaching this is easy and the best time to do it is when grooming him. Standing on the colt's left, grasp the halter or lead-rope to prevent him from moving forward; then press your right fist firmly against his flank slightly behind where the cinch would be. With some colts it may be necessary to poke the flank lightly with one's thumb, but the "punch" should be a mere tap, certainly not forceful enough to merit being called a blow. As you press his hindquarters away from you make a point of drawing the colt's head slightly toward yourself, though not so far or so forcefully as to make him move his forefeet in order to maintain his balance. If you turn his head too far as you push his hindquarters away from you, you will be teaching him to do a turn on his center; but the whole point of the lesson is to make him turn on his forehand, moving his haunches around circularly. The slight turning of the head puts the colt in position to do this naturally and hence helps him more quickly to grasp the lesson.

The instant the colt moves his hindquarters even a slight step away, stop, pat him and let him know that he has done well. Then repeat from the opposite side. Do this frequently whenever you handle the colt, but demand only one sidestep at a time. Eventually you should be able to turn the colt step by step in a full circle in either direction.

Another way of teaching this turn on the forehand is to tap the colt with the butt of a whip or with a crop.

Be sure to practice the lesson to both sides.

It is also about time now that in our daily ground driving we should begin to demand a little more of the colt than hitherto we have expected of him. We should begin to drive him in figure

8's and serpentines at the trot as well as at the walk.[1] To do this we shall find it best to raise the reins so that at each change of direction the lines will clear or lightly slide over the colt's croup.

If you have been using a training surcingle, you have nothing to change. The reins, run through the side rings, are placed high enough to enable them to clear the colt's back if we merely elevate our hands.

If you have been driving in a buggy harness, run the reins through the terrets instead of through the tugs.

If you have been using an English-type saddle for driving purposes, take off the stirrups, shorten the leathers to the last hole, and run the reins through the loops thus formed by the stirrup leathers. This is preferable to threading the reins through the irons when they are run up on the leathers so that they lie near the pommel, for the flexible leather loops permit more delicate handling of the reins than would the heavier irons—an important point, once we begin driving from the bit.

If you have been using a lightweight stock saddle, with the reins held low by being run through the stirrups, there are several ways you can now fix the rig to elevate the lines high enough to clear the colt's croup when he changes directions in a figure 8 or a serpentine:

Tie the stirrups together above the seat of the saddle with a cord, a thong, or a spare curb strap; then loop the cord, thong, or strap around the saddle horn. Held thus, your stirrup leathers will form loops on both sides of the saddle through which you can run the reins.

Run two straps, such as English-type stirrup leathers, through the hole in the fork of the saddle; buckle them loosely, letting a loop hang down on each side of the fork. Put the reins through these loops. You can also use short lengths of rope this way.

Fasten a figure 8 hobble securely to the saddle horn and thread a rein through each loop.

How you rig the reins makes no difference as long as they will clear or easily slip over the colt's croup when he changes direc-

[1]It is possible to drive a colt in figure 8's and serpentines at a canter also, but unless the gait is much slower than it is fair of us to expect of the average yearling or two-year-old, the job is usually too strenuous for all except athletic young folk—and even they need a great deal of enthusiasm to keep them at it. It is impractical for most persons because the task necessitates too much running from one point to another. Therefore, I omit it here. If a colt will take the correct lead on a circle in either direction, we may safely leave the figure 8 at a canter until after we have been riding him for a while.

tions; but unless the fork of your saddle is unusually high, don't thread the reins through the hole in the fork. This will hold the reins too closely together and will not permit them to come back from the colt's mouth to your hands in a straight line even when you are directly behind him; the small diameter of the hole will cause a good deal of friction on the reins and hence an unnecessary drag on the colt's mouth.

Now with the reins attached as usual to the cavesson or hacka-more, and with the colt carrying his mouthing bit, take him into the largest corral you have available and start working him in circles, *on very long reins,* first at a walk, then at a trot, and finally, but briefly, at a lope. This time do not make any attempt to follow behind the colt. Stay as near the center of the circle as you can, just as you would do if longeing him. If you can actually pivot in place, that's fine. The colt's obedience to voice and reins should, usually, enable you to do this and still control him. Sometimes, however, a sluggish colt, upon finding himself so unusually far away from you, will be inclined to slow down or stop, either in slight puzzlement or with some vague idea that he is beyond your reach. If this should happen, disillusion him immediately; if necessary, get out the whip to convince him that this is a regular schooling session, no matter how long the lines are.

Whether it takes a couple of days or a couple of weeks, see to it now that the colt moves briskly at walk and trot and will take and hold an easy lope without getting excited. Work him in both directions, changing frequently. Be sure that he maintains the diameter of the large circle you've started him on, keeping the lines gently stretched at all times. Don't let him gradually veer in toward the center or start moving sloppily in an eggshaped course. He has had plenty of practice now and he should know better.

When he goes really well at all three gaits in either direction, begin teaching him to do a figure 8 at a walk while you move, not directly behind, but in a straight line from the center of one circle to the center of the other and then back again to your original position. Though this maneuver may seem complicated when you read about it, in practice it is quite simple. The accompanying diagram (Fig. 2) should serve better than words or photographs to show clearly how it is done. Bear in mind, however, that before it can be done efficiently the colt should first have been worked on large circles, with the trainer remaining near the centers of the circles instead of following along behind the colt, as was first done.

In the beginning, keep your 8's as large as the length of your reins or the size of your corral permits. This, of course, necessitates that you move a greater distance from center to center, but it also allows you more time in which to move.

When the colt starts changing directions near the middle of the figure 8, if necessary raise the reins to clear his croup by elevating your hands. Do not try to flip the lines over his back. Simply lift them by raising your arms.

When he does the figure 8 well at a walk, shorten your reins and drive him in a serpentine up and down the length of the corral.[2]

In both movements the colt should not change directions until you cue him to do so with voice and rein. It is you, not the colt, who must determine and maintain the size and regularity of the figures.

Do not hurry through this phase of the schooling. Take plenty of time. Be attentive to details. Do your utmost to get the colt moving through these figures correctly. Strive for smoothness and precision.

Only after the colt does these figures well at a brisk walk should you let him try them at a trot.

Before ending each schooling session now, lower the reins and teach the colt to back. Standing directly behind him and holding the reins about waist-high or lower, command, "Back!" and pull lightly first on one rein so as to turn his head slightly, then firmly and evenly on both reins. The instant the colt responds, even if he steps backward only a few inches, slacken the lines. Then drive him forward a few strides before you try again.

The purpose of turning the colt's head slightly with one rein before using both reins simultaneously is to upset his foursquare balance just enough to lighten the weight on one foreleg and on the opposite hind leg. Thus slightly unbalanced, the colt will naturally step backward with those two diagonal legs when both

[2]Until now I have taken it for granted that the reader realizes that small circles and sharp turns are more difficult, particularly for a green colt, than larger ones done at the same pace, since they necessitate more abrupt changes of balance and hence greater muscular effort. For this reason it is important to work a colt on circles, figure 8's, and serpentines in that order, with each successive movement being made slightly smaller than the preceding one. Small circles and sharp turns done at speedy paces should be demanded only of mature horses.

reins are immediately pulled. Backing is a diagonal movement; that is, the near fore and the off hind move together and then the off fore and the near hind; but the movement always starts behind. Generally it makes little practical difference to which side you first turn the colt's head, but if you want to be precise and perfectly logical about it always turn the head to the side opposite whichever hind leg is in advance of the other.

The reasons the reins should be held low are, first, to lower the colt's nose and, second, to prevent the hindquarters from swinging outward when the head is turned.

Correct backing is not just scrambling or stumbling backward any old way. It should be done fluidly, one smooth step after another. Except for the very slight turning of the head from side to side when first teaching the lesson, make a point of keeping the colt as straight as possible so that he learns to back in a straight line, almost as if he were mounted on rails.

Every time you stop him after reining back, drive him forward at least a step or two, so that the colt will never have the slightest excuse for acquiring the bad habits of running backward or balking, vices which invariably originate as defenses against heavy hands.

Perhaps some readers may wonder why I have postponed teaching a colt to back until now. I did not suggest it before because it is a simple lesson to teach but chiefly because the paramount idea that should be stressed in schooling a colt is that of free forward movement. The importance of this free forward movement cannot be overstressed.

In general, I do not recommend the use of side reins, even when they are attached to a cavesson or a hackamore instead of a bit. It is far more important to encourage a colt to move forward with head and neck fully extended than to worry, at this stage of the schooling, about a proper head-set. Anything even faintly resembling collection should be avoided in handling a young colt; there is too much danger of inducing overflexion and developing a rubberneck. At this stage and for some time to come we want our colt to have a firm, even a rather stiff, neck, with no more than a slight natural lateral bend when circling or turning. Side reins, unless too loosely adjusted to be effective, would only hinder this complete extension and natural bending. I admit that side reins if properly and carefully adjusted by a horseman experienced in their use can sometimes be used to good effect, or at least without harmful effects; but I am convinced that they do not enable a

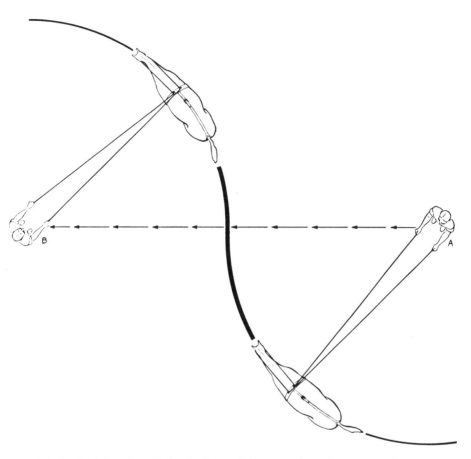

Fig. 2. —Driving the colt in the figure 8 in long reins. Heavy curved line indicates point between completion of first circle to right and start of second circle to left. When horse enters this area, trainer must begin to move from A to B. The faster the horse's pace, the more quickly must the trainer move and the more deftly he must handle the reins. *(Drawing by Larry Kumferman.)*

good trainer to achieve anything which he could not achieve without them in handling a green colt. They are more suitable for horses that have already acquired faults which need correction. I take a dim view of any sort of bitting rig designed to "set" a colt's head mechanically. I believe that the best way to develop a good carriage is by the coordination of educated legs and hands.

The legs create impulsion, driving the horse forward on the bit; the hands regulate the impulsion to accord with the pace or movement. The position of the head and neck automatically takes care of itself in a natural way that no bitting rig can achieve.

While carrying on this ground driving on figure 8's and serpentines, give the colt two or three workouts a week in heavy going such as plowed land or deep, loose sand. It will not only muscle him up a lot; it will also tone down his eagerness at times to go too fast by forcing him to get his hocks under him and to move in better balance.

Never hesitate to take the colt out of the corral and drive him on walks over the ranch or farm. When bad weather, lack of time, or your own or the colt's "staleness" and hankering for variety makes you reluctant to work him as usual, put the colt's mouthing bit on under a strong halter, mount a quiet horse, and lead the youngster on a sight-seeing jaunt about the countryside. The break will do him good, and learning to handle himself across country, as well as going quietly in company and in traffic, are necessary phases of his training.

When you feel that he is going as well as you can drive him, now it is time to begin driving him in the bit.

If your snaffle is of the type illustrated in Plate 15-A, it should be fitted with leather guards to protect the corners of the colt's lips. A chin strap—similar to the one shown on the bit in Plate 15-D—holds the guards in place. A racing type snaffle with large swivel D's needs no guards. A bar bit usually does. Some mouthing bits are equipped with cheeks designed to prevent the bit from being pulled sidewise partly into the colt's mouth; but with a colt that has learned obedience to the reins while wearing a cavesson or a hackamore, there should be very slight danger of this, for hard pulling on the reins should be unnecessary.

With the colt rid of the cavesson or hackamore and wearing an ordinary bridle with the reins attached to the bit, proceed now to rehearse step by step *everything* that you have schooled him to do in the long reins. Revert to the first lesson, driving him at a walk in a large circle with the inner rein coming back directly from the bit to your hand. Then do the same thing at a trot; do it at the lope. Run the reins through the side rings of the surcingle (or through the tugs of the harness or through the stirrups of the saddle) and repeat. Take the colt step by step, first at a walk, then at a trot, and finally at a lope, through his

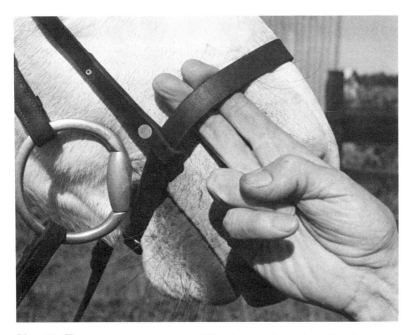

Plate 39. THE DROPPED NOSEBAND. The dropped noseband is almost essential in developing a colt's mouth or in remaking a poor mouth. At least, it makes the trainer's job much easier. It foils a horse that tries such evasions as opening his mouth and yawing. But you must adjust it carefully. If it is uncomfortably tight, the horse will be distracted from learning; if too loose, the noseband has no effect. Two or three fingers should fit inside the noseband easily. Observe that the strap fits in the chin groove and is worn *below* the bit.

Photograph by Gene A. Pearson

entire program of schooling in the long reins. Skip nothing. Don't hurry. Repeat everything from beginning to end.

Since the colt now knows the rein signals and obeys oral commands, you should have no trouble at all, if you handle the reins delicately. The colt should go as well and as calmly as he did in the cavesson or hackamore.

If he does not, if he frets, seems to be confused, balks or tries to rear, you may be absolutely sure that you have not fitted his bridle correctly and comfortably or you are being heavy-handed. Check his bridle carefully. Get the lead out of your hands.

Under ordinary circumstances, with everything going as it should, and even with time out now and then for brief rests, you should be able to put the colt through his complete driving routine in less than half an hour.

Now that you have begun to work the colt in the bit you will realize the real importance of the voice commands that you have taught him. The colt's prompt obedience to your spoken orders will greatly aid you in working him without unnecessary pressure on his tender mouth. This is important now because you are beginning the process of "making" his mouth and you cannot afford to mishandle it or make mistakes.

While you work the colt in the bit for the next several months, concentrate on lightness of rein and on obtaining from him as fine a degree of smoothness and precision in every movement as you have learned the colt is capable of achieving. Be patient, be calm, but be demanding—and *do not pull!* Never let him get away with sloppy work. Do not expect him to handle himself with the finish of a mature horse, but do insist that he work to the best of his ability, as well as you have learned from experience he is capable of doing.

Work mostly from near the center of the corral with long reins. In this position you can observe the colt best, as well as change directions with a minimum of moving about.

It is a good idea to finish each schooling session by driving him about outside the corral. Stop often; make him stand. Don't neglect reining back. Keep him used to "strange" surroundings and in the habit of always obeying orders, anywhere.

Above all, avoid monotony. Don't let the colt become bored and get "stale." Give him a day off whenever you think he needs it. If one day you begin working him and he seems to be "cranky" or away off his usual form, call it quits for the day right then. Every horse has off days. Don't provoke a "fight."

Never attempt to do any schooling when a colt is even slightly unwell. When in doubt about his health or soundness, play safe. Skip school for the day.

Above all, remember the vital importance of a fixed and a yielding hand. *Don't pull.*

CHAPTER XIII

Is He Ready?

The rider's grave is always open.
—Arabian proverb

IF you have successfully carried out all the schooling exercises thus far recommended, your colt is
now as far along as you are likely to be able to bring him without
actual riding.

It is up to you now honestly to ponder the question: Is this
colt ready to be ridden?

As far as his schooling is concerned, there is no doubt that
he is ready to be ridden. He is much further along than the vast
majority of colts of his age are when first mounted. He will almost
certainly be easy to mount and pleasant to ride as you continue
with his education. But there are two other considerations which
you should weigh carefully. These are the colt's degree of maturity—his physical development—and your own weight.

If you are a heavyweight, and particularly if your colt is a bit
on the weedy side, stay off his back for at least another year.

If you weigh about 160 pounds and insist on using your stock
saddle, you will be loading from 190 to 200 pounds onto your
two-year-old's back. That is too much weight for a youngster still
several years short of maturity. Certainly the average two-year-old
can carry that much weight; but the chance of serious strain and
even permanent injury is too great to risk the future usefulness
of a promising colt. At least, that is my opinion.

I am well aware of the fact that riding grain-fed two-year-olds
is a common practice today. It is, I think, far too common. There
are even two-year-old cutting "horses." I know that a few ex-

ceptional colts can stand up under considerable work. But they are exceptions. I am unalterably opposed to the practice of riding two-year-olds as a general rule because I have known of too many youngsters, thus rushed and overworked, to break down and end their days needlessly blemished or crippled. Even if they recover from the physical abuse inflicted on them and the emotional trauma, their convalescence has set them further back in their education than they would have been if brought along slowly.

Colts, like children, differ; some develop rapidly, others lag until we begin to think that they will never catch up. Stuffing them with grain is *not* a universal, sure-fire cure-all. It can, in fact, if overdone, be a real detriment to their ultimate development and soundness. Some breeds, such as the Arab, mature more slowly than others; they are usually breeds noted for their longevity.

If I had to give a general rule, I should say that no two-year-old should ever be ridden except by a small child or by an adult rider who weighs no more than 135 pounds—and even such a lightweight rider should refrain from using a stock saddle of average weight except for very brief periods at a time. I believe that all colts should be only lightly ridden—that is, never worked hard—until they are a full five years old.

I know that many horsemen will disagree with me and that some will scoff; they will consider me too "soft" or too "impractical." I readily concede that what I say here must seem, from the viewpoint of the commercial breeder, quite impractical; but that—the commercial breeder's canny eye for profit and loss—does not prove me wrong. A horseman who really has his colt's welfare at heart will never be hurried by either his natural eagerness to be well-mounted or his desire for profit.

Between 1919 and 1926 the American Remount Association, in co-operation with the army and a number of horse organizations, sponsored annual endurance rides for the chief purpose of determining by practical tests which breeds and types of horses were most suitable for cavalry purposes. The conditions of the tests, which varied from year to year, stipulated at first that competing horses were to carry 245 pounds each, including saddle and rider. This weight was later reduced to 225 pounds and then to 200. Horses were to cover 300 miles at an average of 60 miles a day for five successive days in not less than nine and not more than eleven hours each day. They were to be judged along the route as well as at the finish on condition as well as speed, with condition counting 60 per cent and speed only 40.

One of the foremost conclusions resulting from this series of endurance tests was that horses less than seven years old, even when carefully conditioned, were too immature for such work. They simply could not stand up to a steady grind of sixty miles a day for five days in a row under real weight. If they did not go lame, they became so fagged out that the humane conditions of the contests forced their withdrawal.

Is the task of traveling at a walk and trot sixty miles a day along roads and good wide trails more severe a test of limbs, wind, and muscle than the stock-horse type of fast work many of us expect of two-, three-, and four-year-olds? It may be a severer test of stamina and endurance; but I doubt that it is any harder than fast work on bones, tendons, and muscles. It seems to me that Thoroughbred-racing men, who break down colts with a callous wastefulness that is criminal, prove my point.

You and only you must decide now whether your two-year-old is fit for you to ride. Only you know all the factors involved. If you are in doubt, wait a while. Continue to work him on foot; it won't hurt him at all. Meanwhile, let's consider how, when we do mount, we should try to ride.

Part 3

Man in the Saddle:
Fundamental Principles

CHAPTER XIV

What Is a Good Seat:
Some Fundamentals

Most persons do not ride;
they are conveyed.
— M. F. McTaggart

SOME years ago a professional horseman wrote an article advising riders to "sit tall in the saddle." I doubt that he intended to start a controversy; he was simply aware of the shortcomings of modern stock saddle design and of some common faults in modern riding practices and wished to help whoever cared to heed his remarks. However not everybody did. At least two prominent Western horsemen took the trouble publicly to criticize his views, not without some overtones of scorn. A cartoonist-writer with a fine sense of humor eventually set forth his side of the argument with some drawings worthy of Rube Goldberg.

If the controversy settled nothing else, it did prove one thing conclusively—that some horsemen experienced and skilled enough to be classed as professionals do not understand what a balanced seat is. If they ever achieve it in action, they do so unconsciously and by actions of which they are not aware. If they do not achieve it, they have no idea of how unnecessarily hard they make their horses work merely to carry them.

However, I always find these perennial seat controversies of absorbing interest. If they do not reveal much about what a good seat really is, or at least enough to be helpful to novice riders, they certainly do show the unreliability of human observation, as well as the infinite number of ways people can interpret simple words to agree with their own personal prejudices.

Among the fallacies these perennial seat arguments invariably reveal are the quite common notions that:

1. The forward seat and the balanced seat are not one and the same.

2. The forward seat is just another name for the monkey-on-a-stick crouch of the race jockey.

3. The forward seat, in the exact words of one scornful critic, is suitable only "for steeplechase riding, hunting, polo and sitting a cavalry charger." For any other form of riding, particularly for riding stock horses, it's no good.

4. The forward seat consists merely of the rider getting his weight far enough forward for it to be over the horse's withers, regardless of what the horse at the moment may be doing.

5. There is no such thing as a state of balance, because there are many different kinds of balances. (This idea is not stated; it is implied.)

6. It is more important to keep a horse's forehand relatively unburdened by the rider's weight than to keep the weight off his loins—in spite of the fact, which no one denies, that the hindquarters furnish almost all a horse's power of propulsion.

7. It is "impossible" to maintain the forward, or balanced, seat in a stock saddle. It can be ridden only in a "flat" saddle or bareback.

8. Finally, any set of rules or principles formulated to guide a rider in developing a balanced seat can never be of any value, for individuals differ in their physiques and horses differ in conformation, so that rules which may prove satisfactory for one rider mounted on a certain type of horse will not help another man on a different type of mount; they may, in fact, be even a handicap to him. So the sensible horseman should ignore any rules or principles except those of his own making.

It should be obvious to anyone who ponders these contradictory ideas that any would-be horseman who takes them all to heart can end up only in utter confusion. If a seat is good for one kind of riding, why is it wrong or "no good" for others? Didn't any horseman ever ride forward or balanced seats before the modern English-type "flat" saddle was designed? How many kinds of balances are there? Where is the logic in worrying about overburdening a horse's forehand if the hindquarters furnish the power?

If there are no rules or principles to go by, how can a novice learn, how can any rider improve himself?

It might be simpler to consider how such a way of thinking which reaches no clear-cut conclusions ever developed. In spite of overwhelming evidence disproving all the fallacies enumerated, we are still suffering a hang-over from this confused way of thinking.

Few old-time horsemen, particularly horsemen whose primary business was stock raising, ever gave a thought to the physical principles of skilled riding. The minority who did invariably thought in terms of cavalierly "elegance": if a man looked grace-ful on horseback, he was generally considered a good horseman; it was taken for granted that he had a good seat. There were no fast-action cameras available to show what he actually did, or what happened to him, in action. The human eye missed much and no one was aware of it.

The majority of Western horsemen learned to ride early in life, and usually learned the hard way: climb on and stick. Usually by the time they were mature enough to reason things out logical-ly, they had already developed their riding habits; "sticking on" was second nature to them and they never gave it another mo-ment's real thought. Exceptional youngsters who did give riding — though not necessarily good horsemanship — a good deal of thought usually turned out to be bronc-fighters. They developed into su-perior riders not alone because of natural talent but also because they made deliberate efforts to ride well.

The average stockman was quite content to ride just well enough to do his work. He may have employed a Claude Jeffers, a "Booger Red" Privett, or a Will James, but he himself was not in their class. Though he may have enjoyed riding, he was not a pleasure rider, as we use the term today. He rode to do a job. "We didn't work *at* riding," one of these old-timers told me years ago. "We worked *while* riding." Once he retired from the stock raising business, many a rancher seldom or never rode a horse again, and had no desire to.

There was another way in which most of these old-timers differed from the modern horseman. Few of them, in those days of long working hours and large *remudas*, ever gave a second thought to the idea of *helping* a horse do its job more easily. Horses were cheap and plentiful. They were also, I think, gen-erally tougher, hardier; not because they were better bred than

stock horses of today, but because they had a greater proportion
of Mustang blood that endowed them with stamina and endurance; and because they were raised under more nearly natural
conditions, rustling for themselves out on the range, than most
horses enjoy today. They were also given more time to grow and
develop before being broken, usually as four-year-olds, in contrast
to the modern practice of stuffing a colt with grain as soon as he
is weaned and then riding him, often in competition, as a two-
year-old.

When, however, the old-time cow horse was caught up and
broken, he was worked without any pampering and was worked
hard. His reward came in the form of frequent vacation periods
when he was turned out on the range to rest and fatten up.

As a result of this system built around large *remudas*, the notion of a rider positively trying to help a horse do its job more
easily hardly ever entered a cowboy's head. On the contrary, a
horse that couldn't do the work in spite of handicaps imposed by
a thoughtless or inept rider just did not last on a cow outfit.

All these remarks are equally applicable to the great majority
of flat-saddle riders also. They learn to play polo or ride to hounds
or just trail ride without ever being exposed to planned riding lessons designed to make them "thinking riders." They learn simply
by doing, and never know that many of the things they do are
wrong. If eventually they wish to specialize in, say, dressage or
eventing, then, in spite of all their experience on horseback, they
have to learn all over, mastering fine points of technique of which
they had never before even thought.

However nostalgic we may feel over the passing of the old days
and ways, we might as well face the fact that conditions are considerably different today. Horses are fewer and more expensive.
In most localities, just keeping a horse runs into real money. Most
horses today are sports and pleasure mounts. Real working stock
horses have decreased in numbers even on the largest ranches.
Today's horseman, excluding a small minority of professional
trainers and rodeo contestants, does practically all his riding for
fun—usually just plain fun, but often competitive fun in local
rodeos, horse shows, and riding club competitions.

It is in this field of competition, whether amateur or professional, that a rider's skill in helping his horse to do a job really
counts.

This ability to make work easy for one's mount is a mark of
a true horseman. Most of us have been impressed by the observa-

tion that some men, though they are lightweights, seem to wear a horse out quickly, while some big men seem to ride lightly, enabling their mounts to do as much work as the little fellow's, or even more, without sweating a hair. Maybe we also have observed at the same time that almost always the "light" rider looks better on horseback than the "heavy" rider who actually weighs less. He looks more graceful in the saddle, more "a part of his horse."

"Buffalo Bill" Cody was an excellent example. A Pony Express rider in his youth, Cody developed into quite a hunk of man; but he was always, though he probably never heard of the forward seat or gave the problem of balance a second thought, a magnificent figure on horseback, erect, supple, springy in the saddle. Frank T. Hopkins, probably the greatest long-distance rider who ever lived, considered Cody one of the finest horsemen he ever saw. Hopkins spoke with authority, for he won distance races all over the world, losing only once, when he was disqualified on a technicality—and even then he finished first. Hopkins believed that Cody would have been a great competitive long-distance rider if he hadn't grown so big.

What is the chief characteristic which makes one horseman's seat light and easy on his mount but which is lacking in the seat of a smaller man who, in spite of the best intentions, rides heavily on a horse? The answer may be put in the form of another question: Why is live weight easier to carry than dead weight? Live weight has spring, resiliency. Dead weight is the essence of a burden. The true horseman's seat is light because his body is supple and springy. He rides *with* a horse, instead of merely being toted along on its back. He can do this because, as a general rule, he sits tall in the saddle and has a natural sense of balance and rhythm which enables him to go along with the horse's movements. The "heavy" rider rarely sits in balance and too often has a poor sense of rhythm, or even none at all. To the horse, this second rider is as uncomfortable as a dummy or a couple of sacks of grain tied to the saddle, a tiresome burden and nothing else.

Sometimes, it is true, you will see a rider who sprawls and slumps in the saddle and appears to do everything wrong; yet he is a "light" rider, easy on the horse. Such a rider always is blessed with an exceptional sense of rhythm that more than makes up for his sloppy seat. If he would just take the trouble to improve his seat—though often such men don't even know they are doing anything wrong—he could develop into a ring-tailed wonder.

Can rhythm be taught to a person who lacks it? I doubt it.

Apparently, you either have it or you don't. Fortunately, however, most persons have at least some sense of rhythm. If you can keep time to music, you have it. By practice we can develop our natural sense of rhythm to an astonishing degree. But in riding we can make the most of it only if our seat on a horse is, first of all, *balanced*. Balance is the foundation of skilled riding. It is the first fundamental of a good seat.

This brings us to one of the confusing problems already enumerated: How many kinds of balance are there? Many riders of lifelong experience—men who often like to brag that they "was borned in the saddle," and who are prone, it seems, to think as if they were raised in a barn—cling to the belief that the "right" way to sit a horse depends entirely on the rider's build and his mount's conformation. But obviously there is, there can be, only one kind of balance. Either you are balanced or you are off balance. There is no halfway point or state between the two extremes.

However, since this is so, regardless of your own peculiar physique or your horse's shape or what sort of riding you do, there must be only one right way to sit in a saddle—a way which will enable you to ride comfortably in balance at all times, at all gaits, at all paces, instantly able to shift your weight to go with your mount as he turns, stops, jumps off, slows, or speeds up. This is what is meant by a balanced seat.

The common use of the term "forward seat" is unfortunately ill-chosen. It misleads too many people into visualizing a rider crouched forward over his mount's neck like a jockey. Naturally, they conclude that such a seat can be of little use except in racing and jump-riding. Discussions of the subject would not so often split on a confusion of terms, and consequently settle nothing, if we always used the term "balanced seat" instead of "forward seat." For the true forward seat is a balanced seat. The jockey's crouching position, with his seat entirely off the saddle and all his weight supported by shortened stirrups, is basically the same as the jump-rider's seat. The jump-rider's seat in principle is precisely the same as the good school rider's. Each rider places himself as nearly as possible over his mount's center of gravity. The only differences in the three variations of seat are the respective lengths of the stirrup leathers and of the reins; for these are adjusted in relation to the degree of forward inclination of each rider's torso, which is governed by the location of the horse's point of balance.

Thus, the racehorse, working at top speed, and expected only

Plate 40. THE RACING SEAT. The horse, fully extended at speed, has his balance far to the front. The jockey must lean well forward to "go with" his mount, staying over the center of gravity.

Photograph by J. C. Meadors

to run straight ahead, has his point of balance extremely to the front. Therefore, the jockey in order to keep his own weight over his mount's center of gravity rides an extreme forward seat which might more accurately be called a "perch." The hunter or cross-country jumping horse does not need the extreme speed of the runner, or even of the steeplechaser; he goes at a hand gallop and, though he may put forth great effort in clearing an obstacle, he must be readily collectable, able to check and turn quite sharply and at times adjust his balance over uneven ground that the race-horse never encounters. Hence, the jumper gallops with less of weight on the forehand; consequently the rider can maintain a balanced seat without adopting the jockey's crouch, except perhaps momentarily over really big jumps, when he must lean farther forward from the hips just before and during the take-off to avoid being "left behind." The jump-rider's seat is intermediate between that of the jockey and that of the school rider.

The school rider, whose horse works at relatively slow paces and while highly collected, can maintain a balanced seat riding with longer stirrup leathers and with torso nearly vertical. His mount's center of gravity at all times remains much nearer the haunches than the runner's or jumper's. In certain high school movements, such as the piaffer and the levade, the horse's center of gravity may be as far back as the cantle of the saddle or even behind it. Even when the horse is executing such movements, however, the good rider does not lean back; almost always he leans slightly forward, his torso erect or almost imperceptibly inclined ahead of the vertical. Thus, his balanced seat is actually a forward seat; he is riding over his mount's center of gravity, never behind it. But to use the term "forward seat" instead of "balanced seat" can lead to confusion unless the reader clearly understands and constantly remembers that both terms mean the same thing. *The jockey, the jump-rider, and the really skilled school rider are all doing essentially the same thing—keeping their own weight as nearly as possible directly over their mount's center of gravity.*

Quite a number of horsemen, handicapped by old-fashioned ideas, misinterpret the term "balanced seat" as meaning the precarious position of a rider who attempts to ride *entirely* by balance. But nobody rides entirely by balance, and nobody with a grain of common sense would try. Even circus trick riders who stand on their mounts' backs depend to some degree on "grip," as proved by their liberal use of powdered rosin on their animals' backs. So-called "grip" must always supplement balance to produce a good seat.

It has been argued that riders of stock horses who use the forward seat cause their mounts to work on their forelegs instead of in the balanced way a stock horse should carry himself. When, however, this actually happens it is a consequence not of the forward (i.e., balanced) seat but of the rider not understanding what the true forward seat is and therefore conscientiously leaning too far forward, ahead of his horse's point of balance.

When a stock horse rider, in order to get over his mount's center of gravity, must lean far forward over the withers, isn't it obvious that the horse already *is* working on its front feet? If the horse were properly balanced as a well-trained stock horse, or any other riding horse, should be, the rider could easily stay in balance with his mount without having to "ride the withers" at all.

Any riding horse of any type, whether stock horse or show jumper, that merits comparison when in action with a race horse, whose weight is completely to the front, has not been correctly

Plate 41. THE BALANCED SEAT AT A SLOW GALLOP. The author has adapted his balance to stay over the center of gravity at an easy canter. Note light, "floating" rein: the horse is extended but more readily collectible than loose, flopping reins would permit.

Courtesy J. D. Harper

schooled. He has not been taught to carry himself in correct balance to do his job most efficiently.

Most of the world's best jumpers, horses good enough to win or place in the stiffest international jumping competitions, receive considerable dressage training to fit them for their work. Though they are usually big horses—some of them veritable giants, by stock horse standards—and work at a fast gallop, they can be halted within their own length just before gathering themselves to take off over a big jump; they can be stopped smoothly, in

Plate 42. The balanced seat at the fast gallop. Fred Albright, Knox City, Texas, on Steeldust's Little Sister, beautifully illustrates both balance and spring. Fred and "Little" have won reining contests. Their performance adequately answers the "sit backers."

Courtesy F. Albright

balance, on their hocks—and often with slack reins—by riders using the forward seat with shortened stirrup leathers.

If big jumpers working at speed can be handled in this way by horsemen who accept the balanced seat as the only sensible way to ride, we need lose little sleep worrying over the bad effects of "riding over the withers" of our stock horses and thus forcing them to work on their front legs.

Persons who advance such arguments apparently cannot distinguish between a horse's withers and his center of gravity or point of balance. A horse's withers do not change position; they are where nature put them. But the animal's balance, the location of his center of gravity, depends on what he is doing and how he is doing it. Balance is fluid.

It may be helpful to some of us if we think of the balanced seat in a stock saddle as signifying not the rider's degree of forwardness over the horse's withers but the forwardness of the rider's position in the saddle. In other words, the rider sits as

Plate 43. THE BALANCED SCHOOL-SEAT. Colonel Alois Podhajsky, of the Spanish Riding School, Vienna, Austria, presents a Lipizzaner at the piaffer, a slow, cadenced trot in place. Here the horse's balance is nearer the haunches; hence, the rider can sit erect, yet still be over the center of gravity. All the seats shown in Plates 40, 41, 42, and 43 are basically the same forward seats. All riders are balanced over their mounts' centers of gravity.

Courtesy Oesterr. Gesandtschaft, Washington Photo-Archives

far away from the cantle of the saddle as he can comfortably get; he strives to place all his weight directly over the stirrups. How far ahead of the cantle he can comfortably sit depends on where the lowest point of his saddle seat is; as well as, of course, the rider's own bulk and the length of his saddle tree. On the average stock saddle having a built-up seat that lowest point of the seat will be nearer the cantle than it would be on a Mexican or a McClellan or an old-fashioned A-fork tree. There is nothing the rider can do about that (except get a better saddle), particularly if his stirrup leathers are hung as far forward as they invariably are on most modern stock saddles. The built-up seat, sloping upward toward the fork, and with the lowest part of the seat too far behind the stirrups, will force him back against the cantle and behind his mount's center of gravity. He will have to "fight the saddle" at every stride.

Exactly the same principles hold true in the design of any so-called "flat" saddle, whether it is used for work on the flat or over fences. Unless the lowest point of the seat is within a certain distance of the location of the stirrups—a matter of inches—the rider cannot have, or cannot easily and naturally maintain, a truly balanced seat when his horse is in motion. This is why the old English hunting saddle, which was designed for a "backward seat," is practically obsolete for any form of riding, except in gaited horse classes, today.

With a saddle properly placed on a horse of average good conformation, we shall never have to worry about "riding the withers" if we think of the forward seat as meaning *forward in the saddle* instead of forward out of the saddle as a jockey rides.

The great value of the balanced forward seat is that it enables the rider to "go with" his horse, thus helping the animal work as nearly as possible as if unburdened by any weight on his back. Ideally, the two centers of gravity should be exactly together. Of necessity, the rider's center of gravity is above the horse's. It is the rider's job to keep them that way, neither falling ahead of, nor behind, nor to either side of, the horse.

The only exception to this fundamental rule is when the rider "leads" or anticipates the horse's change of pace or direction, as when riding a cutting horse; or when he "weight cues" a trained horse by shifting his own weight in the direction of desired movement. A trained horse responds to such subtle signals by instantly "catching up" with the rider's weight. In effect, the horse prevents the rider from overbalancing and falling by instantly moving back under the rider. Then in a moment the two are in perfect co-ordinated balance again.

I have spoken repeatedly of a horse's center of gravity. Just where is this point of balance?

The exact center of gravity of any individual horse depends on his conformation and the way he happens to be carrying himself at any given moment. A coarse-headed, thick-necked horse, standing normally in repose, has his center of gravity farther forward than does a well-built horse possessed of good "britches" and a fine head and neck, standing in the same position. When either horse raises his head high, the center of gravity shifts rearward toward the hindquarters. If the head is lowered, as when the

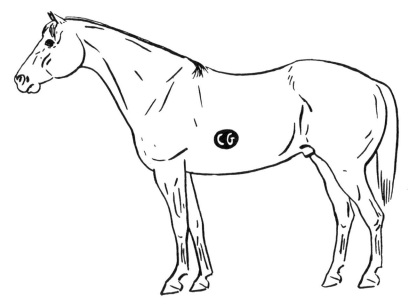

Fig. 3.—Center of gravity of horse. The black area indicates approximate center of gravity when horse is standing normally. (*Drawing by Randy Steffen.*)

horse is grazing, the point of balance moves forward over the forelegs.

Fortunately, we don't have to worry about any horse's exact center of gravity—even if we could determine it without skewering the animal or balancing it in a sling. For practical purposes it is enough for us to know that when the average riding horse of good conformation is standing naturally with head and neck in a normal position, his center of gravity is approximately three or four inches behind the withers, slightly less than midway up the girth, as indicated in Figure 3. When a rider's weight is balanced directly over this spot, he finds it easiest to "go with" his mount in any direction, and the horse can carry the rider with least effort and fatigue.

Once the horse is in motion, his center of gravity moves away from the spot indicated in Figure 3. When he backs up, with head raised and nose tucked in, his balance shifts toward the hindquarters. When he breaks into a walk or trot, with head and neck fully extended, it moves ahead of the dot. When he gallops, it moves still farther to the front; when he races at top speed, the center of gravity shifts as far forward as it can normally go.

A rider who can stay over his mount's center of gravity at all gaits and paces not only conserves his horse's strength and enables the animal to work most efficiently, but he is also riding in the position of greatest security. A strong seat is never an unbalanced one. The balanced rider is firmly placed in the saddle to enable him to stay there whatever the horse may do.

The balanced rider is also in the best position to prevent the horse from doing something wrong, or to correct him quickly if he should slip over a fast one. A rider who himself is off balance cannot control his horse well.

CHAPTER XV

What Is a Good Seat: Grip

*If we can train a horse to stop and turn when
we are on his back only half as well as he does
when left to himself, we shall have gone a long
way in our schooling.*

　　　　　　　　　　　—M. F. McTaggart

To achieve real firmness of seat balance alone is
insufficient. It is so easy to be caught unaware
by a frisky colt or a crafty old rogue and find yourself caressing
a near-by rock with your tender noggin or embracing a cactus.
It is even easier to be surprised by an ordinarily reliable horse
that has suddenly spooked in fright. Obviously, a good seat must
put the rider not only in balance but in the best position to apply
a strong leg grip instantly in an emergency.

Elementary? Perhaps. But bear in mind that I say a *strong* leg
grip that can be applied *instantly*.

Astonishing as it may seem, many riders confuse a strong grip
with straining, and often strained, thigh muscles. Yet the two
need not go together; in fact, they shouldn't. Charley horses don't
belong in any barn. The trouble is that this gripping business is
commonly misunderstood.

As a rule, grip is confused with leg pressure—the normal clinging friction of one's legs against the saddle and the horse's sides.
But the two are not the same. The confusion apparently stems
from the fact that many riders have been taught to ride with the
lower legs well away from the horse's sides. This precept—when
not the result of old-fashioned ideas on how to sit a horse—is
based on the idea of not "dulling" the horse's sides so that when
you do give him a leg signal he will hardly feel anything less
than an emphatic kick or a jab with the spurs. However, riding

with one's lower legs close to the horse and actually gripping him with the legs are by no means identical.

Grip is a brief, intense pressure that cannot be prolonged for more than a few minutes at most without the gripping muscles becoming cramped to the point of uselessness. Anyone can develop the strength of his grip on horseback, but no one has to be taught to grip. In emergencies, it is instinctive. When your horse bucks or shies unexpectedly you will grip whether you want to or not—your sense of self-preservation will see to that. In such an emergency you will grip faster than you can think. If you first had to decide to grip, the horse's sudden lunge or jump would send you flying through the air before your muscles could act to carry out your mental order.

This, however, is not what horsemen usually mean when they speak of a strong grip or of the necessity of a well-developed grip to a firm seat. However loose their terminology may be, what they are really talking about is ordinary leg *pressure* against the horse's sides.

With some jittery horses, it is true, it is sometimes necessary to make a point of keeping the lower legs away from their sides except when employing a leg aid; but such ticklish animals are exceptional and virtually all of them can be cured of their hypersensitivity by progressive schooling—and they should be, without any maudlin nonsense; for their flighty reaction to gentle leg pressure is really a form of rebellion, an evasion, entirely different from the well-schooled horse's developed sensitivity to almost imperceptible leg aids.

Most of us have been advised at some time, "Grip with your knees." When I discovered that gripping with the knees is quite the proper thing to do if you are trying to slow or halt a cold-jawed puller, I began to ask my advisers, "Why grip with your knees?" But the question never got me any reply more illuminating than a dirty look or, at best, some incomprehensible double talk that boiled down to nonsense. Whenever I read that good old stand-by of the fiction writers, "He gripped his horse with his knees," I always wonder, "What did he do with the rest of his legs?" One feat that really fascinates me is a magic stunt often performed by fictional heroes: "He guided his horse by knee pressure," it says here (while knocking over bad men with two blazing six-shooters); or, "He kneed his charger against Sir Marmalade's palfrey." I have never been able to master these stunts or find anyone who could show me how. Every rider who ever tried to demon-

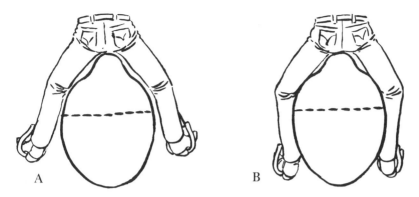

Fig. 4. — "Kneeing" and gripping. *(Drawing by Randy Steffen.)*

strate did his "kneeing" with the calves of his legs and often with
his heels as well. Actually, you can grip with your knees until
you're blue in the face and still have a weak seat.

Maybe Figure 4 can help us understand more about this "kneeing," gripping, and pressure business.

Each of these drawings represents a cross-section rear view of
a horse's barrel straddled by a rider. Observe, first, that each
rider's knees are *above* the widest diameter of the horse's barrel.
This is where the average rider's knees rest against the average
horse. Only a very long-legged man on a weedy horse, or a rider
of average size ludicrously mounted on a small pony, could sit
with his knees placed below this widest point. A short-legged
rider on a chunky horse would find his knees even higher above
the widest part of the barrel. Obviously, a high stock saddle
cinched over a thick, folded blanket would raise the knees even
higher.

Rider A is really gripping with his knees. This forces his lower
legs outward from the horse's sides, thus rendering them virtually
useless to him. With his legs thus placed, would you say he had a
strong grip? Isn't it evident that if he could squeeze with enough
force, this rider would squeeze himself right up and out of the
saddle? If his mount shies, bucks, leaps over an obstacle, or suddenly jumps into a run, then swerves or stops sharply, is Rider
A's knee (and thigh) grip going to help him to stay firmly in the
saddle? It seems quite clear, on the contrary, that *if* he stuck to
the saddle, he would have to do so in spite of his grip, which is
exactly like that of a straight-handled nutcracker.

Nutcrackers, you may have observed, have serrations inside the jaws to hold the nut firmly and prevent it from "squirting" out of the cracker when you apply pressure on the handles. Unfortunately, riders who depend on this sort of knee grip do not come equipped with serrations inside their knees and thighs. Even if they wore wet chaps dusted with rosin, their knee grip would be far from efficient.

This knee-gripping business is one of the principal reasons why saddles with undercut swell-forks were invented. A tight knee grip, being effective only above the widest diameter of the horse's barrel, tends to force the rider's thighs upward. An undercut swell-fork will serve to stop this upward movement, but a rider who resorts to one is *not* gripping effectively with his knees and he is *not* gripping the horse. He is gripping the swell of the saddle with his thighs. If the swell is wide enough and the undercut deep enough, the rider will, indeed, have a firm seat—dangerously firm in the event of a fall by the horse; but the firmness is as artificial as if the rider's boots were screwed down to hobbled stirrups. A rider who relies on this type of saddle to give him a feeling of security and a firm seat is lost on horseback when deprived of his "mumps."

Rider B is not trying to depend on knee grip. He is really putting on the pressure by gripping with his entire legs all the way down to the ankles. With toes turned out slightly, this rider can really hook onto a horse, whether he is riding a swell-fork, a slick-fork, or bareback. The important thing to observe here is that the rider's calves, being *below* the widest diameter of the horse's barrel, give him a much stronger grip than he could have if he rode as Rider A does, gripping only with the upper part of his legs. Rider B's legs are hooked firmly around the horse like the curved jaws of pliers almost completely encircling a man's finger. To shake loose Rider B a horse would have to move with much more speed and violence than he would have to exert in order to unseat Rider A.

Remember that so far we have been discussing only grip, which is for use in emergencies. Bear in mind, too, that grip and normal leg pressure against the horse's sides in ordinary riding are two different things. So many riders, however, confuse them, identifying one with the other, because grip and pressure are the same in principle; they differ only in degree of intensity or force. To grip you must really exert your leg muscles. To ride with firm leg pressure you need only to ride with a balanced seat. Then, with stirrups of normal length for ordinary paces, your legs are down where they belong, snug against the horse's sides almost to the ankles.

The reason I discuss grip in such detail is to emphasize the correct position of the rider's legs in the balanced seat. The feet in the stirrups are the foundation of the balanced seat. Misplace the lower legs and the whole seat becomes wrong. Take away the stirrups, which support most of the rider's weight, and you have not the true balanced seat but the "bareback seat." (Contrary to the opinion of many weightier authorities than I can ever hope to be, I maintain that riding without stirrups does *not* help to develop a stronger, balanced seat. It merely helps to confirm, as a rule, the habit of riding a "bareback seat" and thus being always at least slightly behind the horse's point of balance.)

When the lower legs are close against the horse's barrel, the rider not only has greater firmness of seat; he is also in better position to grip suddenly, when necessary, without undue waste motion or loss of time. This is something that men who sit as Rider A does cannot do. To apply the strongest possible grip, they must first bring their lower legs in against the horse's sides. Rider B, however, already has his legs properly placed there, in position for instant use; in a sudden emergency, he can clamp on the pressure instantly. This may seem like a small matter, but in skilled horsemanship small matters often loom big. In an emergency, this split-second difference, when a horse acts up unexpectedly, can mean the difference between landing on your head or successfully getting the horse under control.

This is also true of the time element in the important act of applying leg aids. Rider A cannot give his horse any understandable leg cue until he has first moved his leg in close enough to contact the animal's side with calf, heel, or—as is most usual with him—spur. Rider B, however, can cue his mount with a minimum of motion and wasted time, so that often, on a trained horse, you cannot even see the slight movement; the horse appears to act independently.

Why do riders who sit like Rider A so exaggerate the importance of knee grip? Generally, it is because they don't pause to think; they don't ponder, reflect, analyze. They blindly accept what they are told by "more experienced" persons. Then they go on parroting to others what has been parroted to them. Some of them in youth have had the hoary old jingle dinned at them:

> *Your head and your heart keep up;*
> *Your hands and your heels keep down.*
> *Keep your knees into your horse's sides*
> *And your elbows into your own.*

Once upon a time people really did believe in riding like that. They made almost a fetish of riding with knees pressed tightly against the horse and lower legs held well away from the barrel. Probably it was an anachronism left over from the days of chivalry when cavaliers in hardware suits wore long, roweled spurs and, in earlier times, daggerlike spurs similar to cockfighting gaffs, stickers that could easily puncture holes in a horse.

If you will look at photographs or tintypes of old-timers actually riding (not just posing), especially pictures of them leaping their horses over obstacles, you will see at once what we are trying to avoid. Almost every one of those old-timers in action, even over very small obstacles, rode with a death grip on the reins. Sitting back against the cantle, with their torsos well behind the vertical and their feet thrust forward almost to the horse's shoulders, they had to hang onto the reins to keep from falling off, because they were away off balance, far behind the horse's center of gravity. (Any reader who doubts this and has no old pictures to refer to can easily convince himself by looking over a few photographs of modern English steeplechase riders, who still ride the same way.) But as long as they had their knees pressed against their horse's sides, they thought that they were doing the right thing. Some old horsemen even used to "test" their youngsters' presumed "firmness" of seat by making the children ride with coins inserted between their knees and the saddle. If the young rider lost a coin even when riding over a jump, he was assured that he still had a long way to go before he could claim "a good seat," like father's.

Riders taught to think and ride in this way invariably turned out to be strictly bit-and-spur riders. They never learned the first elements of the correct use of their legs. As some of them aged in the wood, they liked to brag about their "reined horses" and yearned nostalgically for the good old days when dashing *caballeros* forked their "reined horses" like spurred clothespins and, to quote one soft-hearted, nostalgic writer, "loved their horses" so much that they were wont to "ride their favorite mount until he was ready to drop." The spur and the quirt represented their idea of impulsion.

If you really want to be a horseman, however, and wish to ride in balance and in comfort, forget about keeping your knees pressed into your horse's sides. There is no more sense to the idea than there is in straining to ride pigeon-toed. The so-called "fatal triangle" of light between the rider's knees and the saddle is a myth, a leftover from the good old days when cavaliers wore longshanked, sharp spurs. The important thing is to have your lower legs close to the horse's sides where you can use them instantly.

CHAPTER XVI

What Is a Good Seat: Saddles

The majority of men ride so very badly, that
when selling a horse, I always put on him a
particular saddle which is the most comfortable
one I have ever seen. Time after time I have had
men who had bought a horse from me come on
the following day and entreat me to sell them
my saddle, which, some of them were shrewd
enough to observe, had been the means of selling
the horse.
— *M. Horace Hayes*

SINCE some forgotten barbarian first flung a pelt over his horse's back, men have been designing saddles. The designs have ranged from the simplest to the most ornate, but almost all have had one feature in common: beyond the basic idea of not galling the horse's back — and even that has sometimes been overlooked — saddles have been designed primarily for the comfort of the rider. Until relatively recently, few saddle makers ever spared a thought to improving the comfort and the efficiency of the horse. Probably the only exception to this rule is the racing saddle; in racing, the horse's working efficiency is everything and the rider's comfort hardly matters.

As a result of this careless attitude by horsemen — whose ideas saddle makers merely reflect — even many modern saddles, the products of centuries of experience, are far from perfect. Yet the saddle is an integral factor in the development of a rider's seat. It can help or hinder even the most skillful horseman in his effort to ride in balance with his mount. It may, indeed, be said without exaggeration that saddles *make* seats. This is true not only of novice riders but also of experienced horsemen with firmly fixed habits developed by years of riding.

As an illustration of this I offer the following instance, which could be multiplied almost as many times as there are riders:

In gathering the photographs for this book I was especially eager to include at least one picture, and preferably a series of action pictures, of one particular horse, a splendid stallion of excellent conformation and airy grace of movement. I hoped to publish photographs of this horse carrying a rider in a modern stock saddle built on a low roper's tree having a built-up seat such as a majority of riders now favor; then I wanted to show a comparable series of action pictures of the same horse carrying the same rider in a well-made Mexican saddle which did not have a built-up seat and on which the stirrups were hung not so far forward as on the North American saddle.

It seemed to me that such a double set of photographs would clearly prove to the reader beyond any shadow of doubt the importance of saddle design on the rider's position.

The young man selected as model for the pictures was an experienced rider. Like most of his generation, he was accustomed to saddles with built-up seats.

The first photographs taken, using the North American-made stock saddle, turned out exactly as expected. With feet thrust forward and buttocks pounding the cantle, bumping along on his mount's loins, the rider perfectly demonstrated the faults I wished to stress. When the horse was standing still, the rider had a fairly good position in the saddle; most horsemen would have described his seat—as long as the horse remained motionless—as "a good practical seat." In fact, worse positions have been held up as ideal. However, once the horse started moving, the rider very obviously started to do the same—but in the opposite direction, toward the rear. At the trot, the faults became more exaggerated than at the walk, as the rider's feet slipped farther forward and his balance farther back. When the horse galloped, the pictures became caricatures of how to ride. With feet thrust forward almost to the horse's shoulders, arms flapping like wings and his rump bumping the cantle at every stride, the rider fell so far "behind" his mount that he appeared to be on the point of toppling over backward.

In short, he looked exactly as thousands of riders look in action when they are blissfully unaware of looking like anything but dashing cavaliers.

When, however, we switched to the Mexican saddle, our photographs became anything but perfect. Everything went wrong. For the rider continued to do everything in exactly the same way. Even when carefully instructed what he was supposed to do to remain in balance with his mount, he could not maintain a balanced seat except when the horse was standing still. Once the stallion started

Plate 44. EFFECT OF A SADDLE ON BALANCED SEAT. The semi-slack stirrup leathers betray this rider's difficulty. He cannot stay over his mount's center of gravity without having to "fight" the built-up seat that forces him back against the cantle.

Courtesy J. D. Harper

off, even at a sedate walk, the rider was utterly incapable of "going with" him. Only a great deal of conscientious practice could have enabled him to correct the sit-back habits he had built up over the years.

This young man had never had any riding instruction; he had learned to ride "naturally," without bothering his head about whys and wherefores. Unfortunately, like thousands of others, he had done virtually all his learning in modern stock saddles with built-up seats. Such saddles almost force a rider to assume an unbalanced, sit-back, behind-the-horse position and to develop riding habits that often are extremely difficult to alter. Once acquired, they can never be broken except by the rider's deliberate, persistent effort.

The chief reason why there has been so much bitter opposition to the "forward seat" is that all the old-timers with firmly fixed habits contrary to the forward impulse have not yet died off. Horsemen hate change and changing one's whole way of thinking is a difficult task—as difficult as thinking logically, unfettered by personal prejudices.

But even if all the old-timers were forever silenced, there would still be opposition because the old-timers have left so many spiritual descendants, young people to whom the American Cowboy looms through mists of myth and fable as a heroic ideal who could do no wrong, and who certainly could not err in his choice of his saddle, a most important part of his working equipment. Even many people who do not regard the cowboy as a heroic figure still try to emulate his style of riding. They will vehemently defend the stock saddle for general riding purposes, not as it might be made but exactly as it commonly is. One such enthusiast—who admits that he has not been on a horse more than half a dozen times in his life—states unequivocally, "All those flat saddles are for the tea-and-crumpet set. Those tea-drinkers can't ride like cowboys." Another, with stars in her eyes, writes of the "pure grace that comes only to the man raised in the old Western tradition, on a stock saddle." Just what this "old Western tradition" is she does not explain. Perhaps a careful study of some of the photographs taken by the late Erwin Smith and by Dane Coolidge, showing cowboys of a hundred years ago in action on horseback, might convince her that it is the same romantically hazy tradition to which the spade bit cultists like to refer.

As far as the balanced forward seat is concerned—and that is the seat most conducive to a horse's efficiency in action—the average modern North American stock saddle is wrongly designed. It is faultier in construction than stock saddles made before the introduction of the built-up seat.

A fundamental, universal precept of skilled riding the world over is this one rule: a rider should sit on the lowest part of the saddle seat. That is why the seat of almost any type of saddle, when viewed directly from one side, presents a concave surface instead of a flat surface. The lowest part of that curved seat is where the designer, in his wisdom or in his ignorance, believed that the rider should sit.

With this idea in mind, let us consider the saddle shown in Plate 45. This saddle is typical of average modern stock saddles; it presents no extremes of design. There are many stock saddles with more steeply built-up seats than this one and some with more shallowly sloping seats. Yet one need only glance at this

Plate 45. A TYPICAL STOCK SADDLE. The built-up seat slides the rider back against the cantle and behind the horse's normal center of gravity.

Photograph by D. Strassman

saddle to realize that when it is properly placed on a horse's back the curve of the seat, with the lowest part back near the cantle, will not enable the rider to sit easily and naturally far enough forward, close to the fork, to be over the horse's center of gravity. The lowest dip of the seat is too far back; it is far behind the location of the stirrups. One cannot sit in such a saddle without having his feet ahead of his center of gravity instead of directly under it. This is the worst fault of the average stock saddle. It is made-to-order for *frustrating* a balanced seat. Such saddles cause the rider to sit back on his buttocks, with the greater part of his weight from six inches to a foot behind his mount's center of gravity even when the horse is standing still. The only way the rider can easily get foreward where he ought to be is either to stand nearly erect in the stirrups, assuming a "clothespin seat," or to lean forward excessively from the hips.

Quite as bad as the built-up seat of this saddle, the stirrups are hung too far forward in relation to the lowest point of the seat, another common fault found in most stock saddles. This wrong location of the stirrups too far ahead of the lowest dip of the seat is itself sufficient to force the rider's weight back onto his buttocks, too far behind the stirrups. This violates a fundamental rule of the truly balanced seat—that the rider's weight should be directly *over* his stirrups so that, without having to lean forward from the hips, he can stand in his stirrups at any gait or speed simply by opening his hip and knee joints slightly. In other words, in a properly designed saddle the rider, without finding it necessary to learn forward, should be able to clear the saddle with the seat of his pants while remaining in balance. In effect, he rides as if he were standing over the horse with knees more or less bent. A rider's ability to do this at all gaits and speeds is the chief ingredient of a light, springy seat that is easy on a horse.

If all stock saddles were so designed as to make this easy maintenance of balance possible, we should never hear any objections to posting at a trot "because it looks so awkward"; for it wouldn't look awkward. Neither should we see so many stock saddle riders awkwardly trying to minimize the jars of a rough trot by clinging to the saddle horn in order to hold themselves in a standing position in the stirrups, or by leaning on the horn. Were such riders really in balance, they would not need the saddle horn as a "crutch."

If the stirrups of this saddle in Plate 45 were hung several

Plate 46. The stand-up seat. "When riding, always be in a position to stand up." The author in the Montana mountains, where the going can be rather rugged. Uphill—downhill—all day long—this is the only truly comfortable, because it is the balanced, seat.

Photograph by Dawn Young-Hansen

inches farther back nearer the lowest point of the seat, it would be considerably better, for then the rider's feet would be closer to a point directly under his own center of gravity. But, because the low point of the seat is so close to the cantle, he would still be "behind." However, as the stirrups are located—and as the stirrups of practically all modern stock saddles are hung—the rider finds himself pressed against the cantle with his feet so far ahead that only his most conscientious efforts to "sit forward" can prevent him from being overbalanced to the rear and hence "heavy" on his mount.

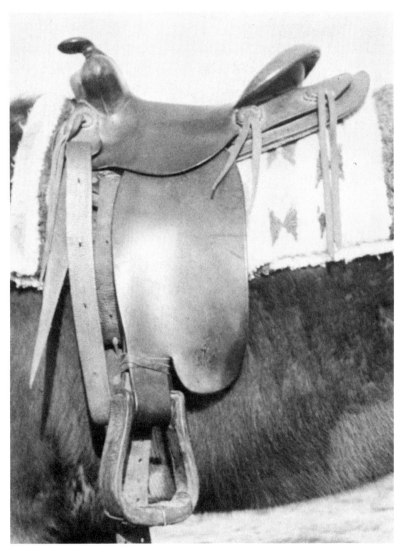

Plate 47. JRY YOUTH SADDLE. The tree is a Little Wonder with a 13''
seat. Note the relative flatness of the seat compared to the usual stock
saddle and the location of the stirrup in relation to the seat.

Photograph by the author

Plate 48. JRY YOUTH SADDLE RIGGING. The flat plate built into the skirt eliminates superfluous bulk between the rider and the horse.

Photograph by the author

This condition of being "behind the horse" and riding "heavy" increases in proportion to the horse's forward speed. A rider who is overbalanced to the rear when his mount is merely standing still or walking will be even more unbalanced—and hence less able to control his horse—when the animal trots or gallops.

A youngster who learns to ride in a saddle having a built-up

Plate 49. THE "FORWARD" SEAT! The author riding up a gentle slope in a so-called "forward seat" stock saddle that has a good "flat" seat but has the stirrups hung far to the front, almost underneath the fork. I was not trying to sit back on the cantle, and my torso was vertical; but where else could I sit, with my stirrups so far ahead of my center of gravity? Such saddles are passably good on the flat; they are fine for riding downhill. But here you see what happens when the horse has to work hardest, going uphill.

Photograph by Gene A. Pearson

seat, or indeed anyone who habitually rides such a saddle, labors under the same sort of handicap as one who sets out to master the piano or the violin while wearing mittens. Kids who are taught to rely on so-called "equitation saddles" never learn even the basics of true horsemanship.

This relationship of stirrup location to the lowest point of the seat is critical in the design of a saddle, any kind of saddle— so critical that it can hardly be overemphasized. The horizontal distance between the rider's feet in the stirrups and his seat bones in the saddle measures his base of support. If this distance is too great, so that the feet are too far ahead of the seat bones, the greater part of the rider's weight will be on his buttocks even when the horse is standing still; he will ride heavily, being seated too close to the loins, where the horse can least efficiently bear weight. The greater the horse's speed or his effort in performing any movement, the more forcibly will the rider be pushed back against the cantle. The only way he can overcome the inertia is to lean forward and stand in the stirrups, which is hardly conducive to a firm seat—an essential in schooling. If, on the contrary, the distance between stirrup and seat bones is too short, the rider's feet will slip too far back; his base of support will be minimal, his balance precarious, and his whole seat unstable, particularly when the horse sharply slows, stops, or turns, or is moving downhill.

Simple as it seems on the surface, this problem of stirrup location frequently confuses even horsemen who have done considerable thinking about saddles. In their efforts to get away from the awkward "backward seat" they go to the opposite extreme. One frequently sees advertisements of so-called "forward seat stock saddles" which, though the saddles have different name tags, stress that the stirrups are "hung forward" directly underneath the fork. The implication in all these ads is that this extreme forward position of the stirrups puts the rider over the horse's "carrying spot," enables him to "ride a balance," or whatever similar catchy sales term the advertiser dreams up. What the ads do not point out is that this is possible only if the horse is worked at speed and only on level or uphill ground. Nor does the advertiser tell the novice rider that this exaggerated stirrup location also puts the rider's legs too far ahead for them to be of much use in controlling the hindquarters; to ride both ends of the horse the rider must move his legs back quite far. But who wants to work a horse always at speed, or would attempt to school that way? For everyday riding and schooling such saddles are as impractical as the built-up seats they are meant to replace.

It is natural to wonder why professional horsemen should fall into such errors. One can come up with a variety of explanations without finding any one that alone answers the question fully. Various intangibles are involved which are difficult, or impossible, to pinpoint and measure—such things as personal limitations and prejudices, professional pride and jealousies; factors that loom larger behind the scenes in the horse business than some idealists would like to admit. However, I believe a fair answer boils down to something like this:

Horsemen in general, like athletes, are doers rather than thinkers. Very few of them could be described as intellectual types. Basically, many of them are almost as mentally herdbound as horses are. Most of them are specialists in some field of horsemanship. The versatile all-round trainer with a wealth of broad experience in different fields is even rarer than the horse that can do it all. The overwhelming majority of stock saddle riders have no experience whatever with jumping horses—and it was in this domain that the forward seat originated, or at least was popularized by the great Italian horseman Captain Frederico Caprilli. Hence, they not only have a very muddled notion of what the true forward seat is but they have no idea whatever that this seat is merely a part of *a system of schooling—forward schooling—* that is absolutely opposed to the type of schooling or training necessary to produce a good stock horse. When stock saddle riders talk about the forward seat or of "riding forward," as a rule they are just parroting a term of which they have no real understanding; it is totally beyond their limited experience. If they really understood the system of schooling and riding of which the forward seat is simply an integral part, they would be the first to condemn it as unsuitable for stock horses.

Besides their lack of experience with hunters and jumpers, these merchants of "forward seat stock saddles" have almost no interest in and less knowledge of what goes on in the world of horsemanship on an international level. Dreaming up their misleading advertisements of their "forward hung" stock saddles, they remain blissfully unaware that the world's best international riders discarded as impractical the extreme forward seat decades ago. Today one can see it occasionally only in greatly modified forms—so modified that probably Caprilli himself would hardly recognize it. The original forward seat as conceived by Caprilli was superseded many years ago by the more efficient balanced seat.

As early as the 1920s, long before stock saddle horsemen ever heard of the term "forward seat," American cavalry officers studied forward riding and schooling at its seat of origin, the Italian Cavalry Schools. Returning to the U.S. Cavalry School at Fort Riley, they wasted no time modifying, adapting, and changing the methods—and the seat—they had learned in Italy. General Harry D. Chamberlin, probably the most widely known and most influential of these officers, and generally acknowledged as one of the best horsemen and teachers America has ever produced, laid down this dictum as a basic principle of good horsemanship: "When riding, always be in a position to stand up." But a rider is in a very awkward position if he must stand up in stirrups that are so far forward that his feet are beside, and at many times may even be ahead of, his horse's elbows. Chamberlin specifically illustrates such a faulty seat in one of his books. He taught a balanced seat that places the rider firmly in the center of the saddle, and he called it a balanced seat.[1]

Probably the most consistently successful riders in international competitions have been the Germans. German riders have always been among the big winners in the Olympic Games, across country as well as in the ring. In the 1936 Equestrian Olympic Games German riders made a clean sweep: they won all the individual and team gold medals. Of course, many factors played a part in this singular performance, but not the least of them was the German riders' horsemanship. Commenting on this after the 1936 Games, the Chairman of the German Olympic Committee for Horsemanship, who was also the manager of the team, had some pertinent things to say about how to sit a horse and about the extreme forward seat:

The rider must at every moment have his horse under absolute control. And this control can be achieved only if the horse is quite supple and the rider is correctly seated.

The rider must sit deep in his saddle, both legs always close to the horse's body. . . .

A forward seat is advisable so long as all goes well, but when the horse has to be driven forward the rider must sit back.

The German system also permits the forward seat (to make it easy for the rider), but he is taught that the deep seat is the fundamental

[1]*Riding and Schooling Horses* (London: Hurst & Blackett, Ltd., 1947).

principle of successful horsemanship. Only when a rider is deep in the saddle can he successfully maneuver his horse by the pressure of his seat and the squeeze of his legs.[2]

This basically is the balanced seat that virtually all world-class riders use today. Today even show-ring jump riders, as well as cross-country riders, sit as deep in the saddle as polo players or contest calf ropers. Many of them really "ride forward" only when actually clearing an obstacle.

This is not a recent development. It will be news only to the "forward seat stock saddle" merchants. Concocting catchy copy about their "forward hung" stirrups and their "Californio-forward seats" to sell their "new" saddles to gullible novices, they do not know that they are about fifty years behind the times.

As an object lesson on the important influence saddle design has on a rider's seat I ask the reader carefully to study and compare Plate 44 and Plate 41.

In the first picture my friend "Monty" Harper has effortlessly assumed a "natural" position in a saddle made with a steeply built-up seat as well as with the stirrups hung too far forward. Notice that, while he is sitting erect, his weight is back against the cantle, a natural result of his feet being too far forward. Even at a slow trot he is behind his mount's center of gravity, which is approximately near the rider's shin, midway between his knee and ankle.

In Plate 41 my saddle is a low roping tree with a very moderately sloped seat, not ideal but not steep enough to prevent me from sitting forward with most of my weight *in the stirrups* and almost directly over my horse's center of gravity. Though riding only at a walk, I am farther forward than Harper is at a trot.

Now lay a straightedge on this photograph so that it vertically bisects the ball of my foot in the stirrup. The edge will pass through the middle of my knee and my ear. Now lay the straightedge on the other picture so that it vertically bisects Harper's stirrup. Then draw your own conclusions about the influence of the saddle on one's seat and balance.

(The reader should not misinterpret my remarks here. I am criticizing only saddles. Monty Harper is a skilled horseman. I use his picture, with his generous co-operation, merely to illustrate a point.)

[2]Gustav Rau, "The German System," *Horse & Horseman*, July, 1938.

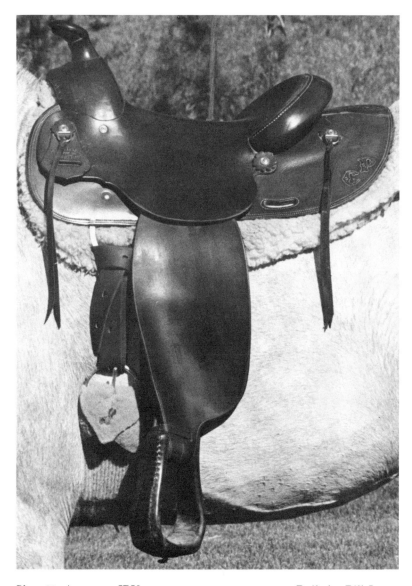

Plate 50. ANOTHER JRY SPECIAL SCHOOLING SADDLE. Built by Bill Long, Spokane, Washington, on a 3B Visalia tree. Some details are different— a matter of choice—but the dynamic principles are the same. Note the single housing, which reduces weight. The owner, whose interest is dressage, calls this saddle "a delight to ride."

Photograph by E. O. Ploeger

Plate 51. The author's daughter Kristen using the saddle shown in Plates 47 and 48. Observe that her feet are right under her and she is not "riding the cantle." She could balance in the stirrups without having to lean forward. This is what makes a light, springy seat, easy on the horse.

Photograph by the author

It is disillusioning to admit that our most expensive saddles, as a rule, simply are not designed for a balanced seat. It is disillusioning because the fault is not that of the saddle makers. It is our own fault, the fault of horsemen in general. If saddle makers manufacture a product that completely destroys easy maintenance of a balanced seat even before we put a horse in motion, they do so because we who ride demand it. The business of saddlers is to sell saddles. Consequently, they give us what we demand. They do not try to tell us what we ought to have. As horsemen we should know that. But we don't. We are slaves to fads and fetishes. We ape the contest professionals, who usually know exactly what they want in their business and will spare no expense to get it. Why any rider interested in skilled horsemanship should think that the style of tree required by a contest bronc rider in scratching out a money ride on a limber-backed outlaw, or the kind of tree favored by a professional roper whose work is measured in split seconds, is just the kind of tree for *him* seems a mystery. But we cannot blame the saddle makers.

These same saddle makers have been building rigs for years, and if there is one way the old-time range riders had it all over us, it was in the saddles they rode. The built-up seat and too-far-forward-hung stirrups are comparatively recent crimes. The old-timers never even dreamed of such things. Many old-timers rode well-balanced seats without ever even thinking of their position in the saddle. They could sit in their saddles without being jammed back against the cantle; they could stand in their stirrups without having to lean forward to attain that position, as we must do with our built-up seats. Their saddletrees—usually longer than ours are today, sometimes seventeen inches long—were very similar to the prototype Western stock saddle, the Mexican, and to the McClellan army saddle, which remains one of the most practical saddles ever designed.

Compare the old-time Collins saddle shown in Plate 52 with the modern stock saddle illustrated in Plate 45. This old saddle was designed for men who worked daily on horseback and who often rode from sunup to sundown. If you happen to find an heirloom of this kind among your family antiques, you will be wise to hang onto it.

Both early stock saddles such as this Collins saddle and the McClellan army saddle were patterned on the Mexican tree.

Another desirable way in which such saddles as these differed from so many modern stock saddles was that the "throat" or "twist"—that portion of the seat under and just ahead of the rider's crotch—was relatively narrow. A rider did not feel as if he were straddling a barrel, with his thighs forced too far apart.

If saddletrees such as these were widely marketed now, their popular use would greatly improve Western horsemanship. To the best of my knowledge, however, it is a rare saddle maker who knows enough about practical horsemanship to have a real desire to wean customers away from the built-up seat.

It has been my experience that the most perceptive saddle makers are not those who began their apprenticeship in early youth and who never have done anything else but those whose primary interest in horses and riding led them to take up the craft, often first as a hobby which developed into a fulltime business. In other words, they were riders before they became

Plate 52. J. C. COLLINS SADDLE. Built in the 1880s with a 15'' tree and a 4'' cantle. This old saddle is still in use.

Photograph by Conant

saddle makers, and often their first efforts were directed just to making themselves a better saddle than any they could buy. They understand a rider's problems because they experienced them. These are the craftsmen who truly understand what saddle making is all about.

Sometimes, however, an old-timer ripe in experience, who has grown rather set in his ways, is not the easiest person to convince. A rather amusing example of this occurred when I commissioned my friend Ed Ellestad to make the JRY Special Schooling Saddle shown on Plate 53.[3] When Ed had all my specifications, he turned the job of actually constructing the saddle over to his chief saddle maker, who had started life as a working cowboy and had been a rodeo rider.

The old-timer was skeptical of certain features of my design. Being an independent, opinionated spirit, like most of his kind, he did not hesitate to say so. He could not understand why I wanted certain features of the saddle precisely as I specified instead of as his years of experience had convinced him they should be made. But Ellestad was adamant; he was also the boss, as well as a horseman himself. I was the customer and the job had to be done my way.

Grudgingly, the old ex-cowboy turned craftsman followed my specifications. He built the saddle exactly as I wanted it, but he made it plain that he just *knew* some of my ideas were wrong.

One day, shortly after the saddle was finished, Ed Ellestad left the shop on other business. That was when the old-timer got a smart idea: he would prove, at least to his own satisfaction, that this JRY Special, however suitable it might be for a pleasure rider, would never pass the acid test of real cow work.

The old-timer tossed my new saddle into the trunk of his car and lit out for a nearby ranch run by one of his old cowboy pards.

He found another one of his old buddies visiting at the ranch. The three old cowhands spent most of the afternoon taking turns test riding my saddle. They gave it every test they could think of—reining, cutting, roping, riding up hills and down. Their final general agreement was that this was the kind of saddle they had been looking for all their lives.

But would the old saddle maker frankly admit this to his boss? Never! That would have been too humbling to his professional pride. The closest the old-timer ever came to admitting that he had been wrong, Ed Ellestad told me, was to concede that after all the JRY Special was a pretty good saddle. A little later he casually remarked that he planned to rework his own favorite saddle, making some changes he had in mind. . . .

[3]Any reader who wishes to obtain a JRY Special Schooling Saddle should write the author, care of the University of Oklahoma Press.

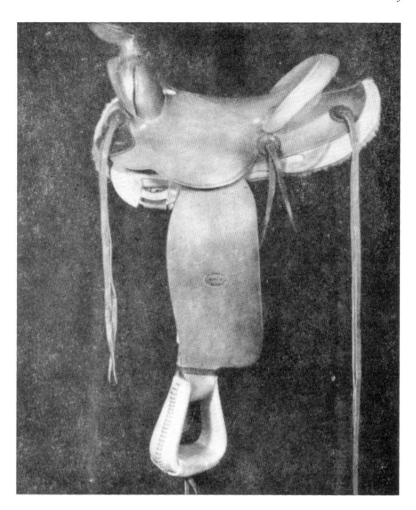

Plate 53. JRY SPECIAL SCHOOLING SADDLE. This rugged, lightweight saddle makes a balanced seat easy and natural. Note location of stirrups in relation to shape of seat. In a saddle of this design one does not have to "learn" to sit in balance. That comes naturally.

Photograph by Smith

Unfortunately, before he could carry out his plan and enjoy using the kind of saddle he had always wanted, the old-timer fell ill and died.

Since many of us may have to do with the saddles we have, at least for a while, a natural question comes up: Can we ride a balanced seat in our present saddles, even in spite of built-up seats and wrongly hung stirrups? Yes; it can be done. To do it really well, however, requires practice and constant vigilance in correcting one's faults until sitting properly becomes a fixed habit —and even then, in the wrong kind of saddle, it will still be easy to slip off-balance and fall "behind the horse." Like anything else worth doing, you may have to work at it for a while. If you are a novice rider, you should have little trouble; you'll have no bad habits that you will have to unlearn. If, however, you have been riding for years and have developed a set of firmly entrenched habits—and ideas—contrary to the principles of balanced riding, breaking down those established habits and relinquishing those pet ideas will be the most difficult part of the job.

Probably the most important fundamental to keep in mind is that when you are mounted your stirrup leathers, viewed from the side, *must be vertical.* This means that when you have placed your feet in the stirrups you do *not* shove your lower legs even slightly forward, thus forcing the leathers ahead of the vertical. The instant you do so, even at a standstill, your weight moves back onto your buttocks which press against the cantle, you immediately fall far behind the horse's center of gravity and your stirrups get ahead of your own center of gravity. The only purchase you have on the stirrups then acts to push your weight even farther to the rear. With your feet out ahead of you, any pressure on the stirrups helps only to jam you tighter against the cantle. This is the commonest fault of which most riders are habitually guilty, because their built-up saddle seats encourage them to assume this behind-the-horse position.

If you do fall into this faulty position, you automatically make another error: you move your lower legs out of position for best control of the horse, for almost always the legs move not only forward but outward, away from the horse's sides, the error most typical of the knee-gripping rider. When this happens, you are in no position to give your mount any leg aids or cues, without first moving your legs back and in close to the horse's sides.

Because you have to "fight" that built-up seat which slides you back toward the cantle, you must make a special effort to sit as far forward in the saddle as you comfortably can. Even though using the cantle as a comfortable backstop seems the natural thing to do, don't do it. Instead, try to sit away from the cantle, as if it were red-hot.

Probably the easiest way to be sure of both the vertical stirrup leathers and sitting well forward in the saddle is to stand straight up in your stirrups, balancing for a moment, and then simply sit down. Make a note of that: sit down, straight down. Do not sit back. Keeping your torso erect, simply let your body sink straight downward by relaxing your ankle, knee, and hip joints. To test your balance, see whether you can immediately stand up again, without having to grab the saddle horn or incline your torso farther forward. If you can't, you are not truly balanced.

If this seems difficult or rather awkward at first—blame your built-up seat which is pushing you back toward the cantle. In saddles with extremely built-up seats and stirrups hung far forward, this balanced position can be only approximated with any degree of comfort; but in a saddle of proper design, or with a seat only slightly built-up toward the fork, this balanced seat is not only easy; it is natural.

Another way of getting yourself forward in the saddle, which some riders might find easier, is to sit erect with your legs dangling loosely, your feet free of the stirrups. Grasping the saddle horn, pull yourself slightly forward so that your weight rolls off your buttocks onto your relaxed thighs and crotch. Now, without moving your upper legs away from the saddle, draw your lower legs backward until you can place your feet into the stirrups. In other words, after rolling forward onto your crotch, try to put your feet into the stirrups by moving your legs only *below* the knees.

A good way to check your seat now is to glance down at the points of your knees, without tilting your head or your body forward. Can you see your own toes? If you can, you probably have unconsciously slipped backward again, or your stirrup leathers are too long. Double-check by trying to stand in your stirrups without leaning forward. You should be able to do so.

Now you will find that your weight is evenly distributed directly over your stirrups—and your stirrup leathers hang vertically. You are balanced almost directly over your horse's center of gravity. You are seated not only on your buttocks, as when sitting in a chair, but also on your crotch. Your spine should be erect or inclined slightly to the front, with your chest out and your waist supple—exactly the opposite of the slouchy seat. Seated thus, with plenty of weight in the stirrups, you cannot help but ride lightly, springily. In action, your ankle, knee, and hip joints work together to absorb every shock of the horse's movements. With your weight jammed down into your heels, you have firm, clinging leg pressure which aids your balance more than mere knee grip ever can.

Plate 12 illustrates this seat—the balanced seat in the stock saddle.

The riders in Plates 3 and 41 are both using saddles that have built-up seats and stirrups too far forward.

CHAPTER XVII

Tiedowns and Martingales

*Long ago I came to the conclusion that the great-
est obstacle in the way of progress in riding is
the reluctance of so many riders to think. . . .
Only if riding is done with the head as well as
the breeches do real horsemen result.*
— Vladimir S. Littauer

T HE other day an ordinarily amiable friend just
about chewed my ears off. I found him unsad-
dling after a ride. He was hot, red-faced, and scowling. His horse
was lathered; he appeared to be scowling, too.

I said: "You working for the Pony Express now, Dave?"

"That glue-fingered Hinky!" Dave turned his hot mount loose
to roll. "The bum borrowed my tiedown, spoiled my whole ride."

"What do you ride, Dave—the tiedown or the horse?"

Dave whirled on me angrily. "When I go for a ride I want to
enjoy myself. I want to relax, forget. I don't want to be riding
a horse that jigs and jiggles and tries to put his head in my lap
and butt my nose behind my Adam's apple. When I see that guy
Hinky——"

"Why don't you train Baldy——" I began.

"Baldy's used to a tiedown and so am I."

"I hope you're not bragging, Dave."

"Why not? Better riders than you use tiedowns. Look," Dave
said, "at all the top rodeo professionals."

"I've looked. Is that why you use that fancy breast collar—to
make you look like a professional? If not, what is it for?"

"What for?" Dave knew as well as I did that he had no real
use for a breast collar on his horse. "Why, that's part of my outfit. All the best professionals use 'em."

I wish I had a dollar for every rider who shares such ideas

229

as Dave has. Americans just can't resist gimmicks and gadgets. Sometimes for appearance's sake, often because we think they help us ride better, we squander money on equipment for which we have no real use. Sometimes we don't even understand what a thing's real use is, its original purpose or its limitations. We fancy it simply because, we think, it makes us look "professional."

One of the chief offenders in this respect is the tiedown or martingale. Youngsters see their favorite rodeo contestants using them and aren't satisfied until they have the same equipment. Riders old enough to be past the hero-worshipping stage act just as blindly.

Rodeo contestants are businessmen first and glamour boys only incidentally. They and their mounts are specialists, members of smoothly functioning teams. The one and only purpose of such a team is to win money. Anything that interferes with this business is ruthlessly eliminated from the team's action and equipment. Anything that helps to win is adapted and used.

To cite a few common examples, contest ropers have discarded high heels for the sake of greater speed and agility afoot. Their saddles are almost slick-forked, with low cantles and especially deep stirrups for speed in dismounting. Some ropers find it faster and more natural to dismount on the right side; therefore, ignoring hidebound custom that says the right side is the "wrong" side, they do so. In training their mounts contest ropers are concerned not with fine horsemanship but with sheer speed. They don't care how a horse carries his head as long as it doesn't get in their way. They want no part of the flashy reining horse's spectacular sliding stop; it would waste precious seconds when fractions of a second might mean the difference between a jackpot or winding up with empty pockets.

Above all, contest ropers, playing for keeps, don't want to risk any unnecessary chances of losing. They want a perfect performance every time they throw a loop. However, horses being horses, perfection is impossible to guarantee. So your contest roper does all he can do to reduce chances of mistakes to an absolute minimum. Let the purists sneer at his tiedown and neck-rope, at his freakish bit and at his apparent disregard for his horse's mouth. Any contestant will cheerfully endure such criticisms if he is first in line at the pay window.

Contest bronc riders don't try to emulate ropers. They stick to their high heels or whatever suits them, wear chaps, use bronc stirrups. The all-round contestants suit their equipment to the event.

Why aren't more amateur horsemen as sensible in their outlook as are the contestants they so often try to emulate? It is as silly for a pleasure rider to adopt a professional roper's gear or a bronc rider's technique as it would be for the roper to ape the bronc rider or vice versa.

Tiedowns have their place among the equipment of professional ropers who are out strictly for the big money; but any amateur horseman who professes to be interested in skilled riding should be ashamed to be seen using a tiedown, except when schooling a spoiled horse. For any horse that needs a tiedown or martingale needs more training. He would not require any such gimmick if he were taught to bridle properly, to yield his jaw to the rider's hand, and flex at the poll. Hence, with an untrained horse a tiedown is often useful; it may save the rider a bang on the nose, assist him in preventing the horse from getting its head out of position, as well as teach the horse that trying to evade the bit by jerking the reins out of the rider's hands will result only in self-inflicted punishment. However, to make a regular practice of using a tiedown on a horse that is supposed to be schooled amounts to a tacit admission that the trainer has completely failed. To argue that he "goes better" in a tiedown than without one is to admit that the horse resists and evades the hand by getting his head out of position—a fault for which the rider or trainer is to be blamed.

A rider who prefers to resort to a tiedown or martingale instead of to corrective schooling thereby admits his own laziness or lack of ability. If he is a businessman who clambers onto a horse merely for exercise, he need apologize to nobody, not even his patient horse; let him loll back in a howdah, if he wants to. The average amateur, however, rides for fun, presumably because he likes horsemanship. His main idea, therefore, should be to ride as well as he can. But he defeats this end when he depends on a martingale or a tiedown as a substitute for skill.

It is worthy of note that in reining and cutting contests tiedowns are prohibited. It is taken for granted by the experienced horsemen who write the rules that a horse that needs to have its head tied down is not fit to compete in a contest worthy of the name. Following the same line of reasoning, the rider or trainer of such a head-tossing mount has yet to master one of the basic, most important elements of horsemanship—the art of making a good mouth. A rider who always relies on a tiedown to keep his mount's head where it belongs will never learn this art. He will never be a finished horseman.

Tiedowns can be recommended for persons like my friend Dave, those whose idea of a pleasant ride is one on which they can "relax" with an utterly blank mind, letting the horse take care of himself—as well as of them—while they absorb scenery or flap their tongues. Such persons generally regard schooling as tiresome work, or as a mystery; they lack the right sort of temperament ever to become good at it. They do not ride horses; they are merely passengers in the saddle. For them the tiedown is a boon. Horsemanship remains forever beyond their reach.

Sooner or later most of us ride, and some of us own, an aged horse that does a particular job excellently, and for this work we find him most useful; but as an all-round mount for either show or pleasure he leaves much to be desired. Before we met or acquired him the beast had become thoroughly set in his ways. We discover that he has a nosebagful of unpleasant little habits and no mouth worth mentioning. If he belongs to us, or if we have to ride him much, the first important question we have to answer is: Shall we let him do things the way he is accustomed to doing them so long as he performs his job well, or shall we reschool him to our way of thinking? In short, is this elderly character worth the effort of reforming? If the task would require more time than we could spare or more patience than we have, or if even the most optimistic possible results would not make up for the time and effort expended in re-educating him, then we may find a tiedown a useful prop to hang on the old horse. At least, it may serve some day to keep his cranium out of our teeth, and that's always worth while.

One other situation in which use of a tiedown may be excused, but only temporarily, is when an inexperienced rider acquires a horse whose previous faulty schooling has resulted in the animal's acquiring the bad habit of stargazing or head-tossing. The new owner cannot be blamed for this fault, nor if he is a novice can he be expected to know immediately how to eradicate the bad habits and set about at once developing the horse's mouth. Perhaps a tiedown, during the first few rides while he is getting used to his new mount and gaining confidence, will help the new acquaintanceship get off to a smooth start. As soon as this has been accomplished, however—and it should not take more than half a dozen saddlings—the young rider should be able to proceed with the necessary course of schooling without the aid of a tie-down. In fact, if there is the slightest chance of his learning to rely on the contraption as a permanent part of his gear, he will do better never to use it at all.

The important thing to remember about martingales and tie-downs is that, though they sometimes have their special uses, at best they are mere palliatives. Like crutches, while they may at times be useful to lean on, they cure nothing. They do not get down to the root of the trouble which calls them into use. That trouble, always and every time, is that the horse which needs a tiedown or martingale simply does not have a good mouth; he is not a trained mount.

CHAPTER XVIII

Bits

*For no person can alter or improve his horse's
mouth beyond the capacity of his own Hand.
Hence, if your Hand is bad, you can never
make your horse's mouth good; and if your
horse's mouth is good you will soon reduce it
to a level with your Hand.*

— *John Adams*

THE use of severe bits of any kind is not only
unnecessary but is a positive handicap in developing a horse's mouth. You cannot obtain true lightness by
means of force; the two are incompatible. Of course, if you happen to be a genius, you may be able carefully to use the severest
kind of bit and still get good results; but if you are a genius you
would never have any need for such a bit, because you'd get better results without it.

It is difficult enough to cultivate delicate responsiveness in a
horse's mouth without compounding the difficulty by using a
severe leverage bit. The greater a bit's leverage, the more delicately it must be used. The average rider can hardly realize the
lightness of touch and the delicacy of hand and arm reflexes
which competent use of a severe bit necessitates.

Severe bits are commonly regarded as contraptions that enable
a rider to "hold" a headstrong or cold-jawed horse. That they
actually make this possible no one can reasonably deny. Archimedes, who first clearly formulated the principle of the lever,
stated that, given a sufficiently long lever, he could move the
world. Man could devise a bit with sufficient leverage to "hold"
a charging bull elephant. But when we begin thinking of a bit
as something that enables us merely to "hold" a horse, we have
got completely off the right track that leads to our original goal —
horsemanship.

The bit is not simply a mechanical contrivance with which to forcibly stop a horse. The bit, acting with the legs, is a means of communicating to the horse the knowledge that we wish him to stop, or to turn or slow down or flex or whatever else we may desire. Force—except as slight differences in degrees of light rein tension inform the horse of various responses expected of him—does not enter into the problem at all. When we think in terms of force, we cease thinking in terms of controlled lightness, which is the essence of horsemanship.

Almost invariably the consequence of using a severe bit is not the superlative lightness we hope for but instead an unnecessarily heavy pressure on the horse's mouth that results in either over-flexion or a "cold jaw." The honest rider must then face the unpleasant truth that the delicacy of his touch has not been commensurate with the powerful leverage of his bit. This, how-ever, is the one sin that few riders will admit, even to themselves: that they have poor hands. They find it less ego-deflating to blame the horse—and try a harsher bit. That's why there are a hundred and one different and unnecessary bits on the market, each adver-tised as a universal cure-all for hard mouths. The advertisers never say anything about heavy hands. Men search for "the right key to a horse's mouth" without ever realizing, or because they will not admit, that the "key" usually lies right in their own hands.

I regard the spade bit as an archaic instrument that should be seen only in museums along with such similar relics of semi-barbarism as chastity belts and brain squeezers. I do not mean to imply that I think men who believe the spade bit is good and who use it intend deliberately to be cruel to their horses. Neither do I maintain—as I have been accused of saying, or at least implying—that some horsemen, a very few, cannot get fair results with so severe a bit. Centuries ago, long before the spade bit was invented, early horsemasters such as Federico Grisone, Pignatelli, La Broue, and the Duke of Newcastle managed to train horses to much more advanced states than any spade bit expert has ever even dreamed of achieving, and they accomplished results using more brutal methods and severer bits than any competent spade bit trainer would advocate or approve. But I do maintain that any horseman whose firmness of seat and delicacy of touch enable him to get fair results with a spade bit should be able to achieve excellent results without the spade. I believe the con-fidence of confirmed spade bit men in their favorite freakish instrument is always based on sheer ignorance, particularly mis-understanding of what constitutes an excellent mouth in a trained horse.

Once I got fed up with the blatantly boastful articles spade bit fanatics like to write extolling their own marvelous skill. To hear these modest *Californios* blow their own whistles, the world has never seen and never will see as finished a horseman as the Mexican *vaquero* and his *patrón*, the Spanish don, who flourished in early California. Their only near rivals, if you would believe some of the nonsense published in certain West Coast magazines, are their own descendants, who apparently yearn for the good old days when everyone was a silver-spangled grandee. One day, after wallowing through one too many of these printed brags, I felt compelled to try to cast at least a glimmer of truth on the subject of spade bits. I wrote an article attempting to explain and analyze as clearly as I could, and without too much prejudice, how a spade bit really works, the logic of those who use it, and the effects the spade has on a horse.

"Calling a Spade a Spade"[1] exploded in print with the effect of a small A-bomb. For months after it had appeared, readers continued to write letters about it, both to the editor of the magazine and to me. Most of the writers applauded the article, but if hell hath no fury like a woman scorned, a woman scorned, we soon realized, hath no fury like a spade bit fanatic forced into the position of being challenged to discuss his specialty with some semblance of calmness and logic. Many of the letters I received from the spade bit warlocks were little more than vitriolic vituperation. The fact that I had cited authorities to back up my views made no difference to them. They did not know who my authorities were.

The article did have a least one good effect. It served to help convince officials of the American Horse Shows Association that Rule XIX, making mandatory the use of spade or half-breed spade bits in stock horse classes, deserved to be abolished. Over the angry protests of some California directors, the much resented Rule XIX was deleted from the rule book.

Several amusing incidents followed in the wake of the article's publication. A California woman sent the magazine an action photograph of herself, taken at a show in which she had won a stock horse championship on her favorite spade-bit-trained horse.

[1] *The Western Horseman*, March, 1950. See Appendix.

In the photograph the rider had a death grip on the saddle horn with one hand and on the reins with the other, while the horse was sliding to a quick stop with its mouth painfully wrenched open by the heavy bit. The lady submitted the picture as incontrovertible "proof" that my ideas about spade-bit horses and riders were all wrong.

Immediately thereafter a spokesman for a California horsemen's association cited the same photograph as an excellent example of a top spade-bit horse's performance, adding "There are plenty more [such horses] in this *manana* land."

Actually, the photograph was a perfectly "horrible example" of just about everything I had said about spade-bit horses. It offered incontrovertible proof that neither the proud rider nor the A.H.S.A. director-judge had the faintest idea of how a horse properly flexes or what skilled horsemen mean when they speak of a "good mouth."

Some time after the appearance of this controversy, a well-known California trainer of the hackamore-spade-bit school stated in another magazine that a noted California horsewoman had greatly influenced and improved the "traditional" California system of hackamore-spade-bit training and was responsible to a great extent for the success of a number of trainers who had learned their business while working for her. This horsewoman had improved on the "traditional" system—which was supposed to be already perfect a century ago—by introducing the bitting rig in the training of spade-bit horses. Having learned about bitting rigs in Vienna, she had introduced the innovation in the training of her own horses, with the result that she had succeeded in teaching her show-ring competitors a few elementary facts about making a horse's mouth that they had never known—though it was all old stuff to the horsemasters of Vienna and the rest of the civilized world.

Here we have an acknowledged spade-bit expert admitting that he and others learned some of their most valuable lessons from a woman trained in Vienna, the home of the world-famous Spanish High School; yet all she taught them was the use of a bitting rig. If any innovation so simple and so universally known could have so greatly improved the training of spade-bit horses, could we find more convincing proof that the old-time Spanish *Californio* was far from the "peerless" horseman that his admirers boast he was?

Every so often one meets or hears of a rider who proudly breaks down and admits that, though he grew up using curb bits and perhaps was even taught to despise men who would put a spade into a horse's mouth, he promptly changed his ideas after seeing good spade-bit horses in action. Suddenly he saw the light. Overnight he became a convert to the cult of the spade.

What such converts really are admitting is that they were impressed by the results achieved by somebody who knew more about teaching a horse and who devoted more time and patience to the job than they had ever learned to. "Cow country horsemanship," the late Dick Halliday—himself a confirmed spade-bit man who dearly loved the California tradition—pointed out, "is not a finished proposition. The cowboy only thinks his horses are trained. They are not, but are so used to the work they do that they really know more about it than their riders."[2] But by a bit of illogical thinking the newly converted spade-bit cultist convinces himself that the method, instead of the trainer *in spite of his method,* achieved the results the convert admires. This is one of the worst errors in thinking a horseman can make. Methods, although they vary in efficacy, do not, regardless of the human element, produce finished horses. Only men can accomplish that. A poor horseman gets poor results regardless.

I consider the spade bit as crude a piece of equipment as the Chilean ring bit. "No horse will keep a soft jaw unless he is well ridden," wrote the late General Harry D. Chamberlin, internationally known as a member of three United States Olympic equestrian teams and one of the most skilled horsemasters this country ever produced. "When bridled with a brutal spade bit, such as is often seen in the 'modern west,' the jaw, because the tortured mouth is open, appears soft. The horse is actually 'behind the bit.'"[3] To believe such a bit is suitable for any kind of riding whatever is parallel to traveling by oxcart.

I regard most types of Pelham bit as clumsy contraptions for schooling. I dislike the Pelham because it is an aborted attempt to substitute for a full double bridle consisting of curb and bridoon. When we exert tension on the upper reins of a Pelham, the "snaffle" reins attached near the mouthpiece, we lift the bit too high in the horse's mouth for the curb action by the lower reins to be properly effective. When we use the curb reins, the bit is

---

[2] *The Horse,* November–December, 1947.
[3] Harry D. Chamberlin, *Training Hunters, Jumpers and Hacks* (New York, D. Van Nostrand Company, Inc., 1952).

shifted downward in the mouth so that it is improperly placed for most effective snaffle action. If we use both "snaffle" and curb reins at the same time, as with a full double bridle, it is virtually impossible to keep the bit exactly where it should be for both snaffle and curb action to be properly effective at the same time.

These faults of the bit can be slightly corrected by the rider raising or lowering his hands to compensate for the movements of the bit, but if we want the action of a double bridle why not simply use a double bridle and get the job done right?

Some pro-Pelham riders maintain that the Pelham is good for "holding" a horse which, when excited, cannot be easily held in a snaffle or a straight bar bit. Others say that it is a good bit because it is "less of a mouthful" than a bit and bridoon. However, we are not concerned in this book with "holding" rambunctious horses; we are concerned with schooling them so that they don't need to be controlled by mere leverage and strong arms. As for the second argument, any horse can be accustomed to a double bridle in a short time. It is much less of a "mouthful" than a spade bit or most half-breed spades.

If the Pelham is used *without a curb chain*, then it is satisfactory for use on a colt before he is put into the double bridle, for then it acts almost the same as a straight bar bit. It has the additional advantage, if used without a curb chain, of giving a novice rider who is not accustomed to handling four reins a chance to get used to handling them without doing the colt's mouth any harm; though the same practice can be gained, of course, by attaching two pairs of reins to a plain bar bit or a jointed snaffle.

The one type of Pelham that I have found to be an exception to the general rule, quite useful in mouthing a young horse, and in helping a novice rider learn to handle four reins with little risk of hurting the horse's mouth is the SM Pelham, usually called the SM polo bit. The SM has loose cheeks and a flat mouthpiece about an inch wide with a low port. The wide, flat mouthpiece helps to keep the bit positioned in the mouth without much shifting about; its effect is mild, and most horses respond well to it.

Normally, however, the only use I have for a Pelham as a training bit is illustrated in Plates 54 to 58.

Either a bar bit or a jointed snaffle is all that is necessary during the early months of elementary schooling. Both enable a rider who knows his business to "place" a colt's head and to correct faults.

Plate 54. STARGAZER. This mare was the worst stargazer I have ever handled, an absolute lunatic in her reaction to the reins. This is the sort of performance she put on the first time I mounted her. She needed a drastic cure.

Photograph by Gene A. Pearson

I am not exactly against the use of a running martingale to lower a high head, but whenever possible I prefer to get along without one. The martingale looped to the reins is anything but helpful to real delicacy of touch. It should almost never be needed in mouthing a green colt and only rarely in remaking a spoiled horse. No genius has ever invented any gadget that can adequately substitute for good hands.

The ideal training bridle, in my opinion, is the Weymouth, the full double bridle, with a low-port, short-shanked curb and a

Plate 55. THE CURE. In horsetraining, there are very few infallibles; what helps one horse may utterly fail with another. But this rig for curing stargazers and headtossers has never failed me. It is a Pelham bit with a curb strap looped through the lower rings and attached to a standing martingale. The martingale is just long enough to hang slightly slack when the horse keeps its head in a normal position. But the more violently he flings his head up the harder he hits himself in the mouth. When he drops his head the tiedown falls slack. It's the basic principle of instant correction and instant reward.

Photograph by Gene A. Pearson

small snaffle or bridoon. (An excellent type is the Ward Union; the shanks of the curb bit swivel on the mouthpiece.) With no other bridle, I believe, is it so easy to develop a desirable head-set, for the trainer can work on the mouth with either the snaffle or the curb alone, alternating the effects as rapidly as he can use his hands, or he can use both bits at the same time but independently of each other.

An expert horseman having much experience and blessed with great tact can successfully start a colt in a full double bridle as

Plate 56. Big surprise! I put the Pelham tiedown on the mare, turned her loose in a small ring and spooked her into a gallop. This is what happened to her the first time she flung her head up to fight the bit. She made just two more halfhearted attempts before she quit. She is cured—permanently.

Photograph by Gene A. Pearson

soon as the colt has become accustomed to carrying a bit—but this is not an accomplishment the average rider should even think of trying.

"Who," I can hear some cow country critics snort, "ever heard of training a stock horse in a double bridle? What a crazy idea!"

Plate 57. Here I am riding the mare, a few minutes later, with the tie-down off. It is hooked to the throatlatch of the bridle, just to keep it from dangling. But the mare does not know that—and she has no intention of trying to find out!

Photograph by Gene A. Pearson

However, the idea is far from crazy. It not only can be done; it should be done as often as the trainer's skill permits. More widespread use of the double bridle for training purposes would greatly improve cow country horsemanship and would produce more finished and better-finished stock horses.

Let me give a specific example of how this unorthodox system of basic training of real cow horses actually works.

Once upon a time I wrote a series of magazine articles setting forth my ideas on how properly to develop a horse's mouth. In one of the articles I recommended the use of a double bridle after the colt has become accustomed to working in an ordinary snaffle. The artist who illustrated the articles, and who should

Plate 58. Here I am riding my ex-stargazer over cavalletti scattered at random on the ground. Note that I have contact with her mouth, and her head is where it belongs. The bars scattered at random induce her to look where she places her feet, and never mind the stars.

Photograph by Gene A. Pearson

have known better, interpreted "double bridle" in the usual Western sense as meaning anything that can be put on a horse's head as long as it has four reins. He drew a picture of a horse being schooled in a Pelham bit.

A number of discerning readers immediately caught this error, and some of them took the trouble to write to me about it. I lost no time informing each and every one of them that "double bridle" in my horseman's lexicon emphatically does not mean a Pelham.

Time passed. I forgot the incident. (But from then on I made it a point to have a voice in the selection of the artists who illustrated my magazine pieces. A popular artist in the horse-illustration field is not necessarily a good horseman.)

About a year later, one day I received a letter from a working ranch hand in Texas. He was employed as a horse-breaker on a large cow outfit. The ranch had a remuda of about four hundred horses, and this man's job was to pick the best potential mounts and develop them into cow horses—not the show-ring variety of "stock horses" that seldom or never see a range cow in the open, but range-raised broncs bred and reared for no other purpose than to work cattle, horses whose training began when they were on the verge of maturity.

Obviously, in a remuda of this size it was not difficult to find horses of widely disparate dispositions, temperaments, and talents. My correspondent had ample opportunity to handle all kinds. He had read and pondered what I had written about developing a good mouth, he informed me, and despite the ridicule of the other riders in the outfit, he had commenced using a double bridle as soon as each horse was sufficiently advanced in the snaffle stage of training.

He just wanted me to know, he said, that the results of the "experiment" were astounding—particularly to those same cowboys who had laughed at him for trying it. Most of these riders were Mexicans, seasoned *vaqueros* of mature years; they had their own ways of doing things and they were quite set in their ideas of how a cow horse should be taught to work. But when these young horses, trained in a double bridle, were turned over to the men and put to work, the horse-breaker wrote, the *vaqueros* "are looking at the results with a different attitude now." For the double-bridle horses turned out to be better cow horses than any mounts the cowboys had known before. In fact, the two top horses on the ranch were a couple of reformed outlaws.

If this seems unusual, here is another fact the skeptic might well ponder: A well-known trainer of so-called spade-bit horses actually trains his mounts in a double bridle—a fact he is careful not to publicize. When they are finished, he shows them in a spade bit.

This, I think, speaks quite adequately for the efficacy of the "unorthodox" method of schooling that I advocate. Actually, it isn't unorthodox at all; it is only strange to most stock horse riders. But when a system of training produces cow horses whose work quickly changes the skeptical attitude of veteran Mexican *vaqueros*—men who invariably have pretty emphatic ideas of how a good cow horse should work, ideas based on lifelong experience in the saddle—the system merits at least a trial before being rejected.

If this horse-breaker's experience were unique, it probably would not be worth citing as proof of the usefulness of a double bridle on stock horses. But there is nothing unique about it. It is quite commonplace among the relatively few Western horsemen who have tried schooling in a double bridle, and knew how to use it.

Unfortunately, too many Westerners have developed a superior disdain of anything that smacks of "English riding." But the double bridle is no more peculiar to English horsemanship than is the snaffle or the stirrup. Only the wilfully ignorant prefer to think so.

In inexperienced hands the double bridle does have a potential danger or drawback, the same drawback any curb bit has: novice riders are prone to use the curb too much and neglect the snaffle. This overuse of the curb very easily develops a horse with a "rubber" neck; it encourages a colt to acquire the habit of getting behind the bit, refusing to extend his head and neck, and hence ruining the free-striding forward movement we want to cultivate. To safeguard against this error a good schooling rule to follow always is: Ride generally on the snaffle; use the curb only correctively, and always very gently.

A lot of exaggerated fuss is made, however, about the difficulty of properly using a double bridle. Like spurs, double bridles should be used, we are told, only by experienced riders. But how do you acquire experience, in using double bridles or anything else? You have to do a thing in order to learn how to do it well. Any rider with hands and a little common sense can easily and quickly learn to manage four reins as well as he can handle two, if he will just

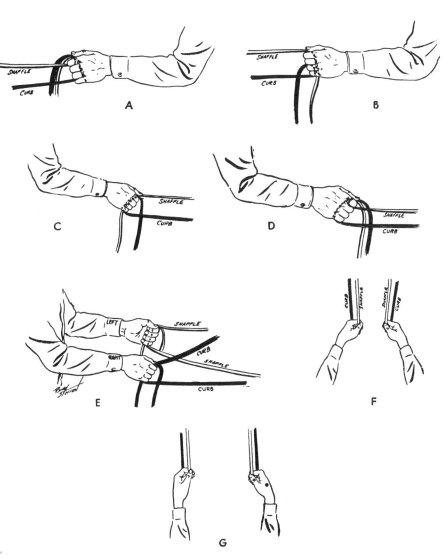

Fig. 5. —Correct ways of holding double reins. *(Drawing by Randy Steffen.)*

take the trouble to hold the reins in a simple, sensible manner, adjusting his way of holding to suit himself, the peculiarities of his mount, and the work he is doing at the moment. About the only rule I would bear in mind is this: The curb rein should not enter the hand above the snaffle rein. You will sometimes see good horsemen holding their reins with the curb rein above and the snaffle rein below so that the leathers cross between bit and hand; but I have yet to meet a horseman who could satisfactorily tell me why. The bridoon lies above the curb bit in the horse's mouth, and it is the curb that is commonly used to lower the horse's head while the bridoon usually serves to elevate it. Why then reverse the positions of the reins in the hand?[4]

Figure 5 illustrates several ways of holding double reins.

It seems hardly necessary to emphasize that in schooling a colt or a green horse the rider should use both hands. Though a finished horse can be easily controlled at all paces with one hand, he will never reach that stage under a one-handed trainer, unless the rider goes to the trouble of holding one rein—on the side to which he intends to turn the horse—shorter than the other rein. This method, however, necessitates always readjusting the lengths of the reins according to the direction in which the horse is to be turned. It is easier and simpler to use both hands with a rein in each.

The importance of one feature of any curb bit cannot be over-emphasized. This is the length of the cheeks above the mouth-piece—specifically, from the center of the mouthpiece to the center of the loops to which the curb chain or strap is attached. Regardless of the type of curb bit used, this dimension should not measure less than one and three-quarter inches for a pony or a small horse or more than two and one-quarter inches for a large horse. Two inches may be considered ideal for the average horse. Any bit that measures less than an inch and three-quarters from the center of the mouthpiece to the center of the curb loops—as many bits do—belongs in a junk yard or on a tackroom wall as an ornament. For it will frustrate your most careful attempts to give your horse a good mouth.

Some bits are made with the headstall loops slanted or bent outward, so that they will not pinch the corners of the horse's mouth when the reins are used. This is as it should be. If your bit is not bent like this above the mouthpiece, clamp it in a vise

[4]Probably the soundest answer to this question was given to me recently by my friend Charles E. Osborne, Jr., an accomplished dressage rider, of Fort Worth, Texas. A finished horseman, Osborne points out, rides on the snaffle more than the curb. The snaffle is dominant and is used first; then the curb, when necessary, reinforces the aid. Hence, with the snaffle rein outside the hand, the rider has merely to flex his little finger to give an aid; then, if necessary, the ring or middle finger controlling the curb rein also acts. In principle, I agree. It is wrong to depend primarily on the curb bit, no matter how the reins are held.

and bend the headstall loops outward about half an inch. Pinching bits defeat even the most skilled rider's gentlest attempts to induce a horse to relax his lower jaw. Instead, they cause the horse to resist the bit and toss his head up, simply to escape the discomfort of the pinching bit.

The length of the shanks of the bit below the mouthpiece does not matter, except that the longer the shanks are, the more carefully must the rider use his hands because he commands a greater leverage. For this reason extremely long shanks are not desirable, and whenever you meet anyone who tells you that they are necessary to "hold" a particular horse, you might as well change the subject, for you will be talking with a ham-fisted mechanic whose talents make him better fitted to handle a monkey wrench than a pair of reins.

Many bits, particularly Western grazing bits, are useless and some are worse than useless for the delicate work of properly developing a horse's mouth.

CHAPTER XIX

What a Good Mouth Is *Not*

Briefly, all training is this and nothing more:
the legs to provoke action; the hands to
direct it.

— *E. Beudant*

THE making of a riding horse's mouth is a sadly neglected art—any kind of riding horse, from the show Saddlebred, that much admired equine peacock which usually has no mouth at all in the true sense of the term, straight through the equine ranks down to the child's pet pony.

Too many riders lack the patience ever to master the art, even when they understand what it is. Others never develop the necessary skill that comes from years of painstaking practice riding all kinds of horses. Some riders, who have both the patience to learn and the requisite delicate reflexes that nature may give but that only much practice can sharpen, never can "make" a really good mouth because they lack that priceless intangible, *tact*. These riders progress just so far in their schooling of a horse; then, without realizing it, they start sliding backward. They never achieve the results they hope for because, lacking tact, they persistently commit errors that upset the horse. If horses were automata, reacting like mere machines, these unimaginative riders would be excellent horsemen; but horses are sentient beings, each individually different from all others.

Probably the majority of errors committed in mouthing riding horses, however, result from complete misunderstanding of what a good mouth really is. Most Western horsemen especially, it seems, commonly confuse developing a good mouth with "putting a good rein on" a horse. A good mouth and a so-called "flash rein," however, are quite distinct from each other.

A horse with a good mouth *must* be well-reined, for obviously, having a good mouth, he is lightly and instantly responsive to his rider's slightest aid. He can stop, turn, spin, and jump out into a headlong run just as fast as the rider can cue him to do so.

In contrast, a trained hackamore horse that has never had a bit in its mouth can be well reined, capable of going through all the maneuvers of a show-ring stock horse in response to only the slightest rein signals. In fact, such a horse, according to trainers who prefer the hackamore and spade bit system, should be excellently reined before a bit is ever put into his mouth; and for a long time after he has grown used to the feel of the bit in his mouth, the rider continues to rein him by means of the hackamore.

But can we say that such a horse has a good mouth? Actually, he has no mouth at all. His mouth remains as undeveloped as that of a yearling colt.

The same may be said of an exhibition cutting horse, trained to work on an absolutely loose rein. Depending on the basic training he received, the horse may or may not have a good mouth. But he has no need of it in doing the job expected of him in the arena.

A good mouth, contrary to the popular idea, does not mean merely a sensitive mouth. A good mouth must be developed, cultivated.

It is a discouraging fact to horsemen interested in true horsemanship that a horse with a "green" mouth can win a reigning contest. Plenty of horses have done so and will continue to do so, particularly where the cult of the spade bit flourishes; for in such localities, generally speaking, the local horsemen, who like to style themselves "reinsmen," have no comprehension whatever of what constitutes a good mouth. These "green mouthed" animals go through a whole reining performance without once yielding or relaxing their lower jaw. If they have been drilled enough in the various maneuvers which the rules require, they can put on precise, cut-and-dried performances quite as interesting to watch —or as dull, depending on one's viewpoint—as the standardized routines of circus horses or of American Saddle Horses.

Such horses, however, are not light in hand, balanced, or collected. If you were to sit on one of these mouthless wonders, pick up the reins and cue him to do nothing more than "give" his jaw to you and flex at the poll, the horse would respond by doing at least one and possibly two of three things:

He might set his jaw in resistance to your light tension on the reins, probably throwing up his head and poking his nose out as well.

He might tuck his nose into his chest by arching his neck along the crest instead of flexing at the poll, and open his mouth stiffly, with the lower jaw contracted.

He might start to back up.

Your real intention in fingering the reins — to have him relax his lower jaw and flex at the poll — would be utterly incomprehensible to him, for horses so trained know no more about lightness than do five-gaited show ring stars.

I have seen a horse that was *always* behind the bit win a state stock horse championship two years in a row. His training ordeal, if you can call what he went through a system of training, interested me so that I followed his briefly successful show-ring career rather closely. Perhaps a summary of it is appropriate here, for this little stallion ideally misrepresented what many amateur riders would consider an excellent show stock horse.

The first time I saw this young horse in competition, his rider had to jab him vigorously with spurs in order to make him jump off into a fast run; but I observed that the horse never really let himself go all out, even when allowed an absolutely slack rein. Neither would he hit a fast, free, long-striding walk; he would mince and prance along with short, choppy steps, his neck arched and his face well behind the vertical. He was, in fact, always out of control, for he was always behind the bit. He would tear up the tanbark, however, in a most spectacular sliding hind-leg stop. I have never seen another horse that could be made to rear with such dangerous ease. Riding him must have been rather like straddling a rocket which at any moment was likely to go into reverse.

I couldn't help wondering what the judges were thinking of, or what they had been looking at during the performance, when they awarded him the championship trophy.

The following year he repeated his victory, this time before a different judge, and did it the same way, but worse.

In his third year of competition this little stallion's travesty of schooling finally caught up with him. Or perhaps the show management finally found a judge who had some vague idea of what a stock horse should be. The horse went unplaced against many of the same competitors, quite ordinary animals, which he had previously won over.

In the grand parade, however, this stallion looked like a million dollars to the average spectator. Prancing along with neck bowed, chin almost touching his breast, jigging, jogging, and sidling, he drew plenty of admiration. He was the essence of what the average person thinks of as "spirited," the kind of horse you frequently see leading parades celebrating some such foofaraw as La Fiesta de las Cucarachas or the Tournament of Cockleburrs.

Yet within approximately two hundred yards along the parade route I saw the horse rear once and try the same dangerous stunt twice more only to be prevented by his rider's quick use of her spurs. Furthermore, the horse was doing all this prancing, jigging, and jogging while merely keeping pace with other horses that were walking. Had the other animals expended half as much energy unnecessarily, they would have left the beautiful one far behind.

Finally, when the competition got under way in the ring, the little stallion's rider could not even spur her state champion out of a high, rocking-horse canter. Neck arched and tail switching nervously, the bit-shy animal simply would not extend. His performance left one with the impression of having watched, slow-motion, a stock horse attempting to put on a dressage exhibition.

Yet all the while in the ring (until the winner was announced), as well as in the parade, the rider responsible for this horse's pitiful showing looked extraordinarily proud of herself. She was obviously confident of winning again. The girl looked thunderstruck when her mount did not even place.

Watching her face as she rode out of the ring, I realized suddenly that the girl actually believed her horse to be better than ever, when in fact he had become worse. The horse was doing exactly what the rider had, in her ignorance, trained him to do.

She could not understand why she had lost. "Why, King was the only horse in the ring that was fully under control," she complained bitterly after the show. "All those others just rushed headlong, cold-jawed. What's wrong with that judge? Why, I've been giving King dressage training for two years."

And just how, I asked in a roundabout way, carefully concealing my thoughts, can you teach a horse dressage when he won't even accept the bit?

The girl withered me with a stare of pitying scorn. "Why, that's *collection*. Don't you know what collection is? When you can't feel any pressure on the bit, the horse's mouth is perfect."

I have sketched the career of this horse in such detail because his example perfectly illustrates a whole combination of errors and misconceptions.

First, the young woman who spent years painstakingly schooling the horse to get behind the bit did so because she completely misunderstood what a good mouth is. She did not know the difference between a mouth that is merely sensitive—as any green horse's mouth is—and the cultivated, carefully developed mouth of a finished mount.

She thought that she understood what true collection is, but utterly failed to attain it because she did not know what over-collection is or what false collection is.

Having developed in her mount the bad habit of getting behind the bit, she then proceeded to confirm and exaggerate the fault by further advancement and refinement of the same erroneous training along the lines of what she misconstrued to be "dressage." Actually, the ultimate purpose of dressage stands for everything which her method destroys.

(Yet it was not until the girl had completed her masterpiece of error, producing a horse that would not extend even into a fast walk, that the men who were supposed to be qualified to judge those stock horse classes could finally see what should have been clearly evident to them from the beginning of the horse's competitive career.)

This horse's development, or retrogression, illustrates not only the utter ignorance of too many stock horse judges but also the reason why so many horsemen scorn advanced dressage—which is just another name for training—as mere "fanciness" of no practical value, and sometimes even condemn it as harmful. They have seen the bad results of misdirected training based on wrong ideas, often without ever having had a chance to see a properly dressaged horse in action. For, unfortunately, such horses are relatively rare—horses like Farana, an Arabian that was so superior to the general run of stock horses that he was finally debarred from competition in California, the much publicized home of the self-styled world's finest horsemen, the spade-bit wizards.

Such horses are rare because it takes a skilled, experienced trainer to finish one, and we aren't all that good. We need not be ashamed to admit it; we can only do our best. But, unfortunately, most of us do not do our best. That requires real thought, study, and effort.

Another important reason why horses with really good mouths are few and far between is that the great majority of Western horsemen have been trained from youth to a system of riding that makes development of good mouths almost impossible. This is the system of riding with loose reins. You cannot school a horse and achieve a good mouth when you deliberately seek to avoid all contact with his mouth except when signaling him to slow, stop, and turn. For a good mouth must be "made"; it is the result of careful training, training that seeks not to avoid contact but to encourage the horse to accept contact willingly, calmly, fearlessly, with no dread of being hurt.

No matter how sensitive a colt's mouth is, to make it a *good* mouth the trainer must cultivate and develop it.

CHAPTER XX

The Marks of a Good Mouth

*The rider must reduce his actions to the
very minimum and leave the horse the
greatest possible freedom in his.*
— *E. Beudant*

I F a good mouth is not merely sensitive, so that a
horse is, as novices say, "easy to stop," how can
you recognize a good mouth, either when watching a horse and
rider in action or when trying out a new mount yourself?

A good mouth is "educated"; it is responsive to the rider's
hands and legs. When the rider's hands take, the horse gives.
When the rider gives rein and drives with his legs, the horse
lightly takes up the slack, extending without any fear of having
his mouth hurt. If the rider sets his hand but does not increase
the drive of his legs, the horse goes "off the bit"; he works on
"floating" reins. If then the rider, with hands still fixed, applies
his legs, the horse does not "fight" the bit; but neither does he
shrink from it in an effort to avoid contact and get behind it.
He increases his state of collection by bringing his hind legs
farther under him, while yielding his lower jaw softly and flexing
at the poll to the rider's hands. At no time does he either resist
the bit or shrink from it. When you see a horse that can be ridden
in this way, you will be looking at a horse with an educated mouth.

It is of primary importance to understand clearly that a horse,
in yielding to the rider's hand, does not merely arch his neck.
This is a bad fault which greenhorns mistake for a virtue, perhaps
because it is a common sight in parades, where one sees expensive,
handsome horses presumably at their best. Artists also can be held
partly responsible for this popular misconception, for over the

centuries they have liked to exaggerate the swelling crests of stallions and the position of the horse's head known as *ramener* in school riding. Actually, only arching the neck in response to tension on the reins is a form of evasion; it needs very little encouragement to become the habit of boring or the trick of getting behind the bit.

In properly yielding to the rider's hand the horse more or less relaxes his lower jaw, the degree of relaxation depending mainly on the pace, the speed at which the horse is traveling forward—the slower the speed, the greater should be the degree of relaxation. This is the first reaction the well-schooled horse shows in response to rein tension. This relaxed lower jaw is the basis of all flexion and controlled lightness. Without it, you achieve nothing except resistance. The horse must first of all "give" you his jaw without opening his mouth. This—not mere physical sensitiveness based on the horse's natural instinct to recoil from possible pain inflicted by the bit—is the essence of the soft, "velvet" mouth.

If, after the horse has thus relaxed his jaw, the rider immediately closes his fingers and urges the horse on with his legs, demanding more collection, the horse with a good mouth, still maintaining the relaxed jaw, yields further by flexing his neck *at the poll*. This flexion at the poll, with the "break" occurring just behind the ears, is a very different reaction from the fault of arching the entire neck. In arching the entire neck the horse brings his chin in *low* nearer his breast. Since this necessitates lowering his head, the horse shifts more of his weight onto his forehand; he thus becomes heavy in front, which is the exact opposite of the balanced lightness flexion seeks to achieve. If the horse lowers his head sufficiently to get his face behind the vertical, then he is behind the bit, any rearward tension on the reins only accentuates the fault and we end up by losing control of the mouth entirely.

When flexing properly, the horse brings his chin in toward the breast by raising, not lowering, his head. The horse "gives" to the rider's hand first by relaxing his jaw and then by bending at the poll. The lower part of the neck running into the withers remains firm, a base of support.

The rider achieves maximum control over the horse when the animal's face is vertical to the ground. This extreme degree of collection, however, is rarely needed or useful for ordinary riding. For a stock horse its only practical use would be in performing a quick-stop from a gallop and in reining back. However, it

Plate 59. ON THE BIT AND STRAIGHT. This picture well represents the ideal we should strive for. This young horse is softly on the bit and flexed. His calm eyes reflect his inner tranquility, though he is alert to the rider. The rider is down in the saddle, legs close to the horse, arms and hands elastically relaxed, with straight line from elbow to bit. This is Carole Ploeger on her Arabian, Sam.

Photograph by E. O. Ploeger

Plate 60. HARMONY. Compare this picture to the preceding photograph. This rider's position shows a few minor faults; for example, her lower leg is too far forward. But there are more similarities than differences. Both riders are in perfect harmony with their mounts. That, above all, is what counts. Don't try to be a picturebook–perfect "wooden soldier." Minor details matter little, if horse and rider are in harmony.

Photograph by Gene A. Pearson

is important for us to understand clearly just when this maximum degree of control is possible so that we shall never fall into the error of letting our mount overflex, getting his face behind the vertical and hence falling behind the bit.

Obviously, the higher a horse elevates his head when flexing, the farther back toward the hindquarters must he shift his center of balance. This transfer of more weight to the haunches results in shorter strides and loftier action. Urged on by the rider's legs but gently restrained by the hands from expending the impulsion in faster movement forward, the horse expends energy in moving with high, strutting action. This collection, when carried to its extreme form, as it is in high school riding, can result in a horse

being made to walk, trot, or canter in one spot, with no forward
movement whatever; or even while backing up.

No one except a school rider would be much interested in
obtaining such extreme collection, which demands a great deal
of painstaking practice by both horse and rider, and serves at best
merely as an exhibition of the rider's skill. Yet it is the mere possibility of accomplishing such rare results that causes many ordinary horsemen to disapprove of such training entirely. They do
not think of the training as a means of making a horse light and
balanced, precisely responsive to the rider's gentlest control. Instead, they dogmatize: "That fancy stuff's no good for anything
but a Sunday park rider's hobbyhorse. We want horses that can
do some practical work and cover ground."

Such reasoning is as logical as would be condemnation of, for
example, weightlifting because it might make a boy too strong.
Any form of physical training, for either horse or man, can be
abused. A horse with an excellent mouth need not become a
"hobbyhorse"; he can work on an absolutely loose rein, fully extended at top speed, if such work has been part of his basic training, as it should be. Developing a horse's mouth properly does not
lessen his agility or his ability to run. No better proof of this can
be found than the horses that compete in the Three-Day Event
in the Olympic Games.

The first phase of this grueling test of equine athletes consists
of a schooling test, a display of dressage, that the overwhelming
majority of horses commonly regarded as well-trained could not
even begin to match. The following day the horses compete
against the clock in a cross-country run of approximately twenty-
two miles, a course studded with formidable obstacles which the
horses must jump; this includes a steeplechase course. This is a
test which would kill the ordinary riding horse and would leave
most race horses crippled. The final phase of the Three-Day
Event is a stadium jumping competition over a tricky course that
would humiliate most show-jumping horses and riders.

The rather common fear many horsemen have of producing a
"hobbyhorse" that will not or cannot extend himself at speed
across country is based squarely on ignorance of correct training
principles When the training produces a "hobbyhorse," the
trainer—not the system—is at fault. He either does not understand
or does not carry out the system of training he tries to follow.
But this is a mighty poor argument to prove the system worthless.

A better argument would be to produce a horse, trained otherwise, that could win an Olympic Three-Day Event.

It makes little difference how sharply you can "set up" a horse from a fast run or how "flash-reined" he may appear to be. If he won't work with a soft, relaxed jaw, flexing when you take and taking when you give, promptly responsive to your slightest aids at any gait or pace, the horse does not have a really good mouth.

I hope no one will misinterpret these remarks as a plea for universal high school training for all riding horses. On the contrary, I am strongly against any such attempted training except by experienced horsemen who know exactly how to do it. I am discussing here simply the art of giving a horse, any horse, a good mouth; and it is a serious error, leading to disappointed riders and ruined horses, to confuse that with training a high school horse.

A first-class school horse must of necessity be a specialist. Rarely, if ever, ridden outside of a level schooling ring or a show arena, he has usually been robbed of most of his natural initiative. He rarely thinks of where he will place his feet, for he has learned that on level footing it does not matter; he need only rely on guidance from his rider.

A stock horse or pleasure horse, on the other hand, no matter how delicately responsive a mouth he may have developed, must never have his natural initiative destroyed. He must always be willing, as a matter of course, to go at any gait or pace over any kind of ground on an absolutely slack rein, picking his own way and watching where he puts his feet without any guidance from the rider. An ordinary riding horse that won't or can't do this is worse than useless; he is dangerous to ride.

Such a clumsy horse, assuming that his vision is normal and that he is not suffering from debility or unsoundness, should be turned loose for several weeks in the roughest, hilliest pasture you can graze him in. Having to scramble up hill and down like a mountain goat's cousin in order to graze will give him plenty of opportunity to develop handiness and to acquire the habit of watching where he puts his feet. (If by some unfortunate chance the horse breaks his neck before having learned this important lesson, the crestfallen owner can always congratulate himself on probably having escaped a similar fate while riding the animal.) After a few weeks of this preparation unburdened by the weight of a rider, the horse should be frequently ridden over the same rough terrain, slowly at first, then gradually at increasingly faster paces, but always on an absolutely slack rein, with the rider allowing the horse complete freedom to rely on his own judgment and to adjust his own balance.

This sort of free-and-easy walking, trotting, and galloping over rough ground on a slack rein is an essential phase of every riding horse's training, with the possible exception only of school horses, dressage specialists; and there is no adequate substitute for it.

The important thing to bear in mind is that it is the rider, never the horse, who always decides when the horse shall be free to go on his own; it is always the rider, never the horse, who decides when to pull up. When the rider takes the slack out of the reins preparatory to taking over, there must be no hotheaded stampeding, no monkey business about snatching the reins, no head tossing or boring on the bit, by the horse—not even when other horses are running ahead. Once the rider indicates that the free galloping is over, the well-schooled horse yields his jaw immediately; he "comes back to the hand" promptly, smoothly. The rider is always in control or able to resume control instantly.

This kind of control cannot be achieved by habitual slack-rein riding, to which most Western horsemen are accustomed; for a horse trained to go only on a slack rein, except when the rider wishes to pull up or turn, never has a chance to develop a really good mouth. When reined in, though the horse may have learned from painful experience to stop or turn sharply, he does not yield his jaw or flex, slowing or stopping smoothly, in balance. The rider may be able to "set him up" as if they had run into a stone wall, but the stop is invariably rough, jerky, awkward. The same rider could not, instead of abruptly halting, smoothly rein in his mount, in a length or two, from a headlong gallop to a collected canter or a slow balanced trot or walk, whichever—*and exactly whichever*—the rider decided upon.

To respond to such precise control a horse must have a made mouth. Habitual slack-rein riding simply cannot make it.

One of the principal differences between the majority of Western horsemen who favor curb bits and that infinitesimally small minority of riders who are really good with the spade bit is that the spade bit men do realize the importance of keeping a constant light contact with and control of the horse's mouth. Even if the spade bit experts—and they are very rare—do not always accomplish what they strive for (and who does?), in this respect at least they are nearer the right track than the slack-rein riders who remain blissfully unaware that a good mouth need be anything more than merely sensitive.

A good mouth must be developed and cultivated.

Part 4

Finish:
Commencement

CHAPTER XXI

The Three-Year-Old

*People who do not school can never
really ride.*
                    —M. F. McTaggart

F EW horsemen are so blasé that they do not find
the first ride on a promising colt that they have
carefully brought along an occasion charged with anticipation
and the element of surprise.

The best place to mount a colt for the first time is inside the
high-walled circular breaking pen or in a small corral. Before
mounting, longe or drive the colt briskly for about fifteen minutes
to warm him up, as well as to take the edge off his freshness.
Never skip this warm-up or you might regret it in more ways
than one.

Don't worry about being bucked off. The ground isn't far away
and there's a lot of it; you can't miss it. Besides, it is very unlikely
that even a high-strung colt that has been schooled on foot according to the system suggested here will blow up at this stage.

However, if you have anyone to help you, have him stand in
front of the colt and hold the reins lightly while stroking the
youngster's neck as you swing up. If you are alone, adjust the
reins so that they are very slightly *slack*, not taut, and be ready
with the command, "Whoa."

As you place your foot in the stirrup and step up, be very
careful not to dig the colt behind the elbow with your toe. Mount
smoothly and quickly and sit down lightly. Avoid dropping into
the saddle with a jolt.

Mounted, keep your heels clear of the colt's flanks. Try to be
relaxed. Don't grip the colt tightly as if you expect him to take

off—even if you do. If he senses your expectation, he'll probably try to oblige.

Leave the reins slack enough for the colt to hold his head normally, but not slack enough to allow him to get his head down if you should accidentally do something to startle him.

The instant you are settled in the saddle command, "Walk."

Rarely, unusually high-strung colts, particularly if they sense that you are nervous, might stand still, their muscles tensed up. If this should occur, don't try to leg the colt straight ahead. Untrack him by gently but firmly turning him in a quarter-circle, holding the rein with which you turn him out wide to one side and with as little rearward tension on it as possible. As he comes around urge him into a trot. The sooner you get him moving, the more quickly he will relax.

It is important now to keep the colt calm and unafraid. Sit as still as you can. Remember that your weight upsets the colt's balance. Give him time to adjust.

Keep him moving and sit still. Urge him to trot. Leave the reins slack; there should be absolutely no tension on them that might discourage the colt from moving forward with free, extended strides.

With the unaccustomed weight on his back, the colt will probably trot rather awkwardly. He might even drop to a walk. If he does not respond to the rider's legs when urged to trot, it is because he does not know what leg pressure means. For this reason you should have your short whip or switch in hand. Squeeze him with both legs and tap him lightly on the flank just behind your leg. Be sure to use your legs a moment *before* you apply the whip. In this way the colt will quickly catch onto the idea that leg pressure means to move forward.

For at least the first five, or even the first ten, minutes do not ask the colt to do anything except trot around and around the enclosure. Leave the reins absolutely slack.

When he has settled down and seems to be quite casual about your presence on his back, try turning the colt toward the center of the corral with a leading rein. *Do not pull on the rein.* Put no rearward tension on the rein at all, for that might cause him to slow down or halt. Merely take the slack out of the rein and move your hand out to the side toward which you wish to turn him. In effect, try to *lead* the colt into the turn without slowing his pace at all. As you do this, shift your weight slightly onto your inner stirrup; this will unbalance him slightly and encourage him to turn.

After all the longeing and driving you have put him through, the colt should respond to this simple demand almost automatically. However, if for some reason, such as extreme nervousness, he doesn't do so at once, don't make the mistake of trying to pull him around. Instead, move your rein hand out still farther, add more weight on the inner stirrup, and press the opposite rein against the side of his neck to "push" him around.

When he does turn, trot him across the corral almost to the fence; then turn him to the opposite side. Be sure to begin leading him into the turn *before* he reaches the fence, keeping the turns wide and maintaining a free, steady trot.

In a square or a rectangular corral, it is easy to teach the colt prompt response to the leading rein and the slight shift of the rider's weight by riding him down one side of the enclosure and cuing him to turn a moment before he reaches the corner, where the end fence forces him to turn or stop.

After not less than five minutes of constant trotting, say, "Whoa"; give the colt a few seconds to obey the order, close your legs, and feel the reins just lightly enough to make him halt.

Leaving the reins slightly slack and being ready to check any movement with a sharp "Whoa," dismount. Pat the colt on the neck; speak to him approvingly. Observe him closely. If he is a little warm, lead him about for a minute to cool off and to rest his back. Then mount again. Walk him around the corral a few times with the reins slack. Halt and dismount on the off side. Remount from that side—be sure to make him stand still. Walk him about for a minute; then dismount on the near side.

That is enough for this first ride. It should not last longer than fifteen minutes at most. If at any time before that you notice the colt getting hot, cut the ride short at once. Even if you think that you haven't accomplished anything, avoid getting the colt hot.

For a week, or longer if necessary, repeat this same routine daily. You can safely increase the time spent on the colt's back about a minute a day, up to a maximum period of about thirty minutes. Always warm up the colt by longeing or driving him for ten or fifteen minutes before you mount him. Ask nothing more of him than a walk and a trot, mostly a trot, and a few wide turns to each side.

Toward the end of the second week it is all right to put him into a lope once or twice during each session, just to keep him from getting any notion that he will spend the rest of his life walking and trotting only. These canters, however, should be brief and the pace—with loose reins—should be easy. If the colt tries to gallop or run, he should be halted immediately; if necessary, turn him into the fence to stop him in order to avoid pulling the reins unnecessarily. Do not yet ask him to do any turning at the canter beyond circling the corral.

You need not worry about his taking the wrong lead. If you walk him up to the fence or into a corner, turn his head with the leading rein, and let him go with reins slack while you simply sit still, he will naturally take the correct lead, just as he did when being longed and driven in long reins. Be sure not to cant the colt's head to the outside (i.e., to the right if you are about to turn left, or vice versa). Use only the leading rein so that the colt faces the way he is turning. Otherwise, you will be undoing most of the good effects of the longeing and the driving phases of training.

During these first two weeks be especially alert to detect any signs of muscular tension in the colt when you are mounted. A green colt shows this nervous tension chiefly by choppy, irregular gaits. This is the first thing we must set out to eliminate. We want the colt to go at the same easy natural gaits which he shows when free. This means that he must first of all be relaxed. A free-striding trot is the best gait for inducing this relaxation; hence, it is the gait we should chiefly depend on.

How can we tell when the colt is relaxed? The best proof of relaxation is that he will begin to get a bit lazy. That is, when we have him moving at a brisk trot, after a while he will begin to coast, to take it easy. With a colt of good disposition that has been wisely handled from the beginning, or with a cold-blooded sluggish colt, this may happen within the first two or three days, while a nervous colt may not settle down for a week or more.

One of the quickest and easiest ways of getting a high-strung colt to relax is to ride him over cavalletti. Faced with the task of picking his way over a grid of poles on the ground, the average colt will forget his nervousness about carrying a weight on his back because he will have to watch where he is placing his feet. A horse's mind just is not geared to concentrating on two things at once.

Even a calm, phlegmatic colt will benefit from work over cavalletti. He will learn to pick up his feet and watch where he is going.

Both types of colts will learn the basic lesson that they should unhesitatingly go wherever their rider points them. If most of us paid more attention to this fundamental, there would be a lot less fuss and hocus-pocus about training so-called "trail horses."

In addition to this, cavalletti work is the first step in schooling a horse to jump. Relatively few Western riders ever think of jumping as part of their horses' all-round training, but basic schooling in jumping is good for every horse. It develops a horse's boldness, muscles, and agility. It is essential to the training of any practical trail horse, as distinct from the clownish robots commonly seen in "trail horse" classes in shows.

Cavalletti in Italian means "little horses." *Cavalletto* is the singular term. Cavalletti are an Italian invention. They were first used at the Italian cavalry school to teach forward riding and jumping, originated by Captain Frederico Caprilli. This man's ideas revolutionized cross-country riding near the turn of the century.

In their original form cavalletti were wood bars, about 16 feet long, elevated about a foot off the ground between X-shaped standards. About a dozen bars were laid parallel to one another three or four feet apart to form a grid, or a sort of obstacle course, over which the horse was ridden at a walk and trot on loose reins.

If a horse negotiating the grid bumped or kicked one of the bars, the X-shaped standards prevented it from falling over. However, a good bump could knock the bar out of position. Then it had to be replaced.

To avoid this inconvenience, cavalletti have taken various forms different from the original Italian design. The United States Equestrian Team, for example, uses cavalletti made of logs about eight inches in diameter set into notched log end pieces. These are heavy enough to stay put, as well as solid enough to teach a horse to treat them with respect.

I use heavy, squared timbers to form cavalletti because I have such timbers on hand. Old railroad ties laid end to end make serviceable cavalletti. So do old telephone poles sawed to a suitable length. But do not depend on a length of 2-by-4 lumber to make a safe cavalletto. Such flimsy bars can be dangerous to a horse. You don't want anything easily breakable underfoot.

Work over cavalletti forces a horse to watch where he puts his feet. To do this he will have to lower his head and round his back. This is essential first to teaching him to reach for the bit and then to putting him on the bit. By slightly varying the distances between bars, we can teach him both to lengthen and to shorten his stride, which will develop his balance. Finally, he will learn to accept obstacles in his path as something to go forward over without fuss, instead of suspiciously regarding them as something to avoid.

It is best to introduce a colt to cavalletti by first leading him over the bars. This not only gives him confidence; it also enables you to determine whether the poles are correctly spaced to "fit" his normal walking stride. If they are too close together or too far apart, he is almost certain to bump or step on some of them. If he must make an effort not to hit any poles, he cannot maintain an even, normal stride; but that is precisely the way you want him to move now. For the average horse moving at a normal walk place the bars about three feet apart.

Walk ahead of the colt and as you start over the grid do not look back. Act casually as if you expect him to follow you without the least hesitation—and he probably will. Your whole manner should tell the colt, "These things on the ground are nothing. If I can step over them, you can. So let's go."

If the colt hesitates or balks at the first bar, do not try to tug him forward. Use no force whatever. Instead, give him a little slack and *wait for him*, gently encouraging him to take that first step. Once he does start you may be sure that he will go all the way.

When you have crossed the grid halt and praise the colt extravagantly. Pretend that he has done something wonderful. Let him know without any doubt that you are pleased. You might even slip him a tidbit—a small handful of oats or pellets or a carrot.[1] Then immediately turn him around and lead him back over the bars again. Repeat as often as you think may be necessary, but at the end of each trip over the grid praise the colt, showing your approval.

Normally, with any colt that has been halter-trained and gen-

[1]Some experienced trainers believe that handfeeding a horse opens the way to bad habits, particularly the noxious habit of nipping. Their theory is that, if a horse is led to expect indiscriminate handouts, he will show his annoyance when you have nothing to offer him. As a general rule, I agree with this. There is no good reason for handfeeding a horse when he has done nothing to deserve it. However, this is not the same as *rewarding* a horse, letting him know that we are pleased, when he has done something well. For years I have rewarded horses with tidbits, but none of them was ever spoiled. I have yet to find a horse so stupid that he could not grasp the difference between being rewarded and being pampered.

erally handled according to the methods set forth here, this introduction to cavalletti takes only a few minutes. But if for some unusual reason it takes longer, don't fret and don't quit. Stick to it until the colt is as casual about stepping over those poles as he is about walking into his own stall.

Every horse is a unique individual; no two are exactly the same. A wise trainer is flexible. He adapts his methods to get the best out of each pupil. Therefore, if, in spite of the careful way you have brought along your colt, he is still a bit timid or spooky about crossing the cavalletti, do not hesitate to start with only one pole on the ground, gradually adding more poles as his confidence increases. Likewise, if you think it wiser to longe or ground drive him over the grid before mounting him, do that. The main thing is to retain the colt's confidence. Resist the temptation to resort to even the slightest force.

If you do longe before mounting, remember that the colt should walk or trot over the bars *in a straight line*, not on an arc. This means that as you bring him around in a circle, guiding him at the middle of the first bar, you must start moving parallel with him in a straight line. You keep him on a straight line for at least two or three strides after he has stepped over the last bar before you guide him around in a semicircle to return to his starting point. For this reason it is sometimes a good idea to place the cavalletti next to one wall of the arena. In effect, this puts the horse in a chute, guided straight by the fence on one side and by you, whip in hand, on the other end of the longe line.

Serious work over cavalletti begins with the trainer mounted. The purpose of this work over poles on the ground is to improve the colt's balance and to develop his agility. The colt must find his balance himself and learn to adjust his strides with a minimum of help from the rider. Therefore, except to prevent wandering or turning out, the trainer should be as passive as possible. He should sit well forward in the saddle with plenty of weight in the stirrups and give the colt loose reins. Ideally, the horse should negotiate the grid with no help whatever from the rider.

After the colt is comfortable working at a walk the trainer should ride over the bars at a trot. This, of course, necessitates repositioning the cavalletti, moving them farther apart to accommodate the longer stride. Generally, four feet—give or take a few inches—is about the right distance for most horses. You have to determine the correct distance by observing your colt's strides.

If he hits poles with his toes, move them farther apart. If he
bumps his heels or pasterns as his feet touch ground, the bars
are too widely spaced for his normal stride.

A brisk trot over cavalletti is quite similar to the elevated trot
of dressage known as the passage. Therefore, the rider should
be careful not to pound the colt's back by bouncing against the
cantle, an easy way quickly to sour a young horse. If necessary,
assume a jumping position with all your weight in the stirrups
and your seat clear of the saddle.

Cavalletti work, like everything else in schooling, loses its benefits if overdone. Drudgery begets boredom and boredom begets
sourness. This work over the bars is not an end in itself; it
is merely a part of our overall schooling program. Place your
cavalletti somewhere near the center of the ring, proceed with
your regular schooling, and every once in a while—preferably
when the colt least expects it—without pause or interruption
ride him over the bars.

When the colt is going well over the bars on loose reins, the
trainer should slightly vary the distances between cavalletti. At
first, move the bars merely two or three inches farther apart.
(Do not move them closer together, for at this point we want to
lengthen, not shorten, the colt's strides.) With the reins loose,
use your legs strongly to encourage the colt to lengthen his frame
and stretch out. Change the spacings frequently, but do not make
the grid so "tricky" that the colt becomes nervous and tense. He
must remain relaxed.

After the colt carries his bit without any fuss when ridden on
slack reins, he is ready to be put on the bit. He must learn not
only to accept steady, light contact of the bit with the reins gently
stretched, but actually to seek such contact by stretching his neck
and lowering his head as he "reaches" for the bit. This is the first
and an absolutely essential step in the making of a good mouth.

It is most easily done by riding at a steady working trot in a
circle about twenty yards in diameter. If the colt is frisky and
inclined to play up, just keep on riding him until he loses his
edge and settles down. Then, when he is slightly tired, push him
on at the same steady pace, jut a little faster than he really wants
to go. One important reason for this is that you as the rider should
always determine the pace. Always, but particularly in schooling,
never permit your horse to go as fast or as slowly as *he* wants
to. You are the boss.

As you circle, establish a very light, even contact with your

Plate 61. THE CAVALLETTI, STEP ONE. First lead the colt over the poles, even if he is not leery of them. This lets you check the spacing of the poles, which you may have to adjust to fit his normal stride.

Photograph by Gene A. Pearson

inside rein, just sufficient to keep the colt on course. You can forget about your outside rein, as long as you keep it slack. You must give with the outside rein at least as much as you take with the inside rein. Otherwise, your hands will be contradicting each other and you will be cramping the horse's forward movement, the cardinal sin of all training.

As this steady circling just slightly faster than he wants to trot begins to bore the colt, he will relax his neck muscles, lowering his head. This is precisely what you want. He is beginning to "reach for the bit." You are "showing him the way to the ground." Bear in mind that you can only show him how to do this; you cannot force him to. He must learn to do it himself. Encourage him to stretch and lower his neck a bit more by giving him a little more rein. Then reward him with a minute or two of rest before you repeat the same exercise in the opposite direction.

Above all, do not make any attempt to "set" the colt's head or flex his neck in toward the center by moving your hand to the

Plate 62. CAVALLETTI, STEP TWO. Longe the colt over the poles. He should move in a straight line, not in an arc or on a diagonal. The trainer must move along parallel with the colt.

Photograph by Dawn Young-Hansen

rear. Imagine that you are squeezing a few drops of water from a wet sponge by merely flexing your fingers. *You must not try to pull the bit back to the horse.* He must learn to reach for it and "find" it.

The downward stretching of the neck is as important as the lowering of the head. It means that the colt is rounding his back and reaching farther forward with his hind legs.

The horse, stretching forward and downward, seeks contact with the rider's hand. The rider does not pull on or shorten the rein to make contact with the horse's mouth. You adjust that inside rein as long as possible, then with your legs urge the colt forward to meet the bit.

This is the first tiny step toward learning true collection. But don't even think about collection now. That is still a long way off.

This is a step in the education of most horses that is usually neglected because it is so little understood. Trainers who think in terms of pulling a colt to make him turn and to halt, of setting

Plate 63. CAVALLETTI, STEP THREE. Ideally (and eventually, without fail), a horse should go over cavalletti entirely on his own, with no help or guidance from the rider. But sometimes, as here, it is necessary to prevent a green colt from wandering. Do this as briefly and as lightly as possible, then immediately slacken the reins. Unless the horse learns to go on his own and balance himself, cavalletti work is pointless.

Photograph by Gene A. Pearson

a colt's head and teaching him to tuck his nose in while he is still as green as grass, do not understand this at all; it is completely beyond them. They never produce really finished horses, horses that are truly light and on the aids.

In addition to this work on circles in the ring, the trainer should also ride the colt in the open on long straight lines. This is important to developing free forward movement, and work on straight lines enables us to check how well the colt has learned to go on the bit.

Put the colt into a free-striding trot. Close both legs lightly but snugly against his sides. At the same time take just enough

Plate 64. THE LONG STRIDE. This is not a cavalletti exercise, but it proves what such work can achieve. This experienced jumper started over the cavalletti at a working trot and on the bit; then the rider closed her legs, demanding an extended stride—and the mare cleared two cavalletti without increasing speed. This longitudinal flexibility, the horse opening and closing on demand like an accordian, is what cavalletti work— and schooling in general—is all about. Therese Hansen up. Note straight line from elbow to bit.

Photograph by Gene A. Pearson

slack out of the reins to give you the lightest possible contact with his mouth. The reins should have no tension on them at all, but should show a hardly perceptible sag. The rider's hands should be fixed, absolutely immobile.[2] As the colt begins to slow

---

[2]Another reason why the trot is the best working gait during this phase of schooling is that at the trot a horse's head is relatively motionless in comparison to the pronounced forward and backward movements of the head at the walk and the canter. Hence, at the trot the rider in teaching the colt to reach for the bit need only maintain a fixed hand, whereas at the other gaits he would have to give and take, following the colt's head movements, in order to prevent the reins from becoming alternately taut and too slack.

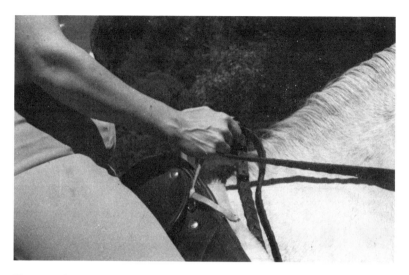

Plate 65. STEADY HANDS. In all stages of schooling, steadiness of the rider's hands is of critical importance. It is particularly important when putting a horse on the bit—and keeping him there. The hands should not move as the rider's body moves with the motions of the horse. Here is a way to acquire steady hands. Tie short straps to the D-rings of the saddle. If you keep the straps taut as you hold the reins, your hands will be steady.

Photograph by E. O. Ploeger

down, the trainer, closing his legs slightly, urges him a shade faster than the colt would trot without urging.

The rider's maintenance of absolutely fixed hands is of paramount importance. For if he gives with his hands while urging with his legs, the natural result is to make the colt trot faster or break into a gallop. If he pulls the bit back to the colt, he shortens the strides, besides going contrary to the fundamental principle of free forward movement in response to the rider's legs, a principle which must always be maintained.

The purpose of teaching a colt to reach for the bit is threefold: to introduce the colt to the aids and to teach him to submit to them, allowing himself to be "boxed" between the rider's urging legs and his restraining hands; to obtain natural, free, flowing strides, a result of the hind legs reaching well forward, instead of choppy, irregular gaits caused by a wrongly tucked-in headset

based on a "caved-in" back; to increase impulsion,[3] which is necessary to eventual lightness.

At first the colt should be taught to reach for the bit only
slightly and briefly. After he has "found" and accepted the bit
for a few strides, the rider should immediately cease urging him
with the legs. But very gradually the length of time of holding
him to the aids should be increased. It should be done mostly at
a trot, later occasionally at a canter, but rarely at a walk and
never at a standstill. The slower the gait, the easier it is for the
colt to lose impulsion and "die on the hands."

This reaching for the bit should not be confused with collection, a state which the wise trainer will not even attempt to achieve
until the colt has been ridden for at least a year and has thoroughly
developed the habit of free going. A collected horse must be on
the aids, but a horse on the aids need not be collected.

This reaching for the bit, however, is the basis of all true collection, whether in its most elementary or most advanced form. If
it is not properly taught to a horse, he can never be made truly
light while submitting to absolute control. At best, he can only
simulate controlled lightness; at worst, his action is a parody of
controlled lightness, as is so often seen in parade horses. Such
horses—weighted down by an excess of silver and carrying fancily
attired riders who sit back against their saddle cantles as if they
had no joints in their legs—can be easily recognized by their
choppy gaits, their stiff jaws and polls, their rounded necks,
and by the absurd positions of their riders' lower legs, which
are usually thrust forward and held well away from the horses'
sides. This last telltale mark is the surest proof that the horses
not only are not truly collected but never have been taught to
extend and reach for the bit; for a truly collected horse is always
"between the legs and the hands." The rider's legs may be passive,
but they are never inactive and futile, as legs held away from the
horse's sides must be because they are in no position to exert any
influence on the horse.

Riders who think that collecting a horse can be accomplished
by pulling the bit back to him are utterly ignorant of what true

[3]Impulsion is often confused with mere speed, but the two are not identical. A
galloping horse may show very little impulsion, while another animal, supple and
well-made, may show lots of it when merely walking. Perhaps the simplest way of
defining impulsion is to say that a horse which has it moves springily and gives the
impression of being able to cover a great deal of ground at every stride with ease
and power.

collection is. It cannot be too often repeated that *the horse must be legged forward against the bit,* for impulsion is necessary to controlled lightness. The rider merely receives the impulsion on his hands. He lets it escape in the form of increased forward movement, or he prevents it from escaping, which results in increased collection.

The importance of this fundamental cannot be overstressed, for it is in this way that a horse not only is ridden forward but also is slowed down and brought to a smooth, balanced stop. The rider's legs push the horse forward against the passive bit; then the legs cease to act while the hands remain fixed. The horse, yielding to the bit and no longer urged by the legs, halts. It is as simple as that—and hardly one rider in a thousand knows it.

It is because of this basic principle of good riding that I stressed handling the reins delicately even when driving the colt in a cavesson or a hackamore. Once mounted schooling begins, there should never be any direct pulling on the reins to slow or stop a horse, or even to make him rein back. All the movements are accomplished merely by *opposition* of the hands to the legs. The legs push; the hands give or resist.[4]

I have often been astonished and perplexed by the number of riders who win stock horse and so-called reining horse classes in shows mainly by the strength and quickness of their arms and the leverage of their bits. Most of them quite obviously merit disqualification for clear violations of the rules, at least when performing a quick stop. I have long ago concluded that if judges strictly enforced the rules they would usually find themselves with more ribbons to award than there were competitors remaining in the ring.

I think that it is a safe bet that if one hundred winners of stock horse or reining horse classes were photographed with a high-speed camera in the act of performing a quick stop, at least ninety-five of them would be frozen in action while pulling on the reins and with the feet braced to the front.

---

[4]Because so many horses are crudely schooled by having their mouths pulled on, some readers may reasonably wonder, "Just what are you supposed to do with a horse whose mouth has been spoiled by pulling?" Obviously, to halt or slow such a poorly schooled horse the rider at first will have to resort to pulling on the reins, since that is the "aid" the animal has been taught to understand. Pulling, however, should be only a temporary expedient; the horse should be re-schooled, and any competent trainer can do the job. But in the schooling of an unspoiled colt pulling should be absolutely eschewed.

Certainly there would be fewer advocates of the barbarous practice of training colts to stop on their hind legs by rasping their forefeet to make them tender in front if more horsemen understood the simple mechanics of controlling and stopping a horse. There would also be fewer advocates of martingales and tiedowns, which are unnecessary to a horse properly balanced and light in hand. Hoof-rasping and the widespread use of tie-downs prove that there must be something radically wrong with most accepted training methods, as well as with the general conception of how a horse should be ridden. If these practices are right, then we should logically approve of the use of severe bits *for the sake of their severity.*

However, I have yet to meet even the most hard-fisted rider who would frankly admit that severe bits should be used because they are severe and hence enable a rider to hurt his mount's mouth without the need of jerking the reins hard enough to blister his own hands. In fact, this is exactly what those who favor severe bits most vehemently deny. This, however, does not mean that they practice what they profess. Yet it is very unlikely that such a rider, confronted with the camera's impartial evidence, will admit his own faults. It is so much easier to blame the horse, who can't talk back.

Curiously enough, Saddle Horses, finished primarily for the show ring, can and do outperform many stock horses at halting sharply and reining back. Yet a quick stop is not part of the Saddle Horse's "act," while it is an essential part of the stock horse's.

Many so-called stock horses are deficient in performing a smooth quick stop chiefly because most Western riders have only a vague idea of what balancing a horse means and what lightness means. If a horse does not actually stumble or try to stampede, the average rider thinks the animal is doing all right.

There is more to this matter of pushing a horse up against the bit than just applying leg pressure. Equally important at the lope or gallop is the problem of *when* to apply the legs strongly. Probably no other factor has so important an influence on how smoothly a galloping horse slows his pace and, in particular, comes to a quick, balanced stop on his hind legs. Even the handiest and most willing colt cannot slow his pace or halt sharply and neatly and without physical discomfort to himself as well as to his rider unless the rider understands exactly when the horse will be in the best position to obey the cue to slow or stop and hence gives the order at the right moment. The rider, whether he sets out to teach a colt an abrupt practical quick stop for real work or the absurd, utterly impractical slide-Kelly-slide skiing maneuver of the show horse, must have a clear understanding of every phase of the gallop.

Once we have our colt moving freely at a brisk walk and trot, willing to hump along slightly faster than he would voluntarily go if we ceased to urge him with our legs, and fearlessly reaching for and accepting the bit with a soft relaxed lower jaw, we can begin working him more frequently at the lope or slow gallop. So let's analyze the movements of a galloping horse while he is taking one full stride in order to determine how best to slow and halt our colt smoothly and in balance.

Two facts which we must keep in mind are important: When the rider applies an aid, the horse needs a momentary interval of time to understand it; then another moment for his reflexes to respond to the order—with a green colt this time element is more than momentary and only practice can reduce it to split seconds. This time interval also applies to the rider; after we decide to give an order, we must act on the decision. From these facts it follows that the rider must apply the aids to slow or halt slightly *before* the colt moves into a position which will make it easiest for him to obey.

Look now at the sketches of the galloping horse in Figure 6.

In Sketch *A*, with the colt at a standstill, the rider closes his legs lightly but firmly, inducing the colt to bring his hind legs up under him while at the same time preventing any other forward movement by receiving on the bit the impulsion thus generated. The colt is thus "gathered" into a state of balance which will let him move easily in any direction.

In Sketch *B* the rider, feeling the colt light and balanced, re-laxes his hand but continues to squeeze with his legs. The colt, no longer restrained, lunges forward into the first beat of the gallop. The leading hind leg alone supports the combined weight of the horse and rider until the opposite hind leg has moved forward and touches the ground farther ahead. Then for a second both hind legs act as supports until the weight is transferred to the nonleading hind (Sketch *C*). The important thing to observe here in both *B* and *C* is that the colt has no "brakes." The respective positions of his hind legs make it impossible for him to check or stop quickly, smoothly, or comfortably. Had the rider signaled for a quick stop while the colt was in the position illus-

Fig. 6.—Leg sequence of a galloping horse. *(Drawing by Claude Johnson.)*

trated in Sketch *B*, by the time the horse's mind registered the
signal and he could begin to respond to the order, this is the
position he would be in—all his weight to the front, his one
supporting leg driving him forward, the other hind leg still moving out behind and both forefeet off the ground. Clearly it is an
impossible position for a quick, easy stop.

In this position, however, the rider can *begin* to stop him now,
though the halt will be neither smooth nor fast. For by the time
the colt can react to the aids he will be in the position shown in
Sketch *D*. In this position, supported by two diagonal legs, his
weight is more evenly distributed fore and hind. If forewarned
while in position *C*, he can stop now; but since one hind leg
is out behind him and still moving rearward, he cannot stop
with maximum efficiency. His halt will be rough, awkward; he
will probably slew sidewise in an effort to bring his left hind
up to take some of the strain.

This position portrays a crucial phase of the gallop. For it is
often in this position that many riders, with their mount on two
diagonal legs, feel most firmly supported. Often unconsciously—
and usually by jerking the reins—they signal for a halt. The result
is that the stop is poor; for before the horse can carry out the
order he has moved into the position shown in Sketch *E*.

In this position the horse has his weight forward to the utmost,
with only one foreleg supporting him. The rider's weight also in
this phase of the stride is tilted to the front. The horse finds it
utterly impossible to carry out the order to stop which the rider
gave him a split second before (in position *D*). Yet it is in this
position that many riders expect their mounts to execute a neat,
sliding stop, which the riders chose the worst moment to demand.

E F G H

This is the phase of the stride, however, when the rider should *prepare* his mount for a sliding stop, or even a decrease in speed. For right now, as the horse vaults over his leading foreleg, his hind legs are momentarily relieved of their principal task, propelling him forward. Right now the rider should fix his hand with the reins gently taut and squeeze strongly with his legs so that his mount, responding to the squeeze, shoots his hind legs as far forward under him as he can—where they must be for a quick, smooth, balanced stop.

Sketch *F* shows the horse completely off the ground, hind legs moving forward, in position to brake firmly as they hit the ground. The more strongly the rider uses his legs, the farther forward those hind feet will hit; therefore, the farther to the rear will be his balance and the easier it will be for him to stop.

In Sketch *G* the horse has begun the sliding stop, yielding to the rider's fixed hand. Sketch *H* shows the horse, weight back and all legs braced, skidding to a quick stop.

This is how a colt should be schooled to slow and stop, long before he will be ready to be worked at speed. The rider's legs drive; his hands give or oppose. But never should the hands pull.

CHAPTER XXII

The Whip

I think that there is no art taught in a
more haphazard way than that of riding.
—*M. F. McTaggart*

THE riding whip in its various forms is one of the most abused and misused tools in horsemanship. Like the bit and the spur, the whip should be an aid to the rider in communicating with his horse. More often than not a majority of riders think of it and use it as a means of punishment.

We have all observed or have read about the stress barrel racing horses undergo, so that they become so over-excited that they are very difficult to control. In my opinion, most of this "stress" is just a polite word for abuse, usually abuse with the bat or whip.

Horses that are properly trained for barrel racing do not exhibit any more "stress" than well-schooled cutting, jumping, polo or event horses. They all work strenuously and at speed, but anticipating or performing their respective jobs does not make them act like frenetic idiots.

Whips can be divided into two general types: cutting whips, and crops or "bats." The former are usually longer and more limber; the latter, short and more or less stiff.

Cutting whips include the long longeing whip, the dressage and polo whips from about three to four feet long, the old-fashioned buggy or driving whip with a shaft about five feet in length and a lash, and the short, slender whip favored by saddle-seat riders. Some whips of this last type have leather poppers at the tip of the shaft, while others are made of bare ash or hickory wood without any covering.

Crops and bats are stiffer and thicker as well as shorter. Used with real force, they can raise welts on a horse's hide. These include the hunting crop, the so-called dogging bat with a popper, the "feathered" bat used by some jumping-horse riders, and the jockey's whip.

It is not by mere coincidence that these short, stiff whips are called "bats" and "sticks." Swung with vigor, they can really make a horse jump—and he is not likely to forget the experience.

There are a few other kinds of "persuaders" that can be used as whips, even though they do not exactly fit the name. These are the wide leather strap, single or double; the quirt; and the spade bit rider's romal. These are specifically designed for more or less forceful hitting.

Of the three, probably the quirt is, or can be, the most severe; a lot depends on how it is made. The romal, properly used by an expert horseman, calls for a double hit—once on each side of the horse as fast as the rider can move his arm, from left to right, assuming the left hand is the bridle hand.

The wide flat strap, I believe, is least severe, but very effective as an accelerator and waker-upper. Making a smacking sound when it hits, the strap does not hurt a horse so much as it startles him.

Whether this startling effect is good or bad, particularly on a colt or a green horse in basic training, is a moot point. A great deal depends on the lesson you want to teach as well as on your horse's individual temperament. Some coldbloods can tolerate a spanking that would make a more sensitive, high-spirited horse almost jump out of his skin, and perhaps ruin him. A stallion is unlikely to react as the average gelding would.

The one unvarying principle I follow in schooling is to teach a horse to *respect the whip but never to fear it.* I consider this as fundamental as obedience to the rider's hands and legs.

If your horse won't stand calmly while you swing a whiplash over his head and let the lash fall gently on his back and then rub him all over with the shaft, he does not trust you. The more violently he reacts, the more he fears you.

In my book, a trainer who gets results by fear is a failure, no matter how excellent the results may appear to be. He may have collected a thousand trophies, but if his horses fear him I mark him zero.

Over the years at various times I have used all these types of whips in training horses. Like everyone else, I had to learn by

Plate 66. THE RIDING WHIP. Every aspiring trainer should learn how to handle the long riding whip, without interfering with his use of the reins. The whip reinforces the legs, stressing prompt obedience. Should your horse sidestep away from the whip instead of moving straight forward, hold a whip in each hand; use both at the same instant.

Photograph by Gene A. Pearson

experience, feeling my way along. I had to find out by trial and error what was good and what was not so good. Now, after more years than I care to count, I have narrowed my choice of training whips to just two—the longeing whip and the dressage, or polo, whip.

On rare occasions, with a horse that is inclined to be lazy—but almost never with a green colt—a quick one-two with a wide strap is a great attention-getter. Except for such rare occasions, however, I think that the longeing whip and the long riding whip are all a competent trainer needs to get any horse started right.

Once a horse learns how he is supposed to respond, a whip is seldom necessary, even in longeing. You might carry it now and then only as a reminder to the horse that you have it and he'd better pay attention. That is all it is—a reminder.

A horse correctly started on the longe line, with respect for but no fear of the long whip, is prepared to accept the riding whip without any fuss when you begin mounted schooling. The first time you touch him with your riding whip he understands what it means. He responds immediately and promptly.

One of the commonest, and worst, mistakes a rider can make is to teach a horse indifference to leg aids. Yet how often we see horses that have to be *kicked* into a lope or gallop, or indeed even a brisk trot! Most of the time this is not because the horse is a slug, but because the trainer who started him did not know when and how to use the whip.

The way to make a horse light to the legs is to be ready with the whip even the first time you ride him. The green colt does not understand that a light squeeze of your legs means for him to go forward or to pick up his pace. It is a grievous error to try to teach him this by squeezing harder or by thumping him with your heels. Instead, repeat the same light squeeze and instantly flick him with the whip just behind your lower leg.

It takes only a few repetitions of this for the average horse to get the idea.

A big mistake so many inexperienced riders make is that, even if they start this lesson right, they do not continue with it consistently throughout all the basic schooling. They may forget to carry their whip each time they school; or, perhaps finding it a bit awkward from lack of practice, they just quit using it. Then when the horse does not promptly respond to a single light squeeze of the legs, the rider squeezes harder or starts using his heels.

This is how insensitive horses are made—gradually.

If a horse has a tendency to go crooked, using two whips, one in each hand, is a wise idea. Obviously, the whips should be used with equal force and at exactly the same moment.

I like the dressage or polo whip for schooling because it is long enough to apply down behind the lower leg by a mere twist of the wrist. There is no need to shift both reins to one hand, as would be necessary if you tried to reach down that far with a short crop or bat.

Why do I consider this important? Because schooling a colt or a green horse—and very often in tuning up a finished horse—is a two-handed job, with a rein in each hand. Only a finished bridle horse should be ridden with the reins in one hand.

Then, of course, it doesn't make any difference if you switch to a crop or a bat. You can apply it where it should be applied. But don't brag about it! A finished bridle horse, if he really is finished, should not need any whip. In my opinion, this applies to barrel horses, too. The use of bats should be outlawed in barrel racing.

Dressage riders school with whips so that they will be prepared to cope with possible evasions, but they are not permitted to carry them in competition. The rules take it for granted that a finished horse, at whatever level, should not require a whip.

You need not remind me that the majority of riders who compete in open jumping and in three-day events always carry crops or bats. They do it for the same reason that jockeys carry whips. Jumpers, event horses and runners have to go all out, sometimes almost to the point of exhaustion. The riders are competing to *win*, and often a lot of money is involved. If a tired horse needs a whack with the stick to get him over an obstacle or to cross the finish line first, usually he will get it—while the rider gets the silver, the cash and the glory.

But we are concerned with inglorious, day-by-day schooling. Good jump riders and eventers patiently school at home, too.

Properly used, the whip is an absolutely necessary aid in intelligent schooling. That means that we should always think of it as an aid, and almost never as an instrument of punishment.

CHAPTER XXIII

The Aids

None of us can learn to ride from reading a book, but we can often discover what to strive for.
            — Singerly McCartney

O NE of the most indicative tests by which we can judge the degree of schooling of a riding horse is the old reliable figure 8 at a gallop. Even when done at a walk or a trot it is a most revealing test to knowing eyes. For stock horses and polo ponies in particular the figure 8 at a gallop is, in theory, elementary; in practice, it often turns out to be a horse's downfall—in more senses than one. "Why is this?" a correspondent asks. "I have seen a figure 8 done *correctly* only once in my life." I can well believe it. Except in dressage exhibitions a well-executed figure 8 at a gallop is a rarity in or out of the show ring.

Yet its rarity is no proof of its difficulty; rather, it is a sad reflection on our horsemanship. For, simple as it appears to be, its proper execution requires a well-schooled horse responding promptly and obediently to hardly perceptible aids applied precisely by a skilled rider. On the surface, galloping a horse in a figure 8 amounts to nothing more than riding him in a couple of adjoining circles, one to the left, the other to the right; but in actual performance to execute the figure correctly the horse must do all the following things when and as the rider demands:

1. Jump off into a gallop on whichever lead the rider specifies.
2. Flex to the inside in obedience to rein and leg.
3. Do a flying change of leads.
4. Flex to the opposite side.

5. Maintain a smooth, even pace throughout.
6. Pull up and stop in balance within his own length.
7. Calmly stand or walk away, as the rider directs.

A horse that will do these things quietly and with prompt obedience may be called a well-schooled mount. Certainly he will be greatly superior to the average nag seen in the show ring, though he will need a really knowing judge truly to appreciate his performance.[1]

It may be instructive for us to examine these things one by one in an effort to attain a clearer realization of how much painstaking schooling lies behind a really good performance. They are listed above in the order in which they are performed, but let's consider them in the sequence in which they should be taught in a well-planned schooling program.

OBEYING THE RIDER'S LEGS

All riding is based on the assumption or the principle that the horse must go forward when the rider so demands. Conversely, the horse must slow down and halt when that is what the rider wants. Going forward from a standstill into a gallop at one stride is only one phase of obedience to the rider's legs.

A horse that has never learned *prompt* obedience to the rider's legs is practically worthless. The only work he is fitted to do is the lowest sort of slave labor. If this sounds as though I am saying that most riding horses are practically worthless as they are commonly schooled (if you can call it schooling) because few of them are promptly obedient to the leg aids, the acoustics are fine and the P.A. system is in working order.

Kicking or spurring a horse into a run is no demonstration of his obedience to the legs. On the contrary, when kicking or the

---

[1] This is not an expression of only my personal opinion. Plenty of competent horsemen concur in this view. For example, one horseman stated in a letter to me: "We have many good riders in the West, but few horsemen. We hardly understand what real horsemanship is. Unfortunately, show judges are often more ignorant than spectators."

This is not meant to imply that even some judges are dishonest. Most of them have a higher regard for the rules than do many of the contestants whose riding and horses they are asked to judge. Too frequently, however, a judge's honest decision is based chiefly on sheer ignorance. This, in a man whose presence in the ring implies that he considers himself qualified for his rather specialized task, is inexcusable.

use of spurs is necessary it is positive proof that the horse has been poorly schooled. A well-schooled horse is promptly responsive to very slight leg pressure, so slight that the movement of the rider's leg is hardly perceptible to the eye. A horse that is *perfectly* obedient to the leg "works in the wind of the boot"; no slightest movement of the rider's legs can be observed.

The colt was taught kindergarten obedience to the legs first when we taught him to side-step in response to pressure of our hand against his flanks. Then later when he was mounted and ridden inside the corral he learned to move forward when squeezed by the legs and tapped on the flank with the whip. At that time, however, we did not demand any real promptness of response, nor did we expect him to respond with a degree of energy commensurate with the force of the leg pressure which we applied. But this is what he must now learn.

This training should be undertaken in a fenced field or paddock that is at least fifty or sixty yards long. Do not attempt it in a small corral, for the colt must have room to gallop straight ahead far enough for him to understand that he is doing what we want him to do, before we rein him in. If no fenced field or paddock of suitable size is available, it is better to work him in the open than in an enclosure that is too small.

After the colt is thoroughly warmed up, ride him to one end of the field (if it is no more than the minimum length mentioned above), turn him so that he is facing the far end and make him stand. If necessary, back him a step to get his hocks under him so that he will be well balanced. Then suddenly give him a free rein, squeeze him hard with both legs and touch him smartly with the whip either in the flank just behind the girth or on the croup. When the colt jumps off into a gallop allow him an absolutely slack rein for about thirty yards before you attempt to slow and halt him.

In teaching this lesson there are several things which the trainer must keep in mind:

The colt should be standing with his hocks well under him. It is not fair to ask him to jump into a gallop if he is all strung out and in no position to do so.

The trainer should give just *one* strong, quick squeeze with his legs, and it should be a squeeze, not a kick. He should not wear spurs.

He should allow the colt an absolutely free rein and take necessary precautions to avoid accidentally giving the colt even a slight jab in the mouth by being "left behind" when the colt lunges forward. The rider should be leaning forward *before* the "take-off"; if necessary, he should "choke the horn" or grasp the pommel of the training saddle to keep his weight forward.

He should squeeze with his legs an instant *before* he applies the whip; never the other way about. For only in this way will the colt quickly understand that a squeeze of the rider's legs means "Go!" and that if he doesn't obey instantly he will be reminded of it with the whip.

Once the colt is galloping the rider should immediately relax the pinch of his legs, reverting to normal pressure. If the trainer neglects this, then he is not teaching the colt the lesson that he is supposed to be teaching him—that extra-strong leg pressure is a demand for extra effort, more extension, greater speed. To maintain the unusual leg pressure after the colt has responded and is galloping would be, in effect, to urge the colt faster and faster until he was going at a headlong racing run. Continued leg pressure under such circumstances has caused more than one runaway.

The colt should be slowed down gradually and brought to a gentle halt. He should never be abruptly pulled or halted sharply. Even if he were physically fit and schooled to perform a quick stop without risk of injury, it would be out of place in this lesson, for we want to be sure that he understands that he did the right thing in galloping. Being checked abruptly would hardly give him this impression, right now.

This lesson can easily be overdone—so easily that I would not even suggest it except that this lesson is absolutely necessary; the colt *must* be taught prompt, unquestioning obedience to the legs. So many riders lack good judgment and equestrian tact, however, that I am not sure that what I say here may not cause some horses undeserved pain. Therefore, I cannot refrain from offering the following advice, addressed particularly to young riders whose vigor and enthusiasm sometimes outweigh their good horse sense:

Do not use this method of teaching leg obedience on a nervous or high-strung colt or on a well-bred one that is always eager to go. It will upset a nervous colt and the eager "goer" won't need it. Such colts will almost always respond to strong leg pressure alone or to a tap of the rider's lower legs, supplemented if necessary by the oral command to gallop which they learned on the longe.

If a colt does not respond promptly to the legs after a few trials, remember that it is only because he does not yet fully understand. The whip is only to help him understand; it is not an

instrument of "punishment." Therefore, do not use it more forcefully than necessary. The touch of the whip should be sudden and
decisive, but not necessarily painful. It should startle more than
sting the colt into a gallop.

Some high-spirited colts and ones with thin sensitive skins resent the touch of a whip. With such colts a flat smooth wooden
paddle or a strap about two or more inches wide is more effective
than a whip or switch. It is less likely to sting and it makes a sharp,
startling noise when it smacks. I have known a table tennis paddle
to work well on horses that resented a whip.

The best place to use a paddle or a strap is on the croup or
haunch.

Sluggish and underbred colts—the ones that usually need this
lesson most—will, as a rule, take this lesson in stride. Three or
four repetitions of it in about ten or fifteen minutes won't upset
them, and may indeed be necessary before they will get the idea
and respond *promptly* to the rider's legs without the stimulus of
the whip or strap. For most well-bred colts, however, two repetitions will be enough for any one day. The third time they will
jump into a gallop the instant the trainer gives them the leg aid
alone. That is when the wise trainer quits for the day. The rest
of the schooling period should be devoted to work at the walk,
preferably across country.

In teaching this lesson the trainer should pay particlar attention to two important things: When he has halted the colt after
a short gallop, he should show his approval in the most unmistak-
able terms so that there can be no doubt whatever in the colt's
mind that he did the right thing. Then the trainer should make
no attempt to repeat the lesson until the colt is again relaxed and
perfectly calm.[2]

Once the colt responds to a strong squeeze of the rider's legs
by leaping instantly into a gallop he will be conditioned to obey
milder applications of the same signal when the rider wishes to
send him forward at a walk, a trot, or a lope. The trainer should
form the habit of using only a degree of leg pressure commensur-

[2]Some readers may wonder why I approve of teaching this lesson with the aid
of a whip or a strap but not with spurs. My answer is that spurs have a different,
and a more severe, effect, because the effect is concentrated in a relatively small
area. Sharp spurs cut or abrade; blunt spurs bruise. The colt's flanks remain sore
long after the lesson is over. Mild use of the whip or the strap does not produce
this aftereffect, and use of either requires no special skill. On the other hand, delicate,
tactful use of the spur necessitates a great deal of skill, absolute independence of the
aids, and a firmer seat than the majority of riders can boast.

ate with the speed or gait he wants. The more responsive the colt
becomes, the less leg pressure will he need. A rider who habitually
uses his legs with unnecessary force will dull the most willing
colt's responsiveness.

In addition to the elementary response of moving straight forward in answer to the rider's legs, the colt must also learn to obey
the application of either leg separately. This involves side-stepping
to the left when the rider uses his right leg and vice versa, and
doing half-turns and full turns on the forehand. Since these movements are properly done with the aid of the reins to control the
forehand acting together with the rider's legs which move the
hindquarters, they may be left until a later stage of the training.

OBEYING THE HANDS:
THE SLOWDOWN AND COMEBACK TO HALT

At the same time that a colt is learning to obey the
legs he must also be taught obedience to the hands. The two lessons are inseparable, for one without the other is futile. In simplest
terms, elementary obedience to the hands consists of slowing the
pace and coming to a halt. (For the present discussion we can
ignore turning.)

The slowdown and comeback represent the most elementary
form of flexing the jaw and the poll. It is the maximum degree of
collection, or semi-collection, which a colt should be taught until
he has been ridden in the snaffle for about a year. If during this
period the trainer handles him well, keeping him naturally soft
and light, when the colt is ready to go into the full double bridle
there will be no difficulty in teaching him complete collection, if
that is what the trainer desires.

During this period the trainer should always keep in mind two
important things: He should never try to slow or halt the colt
by pulling him, in the usual sense of that word; and he should
never attempt to work the colt at real speed. He should teach
the colt to slow down and halt gradually by smoothly "coming
back to the hand." The aim should be to do everything right
rather than quickly. Later, speed will come; but if the trainer runs
into trouble now, he can rest assured that he is working the colt
too fast.

It is not too easy to explain clearly, and it is almost impossible
to illustrate photographically with anything less than slow mo-

tion film, how a skilled trainer correctly slows and halts a horse, bringing him back to the hand literally inch by inch. Describing the action makes it sound complex and very difficult, when actually it is quite simple and all skilled horsemen do it, even though they would usually be baffled if required to explain the action. Let us assume that the rider has legged his mount into a quick gallop and wishes to halt him. Briefly, this is what occurs:

The colt is galloping with the reins slack. The rider takes up the slack until he has a light contact with the horse's mouth.

The rider closes his fingers firmly on the reins, fixing his hands in place.

A moment later he closes his legs, pressing the colt up against the bit.

He prevents the colt from going faster in response to the added leg pressure by maintaining the fixity of the hands.

The colt, pushed forward by the legs but opposed by the hands, collects himself slightly, shortening his stride and hence slowing.

The rider instantly ceases to drive with his legs. At almost the same instant he "gives" with his hands by slightly relaxing the fingers of first one hand and then the other. This uneven giving of the reins causes the bit to move a trifle from side to side in the colt's mouth in a "vibrating" effect that aids in relaxing the jaw. It is more effective than if the rider gave with both hands simultaneously. This yielding by the rider when the colt has yielded is only momentary.

Again the rider takes up the little sag in the reins, establishing contact again and fixing the hands.

Again he uses his legs to push the colt against the bit, shortening the stride still more.

As before, he takes the impulsion produced by his legs on fixed hands.

As soon as the colt yields to the bit, the rider also gives, first with one hand, then with the other.

This process is repeated as the colt is gradually slowed down until he comes to a smooth, balanced stop.

At all times the hands and the legs act separately, not simultaneously. When the legs drive, the hands remain passive, waiting to receive the impulsion produced. When the hands restrain, the legs cease to act. Only in a very advanced stage of training may hands and legs contradict each other.

The important point to note here is that instead of pulling the colt to a strained halt the rider gradually slows the pace by shortening the strides, bringing the colt's hind legs farther and farther under him, so that he is positioned to halt on his hocks with his nose tucked in and can hardly escape doing so. In this way, the halt on the hindquarters eventually becomes habitual.

This kind of slowdown and balanced halt cannot be hurried. It takes time, but is worth achieving. The final result is a smooth, balanced stop with floating reins that pulled horses can never duplicate.

The trainer should keep in mind several points:

The colt should not throw up his head. This would "cave in" his back.

The greater the speed when the slowdown is begun, the firmer must be the rein contact and the first fixing of the rider's hands.

As the pace decreases, so proportionately does the force of the aids.

The quicker the halt, the stronger the aids.

Thus, an abrupt halt from a medium trot necessitates firmer aids than a very gradual slowdown from a gallop.

It is the horseman's tact in applying the aids that develops the colt's sensitivity and responsiveness.

As the training goes on, the aids should become progressively lighter and lighter, as the trainer works toward the final objective —a quick stop from a fast gallop in response to just one squeeze of the legs and a closing of the fingers. Attainment of this goal will be greatly facilitated by, at first, judicious use of the oral command, "Whoa."

The trainer should keep in mind, however, that this final objective is still a long time off. It is a goal toward which the colt must be worked up very gradually. The trainer should be content to postpone fast work until the colt becomes at least five years old and has been worked in the double bridle. Until then, the trainer should work to develop the colt's natural balance and to improve his responsiveness, always striving to keep him naturally supple and light.

Probably the best exercise for developing a young horse's balance and for teaching him to extend and collect himself naturally in response to the rider's legs and hands is riding him with frequent changes of gaits, pace, and direction, frequent halts and occasional reining back. This should be done both in the schooling paddock and, later, across country over varied terrain. Here is an example of such an exercise, which can be varied as the trainer prefers:

Start off at a fast extended walk.
Halt. (Be sure that the halt is straight.)
From the halt leg the colt into a brisk trot.
After about a minute, halt—halt from the trot, without dropping first to a walk. (Halt straight.)
Rein back two steps, being careful to keep the colt perfectly straight.
From the reinback leg the colt into a canter.
After about thirty yards, halt—without any trotting or walking.
Rein back a step; then immediately send the colt forward again at a canter, this time on the opposite lead.
Canter in a wide circle, gradually decreasing the diameter of the circle so that the colt moves spirally in toward the center.
When he is cantering in a circle about fifteen yards in diameter, drop to a walk.
Change directions and leg him again into a canter on the opposite lead, gradually spiralling outward.
Straighten out. Drop to a trot; then to a walk.
Canter.
From the canter halt and rein back; then walk.
From the walk break into a fairly fast gallop.
Slow to a trot and then a walk.
Leg the colt into a fast trot.
Slow to a medium trot.
Do a figure 8 at a slow trot.
Walk.

Nothing can replace this kind of work for developing a colt's balance and teaching him to be alert, ready at any moment to change speed and gait as well as direction. Within the colt's capacity, this sort of exercise can hardly be overdone. Every change necessitates a readjustment of balance, and when the colt learns that the rider might demand a change at any moment he learns to be alert, ready for it.

Many amateur riders fail to get results in their schooling, or become discouraged by how slowly tangible results reward their efforts, because they do not realize that about 90 per cent of

Plate 67. THE REINBACK. Correctly reining back defeats many riders because they don't understand how the movement should be done. The reinback is not a scramble or a race in reverse. It is a cadenced, diagonal movement, like the trot. A horse's willingness to rein back is commensurate with his willingness to go forward. Mollie Cermak on her Connemara pony, Buzzie, does it correctly.

Photograph by Pat Kay

effective schooling is achieved by working the horse on transitions —frequent changes of pace at each gait and repeated changes from one gait to another. When the horse never knows what to expect next he learns to be alert for changes; he develops the habit of "listening" to the rider. Half an hour of such diversified work accomplishes more than slogging along at one gait or exercise until both the horse and the rider are bored, then switching to something else to become bored with that. Frequent transitions get quick results.

Mere collection at very slow paces on level ground is no adequate substitute for this exercise, as some high school fanatics claim or imply. For balance, though we customarily speak of it as of something static, actually is fluid, constantly changing as the horse moves. The faster the pace, the more unstable the balance becomes. Hence, a horse used to balancing himself, however delicately, only at slow paces finds himself unable to cope with his increased instability at speed. As a result he cannot go at real speed; he is "tied in." Only if he has plenty of this kind of work across country in addition to his school work will he prove to be a safe mount.

In this work the trainer should concentrate on riding his horse straight and on smoothness of execution. Acceleration, slowing, and stopping should be smooth and balanced; this fact should never be out of the trainer's mind. Halting roughly, then rushing the colt ahead, forcing him to scramble backward all spraddled out instead of backing smoothly step by step, does more harm than good. Straightness, especially at the halts, is of paramount importance.

Pay particular attention to cantering from the reinback, then halting and reining back again. With colts that are heavy on the forehand or with those that are inclined to get out of hand, no other exercise is so effective in teaching them to get their hocks under them.

MAINTAINING A SMOOTH, EVEN PACE

This means more than it says. A well-schooled horse not only keeps evenly to a pace which the rider has set; he also holds the gait which the rider has put him into, until the rider demands a change. *Gait* and *pace* should not be confused. The sequence in which a horse puts his feet to the ground determines his gait; pace refers to the speed of the gait.[3] Thus, an extended

---

[3] The usual gaits are the walk, the trot, and the gallop. Some authorities distinguish between the slow gallop, or canter, and the racing gallop; the former is a three-beat gait, the latter one of four beats. In both, the sequence of leg movements is the same, but in the racing gallop the period of suspension and the degree of flexion and extension of the limbs are greater. Continental horsemen, however, never use the term "canter" to mean a slow gallop. For practical purposes the distinction between the canter, or lope, and the fast gallop is of little importance. Throughout this book the terms are used interchangeably, with "lope" or "canter" referring particularly to a slow pace.

trot results in a faster pace than a collected canter; which may be no faster than a brisk running-walk. Likewise, a horse with a fast walk can set a more rapid pace than a slower animal performing the same gait can match.

Stabilizing a colt is the process of teaching him to maintain a gait and a uniform pace on loose reins for as long as the rider wishes him to do so. Once the habit is established, the colt must learn to do the same thing first while being ridden "on the bit" and then while going "off the bit." Being "off the bit" means that, after the colt has learned to flex, the rider collects him to a certain degree and the colt maintains that degree of collection, as well as the gait and the pace, with "floating" reins, while the rider's hands and legs remain passive. This step in the schooling process, however, comes a considerable length of time after the colt has learned first to go well on loose reins and then to go on the bit.

Teaching the colt to take and hold each gait on the longe line in obedience to spoken commands was the first step in stabilizing his gaits. Driving in long reins, which allowed better control of pace, was the second step. The third step consists of many miles of slow riding across country on loose reins, interspersed with frequent workouts in the schooling corral.

When I say "slow riding" I emphatically do not mean sloppy riding, just moseying along any old way while the colt becomes more and more slovenly and the rider squanders the time admiring the scenery and dreaming of all the trophies his budding Pegasus is destined to win some day. I mean the slow gaits, sometimes done slowly, sometimes briskly—plenty of fast walking, lots of slow and fast trotting, a very moderate amount of cantering.

During these cross-country jaunts the rider, besides working on the gaits, should make a practice of riding the colt in figure 8's, serpentines, zigzags, etc., at a walk and a trot to develop the colt's balance and to confirm obedience to the aids. He should ride over low obstacles, such as fallen logs, which the colt can merely step over but, if left to himself, might prefer to go around. One important lesson that never should be neglected is teaching the colt to go quietly with other horses—and to go away from them. In this the rider must quietly but firmly insist on absolute obedience to the aids. The colt must learn good company manners, traveling with other horses, going ahead of them and away from them, and continuing on his way quietly in obedience to the rider while other horses pass and go away from him. Too many horses that will go quite well alone become obstreperous knot-heads in company, always wanting to rush along with the crowd regardless of the rider's wishes.

If the rider intends ever to use the colt for roping, he should make use of the time on these cross-country rides to get the colt used to a rope. This lesson should not be put off; the sooner the colt learns it, the more easily he will take to it.

At the same time the rider should "show him a cow."

None of the opportunites these rides across country offer should be wasted. It is the rider's job to see that the colt learns all the time.

In this work on the gaits the rider should make a deliberate effort to improve the colt's walking speed. This is done by en-couraging the colt to stretch his neck on a long rein and rhyth-mically squeezing him at each stride—with the right leg when his left fore is advancing and with the left leg when the right fore swings forward. A simpler though less effective way is simply to squeeze the colt with both legs at every second or third stride. This squeezing induces the colt to bring his hind legs farther forward under him. With sluggish colts light taps of the short whip or switch in co-ordination with the action of the legs help to increase impulsion. Constant kicking or spurring of a colt's flanks, however, is worse than useless; eventually it will result only in completely desensitizing them. The forced fast walk is a very beneficial exercise, but very fatiguing. It should not be prolonged for more than a few minutes at a time.

The trot should never be allowed to degenerate into either a jog or a pell-mell rushing along that might best be described as a diagonal run.

The rider should control the canter carefully. Never let the colt run or even get the idea that he can go all out. Basic work on this gait is most effective when done inside a corral. When he can't go any place except around and around, even the hottest colt will relax and settle down.

During this work on the gaits it is wise to continue with oc-casional longeing and long-rein driving. Longeing or driving the colt in deep going is a great muscler-up without the risk of bur-dening him with weight on his back. Work the colt in gradually decreasing circles and figure 8's. Stop him often and make him rein back; but never let him back more than a step or two at a time before you immediately send him forward again. Use voice commands more than the reins. This work at reining back improves a colt's balance and alertness, but should be employed very sparingly or even omitted until the colt has learned to reach for and accept his bit; otherwise, he might develop the habit of getting behind the bit.

Do not at any time during this period of the schooling attempt to work the colt at speed. He is not ready for it; to rush him now can result only in harm.

Strive at all times to obtain free, flowing, regular gaits.

A horse's gaits, of course, can never be better than his conformation. If he has straight shoulders and pasterns, his gaits will be rougher than those of a horse with sloping shoulders and springy pasterns. Weak hindquarters result in poor impulsion. A thick stubby neck and a coarse head usually mean poor balance, with too much weight on the forehand. However, proper exercises can strengthen weaknesses. Schooling can improve balance, sometimes changing a poorly made horse into a better ride than an animal with greater natural endowments. It is a safe bet that about 90 per cent of riding horses are not schooled up to their conformation. Almost all can be improved.

Exactly what are free, flowing, regular gaits? How can they be recognized? The questions are not as absurd as they might seem. Go to any horse show or riding club get-together and you will see horses, which their owners consider good enough to boast about and enter in shows, that have never learned to carry a rider at the same easy natural gaits they show when free at grass.

Free gaits consist of long, low strides that cover ground efficiently—the opposite of short, choppy strides and artificially high "showy" ones. Long, low strides do not mean that the horse necessarily is heavy on his forehand, with too much weight to the front, for the hind legs as well as the fore limbs must show full "play," reaching well forward at each step so that the horse is well balanced and can easily be collected and have the gaits shortened. Free gaits mean that the horse is supple, relaxed, willing and able to extend fully, unafraid of the bit—the opposite of the horse with jerky, constricted gaits, and an "upside-down neck" and a caved-in back that result in his having his head in the rider's lap. To develop free natural gaits under saddle the rider must deliberately work to lengthen the strides, pushing the colt faster than the youngster voluntarily would go but not breaking the gait.

Flowing gaits are smooth and springy, the result of good balance and strong impulsion from hind legs that work well under the horse.

Regular gaits have cadence, rhythm, timing. This is particularly evident even to an unschooled onlooker in a well-balanced
trot and a slow, controlled gallop.

Flexing a horse to make him light and supple is a
mystery to loose-rein riders. "Why should I try to flex him?" is
a typical reaction. "He's easy to stop, ain't he? I can set him up
with one little pull." Some stock horse trainers even are of the
opinion that a horse when turning or spinning fast should do so
while remaining perfectly straight from poll to croup—which is
on a par with saying that a human athlete should run or jump
with his spine perfectly rigid.

The basic idea of flexing a horse is to make him supple and
relaxed. When a horse contracts or stiffens the muscles of his
lower jaw in resistance to the bit, the powerful muscles along his
entire neck and spine automatically stiffen, too. The set lower
jaw has an effect that goes through the whole horse. He becomes
unyielding to the rider. Conversely, if he can be taught to yield
his jaw softly to the rider's hands, he can then easily be taught to
relax or flex at the poll and, in response to the intermittent squeezing of the rider's legs, round his loins—the opposite of the caved-
in back—and bring his hind legs farther forward under him. He
thus becomes light and pliable, responsive to the rider's most delicate control. A horse like this is a delight to ride which loose-rein
riders never know or can imagine.

A horse trained to go only on loose reins involuntarily stiffens
up the instant he is reined in. When the rider slows or stops him
by pulling the bit back against the jaw, the horse may obey almost
instantly; but no matter how quickly he responds, the horse cannot avoid stiffening. It is natural for him to react so, for he has
been conditioned to it, has never been trained otherwise. Only
when he slows or stops of his own volition, with the reins hanging
slackly—as a good contest cutting horse or roping horse learns
from experience to do—can he remain supple and balanced;
though even then his conditioning may cause him to stiffen involuntarily, a reaction more commonly seen in roping horses,
which in the early stages of their training often have their mouths
jerked, than in well-trained cutting horses.

There are two kinds of flexions—flexion of the lower jaw and of the poll, which are necessary in developing a good head-set; and lateral flexions, by which the colt not only yields his jaw but turns his head and bends his spine in response to rein and leg aids.

A colt should always be taught lateral flexions first; they logically follow the direct rein indications which he learned during the first ground driving lessons and which the trainer has been using in riding him. Even before the first driving lesson, the habit of flexing laterally was implanted in the colt when he was worked on the longe; the mere weight of the line induced him to face in the direction he was turning. Later when the trainer commenced mounted work, the habit was further developed by the repeated use of the leading rein in turning the colt. Thus, by following this system of simple, logical steps, each of which has more than one purpose but all of which are planned with a definite goal in view, we can save time and bring the colt along more and more rapidly as we progress, for we proceed merely by asking the colt to improve his execution of things he already has learned how to do in earlier stages of schooling. We can avoid or minimize the possible confusion that so often results from continually introducing entirely "new" lessons.

Any rider who has brought a colt along from the first lessons on the longe to the beginning of the mounted phase of training according to the system set forth here need hardly concern himself with lateral flexions now. His colt will bend to the rein by force of habit, as much as is necessary or desirable in a horse intended to be used as an all-round mount for general riding purposes or one destined to be given specialized training for a particular kind of work later.

The only practical purpose in this lateral flexing is to instill into the colt the habit of looking in the direction he is asked to turn. School riders and their thoughtless imitators, as well as horsemen who have lots of time on their hands, like to make a fetish of this lateral flexing, as if it were a worth-while accomplishment for its own sake. These pundits go to great pains to teach a horse to move straight forward with his head turned sidewise, or to move obliquely on two tracks to one side or the other with his head turned and his spine flexed to the opposite side, a movement known as shoulder-in. Theoretically, this exercise is supposed to supple a horse, calm an excitable one, make it impossible for him to shy, and benefit any horse mentally as a disciplinary exercise. In practice, it is an illogical movement, directly contrary to the fundamental principle of having the horse look the way he is going. That it ever "calmed" any horse I doubt; that—when done properly—it is proof of the horse's obedience to leg and rein is obvious, for no free horse would do it naturally and voluntarily; but that it supples a horse I deny, for only a horse already well suppled can do it smoothly and softly.

For practical riding such flexing away from the direction of movement is not only useless; it can be positively detrimental. Occasionally it teaches a crafty horse the defensive trick of developing a "rubber" neck which bends to the rein while the horse refuses to alter his course. Why do we turn a horse? Because we want him to face that way or to move that way, and we want him to look where he is going. Why then waste time teaching him to move in one direction while looking in another? Shoulder-in, like riding a horse without a bridle, is merely an exhibition stunt, very satisfying perhaps to the rider's feeling of mastery but completely out of place in the education of a horse for outdoor work.[4]

With a colt well schooled on the longe and in long reins, the rider need concern himself with only two aspects of lateral flexions now: he should not allow the colt to bend its neck more than merely to follow on the line of the curve the rider directs; and he should be careful that the colt does not lower its head and that the neck does not "break" sharply inward from near the shoulders but bends in a uniform arc from the poll, with the head maintaining its natural laterally vertical position. This last means simply that the colt, though bending his neck to the rein and facing in the direction of the turn, should not cant his head to one side so that one ear is tilted lower than the opposite ear, with his muzzle nearer the center of the circle or the turn than his poll.

If the rider detects either of these faults, he should instantly correct them by limiting the degree of flexion of the neck with

[4]One of the greatest master of *haute école* was undoubtedly Captain E. Beudant, a French army officer, whose book *Horse Training: Out-door and High School* (New York, Charles Scribner's Sons, 1931) is not as well known in this country as it deserves to be. After a long lifetime of riding, this expert in the most difficult form of equitation which a horseman can undertake concluded: "I must say, that instead of emphasizing more and more the schooling exercises, I have come to the conclusion that shoulder-in and two-track work are nothing more than amusing diversions, often detrimental to the horse, and of utility only in permitting the mounted soldier to place his horse properly in ranks." To understand the true significance of this statement one must have some realization of Beudant's marvelous skill. The photographs of himself on horseback in his book give an indication of this. Compared to Beudant's pictures, the photographs of James Fillis in his widely known book *Breaking and Riding* (London, Hurst, n.d.) look like those of an amateur.

the opposite rein in a fixed hand that gives only when the colt ceases to overbend. This prompt correction is of the utmost importance, particularly with a colt that has a weak or very slender neck and a fine throat, for such a youngster, if mishandled, is most liable to develop a limp "rubber" neck. With a colt of this type the average rider will do best to demand no lateral flexion at all; he should, on the contrary, encourage stiffness of the neck. Later, when the animal is mature and more muscularly developed, flexing him laterally will not be difficult.

A horse that overflexes cannot be kept straight on a circle or a turn any more than one can that does not flex at all. This matter of straightness is worth some explanation, for a rider should clearly understand exactly what it means.

We know that a horse gallops with one shoulder and two legs, all on the same side, leading. Ordinarily, even when galloping directly forward, this causes the horse to be slightly traversed to the line he is traveling. He gallops with one shoulder slightly in advance of the other, with his haunches carried to one side of an imaginary straight line. If this degree of traverseness is very slight and is kept to a minimum, for practical purposes we are doing all right. For absolute straightness, with the horse's hind feet following exactly in line with the forefeet, is a difficult accomplishment which only an almost perfectly schooled horse can consistently achieve—if he is ridden by a highly skilled horseman. It can be done and it is the ideal for which we should strive; but the average rider not only makes no effort to keep his mount as nearly straight as possible, but usually seems to be entirely unaware that his horse is traveling traversed.

The usual reason for this, besides plain ignorance, is undoubtedly the way most of us have been taught to put a horse into a lope or gallop on a specified lead. For instance, to start off on the left lead most of us were taught to "pull his head to the right" and boot him out. This is certainly the commonest style of taking a lead seen in all saddle classes at horse shows. The horse that does not circle the ring with his nose stuck out towards the rail is an exception.

To be sure, this method works (and that's all many riders care about); but it is crude plowboy riding, as crude as jerking on the bit to halt, and it is fundamentally wrong, for on a curve the horse starts his gallop looking away from the direction in which he is moving. In turning and circling, a horse should always lead with his head. This is what we had our colt do on the longe and in the long reins, and it is the natural way.

Thus it becomes clear at once that straightness on a curved line of movement does not mean actually ruler-straight. It means that the horse is straight in relation to the arc he is following. A horse doing a circle or a figure 8 properly should be bent from poll to croup in the arc in which he is moving. In effect, the rider bends the horse around the rider's inner leg. He does this not only by use of the reins—which, when the horse is finished, the rider uses hardly at all—but by the use of his legs. When circling to the left, for example, the rider keeps his left leg firmly in place at the girth and uses his right leg several inches behind the girth to push, or hold, the horse's hindquarters in. Thus, the right leg has the same effect as the outside rein around the hindquarters when we were driving the colt in long reins. If in schooling a horse to circle or do a figure 8 at any gait or pace the rider fails to get this spine-bending flexion, he is simply wasting his time. (See Fig. 7.)

Colts, green horses, lazy horses, even well-schooled mounts when worked by careless or poor riders, will usually resist this bending at first; some will resort to tricks to avoid it and to fool the rider. For example, one horse when circled to the right will merely thrust his nose in toward the center, canting his head but not flexing at all. Another will "break" near the shoulders, swinging his entire neck inward but otherwise remaining as stiff as a board. At a trot or canter some horses will lean inward exaggeratedly; as if centrifugal force were about twice as strong as it really is. These tricks are nothing but evasions; a trainer should be on the alert for them. He must see to it that the bend begins in the upper part of the neck just behind the poll and that the colt keeps his head laterally vertical from poll to muzzle instead of tilting it to one side.

A good way to teach a colt to bend when turning is to work him in the corners of a corral or paddock. Start at a fast walk close to and parallel with one fence. Ride the colt into a corner, holding him straight until his nose almost touches the fence at right angles to his course. When he must either halt or turn to avoid bumping his nose, and not until then, feel the rein on the side to which he must turn, carrying the hand outward quickly to the side, and at the same moment press the opposite rein against his neck well up ahead of the withers. Use the legs strongly, push-

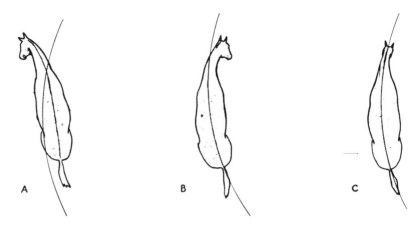

Fig. 7. —Flexion on a circle. *(Drawing by Larry Kumferman.)*

A WRONG

Horse is traversed to direction of movement, moving on two tracks. Head is canted to outside. Center of balance is outward. Horse is not looking where he is going.

B WRONG

Neck overbent near withers. Head is canted to inside. Ribs and spine are not flexed. Horse might change leads in front.

C CORRECT

Horse is flexed truly on circle and is looking where he is going.

ing him close to the fence, the inner leg just at the girth, the outer leg (next to the fence) slightly drawn back, pressing vigorously behind the girth. The effect is to bend the colt as he turns in an arc around the rider's inner leg. Make five or six circuits of the corral, making him bend at each corner; then work in the opposite direction.

Most colts quickly learn to anticipate the turns; they will start trying to cut the corners. The trainer must not allow this. By using his legs strongly he must drive the colt right into each corner. An effective way of checking anticipation and attempted corner-cutting is to ride the colt into a corner diagonally, so that it will be possible to turn in either direction; then turn to the side which the colt does not seem to anticipate. In using this method of catching him by surprise, however, the trainer should allow enough room for the colt to come around without having to fling up his head to avoid bumping the fence.

Avoid roughness; do nothing to excite the colt. But see that he bends. Patience and persistence, an inflexible determination by the trainer to have the colt do it right, and immediate reward when the colt even tries to obey—a brief rest on loose reins— will get results.

Keep to a walk until the colt does well before doing the same work at a trot and later at a lope.

The trainer should remember always to maintain impulsion when going into a corner. He must not let the colt slow down, "die on the hands," or change gaits.

When a horse is traveling traversed either on the straight or on a circle, the easiest way to put him straight is to move his forehand in line with his hindquarters by means of the reins. Needless difficulties, such as loss of impulsion, usually arise if the trainer tries to straighten him out by legging the hindquarters over in line with the forehand.

TAKING A LEAD AND CHANGING LEADS

Some trainers like to make a great deal of fuss about "teaching" a colt to take a correct lead. They make the whole business seem as complicated as advanced calculus. No normal colt, however, needs to be "taught" to lead correctly when circling or moving on a curve. He will do so naturally—if the rider does not "mess him up." Getting the horse to change leads on the straight in response to the rider's signal, however, is, of course, a different matter, for then the colt must be made to understand that a certain aid means, "Change." But once he has learned that, the rest is simple; it depends chiefly on the rider's timing, knowing exactly when to apply the aid.

A horse schooled according to the system suggested in this book will give even a mediocre rider almost no difficulties when it is time—as it is now—to work on leads and changing leads. The longeing, the ground driving, the constant use of the leading rein in turning, and the lateral flexions of the neck and spine have all served to condition the colt to move forward naturally at any gait—walk, trot, or gallop—in the direction in which his head is turned. On a turn or a circle to the left the natural way for any horse to break into a gallop is on the left lead; if he moves to the right, it is natural for him to take the right lead. Consequently, all that is necessary is for the rider to adapt his aids to correspond with the lead which he wishes the colt to take.

The simplest way of doing this—to obtain, let us say, a gallop on the left lead—is for the rider to feel the left rein lightly, just sufficiently to turn the colt's head a trifle to the left, and to squeeze with both legs, demanding a gallop. The right leg, if necessary, may be drawn back a few inches behind the girth and applied with slightly more force than the left leg in order to make sure that the colt's right hind leg moves forward first, as well as to push the hindquarters a trifle toward the left. To start the gallop on the right lead simply reverse the aids.

I could make this sound much more complicated and impressive by dwelling at length on the importance of the rider's fixing one hand, moving the other, displacing his weight in this or that direction and tilting his pelvis while he drives the colt with the muscles of the small of his back. But none of these actions is really necessary merely to put a horse into a gallop on a desired lead; they are merely refinements in which school riders delight.

Probably to a rider brought up in the pull-his-head-to-the-opposite-side school it may seem that this method of reining, which turns a horse's head toward the same side as the leg with which we want him to lead, should discourage a horse from taking the lead demanded, because by not moving the head to the opposite side we neglect to "free" (i.e., shift weight from) his leading leg and shoulder. On the surface, this objection seems logical. Actually, it is of no importance. The important thing in teaching a horse to strike off on a specified lead, or to execute a flying change of leads as when galloping in a figure 8, is to get him leading correctly *behind*. This is the most efficient way to start a lead or to change leads, especially when working at full speed, and it is the way we should confirm a colt in learning until it becomes almost automatic, a fixed habit. When the hind legs start the stride correctly, the forelegs will naturally follow. But it is easy to get a change of leads in front while failing to accomplish the same change behind. Then the horse becomes disunited and his whole stride is wrong.

The one exception to this fundamental rule of starting a lead with the hind legs and letting the forelegs follow is when a horse executes a sharp turn on his hindquarters with both hind feet firmly on the ground, then jumps out in a different direction that necessitates his changing leads in front before his hind feet can leave the ground. However, if the horse has been schooled to start his leads with the hind legs first, as soon as his hind-quarters are free he will change behind in the air and remain united. But a horse not so schooled cannot always be relied on to do this. He is a risky ride.

The trainer's task at this stage is to teach the colt that he must change leads whenever the rider cues him for a change and to confirm the colt in the habit of obeying. This means working him on leads until he becomes so used to responding to the aids that there will rarely be any excuse for mistakes or disobedience.

In the schooling corral or paddock, start the colt at a fast walk parallel to one of the fences, heading into a corner, just as when teaching him to bend. As he goes into the corner and starts to turn, feel the inner rein—it should not be necessary to carry your hand out to the side now—and, with your leg that is next to the fence drawn slightly back, leg him strongly into a canter. Ride down the corral parallel with the fence; two or three strides from the next corner rein the colt to a balanced halt. Again walk him into the corner, make him bend as he turns and put him into a canter again. Halt a couple of strides from the third corner and repeat. Do this for two or three circuits of the corral; then change directions and repeat, working him on the opposite lead.

Do this for two or three days. Then, when the colt is working smoothly, bending at every corner and taking the correct lead from a walk, try a large circle from a straightaway—a gothic figure 9. This should be done well away from the fences and without the aid of the corners. The trainer should begin with the lead which he knows the colt prefers. Let's assume this is the left.

Starting near one end of the corral and well out from the right-hand fence, put the colt into a fast walk. About midway down the enclosure, bend him slightly to the left and leg him into a canter, using the right leg strongly behind the girth. As the colt starts the circle at a canter, the trainer should keep his own legs firmly fixed, bending the colt with the inner rein and the outer leg. The canter should be slow, and leaning inward should be kept to an absolute minimum. After completing the circle, straighten out. Drop to a walk; pat the colt. Then repeat to the opposite side.

After the colt will circle correctly on either lead, get him to do it while following a serpentine course the length of the enclosure. It is in this exercise that the trainer really begins to put over the idea of *changing* leads on cue. With some colts it is wise to do a few serpentines first at the walk and the trot. The important things are that the trainer must make the colt bend freely from side to side as he turns and that he keeps the colt well up on the bit, never letting him slow down on the turns.

In starting the serpentine at the canter it is usually wise to strike off on the lead which the colt does *not* prefer. Then after he has made the first turn and the rider cues him to change, he can change to the lead he likes. After the second change, again back to the lead he likes, the colt is going well and should have a clear idea of what the rider expects.

Start the serpentine at a walk, and as the colt goes into the first turn leg him into a canter on the correct lead, being sure to make him bend his neck and spine. At the completion of the first semicircle, the trainer should rein into a walk for no more than two strides—one stride is better; then, bending the colt to the opposite side, push him into a canter on the other lead.

The trainer should make a special effort to hold the colt to a series of true semicircles and not make the mistake of zig-zagging from side to side or describing hairpin turns, which are more difficult. If at any time the colt fails to change to the correct lead, the trainer should stop him short, bawl him out; then try again. When the colt does change correctly, the trainer should keep the aids on while completing a semicircle, for in this way the colt will more quickly understand that he has done right.

When dropping to a walk for a stride or two just before reversing directions, the trainer should always bend the colt into the new arc *before* putting him again into the canter on the new lead. In other words, the stride or two at the walk marks the beginning of the new semicircle. If the trainer neglects this, he is, in effect, asking the colt to change leads on the straight, a feat for which he is not yet ready.

For the same reason, each semicircle should smoothly follow and blend into another; there should be no straight forward movement between arcs. In this manner, the trainer positions the colt to change leads by letting him start each semicircle while momentarily at the walk.

During this work the trainer should not, when halting or dropping to a walk, allow the colt to put in a few strides at the trot. Neither should he tolerate any trotting when demanding a canter. The colt must learn that when the rider asks for a canter on either lead, that and nothing else is exactly what he wants, and when he signals for a walk or a halt he does not want any trotting.

The next step is merely an advancement of the serpentine. The trainer should canter the colt in a full circle, check momentarily to a walk, bend the colt quickly in the opposite direction, apply the aids for a canter on the new lead, and do a second circle, completing a figure 8. If the preliminary work has been done thoroughly, there should be no difficulty.

When the colt will do several successive figure 8's well, bending supplely and responding promptly to the aids, he is ready to do the figure 8 at a canter from start to finish, with the change to a walk at the center of the figure omitted.

When approaching the center of the 8 where the colt will have to execute a flying change of leads, the trainer must remember to give a clear warning just before demanding the change. This warning consists of a slight check, just as when dropping to a walk; in other words, the trainer merely collects the colt a bit. Just as the colt's leading foreleg is about to strike the ground, the trainer feels the rein on the side to which the change will be made and reverses the leg aids. That is, he calls for the change of leads as the colt's hind legs rise into the air. When the colt does change, the rider should keep the leg aids on firmly until well into the second circle.

Since this schooling work is done at an easy canter, there should be a minimum of centrifugal force compelling horse and rider to lean inward. It might be well to mention here, however, that, later, when the work is done at speed in cross-country or competitive riding the rider should not use the outer stirrup as a brace when making a quick turn. To do so would prevent free use of the outer leg against the horse's ribs. It would also shift the rider's weight to the outside, thereby unbalancing the horse, and it would prevent the rider from using his weight as part of the cue or aid signaling for a turn. With a really well-schooled horse this is important; for a slight shift of the rider's weight is about all a finished mount needs to start him turning. When working at speed, horse and rider should be looking in the same direction and leaning together at the same angle. They should give the impression of aiming themselves as a single unit at a definite target or objective. Therefore, in fast turning and circling the rider should shift his weight onto the inner stirrup and the inner buttock. He should never have to depend on the outer stirrup as a prop.

The wise trainer will spend plenty of time on this figure 8 at the canter, never pushing the colt for speed, always concentrating on doing every phase of it right. Speed will come with practice;

it should be worked up to very gradually over a long period of time.

After the colt has mastered the figure 8 he should be taught to change leads on the straight. This is little more than repetition of the preceding work. The rider decides which lead he wants the colt to start on, collects him slightly so that the colt stands evenly balanced on all four legs, then applies the aids. After a certain number of strides the rider checks slightly, then reverses the aids just as the leading leg is about to strike the ground and while the hind legs are in the air. Eventually it should be possible to change leads at every other stride.

I am well aware of the fact that the method advocated here is not the way many stock horses are taught leads. One trainer who has written a book on leads advises pupils to teach a colt or green horse to take the correct lead by running the animal at headlong speed, thus forcing it to take the desired lead or risk falling on its face. In my opinion, not only is such teaching deleterious, but immature colts so treated would be better off dead. Personally, I prefer a calm, kindly treated horse that works without fear. Such a mount cannot be developed by strong-armed methods.

HALTING IN BALANCE; CALMNESS

These have been so strongly emphasized as requisites of intelligent schooling throughout this book that they need no repetition or elaboration here. It is worth mentioning here, however, that halting from a fast gallop in a quick, sliding stop, as required in stock horse competitions, belongs to a later stage of training. No rider should demand so strenuous an effort from a colt, even if the colt has the necessary finish to do it well. It is a rare colt that shows such finish, though many riders have no scruples about demanding such fast stops; but they cannot by any stretch of the imagination be called horsemen.

CHAPTER XXIV

Collection: The Double Bridle

*No method can aim at making great riders or
great horses; they are made in heaven.*
— *Vladimir S. Littauer*

A REALLY well-schooled horse can be ridden in a figure 8 or in a serpentine without the rider even touching his reins. The horse responds to slight, hardly visible shifts of the rider's weight, as well as to leg aids. For a really finished performance, this finesse in the use of the aids is essential, though it is rarely seen; but for ordinary riding it is not. Some horsemen attach a great deal of importance to weight cues, but I consider them of relatively minor importance, if for no other reason than that very few riders ever acquire the degree of skill to employ them properly—and that includes a majority of those who think them so important. Too often, even in dressage and so-called high school riding, weight cues are so exaggerated that both horse and rider look ridiculous and the performance becomes a travesty.

A good rider naturally leans the way his mount turns; he must do so in order to stay in balance even at slight speed. If he has any sense, he will also look the way he is turning, just as he requires his horse to do. I believe that any horseman by the time he has schooled a horse well enough for it to be sensitive to slight weight cues will have learned how to use his weight as he should. Therefore, all I have to say about weight influence is: When backing a horse, don't lean back; stay slightly forward so as to keep your weight off the horse's loins, or at least sit erect.

Some readers may wonder why I have said nothing yet about teaching a colt to neckrein. Neckreining is contrary to the basic

Plate 68. FINISHED NECKREINING, AT SPEED. This is what novice riders expect to do with a green colt; but fast, easy reining like this is the result of patient, gradual schooling that began with "plowlining."

Courtesy F. Albright

principle of teaching a colt to face the way he is going, particularly when turning sharply. To begin neckreining before the colt is confirmed in this fundamental would be to upset his natural balance and destroy his head carriage. Crossing the reins beneath the neck is no solution. It only destroys delicacy of touch on the mouth. As for the caveman method of "teaching" neckreining by walloping a colt on the side of the neck with a bat or a club, it may have worked fine on dinosaurs, but certainly has no place in horsemanship.

To teach a colt to neckrein but always to face the way he turns can be done only by employing the direct rein first. Later, the rider gradually begins to use the bearing rein lightly in co-ordination with the opening or leading rein. Finally the opening or leading rein effect is omitted.

It has been my observation that the reins of indirect opposition in front of and in rear of the withers mean virtually nothing to the average rider anywhere, and absolutely nothing to the average Western rider, who rarely even knows what they are. Such riders go on the theory that anyone who can find his way home in the dark, or who can stay on top of a horse, should be able to rein his mount in whichever direction he wishes without the aid of diagrams. Hence, we have the "practical" Western-style of neck-reining as the usual method of guiding a horse, a way of "steering" as crude as it is simple. However, any rider will get better results with less effort and trouble, and with a great deal more accuracy, if he knows and can apply the five standard rein effects (Figs. 8, 9, 10, 11, 12) in combination with precise leg aids before he begins to work his horse in a double bridle. For in the double bridle we put the finish on a snaffle colt, and no rider can get real finish merely by pulling or pushing one rein at a time.

Entirely too much importance, I believe, is attached to handling a horse with the reins. To speak in terms of "putting a good rein" on a horse is misleading. The rider's correct use of his legs is far more important — at least 70 per cent more important — than what he does with his hands. Whenever you meet a rider who styles himself a "reinsman," you will be talking with a man who does not understand the importance of legs. He will be strictly a bit-and-spur rider who will tell you all about how to set a colt's head, how to place his feet for a quick stop, and how to keep him "light" by pulling the reins in a certain way. Listen to him long enough and you will probably become a "reinsman" yourself, and be proud of it.

This pernicious misconception that lightness depends on the position of a horse's head is shared by many riders who do not proclaim themselves "reinsmen" or ever even heard the term. They talk of "shaping" a horse, of making him "bridle," of setting his head, of making him tuck his nose in, of forcing him to give to the reins — but never a word do they say about first suppling him. "The face," they proclaim, "should be perpendicular to the ground" — or at forty-five degrees or at sixty degrees or at some other angle which they have mathematically calculated as correct (or have been told is correct) — as if all horses had the same conformation. And these riders diligently try to achieve their ideal by a variety of means which demand more mechanical ingenuity than skill. They leave a colt checked with side reins for hours at a time in his stall, gradually shortening the reins as the animal

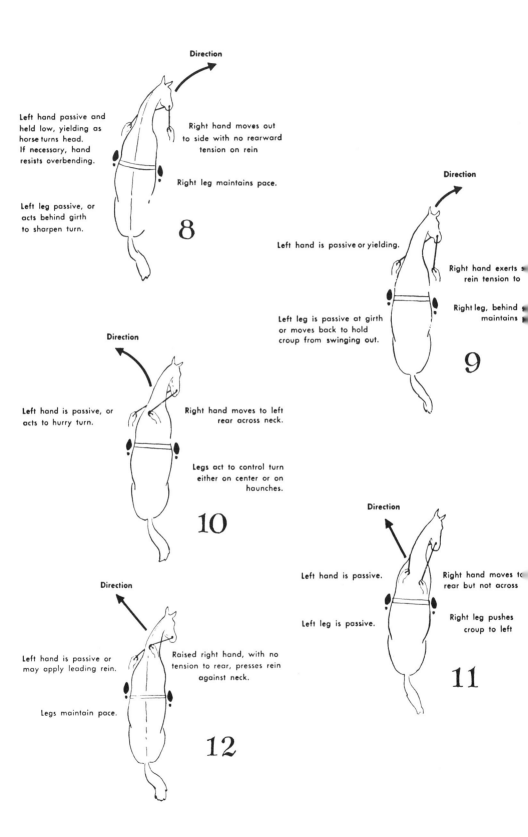

Direction

Left hand passive and
held low, yielding as
horse turns head.
If necessary, hand
resists overbending.

Right hand moves out
to side with no rearward
tension on rein

Right leg maintains pace.

Left leg passive, or
acts behind girth
to sharpen turn.

8

Direction

Left hand is passive or yielding.

Right hand exerts s
rein tension to

Left leg is passive at girth
or moves back to hold
croup from swinging out.

Right leg, behind
maintains

9

Direction

Left hand is passive, or
acts to hurry turn.

Right hand moves to left
rear across neck.

Legs act to control turn
either on center or on
haunches.

10

Direction

Left hand is passive.

Right hand moves to
rear but not across

Left leg is passive.

Right leg pushes
croup to left

11

Direction

Left hand is passive or
may apply leading rein.

Raised right hand, with no
tension to rear, presses rein
against neck.

Legs maintain pace.

12

learns not to hurt its own mouth. They longe and drive the colt in side reins. When mounted work begins they often find it expedient, and necessary, to complete the "mouthing lessons" by using draw reins, which enable them forcibly to pull the animal's head down with the least muscular exertion.

The natural result of such abuse is that the horse usually ends up with a beautifully bowed neck that is as stiff as iron just behind the poll where it should be most supple, a caved-in back, and a seminumb mouth that can best be described as no mouth at all, for the horse has learned either to lean on the bit with his head too low or to stay behind it. Invariably his natural gaits have been ruined; his strides are short and "hobbyhorsey," without elasticity or swing. He may win an oat bucket full of ribbons and trophies as a parade horse, a pleasure horse, or even as a "reined" horse; but to a real horseman he is a man-made caricature of what a riding horse—any kind of riding horse—ought to be. He is a wonderful example of misguided "training."

The errors that cause riders to produce such ill-trained horses always stem from one simple basic fact: they do not understand what true lightness is; they lack the wit to reflect that there is a vast difference between a horse that is merely light and one that is light in hand. They confuse mere lightness with *controlled* lightness and with collection. Somebody ought to tell these misguided amateurs that anyone can make a horse "light" simply by making the animal's mouth so sore that the horse will not only refuse to go up against the bit but will struggle against letting anyone even put a bit into its mouth.

A horse that is behind his bit is light; the trouble is that he is *too* light: he will not bear the slightest pressure of the bit. The same is true of a horse with a sore, hypersensitive mouth. But neither animal, in such a condition, can be truly collected. It first must be taught calmly to accept the bit, to reach for and mouth it softly without fear or flinching. The simple distinction between

Fig. 8.—Leading rein. For turn on large curve. *Fig. 9.*—Rein of direct opposition. For sharp turn while moving or for turn on center in place. *Fig. 10.*—Rein of indirect opposition in front of withers. For sharp turn while moving or for turn on center in place. *Fig. 11.*—Rein of indirect opposition in rear of withers. For left turn while moving. *Fig. 12.*—Neckrein. For simple change of direction without change of pace. *(Drawings by Larry Kumferman.)*

Plate 69. THE REIN EFFECTS.

A. Leading or opening rein, almost no tension to the rear.

B. Left rein of direct opposition, tension to rear.

C. Left rein of indirect opposition in rear of withers.

D. Right rein of indirect opposition in front of withers.

Photographs by Richard A. Lentz

mere lightness and true collection, though it is self-evident to any logical mind, is a truth which the head-setting fanatics appear to be incapable of understanding.

One of the most famous school riders in Europe several generations ago is said to have compared collection to a razor in the hands of a monkey. Few men know what true collection is, can recognize it when they see it, and can succeed in collecting a horse properly. Yet, cocksure in their ignorance, many of them will attempt to decide whether a horse is collected merely by observing the position of his head. They will try to get a horse balanced on his hocks not by moving his hind legs forward under him but by hauling him backward with the reins, apparently in the belief that his hocks will stay in place until they get him there, as if that is all that matters—and their only guide to getting him in "position" is the degree to which he tucks in his nose. This is on a par with trying to play polo with a croquet mallet.

Head position is a result of collection; not the cause of it. A horse that is truly collected is relaxed and supple from jaw to croup; he must be, for the slightest stiffness anywhere destroys collection—and I don't mean the full collection of a school horse; I mean any slightest degree of true collection, such as we should expect in a trail horse or a stock horse when the rider demands it. The position of the head, no matter what it is, has nothing whatever to do with *making* a horse truly light or collected. If the head is forced into a certain position, as is done by means of side reins and draw reins, the horse cannot be light in the sense that he can be truly collected; all the straps and gadgets in the world will not make him so, no matter into what position his head is forced, for the first essential before collection can be obtained is relaxation. Conformation determines the degree to which a horse *can* be collected, and it determines the best position of the head; but lightness does not result from, or depend on, head position. A trained horse, for example, can maintain lightness while extending his neck forward and downward in reaching for the bit, and continue to maintain it while he smoothly raises his head, coming back to the rider's hand. Some horses, having poorly attached, coarse heads on short thick necks, can be made light and can be fully collected to the maximum degree of their individual conformation without ever getting their faces nearly vertical. The same is true of ewe-necked horses. Their conformation makes it impossible for such animals to attain a theoretically "ideal" position without suffering physical discomfort or acute pain. If a trainer persists in forcing them to tuck their noses in too far, the unfortunate animals can obey only by arching their necks (or trying to do so, if they are ewe-necked)—which is a common major fault trainers permit and even unwittingly induce, and then are proud of having achieved.

Schooling can improve a horse's balance, but a trainer is never justified in attempting to alter an animal's natural conformation. It simply cannot be done.

A horse can be suppled and collected only when the trainer works on him as a single unit from croup to jaw, instead of trying to work on parts of him while neglecting other parts. And it cannot be overemphasized that the trainer must work from rear to front, never from front to rear. Even in the highest state of collection the horse must never lose impulsion; he must be always ready and able to extend fully and to move forward at speed. Merely inducing the horse to raise his head and tuck in his nose means nothing; at the same time the jaw must be soft, the poll supple, the hind legs must move forward and the croup must be lowered correspondingly. The rider must always drive with his legs before restraining with his hands. The horse's gaits must give the impression of freedom and elasticity; at all paces he must move with an obvious cadenced "swing," giving the impression of athletic litheness and agility. A well-schooled horse of only fair conformation will develop this pleasing and efficient way of moving more pronouncedly than a better horse that is poorly schooled and badly ridden.

In introducing a colt to the double bridle, be sure first of all that the bit fits; the curb should be neither too wide nor too narrow for the mouth. Before adjusting the curb chain, check to see whether the cheeks of the bit pinch the corners of the lips above the mouthpiece. If they do even though the bit is wide enough for the mouth, bend each headstall loop of the bit outward from about a quarter of an inch to half an inch. This will let them move forward without pinching the corners of the mouth when the reins are used.

Adjust the bridle with care. The snaffle should lie in the mouth above the curb. Be sure that the curb chain—which should be wide rather than narrow—lies flat in the chin groove. Many horsemen use the rule of thumb—or rule of finger—that the chain should be adjusted just loosely enough to allow two fingers to be inserted between it and the horse's chin. But since people's fingers differ in thickness, this is no more reliable a rule than the old method of adjusting the length of one's stirrups by measuring from the fingertips to the armpit. A better rule to observe is this: with reins slack, the shanks of the bit should be approximately parallel to the horse's lips; when the reins are drawn taut, the curb should take effect as the shanks of the bit reach a position between thirty and thirty-five degrees behind the line of the lips. If the shanks cannot be moved this far back without the curb first taking effect, the chain is too tight; if they move back farther, the chain is too loose.[1]

Give the colt time to become accustomed to having the bit as well as the snaffle in his mouth. For the first week or so ride entirely on the snaffle. A rider who is not used to handling four reins should make use of this period to become accustomed to them. He should hold all the reins in any way that suits him (Fig. 5), but should let the curb reins sag so loosely that he can use the snaffle without bringing the curb into play.

When the colt has become used to the new bridle and the rider is sure of his hands, the rider may gradually and very lightly begin to use the curb in conjunction with the snaffle. He should make a special point of keeping his hands as soft as possible, with fingers relaxed and wrists rounded and supple. It is sometimes helpful to think of the arms as if they were rubberbands, always ready to give and take elastically with the movements of the colt's head. Tension on the reins should be increased and decreased as a rule by merely closing and opening the fingers and, if necessary, by rounding and straightening the wrists, and always in co-ordination with action of the rider's legs.

One of the worst mistakes a rider can make is to think of the curb bit as an "emergency brake" with which to slow or halt a horse. If a colt is not perfectly controllable in a snaffle and has not learned to flex at least slightly, he is not ready to be worked in a double bridle, and putting one on him will never compensate for deficient basic training. The double bridle is only a means of refining and polishing what the colt should already have learned in the snaffle. A very few talented horsemen never use a double

---

[1]It is a fallacy to believe that a too loose curb chain or curb strap results in milder action of the bit. On the contrary, it can—depending on the design of the bit—result in discomfort to the horse. Having the chain too loose, however, is better than having it too tight; but the wise horseman will attend to adjusting it correctly.

Many Western horsemen think that a curb chain is more severe than a strap; but if properly made and correctly adjusted so that the links lie flat, it is not. It has the advantage of not becoming stretched with use, as a curb strap will.

bridle at all; their rare tact and genius enable them to produce brilliant high school horses while using only a snaffle. Anyone who believes that he is blessed with this sort of genius is welcome to prove it. His example should help to convince others that, when the schooling is done right, the double bridle is not necessary as an emergency brake. It is simply an aid to lesser mortals in achieving some degree of the brilliant finish which the geniuses can achieve without it.

The first thing the trainer should work on after he begins schooling in the double bridle is increased flexion of the jaw and of the poll, *without any loss of impulsion.* Many riders find it easiest when doing this to hold both snaffle reins in one hand and both curb reins in the other, with the hand holding the snaffle reins placed directly above the other. Thus, when a slight upward tension on the snaffle causes the colt to raise his head, as the rider's legs drive him forward, the curb can be used with a horizontal or downward effect to induce him to drop his nose. If he tucks in a little too far or tries to lower his head, the rider gives with the curb and checks the downward movement with upward tension on the snaffle. Of course, the same effect can be had when the rider is holding the reins any other way he prefers, but for many riders this way of holding the reins works best.

The trainer should always keep the horse moving forward freely at a walk or at a slow trot when demanding greater flexion than the colt was accustomed to in the snaffle alone. He should never try at first to obtain flexion with the colt standing still — though that will be easy to do eventually. Only a very skilled, experienced horseman can mobilize the haunches to a degree exactly commensurate with the degree of flexion obtained when the horse is standing; and if this is not done precisely, either the cardinal rule that impulsion must be maintained is violated or the impulse produced by the rider's legs outweighs the influence of his hands with the result that the colt moves forward insufficiently flexed.[2]

---

[2]Some horsemen prefer to begin teaching jaw and poll as well as lateral flexions while on foot. I do not regard this as either necessary or desirable with a colt brought along according to the system which this book offers. However, some readers may find the method helpful in teaching rudimentary flexions to mature horses that have never been properly suppled. This is how to go about it:

The trainer, standing at the horse's left shoulder, grasps both snaffle reins in his left hand and the curb reins in his right about eight inches from the bits. Moving the left hand out ahead of the horse's muzzle, he starts the animal walking forward. As they move along, the trainer changes the tension on the snaffle reins upward as

With naturally high-headed horses this primary work in the double bridle is relatively easy; in fact, with some types of horses, notably Arabians and Saddlebreds, the trainer sometimes has to be alert not to overwork the snaffle with an upward tension or he will find himself, as the saying goes, with the horse's head in his lap. But with low-headed horses the head must be elevated to its highest *natural* position before the curb is used to bring in the muzzle. Otherwise, the trainer will fail to get flexion at the poll; he will instead teach the horse merely to arch its neck and get behind the bit.

These first attempts at increased flexions in the double bridle should be very brief, no more than a few minutes at a time. The trainer should keep in mind that the job must be done very gradually. Being ridden in the snaffle should have strengthened the young horse's neck muscles considerably so that he has a higher head carriage now than he had in the beginning; but he still needs time and practice in order to respond to the trainer's demands for more collection now. A little of this work at a time goes a long way. The horse must never be tired or made fretful; either is a sure sign that the trainer is overdoing the work or is doing something wrong.

As a rule, with horses to be used for ordinary outdoor work, the trainer should not try to obtain a high degree of collection, such as would be desirable in a horse destined for specialized exhibition work—a school horse. The trainer's chief concern should be to get the horse to work with gradually increased lightness until the reins can "float," regardless of the degree of collection. When the trainer has the horse working like this, "off the bit," increasing the degree of collection is simple, if the rider wants to do it.

---

well as forward. With gentle little jerks he not only keeps the horse moving but induces it to elevate its head. When the animal's muzzle is about as high as its withers, the trainer begins to vibrate the curb reins in the same way, but with tension to the rear and slightly upward in an effort to induce the horse to open its mouth, relax the lower jaw, and flex slightly at the poll. The instant the horse responds even a very little, the trainer slacks the reins and shows approval. However, the oftener the exercise is repeated, the longer should the trainer try to make the horse maintain lightness. The horse must yield its jaw straight downward, not with any yawing to one side or the other, for yawing is evidence that the jaw has not relaxed, hence there is no lightness.

This exercise should never be attempted when the horse is standing still. At all times the trainer must keep the horse moving and keep the animal's head high with his left hand while inducing flexion with the right.

But it should not be attempted until the horse works off the bit at all gaits, with the reins floating. Otherwise, the trainer risks producing short, choppy gaits.

It is impossible for anyone to tell another exactly how to collect a horse properly so that the recipient of the advice and instructions can then proceed immediately to do it as easily as he would assemble or learn to operate a mechanical gadget with the aid of a booklet of instructions and diagrams. The accomplishment can be the result of not only knowing what to do and how to do it but from much persevering practice in applying that knowledge and acquiring a "feel" of horses so that when something goes wrong the rider instantly knows it and knows *what* is wrong and *why*. Neither one who is merely a reader nor one who is only a rider can fully acquire this experience; he must be a reader who rides much or a rider who is willing to study and to ponder. There is no other way to success. All really good horsemen are students. The finest horsemen never cease to be.

During this stage each schooling session should include some time spent rehearsing everything that the young horse learned to do while ridden only in the snaffle. These things should never be practiced in any set routine; the trainer should mix them to suit his fancy. Only in this way can the horse's prompt obedience at all times be confirmed.

The brief periods devoted to work at collected paces should be followed by frequent "intermissions" during which the young horse is allowed to relax with the reins loose. Each schooling session should be followed by cross-country riding during which the trainer should let the horse go mostly on loose reins and let him do some galloping over varied terrain, particularly over reasonably rough, uphill-and-down ground.

In this work in the double bridle the trainer should make a point of gradually diminishing the aids, getting the horse to respond to rein and leg cues as light as possible. In no other way can a young horse be improved. A rider can change bits as often as he pleases; he can put a hackamore on a bridle horse "to rest his mouth" or a bridle on a hackamore horse "to make him work better." But nothing will do any lasting good, nothing will improve a colt or keep a finished horse working well, except skillful application of the aids, gradually diminished.

The trainer should work the horse in responding to the five rein effects. These help greatly in making the horse handle better when eventually he will be ridden in a curb bit only. If more

Western horses were schooled in this way, they would neckrein better.

The trainer should spend considerable time, but only in short periods, working the horse on the following exercises:

1. The half-pass, or diagonal side step, at walk, trot, and canter. This is a good test of the horse's leg obedience. The rider starts the horse straight forward at a collected walk. When the horse has moved about ten or fifteen yards with good impulsion, the rider cues him to move diagonally to one side while continuing to move ahead with his body parallel to the original forward direction. In effect, the horse moves obliquely along one branch of an imaginary X while facing to the front. To side-step from left to right, the rider presses the horse's hindquarters to the right by using his left leg strongly behind the girth; at the same time he moves the animal's forehand to the right by shifting both hands slightly in that direction, with a little extra tension on the right rein to turn the horse's head very slightly in the direction of movement. The rider should sit centrally in the saddle, leaning to neither side, but he may put a little extra weight on the outer stirrup (the one away from the direction of movement) to lessen the load on the horse's legs that have to work harder in this movement.

In teaching this movement the rider should be satisfied if the horse at first takes only two or three steps sidewise while continuing to move ahead. The trainer should concentrate on keeping the horse *straight*, except for the slight inclination of the head toward the direction of movement. The horse's foreleg and hind leg away from the movement should each cross in front of its opposite member.[3] To side-step left reverse the aids.

When the horse side-steps well to either side the trainer should try for more precision by controlling the exact direction and the number of steps to each side and smoothly changing from left to right and vice versa. At first he can make the lesson easier for the horse by allowing the animal to move straight forward for a few strides between changes—for example, six steps to the left, three steps straight ahead, eight steps to the right. Later the changes can be made with the straight-forward movement omitted. At the canter this means a flying change of leads.

If the horse has difficulty understanding or carrying out this exercise, the trainer has not properly taught the elementary les-

---

[3] This simple exercise should not be confused with the school movement known as "two tracks." Though similar, they are not identical.

sons in leg obedience or is using his legs and hands wrongly.

If the trainer desires, he can also teach the full pass, in which the horse while facing to the front moves directly sidewise without advancing at all. This exercise tests the horse's obedience and the rider's precision in applying the aids. It is of practical value in opening gates. If the trainer attempts it, he must remember that, even though the horse does not move forward, nevertheless he must have good impulsion and be well balanced with his hocks under him. This makes correct execution of the movement much more difficult than it appears to be. Many inexperienced riders who think that their horses side-pass well are astonished when told that their mounts do the movement incorrectly: they cross each foot behind the opposite foot. This proof of lack of impulsion makes the exercise worse than useless. The feet should always cross over toward the front.

2. Turns on the hocks in place. In this movement the horse pivots around his inner hind foot. It looks deceptively easy to do, but the first few attempts to do it correctly reveal the deception. It is a real test not only of the horse's obedience but of the rider's co-ordination in using his hands and legs. If the rider uses either hand or either leg too strongly or too mildly and fails instantly to correct the error, the horse immediately gets out of position and the rider has to begin all over.

The easiest way to set about teaching this turn on the hocks is to back the horse into a corner of a corral with his hindquarters only a few inches from the two walls that form a right angle. If the horse is thus placed with his body parallel to the fence on, say, the rider's right, the animal can turn only to the left, and he cannot back up without being halted by the fence behind him. Having placed the animal in this position, the rider should close both legs to collect the horse. Then with the right leg acting slightly ahead of the cinch and the right rein pressing against the side of the neck in conjunction with a slight direct tension on the left rein, the rider induces his mount to take one side step to the left with his forelegs only, starting to pivot around the haunches. If the horse tries to move his hindquarters to the left, the rider must check the movement with his left leg. (The fence on the right side will prevent any movement in that direction.) As the horse starts the first step around to the left, the rider should see to it that the animal turns his head and neck out of line in the direction of the turn only in the slightest degree. He must use the right rein to check any attempt to overbend.

When the horse has taken just one step in the desired direction, the rider must show his approval by relaxing all aids immediately. Then he collects the horse again and applies the same aids, demanding a second step. Each step should be a separate and distinct part of the entire movement, with at least a momentary pause between steps. Under no circumstances should the trainer make any attempt to hurry the horse or to force him around by pulling. The horse must remain relaxed and calm, with his lower jaw and his poll soft and yielding. Otherwise, the exercise has no value for what it is intended to be—the first step in teaching the horse the elements of the balanced quick set and turn and the set and spin.

At each step the rider should try to feel whether the horse has moved his inner hind foot out of position. This leg—the left one when turning left, the right when turning right—is the pivot point of the turn. Obviously, it cannot remain glued to the ground; it must revolve as the horse turns, but only on one spot. Otherwise the horse will form the habit of moving his hindquarters in the turn instead of pivoting on them.

As the horse catches onto the idea and keeps that pivot foot in place, the trainer can turn him, step by step, ninety degrees until his body is parallel with the left-hand fence. If not rushed and if allowed to pause between steps, the horse will learn to take some weight off his pivot leg so that the foot can turn with the movement without being lifted out of position.

When the horse will easily and smoothly turn 90 degrees to either side, the trainer should move out of the corner, place the horse with his tail close to the fence out near the middle of the corral and gradually get a half-turn of 180 degrees. The next step, of course, is to execute the half-turn near the center of the corral without the help of the fence.

A full circle on the hocks with the pivot foot remaining in place requires a great deal of patient practice, and is worth the trouble only if the trainer is a perfectionist with plenty of time on his hands. It is an accomplishment which can quite safely be skipped.

3. Turns on the hocks in motion follow logically from the turns in place. They are the second step in conditioning the horse for the fast set and turn, or the quick stop and rollback on the hocks, and finally the fast set and spin. Actually, these turns on the hindquarters—done first at the walk, then at the trot, and finally at the lope—are slow stops and rollbacks, for the horse must learn

to do them exactly as he will be expected to perform the quick stop and turn and the spin. The chief differences are that at this stage the trainer at first demands only a quarter-turn at a time so that the horse completes the full half-turn of 180 degrees in two movements, and that the trainer ignores speed and strives only for perfection of execution, with the horse working calmly and softly and at all times in perfect balance, well collected. Not until the horse has learned to work this way at slow paces and responds almost automatically to the aids does the trainer try to speed up the turns. By that time he won't have to worry about speed; it will come naturally as the lope is stepped up to a fast gallop.

The trainer starts the horse at a collected walk, moving down the corral close to and parallel with one fence on the side *away from* which he intends to turn; that is, for a turn to the right the fence should be on the rider's left. As the horse takes his weight off the right hind leg preparatory to moving the leg forward for another stride, the rider checks him by closing both legs and momentarily feeling the right snaffle rein. As the horse halts, head turned almost imperceptibly to the right, the trainer instantly applies the aids for a 90-degree turn away from the fence. The aids are the same as for a turn on the hocks in position, but the rider must apply them more strongly, particularly the leg aids; for now he wants not merely a single step to the right but a half-turn pivot on the hocks, with the forelegs lifted off the ground; hence, the horse must be well collected. As the horse swings around, the rider relaxes the aids; but the instant the forefeet return to the ground as the horse completes the 90-degree turn, the rider applies the aids again, demanding another half-turn immediately. Thus, the horse completes the full turn in two separate movements, finishing headed back toward the starting point. The rider should immediately slack the reins and leg the horse into an easy gallop—not a fast run—on the correct lead for five or six strides before slowing to a halt.[4]

In this work on the hock turn the trainer will do well to keep several things in mind:

He should never attempt to pull the horse around or to force him. The horse must remain supple and collected. It is impossible

[4]The correct lead after a turn to the right is, obviously, the right lead, and vice versa. Later, the trainer should demand either lead, as he prefers, regardless of the direction of the turn.

to teach a horse to turn or spin lightly by yanking the reins or otherwise trying to force him. The horse must co-operate willingly. If he has been properly handled up to this stage of the training, he will; he will obey the rider's hands and legs. The trainer has only to give the position; it is for the horse to execute the movement.

Turning the horse into the fence instead of away from it should no longer be necessary. This is a crude, workable way of handling raw colts and some spoiled horses; it is of aid to a breaker who must turn out a string of mounts fit to be ridden in the shortest time. But it certainly should not be necessary in working a horse fit to wear a double bridle. The horse now should turn on his hocks because the rider has him collected and disciplined; not because an obstacle compels him to do so. Even working the horse near the fence should not be necessary, if the rider uses his hands and legs with precision. This, however, is something all riders don't always succeed in doing; hence, using the fence as a "backstop" is, as a rule, a wise precaution at first.

If at first the horse responds to the aids with a partial turn of less than 90 degrees, the trainer should be satisfied; he need only repeat the aids until the horse has made a full turn. If the horse swings around more than a half-turn, the trainer can be happy; it is a good sign that the full turn of 180 degrees in one movement will come easily. The important thing for the trainer to concentrate on is getting the horse to come around on his hocks with his forefeet off the ground. Once the horse understands that that is the main idea, he will quickly learn with practice to complete a full turn in one swinging movement.

Success depends almost entirely on the rider's skillfull co-ordination of his legs and hands.

When a rider sets out to teach this turn on the hocks by galloping a colt, then pulling him up short, turning him into the fence and "hitting him a lick" or spurring him to hurry the turn and scaring him to jump out back the way he came, it is little wonder that so many horses sour on the lesson quickly. From the animal's viewpoint, he is being "punished" — actually, abused — for no reason whatever. The only thing he learns from the lesson is that it's hell to be a horse. Eventually, if the rider uses moderation, the horse does build up the habit of stopping and turning quickly; but is this the way the trainer himself would like to be taught? Is it the way *you* would? Is it the kind of treatment you expect your children to take in school? I am not sentimental about horses, nor do I confuse them with children; but experience has convinced me that the most efficient way to get the best out of the average horse is to shun roughness and force. Treat a horse as you would like to be treated in his place.

Working up to the quick stop and turn, the rollback on the hocks and the spin is a simple matter when the basic movements are taught and practiced first at the turn in place, then at the walk, the trot, and finally at the lope. As long as the trainer never tries to work faster than the horse's progress indicates he is ready to be worked, there is little danger of the horse becoming sour.

Until the horse has mastered a smooth, prompt full turn on the hocks from a walk, he should always, as he completes a turn, be legged into a lope back the way he came. Even if he begins to anticipate the jump-off a little, the trainer may overlook it— temporarily. Once the horse has mastered the lesson, however, the trainer must check anticipation. He must make the horse wait for the leg pressure. Only in this way can he confirm discipline, by deliberately emphasizing that he, not the horse, is the boss. The rider gives the orders; it is for the horse to obey them.

Besides, the next step after the full turn is the spin. This cannot be done efficiently if the horse is allowed to acquire the habit of always jumping out after turning.

The spin is simply two or three full turns put together. It is taught exactly as the two half-turns of 90 degrees each were put together to make one full turn. After having turned the horse once, the rider relaxes the aids until the horse's forefeet return to the ground; then he turns him again, completing a full circle. When the spin is added to the set and turn, the horse makes three full turns, or a circle and a half, before jumping out back toward his starting point.

In this work the trainer must be careful that he, not the horse, controls the pace. At this stage high-strung horses especially are inclined to try to work too fast. The trainer certainly should not try to slow down the speed of the turns and spins, but he must see to it that the horse works smoothly, neatly, without getting out of position or becoming unbalanced and heavy. Form should never be sacrificed to speed. Form makes speed. A young horse permitted to work too fast before he is ready for it loses collection and lightness, and his stops become rough and bouncy. When this happens it is always the trainer's fault.

Stopping short and turning and spinning are hard work; each puts considerable strain on a horse's muscles and tendons. Therefore, a young horse in particular should not be worked at these exercises every day or more than for a few minutes at a time in any one day. He should *never* be worked at them when he is tired. The more he improves, the less he should be asked to demonstrate his new skill. If not rushed, once he is working right he will continue to improve. The wise trainer will do most of his schooling at a walk and a trot and an easy lope. He will strive always for collection, balance, precision, with lightly "floating" reins.

When riding out across country now the trainer need not use the double bridle any more. He may go back to the snaffle or bit the horse in a mild curb, whichever he prefers, or whichever the horse seems to favor. Riding across country or working stock, the rider should give the horse a long rein and, as much as practicable, let him go on his own.

No rider should ever let himself become a horsy scholastic, a pedant of the schooling ring; there is no greater bore, and only a bridlepath cowboy is more obnoxious. Schooling should never be an end in itself; to make it an end is as impractical as pondering how many angels can stand on the point of a needle. Schooling is only a means to an end—the making of a good riding horse and the development of a skilled horseman.

CHAPTER XXV

Spoiled Horses

But there is one rule to be inviolably observed above all others; that is, never approach a horse in a passion; for anger never thinks of consequences, and forces us to do what we afterwards repent.

— Xenophon

QUITE likely some of my sterner readers by this time, I suspect, may have formed the impression that because I advocate training horses gradually and by gentle means I am a bit on the soft side. I can imagine others muttering as they read, "Your system may be fine for anyone who can begin schooling a weanling colt, but what about horses like *mine?* He was three years old when I bought him and wasn't even halterbroke—" or, "—he was ten years old when I got him and had a mouth of iron. He wouldn't stand to be mounted. When I did get on, he reared up—" and so forth and so on.

When I say, however, that I believe in treating a horse as I, if our positions were reversed, should like to be treated, I am not implying that if I acted like a spoiled brat I should not expect to be treated exactly as a spoiled brat deserves.

Writing about spoiled horses is difficult because generalities are inadequate. Every spoiled horse is a special "case" that calls for special treatment; for while many horses develop identical or similar vices, they all do not develop them for the same reasons. Discovering reasons why a horse has developed a bad habit and persists in it is the key to reforming him. To try to eradicate effects is a waste of time. The trainer must figure out the cause of the vice. Once he eliminates that, the effect will disappear. This is simple logic, yet it is usually ignored.

Reforming spoiled horses requires time and patience. In my opinion, the world is so full of good horses that bothering with

337

a badly spoiled one is not worth while except under the following conditions: when the horse is of excellent quality or exceptional potential ability, too good an animal to get rid of or destroy; when the owner finds it economically inconvenient to get rid of the animal at a loss and replace him with a "good" one; when the trainer has both the time and the facilities to effect a cure and, usually, has no objection to taking some risk of personal injury.

I regard either the first or the second condition as essential, and so is the first part of the third condition—having the time and the facilities—as well as considerable experience. Only the willingness to risk possible injury is a matter of personal choice.

Many horses are so badly schooled that from their own points of view their vices are their virtues. With very few exceptions, spoiled horses are ones that have been so badly mishandled that they have developed their bad habits either while trying to carry out demands which bumbling trainers failed to make them clearly understand or in sheer self-defense against abuses inflicted on them by poor or cruel riders.

One exception to this rule is the pampered pet horse, the spoiled brat that has been allowed by an overindulgent owner to have his own way too much. This type of brute is a most obnoxious pain in the neck. However, we need waste little attention on him. All the pampered pet needs are a few lessons on the facts of life or the horse's place in the barn, and a new owner.

The herdbound horse—who is far commoner than most people realize—often presents a quite serious problem to the amateur owner. This vice is merely a natural, uncurbed development of a horse's gregarious instinct. We cannot justly blame a horse for following his natural instinct to stay with his own kind, but the oftener the horse is permitted to get away with this rebellion the more stubborn he becomes. Eventually we find ourselves with a confirmed rogue on our hands, a horse that is useless for anything but consuming feed. He can be ridden nowhere except in company without a fight. Some such herdbound horses refuse even to leave their stable alone. Coaxing and caressing them or feeding them tidbits is a waste of time. What they need is a convincing lesson that vice doesn't pay.

The most overwhelming argument to which there can be no equine back talk, in my opinion, is the "running W" trip-rope. With the running W the trainer can pull a horse's feet from under him at the first hint of rebellion and keep the animal down as long as he wishes. Nothing takes the conceit out of a horse as quickly and as thoroughly as tumbling him over on his side and forcing him to lie with his head pulled around toward his tail while he ponders the error of his ways.

Throwing a horse with the running W is simple. All one needs are a training surcingle or a saddle, a pair of hobbles with rings or D's, and some rope. The trainer can handle the rope either from the ground or from the saddle.

In reforming a barn-sour or herdbound horse with the W rig, the trainer urges the horse away from the stable or from his companions; choosing his own "battleground," he invites the horse to rebel. The instant the animal tries to turn back, the trainer, pulling the rope attached to the foreleg hobbles, tumbles the horse to his knees. If the horse's struggles don't cause him to fall over on his side, the trainer, holding the rope taut, can walk up and easily push him over with one hand.

Often it isn't necessary to throw the horse flat. Holding him on his knees may be sufficient. But if, when he is let up, he balks at going forward again, the trainer should trip him immediately and this time not only hold him down flat but pull his head around and tie it short by the halter to the cinch or bellyband. After five or ten minutes of having his neck held in this uncomfortable position, the average horse will be a lot meeker when the trainer lets him get up.

Very rarely a really stubborn rogue will refuse to struggle at all. He simply lies relaxed, determined to wait until he is let up; he has no intention of being reformed. He is out to wear down the trainer's patience. However, if the trainer keeps him down long enough with his head pulled around and tied short to the cinch or bellyband, the horse will lose his determination. He will finally try to get up, probably with a lot of grunting and groaning. When the trainer does let him up, he should immediately urge the horse to obey the original order, to go where he is driven or ridden. If the horse again refuses — which is unlikely — the trainer should repeat the whole procedure, and keep on repeating it until the horse gives in. The horse *must* learn to submit to control. As long as he clings to the notion that he is the boss, he is useless. The trainer must be willing to stay with him, even if the battle takes all day. But hardly one horse in a thousand will be this stubborn.

As a rule, two or three tumbles will make most horses see the light. Sometimes once is enough. The running W is powerful

medicine because it attacks a horse at one of his weakest points—
his instinctive terror of being deprived of his power to flee.

For this reason the trainer should use the trip-rope judiciously.
If the lesson is overdone, prolonged after a horse has surrendered,
it might make the animal afraid to move for fear of being thrown
again.

The trainer should, of course, take precautions to protect the
horse's knees. If kneepads are not used, the "battleground" should
be preferably a well-grassed field, or plowed ground, or deep sand;
any place where the ground is soft.

The horse should be given a daily lesson—or preferably two or
three brief lessons every day—on the longe line for at least a week
until he is confirmed in going forward promptly in response to
oral commands and the whip. Then the trainer should switch to
ground driving further to confirm the animal's obedience. The
trainer should stress frequent turning and halting in response to
the reins and, above all, alacrity in moving to the front; but he
should avoid even the suggestion of reining back—there will be
plenty of time for that later.

The horse should be longed and, if necessary, driven with the
running-W rig on so that at the least hint of rebellion the trainer
can immediately enforce discipline, but as soon as the horse shows
that he has submitted the rig should be removed. After the longe
work, it may not even be necessary to use it in the ground driving.

After the horse submits to being ridden or driven wherever
the trainer wishes him to go, he should be given a thorough
course of schooling, with particular emphasis on obedience to
the rider's legs. For at least a month, preferably longer, he should
be ridden alone; never in company. At the end of a ride, the trainer
should make a point of riding the horse past the barn once or
twice. After dismounting, the trainer should not unsaddle or turn
the horse into its stall. Put a halter on him, then let him stand
tied for an hour or so with the saddle still on. The horse will soon
learn that returning to the stable does not mean that he will immediately get back into his comfortable stall or be turned loose
with his pals.

Not until the horse seems to be completely cured of his disobedience should the trainer ride him in company; even then,
that should be approached gradually. The trainer should ride the
horse within sight of other animals, but a good distance away from
them. If the horse should show any signs of becoming excited or

getting out of hand, the trainer should turn him around and ride him, forcibly if necessary, away from the other horses.

Should the horse at any time rebel by rearing, balking, or whirling around, the trainer need not be helpless even if he does not have the running-W rig on his mount. He should take hold of one rein close to the bit and pull the horse's head around as far as he can get it—if necessary, he can dally the rein around the saddle horn. Then, using his legs vigorously, he should force the horse to spin, chasing his tail like a dog. After three or four circles he can let the horse straighten out, being careful to release the rein when the horse is facing away from the direction in which he tried to rush.

Firmness and patience will enable a trainer to cure almost any herdbound or barn-sour horse, but he must make a point of developing the habit of obedience in the animal by enforcing the same demands repeatedly.

A confirmed rearer is dangerous to ride. Even when he has no intention of throwing himself—and few rearers do—there is always the likely chance that he will lose his balance and fall on the rider.

Rearers are man-made, usually by riders with heavy hands. It is simple enough to advise such a rider, "Give the horse more rein. Quit tight-reining him." This, however, is somewhat like telling a drowning man, "Don't sink! Swim!" For riding with a long rein is the one thing most heavy-handed riders cannot, or will not, do. Heavy hands are an effect of the rider's state of mind just as much as they are a cause of spoiled horses. Nobody *wants* to be heavy-handed; the worst offenders are invariably the least aware of their own fault. Very few of them are deliberately brutal. Most of them have very little real understanding of horses. Tight-rein riders are usually nervous on horseback. They may wear a brave front, but at heart they are timid; they lack self-confidence in handling horses. That is why they cannot cultivate light hands. When mounted on a frisky, free-going horse, they are afraid to "let him go." They don't mean to hurt the horse; they just want to be sure that he doesn't "get away from them."

An experienced horseman can often recognize a potential rearer before the animal develops its vice. There are plenty of signs by which to forecast the coming events. One of them is a horse's habit of fretfully tossing its head in resistance to the bit. Another is boring on the bit. From either of these bad habits to rearing is often only a step. Sudden shying and whipping around is another indication of a potential rearer. So is balking. When the rider who has been caught napping by these abrupt maneuvers tries to make the horse obey, he quite often finds himself with a rearer under him. If he jumps off to escape a possible backfall—as timid riders usually do—that is all the horse needs to make him realize that by rearing he can escape the rider's discipline.

A rearer has never been confirmed in obedience to the rider's legs. A horse that is on the bit and obeys the legs cannot rear unless the rider compels him to.

It is a common fallacy that a rearer can be cured by being ridden in a tight tiedown that cramps his head freedom. The fact that a horse is temporarily prevented from rearing does not mean that he won't rear when later he is able to do so. The all-important first step in curing a horse of any vice is to find an answer to the questions: *Why* does he do this? What makes him *want* to rear?

Aside from the heavy-handed rider who is the principal cause of rearers, a horse develops the habit of rearing for any of the following reasons:

> Stubborn temper
> Too severe a bit
> Impetuousness, rebellion against restraint
> Being behind the bit or over the bit
> Intimidation of the rider
> Deliberate design to fall backward and crush the rider

Let's consider these reasons and see what can be done to eliminate them.

Pure temper, in spite of the sock-'em-and-spur-'em *caballeros*, is rare. When it does occur, the rider is usually the reason for it. Temper shows itself in two forms: hotheaded resentment of abuse or of demands by the rider which the horse cannot understand or carry out; and sullen, pigheaded, calculated stubbornness.

The first form of temper is characteristic of hot-blooded, spirited horses, quick to resent rough treatment which a coldblood might patiently endure. The second form, sullen pigheadedness, is typical of low-spirited "cowardly" nags that are inclined to be always unreliable and treacherous, and of exceptionally intelligent, cunning horses which have learned that they can successfully flout human authority. This last type of brute includes most of the confirmed rogues and "unbreakable" outlaws, and they are the most difficult of all to deal with.

The explosive tantrum of a high-spirited horse is always the fault of the rider. Often it is an unintentional fault caused by ignorance or momentary thoughtlessness, but much oftener it is the result of a rider's losing his temper and trying to show his "mastery" over the horse. Whichever the cause is, the result is the same: the horse is provoked into a fight, and wins.

The remedy is obvious; it has been stressed throughout this book: don't start a fight. Go slowly, one small step at a time. If you discover belatedly that you have done something that excites the horse, stop it instantly. Do something else. Get the horse's mind off the unpleasantness which aroused his resentment. Later, after he has cooled down, you can go back to the original lesson.

This deliberate avoidance of a fight is one of the most difficult lessons of horsemastership for many riders to learn. Even when they know it, they do not always practice it. It is human nature to blow a fuse when a horse acts "contrary." Besides, haven't we all heard from more experienced horsemen, "If you get into a fight, you've got to win, show the horse who's boss. Otherwise he'll be spoiled forever." But this, of course, is nonsense, just a convenient rationalization of the human fault of losing one's temper and venting our exasperation on the animal that has dared to flout us. If the idea were correct, then logically we must admit that no horse with any bad habit can ever be reformed, for in acquiring the habit he must have outwitted and defeated somebody.

Sulky horses that display sullen, determined temper are usually fainthearted, treacherous, and often thickheaded. Most of them are hardly worth the trouble of reforming; even when forced to obey, they remain always nags at heart. The others of this type, the ones that are not thickheaded, are the intelligentsia of the equine world. They often show a "bump" between the eyes, slightly bulging foreheads indicating unusual braininess. They can be subdued, but they can never be made reliable. Fortunately, these equine Daniel Websters are rather rare. Don't ever buy one, or even accept one as a gift.

About the only way to deal with this type of rogue is to work him over thoroughly with the running W. The trainer should deliberately encourage the horse to rear, then pull his feet from under him and keep him down with his head pulled around to the girth long enough to let him add up the score.

A horse that rears because he is overbitted presents the same problem as one that rears to escape a rider's heavy hands. The solution is to ride him in a mild bit or, for a while, in a hackamore. The idea is not only to give his mouth a rest but to let him know that he no longer need fear having his mouth hurt. During this period of several months in a snaffle or hackamore the trainer should confirm the horse in obedience to the leg aids.

Impetuous free-going horses often resent being made to stand while other horses are going away from them almost as much as herdbound animals. As a rule they start their shenanigans only when warmed up and excited. They are quite willing to move in any direction; the trouble is that they want to ramble regardless of the rider's desire to stay in one spot. This type of spirited horse can easily be converted into a rearer merely by the rider's trying to rein him in. An effective way of impressing on him the idea that he is to stay where he is as long as the rider wishes him to is for the trainer to go down one rein, pull his head around, and force him to chase his tail. The trainer should try to do this before the horse goes up on his hind legs; then let him straighten out, catch him with the other rein, and spin him in the opposite direction. If the horse first succeeds in rearing, the trainer should not think of quitting the saddle for fear of a backfall; for such impetuous rearers seldom go up nearly vertical and almost always have their hind legs well placed under them, for their purpose in rearing is to escape restraint so that they can be free to run. As soon as the horse comes down, the trainer should grab a rein close to the bit and spin him three or four turns in each direction.

A horse that stays behind or goes over the bit is out of control. His persistent efforts to evade the bit shift more and more of his weight onto the hindquarters until rearing becomes a natural, almost inevitable, consequence. This form of rearing is really dangerous. Horses with extremely sensitive mouths or ones that have had their bars injured are prone to this form of evasion. If the mouth is sore, the trainer should substitute a hackamore for a bridle. If the bars are sound, the horse can be ridden in a snaffle or a thick bar bit.

Probably the simplest way to get this kind of horse to shift his weight forward and to learn obedience to the rider's legs is to make him practice turns on the forehand. Most such rearers respond to this exercise very quickly. Riding the horse in circles on two tracks—that is, with the hindquarters ranged outward so that the hind legs make a larger circle than the forelegs—has the same beneficial effect; the only times when these exercises are beneficial, in my opinion.

Light-mouthed horses of this type should always be ridden in very mild bits and only by riders with firm seats and good hands.

Horses that rear in order to intimidate their riders and thus get their own way almost always learn the trick by accident; and, I believe, without exception, they learn the trick under timid riders. A common way this happens, for example, is that the rider gives the horse a jerk in the mouth. The horse rears or half-rears and the rider slips his feet from the stirrups to be ready to jump clear of a possible backfall. Coming down, the horse plunges forward or bucks or whirls. The rider, jarred loose, falls off. The horse gallops off in delight, thinking, "How easy! Maybe I've got something here." Perhaps the horse frolics back to his stable; or probably the rider, if he catches his mount, is hesitant about getting back on; or if he does remount, he is jittery, and the horse instantly knows it. The next time the horse tries his new stunt, even if he doesn't throw the rider or bluff him into jumping off, he succeeds in cutting some fancy didos before the scared rider can get him under control—if he does regain control at all. Thus, the horse has learned that he can disobey with impunity; all he has to do is rear.

All a horse of this type needs is a new rider who isn't afraid of him, one who understands that all such bullying rearers are bluffs. If ever they topple over it is by accident. They don't want to fall for the same reason that they would not want to be tripped by a running-W rig: it is contrary to their instinct of self-preservation. Bluffers of this type are little trouble to reform. A session or two of tail-chasing and they are ready to be good again. Only rarely will one of these bluffers need to be tripped and rolled on the ground. Very often when mounted by a competent horseman who understands just what they are up to and is determined to be on top when they come down, they will go quietly without even an attempt to rear.

A horse that will deliberately throw himself over backward in an attempt to crush his rider is a very, very rare animal. Almost every such genuine outlaw has a mental kink that makes him useless for any ordinary purpose. If not actually insane, he usually has been so thoroughly spoiled and has remained spoiled for so long that reforming him is almost hopeless—and it certainly is no job for an amateur. Even when such a deliberate killer can be reformed, the job is not worth the time, effort, and risk involved. The world is too full of good horses for any sensible horseman to bother with the task. Broncs of this type belong in cans. I have known only one exception to the rule—a beautiful, ordinarily gentle, registered Saddlebred brood mare. In some way that I never learned she had seriously injured a hip in a fall with a rider. After she had recovered, she would go stark crazy when anyone climbed on her back.

CHAPTER XXVI

Children and Ponies

Let us be horsemen first and riders
afterwards.
—M. F. McTaggart

I horsemanship, as in most other fields, young
people are the hope of the future. Indeed, I
sometimes think that they are the only ones whose minds a
serious horseman will find it worth his while to try to reach.
Older horsemen, usually quite settled in their ways, are rarely
interested in changing either their riding habits or their ideas.
Many are incapable of changing. For some, changing their riding
habits would involve rather severe physical effort, and they are
wiser not to bother. For others, it would necessitate scrapping
ideas to which they have clung for most of their lives—and that
is the severest strain of all. I care little whether experts agree
with me or approve of my ideas; I concede anyone the right to
disagree, for I know that there is more than one way to train a
horse, and I am content in the knowledge that the ideas which
I advocate work. But I regard teaching youngsters horsemanship
as a serious business worthy of anyone's best efforts.

As a rule, it calls forth one's best efforts; for while teaching
youngsters is enjoyable, it is by no means easy. It is not always
so simple to impart an explanation of correct principles without
diluting the ideas and thereby giving the pupils either an incom-
plete grasp of what you mean or a complete misunderstanding.
On the other hand, it is the easiest thing in the world to bore
the pupils and lose their interest with a detailed, involved lecture
that drifts far over their heads, leaving them only the impression
that the subject isn't worth listening to, even if they could under-

347

stand, because it is so "dry." A teacher may have several serious faults and still get good results in his teaching, but if he is dull, a bore, his efforts are hopeless.

Another aspect of teaching children that makes the job far from easy is that, after the pupils have progressed to a certain stage, they must have well-schooled mounts in order to continue to improve. This, of course, is true of adult riders too; but while it is reasonable to expect an adult to improve his own mount by intelligent schooling, this is often too much to expect of a youngster from eight to thirteen years of age. It is possible only when the child has a clear understanding of fundamentals, sufficient experience and self-confidence on horseback to put his knowledge into effect, and vigilant supervision to prevent him from making mistakes in his way of handling the individual pony he is mounted on. Lacking any of these factors, a child cannot progress steadily in skilled riding; and of the three factors— knowledge, experience that builds self-confidence, and intelligent supervision—I place supervision first in importance. Knowledge can be learned; time will impart experience; but, without close supervision, neither will come soon enough to prevent the child from first acquiring bad riding habits and letting his pony develop faults.

Many children, whose parents are glowingly proud of their offspring's ability, really know little more about horsemanship than the basic idea of merely "sticking on." This is not any child's fault; it is simply a reflection of the parents' lack of knowledge about horsemanship.

I do not subscribe to the idea that a child will naturally develop into a good horseman if he is merely "started young," allowed to "ride" almost as soon as he can walk. A child of less than seven or eight—and often older than that—cannot even *begin* to learn to ride. At best, the pony will simply carry him about pretty much as it pleases, with little regard for its young passenger's wishes. When there is a difference of opinion about which way to go, the pony can always win with ease. This sort of promenading about is quite all right and can be fun when the pony is amiable and quiet or as long as the child is content to be merely a passenger; but to think of it as riding or as being even remotely related to real riding is absurd. The first essential of riding is control of one's mount, and the source of real control is the rider's legs. Small children simply do not have the legs to achieve control— and giving them a whip as a substitute or teaching them to ride the reins is about the last thing a wise parent should want or permit.

The important thing is that a child should learn right, not that he should begin very young. Learning right, as I conceive it, consists primarily of absorbing the fundamentals of good horse-mastership before anything else. Preoccupation with acquiring a good seat, skill in applying the aids, developing balance and rhythm—these details should be of only secondary importance. For having a good seat, in spite of all that I have said about its importance, does not make a good horseman. A rider can have a perfect seat and yet be unfit to own a horse; he may be almost totally ignorant of how to care for his mount and callously indifferent to its welfare. Many quite skilled juvenile riders habitually abuse their mounts. Their roughness makes one's hands itch to tan their bottoms. True horsemastership is basically a state of mind. It is the first and the most important thing that an instructor should strive to inculcate in his pupils. Should he fail in achieving this first objective, he fails completely; for nothing else that he may be able to teach his pupils can substitute for this.

Parents who are not riders themselves—and many who are, though they fall short of being horsemen—are at a distinct disadvantage in choosing a riding instructor for their children. More often than not the proud parents pay through the nose for lessons without having the foggiest idea of the real qualifications of the charming instructors to teach horsemanship on sound principles. About the only way they can judge an instructor's ability is by observing how many of his young pupils win in shows—and, in my opinion, there is hardly a worse standard by which to judge. However, as long as winning in the ring, even if the competition is mediocre, is of paramount importance, that is the way the overwhelming majority of riding teachers will be rated. We Americans are so competitive that we just have to go out every weekend and try to beat somebody at something, even if it is at something that hardly matters.

What happens every year when our coaches of the United States Equestrian Teams go scouting for fresh talent? At various screening trials in different sections of the country the coaches test and evaluate hundreds of young hopefuls whose records put them at the top of the amateur heap. Yet a coach feels lucky if he finds a mere half-dozen riders who show enough promise to merit working with them further at team headquarters.

Bear in mind that the search is not for finished riders of Olympic caliber. It is just for riders who, with a lot of coaching and much more practise, *might* make the grade.

What kind of commentary is this on our teaching methods, our system of training that should produce our horsemen of tomorrow?

Certainly, there are thousands of young riders whose equestrian interests deviate from the U.S.E.T. and Olympic ideal. They ride stock horses, gaited horses, Arabians, Morgans and all grades in between. Many like endurance riding. Some play polo and other mounted games. A great majority are simply pleasure riders who enjoy the outdoors from the back of a horse.

However, there are several hundreds of thousands of young riders, and they are not all teenagers, whose chief interests are cross country riding over obstacles and show jumping. Many of them have been riding most of their lives, have parents who ride, and have been chasing ribbons since they were in lead-line and short-stirrup classes. They take riding seriously, as they understand riding. Some want to make horsemanship their lifework. They own the best horses they can afford and pay for the best professional help they think they can get.

With what results? With the results that when our Olympic team coaches comb the country from coast to coast and from Canada to Mexico, hopefully looking for prospects who might eventually make it on the international scene, they end up with a select few riders whose training and natural ability make them mere possibilities. The rest of these young hopefuls are not even worth a second look, and the majority don't even get past the screening trials.

How can anyone reflect on this without concluding that in a country the size of the United States, with all our wealth of horseflesh and our competitiveness, something must be lacking?

Somewhere, at the grass roots level, we are producing mere riders instead of horsemen.

The reason, it seems to me, is plainly evident. We pay lip service to the art of horsemanship, but we do not truly understand what that is. We are smugly satisfied to produce only show winners, mere silver collectors. We encourage our young riders to chase points. Winning in the ring, under the most artificial of standards, is our criterion of excellence.

Unfortunately, you just cannot produce skilled horsemen or truly trained horses that way. At best, you turn out mere unthinking robots and monotonously routined horses. The insidious ideal we hammer into our kids is not horsemanship but mere superficial appearance—the picture-book seat or, as Müseler calls it, the wooden-soldier seat.

One of the most accomplished young riders I have ever seen could never win a ribbon in a horsemanship or equitation class simply because she was not built right. A big, husky girl, perhaps a bit overweight, though a superb rider she looked like a lummox on horseback. After one glance, judges ignored her. Judges are not interested in equestrian finesse—but it is very important that a girl should be svelte and have her hair neatly styled.

Young riders do not formulate the artificial standards that dominate the show ring. Instead, they are the victims. The ones responsible for the phony standards are their elders—the rule makers, the judges, the trainers and coaches, and the unthinking parents; the very people who should know better. The kids merely conform, doing what they are told is right and necessary to win. In the chase for ribbons, the basic principles of true horsemanship are ignored.

If the kids don't rebel, as some do, in time they become the pontificating elders of the horse show world, firmly upholding and perpetuating the artificial standards which ruled their lives and aborted their horsemanship.

Probably the greatest asset a teacher of horsemanship can have is personal influence based on example. I do not mean that a good teacher must be a really first-class rider, though he certainly should be a good one; but he must consistently practice the principles of horsemastership which he professes to teach. This seems obvious, but the catch is in that word "consistently"; the teacher must never, in the presence of pupils, let his actions contradict his words. If, for example, he tells his youngsters that hitting a horse is wrong, he cannot ever afford, even under the most exasperating circumstances, to lose his own temper and make that mistake. If he would discourage them from wearing spurs, then he himself should not wear spurs. Even small children are quick to observe inconsistencies between the teacher's words and his actions, and it is his example that they are prone to follow rather than his advice.

For this reason the example set by a child's parents, if they too are riders, is of utmost importance. Parents can be an instructor's biggest obstacle to success, if the example they set goes contrary to the principles he is trying to instill in the child. Youngsters are more likely to mimic or imitate what their father does than

Plate 70. AN EXCELLENT TYPE OF CHILD'S PONY. His sire is a registered Welsh pony, his dam a crossbred Welsh-Arabian. This two-year-old stallion can carry a middleweight man, yet he has good saddle conformation, a virtue many children's ponies lack. Author's daughter Sheilagh up.

Photograph by the author

do as they are told to do. They are always ready with the retort, "But *you* do it."

Suitable mounts for small children are not always easy to find. Mere size, in my opinion, is one of the least important features to look for. Next to good temperament, I would look first for saddle conformation. A well-made pony or small horse that is a bit too tall for a small child to mount easily is much better than a smaller animal of draft-horse conformation such as is found too often among Shetland ponies. The pony that is built like a miniature draft horse will always be relatively "heavy" and rough-gaited; his bulging sides will be too awkwardly wide for the small

Plate 71. RIDING WITHOUT STIRRUPS. The author's daughter Dawn, on Mitzie, sits supple and loose to develop rhythm and "feel."

Photograph by D. Gjermundson

rider's legs, and he will probably always be rather insensitive to the aids. It is almost impossible to teach children to ride really well on mounts of this coarse type.

Certainly a child's pony should have a quiet, even temperament; but too often parents setting out to buy a pony confuse steadiness with sluggishness. Being mounted always on a lazy, insensitive slug will quickly ruin any youngster's riding habits. And who can blame the child, mounted on such a nag, if he wants to be allowed to "wake him up" with spurs or a quirt?

I do not believe that riding without stirrups is at all necessary to the development of a strong seat. The truly balanced seat depends on the rider's feet in the stirrups as the fulcrum of balance. Stirrupless riding, however, does help to develop rhythm and feel and suppleness, *if* the rider does not resort to grip to maintain his seat but lets his legs hang naturally, even rather loosely, and relies chiefly on balance. For children this is excellent training, but any tendency to depend chiefly on grip should be discouraged.

One of the most disheartening experiences for a youngster is to practice diligently for a show, do well in the ring, then see someone else win with an inferior display of riding—simply because the standards of riding which the child has been taught and the judge's standards differ. A sensible adult can shrug off such a defeat and forget it, but it hurts a child and, even worse, it confuses him. How can a parent or an instructor satisfactorily explain such a defeat? The more enthusiastic the child is about horsemanship, the bitterer is the disappointment.

This sort of thing makes it very unwise for fond parents to build up a child's hopes for success in the "show game." On the contrary, they should go out of their way to instill in the youngster's mind that he should expect defeat, take it as a matter of course, and to feel lucky if he wins instead of getting cocky about it. Children should learn to regard showing as a game; not as a serious business, a matter of life or death. Leave professionalism for the professionals. When riding becomes a serious business it too often ceases to be fun.

Parents who approve of having their children take the show game rather seriously should have the good sense to get the youngsters ponies of show-ring quality. It is almost impossible to win, or at least to win with any degree of consistency, otherwise. Though children's horsemanship classes are, in theory, judged on the riders' skill in handling their mounts, plenty of judges are influenced, sometimes perhaps unconsciously, by the ponies themselves. Most Western judges, I believe, favor the miniature Quarter Horse type of pony.

Parents who want their young hopefuls to make a habit of winning should be willing to pay for the type of pony that will catch the judges' eyes.

CHAPTER XXVII

A Last Word

I have wondered many times why it is, when-
ever I make a suggestion meant to help horses
by improving their condition, the very people I
have to fight every inch of the way against are
those who proclaim themselves "friends of the
horse."

—M. F. McTaggart

T HE wife of a well-known breeder of Thoroughbreds once asked an old-time Western friend
of mine, "Well, what *is* a Quarter Horse?"

"A Quarter Hoss, ma'am," replied the old-timer, "is a short-
winded, low-geared race hoss."

I had expected the old fellow to define a Quarter Horse, in
any one of several ways, as a cow horse, the ideal stock horse,
the kind of riding mount the old-timer himself had been raised
on. The more I thought over his definition, however, the more
clearly I realized that the old horseman was too often right; and
that he did not at all like the kind of horse he defined.

One might supplement his definition with the observation that
palominos, the so-called "Golden Ones," could more fittingly be
dubbed "the Silver Ones," judging by the amount of silverware
they are usually loaded down with in horse shows and in parades.

A magazine reader once inquired of the late Dick Halliday,
well-known Western horseman and one of the best authorities
on palominos, by what standards "silver classes" are judged.
Halliday replied: "I don't know by what standards 'silver' is
judged; but certainly not by any standards of common sense or
good taste." He then went on to describe a spectacle which he
termed "the height of human folly" and which he himself had
seen, the spectacle of three strong men straining to ease a silver-
mounted saddle onto the back of a palomino "draught horse,"
and then the rider, practically staggering under the weight of

silver decorating his own costume, mounting the horse from a stepladder.

These two incidents keynote the thesis of this chapter, that in our mania for speed and in our slavish craze for showiness, just plain showing off, as horsemen we have lost sight of true standards of horsemanship, of what makes a good horse good, of what a real riding horse should and must be. We are speed and show crazy; and for our craziness the Western stock horse, and all breeds of light horses, have suffered. We have let flossy appearance influence our taste in riding horses far more than practical utility. In general, how picturesque a horse looks is more important to the majority of present-day riders than what he can do.

Lieutenant Colonel William A. Ranck, writing in *The Western Horseman* of March–April, 1947, states that the stock horses of today are much inferior to the types of riding horses he knew in the West of his youth. "Good working saddle horses . . . were almost as common and plentiful as flies." And he gives some instances of these old-time horses' endurance and stamina which make the feats of our modern trail ride winners seem by comparison as difficult as prancing in a parade. Such instances could be multiplied, I believe, almost indefinitely.

It seems quite clear that within the past several decades our whole attitude toward the riding horse has changed. Note Colonel Ranck's phrase "good *working* saddle horses." Today, as a general rule, riding horses do not work. The vast majority of them are primarily pets, used for play and for show. Mechanization, of course, largely accounts for this changed status; but the fact stands out that this change has resulted in inferior, albeit more finely bred, horses—animals that simply cannot match the performances of their forebears.

For a "horrible example" of what can happen to a good breed we might consider first the American Saddle Horse. The Saddlebred originally was an all-round utility horse, like the Morgan, but he earned his good reputation chiefly under the saddle. He was bred and trained for easy riding qualities. Anyone who ever has ridden a good Saddlebred that was not artificialized for the show ring can attest to what superb riding qualities he has. Men used their Saddle Horses to go places. These horses were as "practical," and just about as tough, as can openers. But what a sad contrast is the American Saddle Horse of today! He is but a show-ring automaton that goes up-and-down almost as much as he goes forward, a miserable brute with a mutilated tail. Even surgery, apparently, cannot elevate the Saddle Horse's tail high enough to please the fancy; the common phrase "full of ginger" really means something to one who knows Saddlebreds. The horse's natural action is ludicrously exaggerated by means of boots, abnormally long hoofs, and toe weights. His extreme "animation," as the Saddle Horse fanciers euphemistically term it, is achieved chiefly by means of the whip.

Mr. Louis Taylor in his interesting book *The Horse America Made* states with aggressive repetitiveness that the American Saddle Horse has more strength pound for pound, more endurance, more stamina, more intelligence, in brief, more of everything, than any other breed, and needs no "artificial" tests like endurance rides to prove it. In fact, Mr. Taylor regards endurance rides as slightly amusing, suitable only for lesser breeds than his favorite. He then goes on to answer the question, "What is the practical value of horse shows and show stables?" His answer boils down to two ideas: first, that high prices "are in reality the backbone of the Saddle Horse breeding industry"; and, second, that show competition produces top horses at the peak of their performance and gives breeders and owners an ideal at which to aim.

Elsewhere in his book Mr. Taylor admits that show horses are untrained and impractical for regular riding use and that they do not, and should not be expected to, accommodate themselves to the average rider.

This book is published by the American Saddle Horse Breeders Association and was planned by and written with the encouragement of the directors of the association. So we may accept the ideas expressed as ex cathedra, and the "ideal" as accurate.

Can any man conceive of a more nonsensical, futile ideal than that of a riding horse whose entire training leaves him unfit for practical use, a horse that should not even be expected to accommodate himself to a rider? This, apparently, is the ideal of the American Saddle Horse Breeders Association; and though it may sound extreme, it is not a unique example of the misguided efforts to which American horsemen in general have gone and are going to get as far as possible from the fundamentals of true horsemanship, and incidentally to help deteriorate the breeds of light horses.

We are doing much the same thing to the Arabian. By breeding chiefly for show points and accepting victories in the ring as the criterion of excellence we are producing a surplus of Arabs that are good for almost nothing but showing. "Headhunters" breed horses with faces so freakishly dished the animals' breathing is seriously impaired—and stupid judges award such freaks blue ribbons. Without any testing for endurance, speed or general trainability, a horse can become a grand champion at halter, earn extravagant stud fees, and be sold for a fantastic price to produce offspring just like himself. Arabian "park horses" are no more than imitation Saddle Horses.

The owner of a well-known Arabian stud in the Rocky Mountain region customarily let even his best purebred Arab horses be used in ordinary ranch work. At high altitudes and in rough mountain country these horses proved that they could "take it." This seems to be so unusual that in every story about this stud which I have read the fact that these carefully bred Arabs could and did perform real work was always stressed. But why? For centuries the Arab has been the "work horse" of the desert.

But it is apparent to any intelligent observer that we are producing many prized Arabians that could never stand up to any real work. If some of them could, they never get a chance to prove it. Many of the finest Arabian horses that do prove their working ability—stock horses and endurance ride winners—would not stand a chance in a halter class. If they had "pinto markings," they couldn't even be registered as Arabians. The color fetishists make sure of that.

How many conformation hunters could stand up to a long day with hounds? Few such horses even get a chance to see a fox or a hound. Their show-happy owners consider them much too precious to run the risk of proving that they are what they're supposed to be—hunters. The animals are just beautiful pictures and the show ring is their frame.

The Thoroughbred has been bred for speed alone so long that good weight-carrying Thoroughbreds are rarer than stake winners. To produce heavyweight hunters with any consistency, breeders must infuse Cleveland Bay blood or cross with heavy draft stock such as the Percheron. More recently, hunter and jumper breeders have been crossing Thoroughbreds with the German Trakehner and with such massive German breeds as the Holsteiner, the Hanoverian, and the Westphalian horses. The idea is to get not only greater size but better soundness and more natural ability.

So great has been the craze among Thoroughbred breeders for speed that a race horse whose best distances are more than a mile and a quarter is considered a "stayer." Yet only a few generations ago three heats of four miles each, all run with only brief rests between heats, made up a real race. How many Thoroughbreds could do that today, without injury? At least, it would take a mature horse. But a five-year-old race horse today is considered "a veteran campaigner." The fashion now seems to be to race 'em at two, break 'em down at three.

If only sound, healthy horses were permitted to race—horses that could perform without the aid of medication and drugs—the entire industry would collapse. But that will never happen as long as "friends of the horse" have bankrolls to protect.

These examples may seem not to concern Western stock horse men or others who breed light horses for pleasure use and for sport; but they do. They are clear-cut examples of what to avoid— examples of mistakes which we are *not* avoiding.

Consider the Quarter Horse. He originated as a sprinter; speed is his essence. Yet there is hardly a Quarter Horse breeder who will not admit, or even brag, that the Quarter Horse is preeminently a cow horse, the best in the world, and that he won his reputation as such the hard way. But as a stock horse he should be able to work with ease carrying at least two hundred pounds, the approximate weight of an average man riding a typical stock saddle. What then is the point of racing Quarter Horses ridden by flyweight jockeys? Lack of weight in the saddle lets a horse run faster, but it does not otherwise prove a horse's quality.

On the contrary, handicapping positively encourages lack of quality. It serves to make a race more "even" in the same way that tying down a skillful boxer's left hand, in order to give his inferior opponent a chance to win, would make a boxing bout more "even." In other sporting contests we formulate rules for all contestants equally with the idea of letting the best man win. But we refuse to do it in horse racing for fear that this would relegate too many horses to the bonepile and thus "ruin the sport."

However, this idea is not necessarily true. Under a system requiring all horses in one race to carry equal weight, inferior animals would quickly prove their unfitness for Class A (i.e., heavyweight) competition, but they could still earn their oats running against competitors of equal quality in Class B (middleweight) or Class C (lightweight) events.

These inferior horses, however, would naturally prove to be unpopular as breeders, and the racing of colts could be, if not eliminated, at least discouraged. Is not this an obvious way to improve the Quarter Horse and the Thoroughbred?

If something of this sort is not eventually done, I believe, we shall certainly end up soon with a type of so-called Quarter Horse that will be utterly unfit either to carry weight or to work stock.

If this idea seems a bit farfetched, bear in mind that we already have three types of Quarter Horses: the racing type, many specimens of which are registered Thoroughbreds, judged solely on ability to sprint on a level track under very light weight; the old chunky bulldog type; and, finally, the popular show and pleasure type with so much Thoroughbred blood and refinement that he is a Quarter Horse in name only simply because he is registered as one. I have seen an alleged Quarter Horse, a jumper, registered, that was 17 hands tall.

Now just which of these three types is the true "Quarter Horse?"

Even this most popular American breed has suffered from the obstructionism and wrongheadedness of the color worshipers, who would have the world believe that a horse's merit should be judged by his pigmentation. Before a lawsuit forced AQHA directors to change the rules, a Quarter Horse of the finest breeding could not be registered if he had too much white—white markings above the knees or hocks or too much white on the face. But those who made the rules evaded the question: What does color have to do with a horse's quality? Some of the most illustrious names in Quarter Horse history—Little Joe, Old Fred, Joe Reed—got colts with "too much" white. That these colts were truly bred Quarter Horses and conformed to the standard in all other respects made no difference. The color fetishists rejected them for registration.

It is an irony of horse history that one of the greatest sires of quality Appaloosas was a Quarter Horse, Joker B. This horse was gloriously spotted, but as a Quarter Horse he was a freak. There was no way under the rules that he could be registered. A breeder of Appaloosas bought him at a ridiculously low price, and Joker B. became perhaps the most famous sire in Appaloosa history.

What, today, is a stock horse? Is he a horse suitable for use in actually working range stock or one that can put on an acrobatic, slide-Kelly-slide exhibition in the show ring? After attending shows, one familiar with range work can only wonder.

It seems self-evident that we horsemen have become slaves to artificial standards of our own creation, a condition which, as Colonel Ranck points out, has resulted in deterioration of all breeds of light horses. We are neglecting a prime requisite of all good saddle mounts for whatever purpose—endurance. Probably the prime example of our shortsightedness is the manner in which we have let the genuine Mustang become nearly extinct; indeed, we actually have helped him to extinction. He wasn't big enough and fancy-looking enough for us. So we ignored the fact that he was one of the hardiest, most enduring horses that ever trod grass. Unlike the South Americans, who have been wise enough to save and improve the Criollo, we let the Mustang virtually die out.

Why?

The answer to that "Why?" seems to be that we Americans no longer think of a riding horse as our forefathers did. They expected a horse to work; they bred him to work. As a result they produced, and enjoyed, animals worthy of kings. With a much more varied choice of breeding stock at our disposal, we are not doing as well. By setting up and slavishly adhering to artificial and unsound standards we are not producing the best possible riding horses.

Calling A Spade A Spade

SOME 30 years ago a hackamore and spade bit expert of the old Spanish California breed admitted to me:

"You know, the spade bit is mostly for show. We *Californios* love to show off. That's why we go in so heavily for the fancy knots, fine braided leather work and silver mounting which we like on our horse gear. We enjoy admiring our own shadows. A spade bit makes a horse put on a show. It isn't really necessary, or even the best bit."

This is the only time I have ever heard of a spade being called a spade by an acknowledged spade bit expert. I doubt that I'll live long enough to hear of its ever happening again. Few, if any, of his fellow experts would agree with this oldtimer, at least in public. On the contrary, they would have us believe that the spade is the ultimate of perfection in bits.

In a way, I believe it is, but not in the way they mean. Omitting freak contraptions with studded spikes and so forth, the spade bit is, in my opinion, a perfect example of what a good bit should not be. The fact that some men, by dint of great patience and care, may achieve good results with it does not cancel out the fact that the spade bit is fundamentally and absolutely wrong in design and in operation.

I realize that in publicizing this idea I may be stirring up a dozen hornet nests, but until someone can convince me I'm wrong, I'll stick to my guns. My opinion is not based on emotion; I'll leave the question of the humaneness of the spade bit, as well as the anti-cruelty lecturing, to others. My conviction is based entirely on the spade bit's design and effect.

A Stock Horse should stop on his hind legs, with neck flexed at the poll, lower jaw relaxed and softly yielding, and nose tucked in. But I have yet to see a spade bit horse ever do this properly from a fast run. True, I have seen some stop as though shot; I've seen some stop on their hind legs. But true lightness was always lacking; the flexed neck, relaxed jaw and tucked in nose with proper head carriage were conspicuous by their absence. Furthermore, I have yet to see a spade bit horse perform a quick stop of any kind *with a calm eye*, the kind of placid, unworried expression you can see in the eyes of a well-handled cutting horse or jumping horse or dressage horse even in moments of extremely fast action. If you don't think a calm eye is important and very revealing, you have a lot more thinking to do.

I consider it utterly illogical even to expect a horse to work at speed with neck flexed, jaw relaxed and nose tucked in, while wearing a bit that is designed to act upon the sensitive roof of his mouth and thereby tends to urge him into thrusting his nose out and raising his head. And herein, I believe, lies the spade bit's inherent fault. It is simply *wrongly designed.* I believe, without exception, that any spade bit horse which even approximates a balanced, collected quick stop from a run flexes because he was taught to do so in the hackamore or snaffle. He flexes *in spite of* the spade bit in his mouth, never because of it; for by its inherent action the spade tends to make him poke his nose up and out.

A Californian, who disagrees with almost everything I say here, objects to this statement: "You imply that good spade bit riders *pull* on the reins. They do not. Pulling is done on the hackamore. Expert vaqueros merely raise, lower and move their bridle hands left or right, without pulling at all."

Well, if this is true, why do they use spade bits? Why do they insist that the spade is the bit par excellent? Why shove a couple of pounds or more of metal into a horse's mouth when, if they actually ride with reins always slack, these feathery-fingered wizards could get the same, or better, results using a light curb or plain snaffle? And if they cannot get the same, or better, results with a light curb or snaffle, *why not*—if they never pull on the bit? It seems downright silly to champion one of the severest bits ever designed, if one never exerts even the slightest direct tension on the reins.

However, Wallace Reames, writing in the January–February 1947 WESTERN HORSEMAN, states:

"The first thing I learned about a spade bit was to set the spade so that it lined up with the back of the holes to which the headstall is affixed. This is done by . . . bending the spade back with a monkey wrench . . . I also . . . bent the copper-tipped spade back to further reduce the danger of tearing the roof of the horse's mouth in case he fell and caught the bit on the ground."

Now if the spade bit is the "scientific" precision instrument its advocates claim it is, why must it be altered with a monkey wrench before it's fit to be properly used? It is interesting to wonder how many users of spade bits know that their "scientific" instruments should be thus altered before use. How many use them just as they buy them?

Let's examine the action of the spade bit and see why it is fundamentally wrong.

When the reins are tightened, the cross-bar of the bit presses on the bars of the horse's lower jaw, as in ordinary curb bit action. If more tension is exerted on the reins, the spade presses upward against the roof of the horse's mouth. This additional leverage increases the pressure on the bars of the lower jaw exerted by means of the curb strap or chain.

In theory, the horse responds by flexing at the poll and yielding his jaw to the rider's hand. Actually, however, the spade pressing against the sensitive roof of the mouth urges the horse *not* to flex; instead of tucking in his nose, the horse instinctively raises his head to avoid the upward pressure of the spade against the roof of the mouth. No one who has carefully observed spade bit horses in action, especially fast action, can honestly deny this.

Let us suppose, however, that a horse is so "velvet mouthed" that he responds instantly to the lightest pressure exerted by the curb strap, yielding his jaw to the rider's hand even before the spade becomes effective against the roof of the mouth. Then the action of the bit ceases to be the action of a spade bit; it is the action of an ordinary curb bit. The spade principle is ineffective and the spoon is just so much excess metal in the horse's mouth.

But, you may be wondering, what if the horse is not so velvet mouthed and does not respond until the spade, even when bent backward as Wallace Reames mentions, does take effect against the roof of the mouth? Well, then, alas, the horse simply does not have the supermouth that spade bit advocates boast their horses always have.

In other words, we see, either the horse yields immediately to the leverage exerted by the curb strap or the spoon forces him to yield. But the moment force enters the picture all thought of true lightness must vanish. This brings us to the spade bit's fundamental, inherent principle—the achievement of lightness by force. It simply cannot be done. The two cancel each other out.

What happens when a horse is ridden in a spade bit without a curb strap or chain? Will a horse with a velvet mouth tuck his nose in then? At a standstill or at a slow parade pace, if his rider is very good, he might; but he will never flex at the poll because of the bit in his mouth. If he flexes at all, it's because he has been taught to do so, he has acquired what trainers call a "proper head set," during the hackamore stage of his training, just as American Saddle Horse colts acquire a set head carriage during the bitting rig stage of their schooling without ever really learning to flex at all. The moment, however, a spade bit horse is called on to produce some fast action entailing quick stops and spinning turns, all semblance of flexion and true lightness vanishes; then we see the elevated head, the thrust up nose, the open mouth, accompanied usually by a wild-eyed expression that speaks volumes.

Belief in the efficacy of the spade bit as a scientifically designed precision instrument is based squarely on wrong thinking. Spade bit advocates almost invariably think in terms of light hands; they seem utterly incapable of understanding that lightness of the rider's hands is NOT identical with lightness of the horse. Thus, they handle, or try to handle, their reins gently, but that does not mean that the pressure they exert on the horse's mouth by means of the spade bit is therefore also gentle. If you use a curb bit with shanks 12 inches long, you surely could ride with "light hands"; but how light would the pressure on the horse's bars be?

Good spade bit riders do have light hands; but that does not mean that their horses are light, flexed at the poll and with softly yielding, relaxed lower jaws. It is a mistake to think the two are the same, or even must always necessarily go together. Anyone who rides with slack reins has light hands; it does not follow that his horse is light. I have been asked more than once to try horses which, I was told, had "marvelous mouths," only to discover that they had no mouths at all. Their proud owners meant, without knowing it, that the animals were merely easy to stop. But a green colt whose mouth is nonexistent can be easily and quickly stopped, or even pulled over backward. His mouth is sensitive, not light. A light mouth must be *made*.

An excellent example of how spade bit riders think was illustrated by Ralph Irving, in the May–June 1948 WESTERN HORSEMAN. Extolling the spade bit as the one and only ideal bit, Irving wrote:

The spade bit "contacts a greater number of nerves as well as nerves of higher sensitivity, especially those in the roof of the mouth, making a stronger telegraphic union between the touch of the reins on one side and the horse's brain on the other, thereby amplifying and rendering more acute the directing signals of the rider. *The purpose and effect is to reduce the force of the pull on the reins for the same result;* and severity is not the standard by which to judge the good of the spade bit . . . regardless of any opinion to the contrary." (The italics are Irving's, not mine.)

Politely overlooking Mr. Irving's typical spade bit fanatic's disregard for "any opinion to the contrary," we see here some hint that spade bit riders do pull on the reins, and clear proof that the author is thinking in terms of light hands instead of in terms of lightness of the horse's jaw. The spade bit results in "*a stronger* telegraphic union," it "amplifies" and "renders more acute" the rider's signals; the sole purpose "is to reduce the force of the pull on the reins."

In other words, says Mr. Irving, the more leverage a spade bit gives you, the more lightly you can handle the reins, which is correct, as far as it goes. But this is NOT the correct way to think about reducing rein pull. The correct way to do that is to work toward increasing the horse's lightness, responsiveness, not by increasing leverage. This lightness is achieved not merely by means of the hands on the reins but mainly by proper use of the rider's legs.

Proper use of the legs to the average spade bit rider seems to be one of life's most baffling mysteries. I don't think I have ever seen a spade bit man who did not sit well back against the cantle with his lower legs well ahead of the vertical, a position in which it is impossible to use the legs efficiently as a means of driving a horse up into his bridle. No one who rides a horse in this manner can really understand what lightness means or how it is achieved. This is the typical seat of those who labor under the delusion that they can collect a horse by pulling on the bit, instead of driving the horse forward against the bit.

Elsewhere in the same article in which he extols the wonders of the spade bit, Mr. Irving objects to those who criticize a vaquero's wicked-looking roweled spurs. These, says Mr. Irving, are merely a vaquero's "persuaders"; he uses them judiciously because when he does "grab" a horse with those hooks he wants the lucky animal to "jump out of his skin."

Any horseman who understands what true lightness is does not have to read these ideas twice to realize at once that neither Irving nor his imaginary ideal vaquero has the faintest idea of what it is. A horse truly light in hand does not have to be "grabbed" with any gut-hooks to be made to "jump out of his skin." On the contrary, he will "work in the wind of the boot."

Yet this kind of reasoning is typical of the spade bit rider, who can talk so fluently about training a horse carefully and gently. If gentleness is the aim, why the spade bit and the Spanish style roweled spurs? It would be difficult to believe that a gent toting a submachine gun was merely hunting for sparrows, or for peace.

To an impartial observer with no axe to grind, it seems evident that Mr. Irving's type of vaquero relies on the spade bit and on his "persuaders" because he simply does not know any better. The American West has probably never produced a more enthusiastic proponent of the Spanish-Mexican style of horsemanship than the late Dick Halliday. Yet even Halliday admitted, publicly, in print, that misuse and abuse of the spur was probably "the blackest blot" on Spanish horsemanship. But he did like the spade, though he preferred the halfbreed spade. With either bit, he assured me, he could "keep a horse in my lap." Could one find a clearer illustration of the typical spade bit man's wrong thinking whereby one naively believes he can make a horse light by pulling the bit back to the horse?

The highest standard by which to judge the "velvetiness" of a horse's mouth is the simplest, most elementary: How lightly does he respond to the pressure of a plain snaffle or straight bar bit adjusted so that it bears directly on the bars of the lower jaw? This is the true test, and here is why:

The leverage exerted by a curb bit multiplies the pressure which the rider applies to the reins. A spade bit, when the spoon comes into play against the roof of the mouth, does this even more than the usual type of curb bit. To illustrate, suppose a rider applies a one-ounce pull on his reins. With an ordinary

curb bit this may result in, say, five ounces of pressure on the
bars of the horse's jaw. With a spade bit this pressure may be
twice that much, say ten ounces. But with a straight bar bit or
a snaffle, a one-ounce pull on the reins, being direct, without
curb leverage, results in one ounce of pressure on the bars of the
mouth.

Thus it is easy to see how a spade bit rider, and a curb bit
rider to a lesser extent, can delude himself into overestimating
the "softness" of his horse's mouth. He is applying more pressure
to the bars of the mouth than he may think he is; and just how
much more it is difficult, if not altogether impossible, to guess.
So test your horse's mouth with a straight bar bit or a snaffle.
You may be surprised.[1]

It makes no difference what type of bit you usually work your
horse in. The leverage of the curb can fool you, start you thinking
deceptively, as spade bit advocates do, merely in terms of "light
hands." Learn to think in terms of lightness of the horse. Achieve
that and you simply cannot avoid light hands.

Advocates of the spade bit like to point out how slowly and
carefully old-time vaqueros proceeded with a colt; in their world
of *mañana* those old boys had all the time there was. Well, with
their system of doing things the hard way, they needed it. But
if other men using other methods could get better results in less
time, it is rather difficult to understand how or why those old-
time vaqueros and their modern counterparts can qualify, as one
writer recently described them, as the world's "peerless" horsemen.

That is a rather sweeping statement, quite typical of the bashful
spade bit boys, to which other horsemen the world over might
find a couple of answers.

[1]At one of my recent horsemanship clinics a young woman rode into the ring
on a breedy, high-strung 5-year-old that, in Mr. Irving's apt phrase, appeared to be
ready to "jump out of his skin." Even with the aid of a very severe curb bit—
designed by a famous stop-'em-on-a-dime trainer of the No Coddling School—the
rider could hardly control her mount. Calling her to the center of the ring, I told
the woman frankly: "Your horse is hardly green broke. He has no mouth. That bit
you are using is much too severe for him."

Irked by my bluntness, she wanted to argue with me. I cut that short by suggesting
that she show me what her horse could do in a snaffle bridle. The result came close
to being disastrous. The instant the horse realized that he was free of the powerful,
painful curb bit he promptly ran away, stampeding around and around the ring at
top speed before we got him cornered and stopped. The rider was more than surprised; she was scared speechless.

Whether she continued to rely on her severe bit or had sense enough to reschool
the young horse from scratch I do not know.

Recently a California writer stated that the spade bit expert's standards are "so high" that a man can feel lucky if he produces even two top "reined horses" in his lifetime. No doubt this is true; indeed, it might well be considered semi-miraculous if any man ever produced even one top horse by means of the crude tools and methods spade bit wizards prefer. But to simpler folk, who have no hankering to do things the hardest way, this sounds like sheer nonsense.

Other horsemen the world over take it for granted and act on the assumption that careful schooling will make a good mount of any average horse, and that if a colt has particularly good disposition and conformation (as thousands do have) he can be made excellent, while a superior colt can hardly miss being tops if his trainer has the skill to carry him that far. So one might wonder whether the California writer was expressing an attitude not based on extraordinarily high standards but stemming from the difficult job of trying to accomplish ordinarily simple things by means of impossible tools and methods.

I doubt if even a spade bit wizard would argue against the obvious fact that no Stock Horse ever foaled needs a better mouth or lighter all around responsiveness to the aids than a good dressage or high school mount. In fact, as Dr. Charles O. Williamson has pointed out, a Stock Horse is fundamentally just a high school horse in the elementary stage of training. But did ever any expert in this advanced branch of riding maintain that he'd be lucky to turn out two top horses in a whole lifetime?

It is curious, too, why experts in advanced dressage, the most exacting form of horsemanship, have never had the wit to recognize the excellence of the spade bit system of making a "reined horse." Are all these master riders, who have usually devoted their entire lives to the study of horsemanship, wrong in having long ago discarded the severe bits of their early predecessors, bits similar to the spade bit? Are they really ignorant of their own art, or simply stupid, while illiterate old-time vaqueros long ago acquired a monopoly of all horse training science and wisdom? The answer is *yes*, to hear the spade bit fanatics tell it.

And if the wizard happens to be a Californian, he is usually very careful to distinguish between a "California reined horse" and a mere Mexican or Nevadan horse trained in exactly the same way. Just what differences there may be only a real *Californio* can tell you. But even Dick Halliday could not tell me; he said there wasn't any difference.

Whenever the subject of spade bit training comes up someone is sure to mention Red Fox. Here, indeed, was a "California reined horse" second to none. The Fox was an exceptional horse, a "natural" with lightning reflexes. With his record, he couldn't have been otherwise. But, though there is no way to prove it now, I say, without any *ifs* or *buts*, the Fox was excellent in spite of the spade bit, not because of it, and I believe he would have been even better without it. The trainer, not the bit, makes the horse, and a skilled trainer can accomplish more even with poor tools than a dub can with the best equipment, a fact few spade bit advocates seem able to grasp.

I have said that my ideas here are not based on emotion aroused by notions of inhumaneness or cruelty. They are based, I believe, on hard facts. However, just to check my own observations and conclusions, I have asked several widely experienced Western horsemen this question:

"Have you ever seen a spade bit horse do a quick stop from a fast run with neck flexed, nose tucked in and lower jaw relaxed?"

Every horseman who replied answered, "No." Some of them, for wise professional reasons, refused to be quoted. But three of them were brave enough to speak right out for the enlightenment of any spade bit expert who wants to take issue.

Dr. Charles O. Williamson, who needs no introduction, says:

"No, I never saw a spade bit horse stop with his neck flexed; furthermore, most of them stop on their front feet. But the hombres who ride and make them will tell you that they do not need to stop with their necks flexed. It will not do you any good to quote James Fillis or any other fine horseman, either. The spade bit boys think they are the finest horsemen in the world, and do not know that any good high school rider can pull the bridle off his horse and have him do, on legs.alone, anything their horses can do. When you show them, they think you have taught the horse like you teach a circus horse to do a stunt."

E. C. Cleveland, U.S. Customs Agent at Nogales, Ariz., a former mounted inspector who has ridden the ranges from Canada to Old Mexico, a horseman of wide knowledge, varied experience and keen observation, answers:

"No, I have never seen a spade bit horse stop with neck flexed and lower jaw relaxed. Furthermore, I do not expect ever to see it. A spade bit horse is *broken*, not trained. He will stop quickly, no doubt about that; but he performs the stop as if slugged on the nose with a baseball bat, and for essentially the same reason.

He learns to do a quick stop not as a result of intelligent, patient training by a rider using a bit adequate for control and designed for comfort, but as a result of being worked in a bit especially constructed to *force* him to stop or suffer excruciating pain.

"I have yet to see a spade bit horse that looked as if he enjoyed being ridden, that was properly collected and yet at ease, and that seemed to have confidence in his rider. But I have seen many colts shrink to skin and bones on their first roundup because they were unable to graze with their mouths torn by spade bits. For me, a spade bit horse is forever spoiled. He will never forget the spade, he can never be fully trusted.[2]

"I believe spade bit men are just as humane and kindhearted as other horsemen; they just don't realize, it seems, that even with the best of intentions they can hardly avoid hurting their horses' mouths with a spade bit. The bit is entirely wrong in design. The spoon is a constant irritant to the mouth and makes a horse fretful regardless of the rider's intentions."

Ward W. Wells, the well-known exhibition dressage rider whose high school horses Sharik and Sharik's Son are known to thousands of horse show spectators, has this to say:

"There is nothing accomplished by the spade bit that can't be better accomplished by a mild curb bit with a straight or low port mouthpiece. Horsemen that resort to the spade bit are working on the wrong end of the horse. A flexed jaw is not accomplished by 'pulling' the mouth open but by a light fingering of the reins. The horse is taught to stop by leg pressure coordinated with a fixed hand, not by pulling back. My Arabian stallion Sharik will make square sliding stops and spinning pivots on the hocks without a bridle.

"I attend many horse shows every year and I have yet to see a Stock Horse class in which a rider using a spade bit has made a sliding stop without the horse's nose high and the mouth open. The spade bit is not suitable for really high class riding."

These statements are just other ways of expressing the main idea of this article: the spade bit is absolutely and inherently wrong in design and operation. Until someone convinces me of the contrary, the imported Mexican spade bit that decorates my mantle will remain there, for show purposes only.

---

[2]While this last sentence may be taken as a personal opinion, it is significant that Red Fox, according to men who knew him, was anything but an affectionate pet. He was a rather cranky horse with a penchant for kicking.

Index

Aids, importance of diminishing the: 329
American Horse Shows Association: 236
American Remount Association: 180
American Saddle Horse: merits of, 56; artificiality of showing, 356–57; Breeders Association, 357
Anglo-Arabs: 38
Appaloosas: 28ff.
Arabians: prejudice against, 31ff.; as Western mounts, 33ff.; types of, 43; as working horses, 358; breeding only for show, 358
Archimedes: 234
Asmis, Carl H.: 43

Balance, improving horse's: 142, 298–99
Balanced Seat: 185ff.; errors in thinking about the, 216–17
Baldy: 42n.
Battell, Colonel Joseph: 45
Battlewagon: 69

Beloved Belinda: 57
Bertha Skillful: 64
Beudant, Captain E.: 307n.
Bit: training, 88, 166–67; mouthing, 89–90; putting tongue over the, 169; disadvantages of using a severe, 234–35; spade, 236ff., 362–71; Pelham, 238–39; correct length of cheeks of, 248; reaching for the, 276, 279–80; behind the, 344
Black Elk: 50
Blistering: 163ff.
Body rope: 124
Bolting, drastic cure of: 107
Bridles, adjustment of: 325–26
Bronc-busting: 4ff.

"Calling a Spade a Spade": 236, 362–71
Canter: scrambled, 74; teaching a slow, 303
Caprilli, Captain Frederico: 217, 271
Cavalletti: 270ff.

Cavesson, training: 86, 128ff.
Chamberlin, General Harry D.:
    92, 93, 218, 238
Children: teaching, 347ff.; impor-
    tance of teacher's example with,
    351; suitable ponies for, 352;
    show riding by, 354
Cleveland, Edmund C.: 50, 370
Cobb, Lyle H.: 66
Cobb's King Gold: 66
Cody, "Buffalo Bill": 189
Coolidge, Dane: 209
Collection: based on reaching for
    the bit, 280–81; false, 321; not
    identical with lightness, 321–24;
    influenced by conformation,
    324; inseparable from impul-
    sion, 325; delicacy of achieving
    true, 329
Corky: 65
Corral, schooling: 84, 85
Cruiser: 14

Dawkins, Joe: 33, 34, 42
Dobie, J. Frank: 33n., 42n.

Ellestad, Ed: 224
Experience, equestrian: 74ff.

Farana: 41, 42, 254
Ferras: 30
Figure 8, teaching the: 291ff.
Fillis, James: 307n., 370
Flexions: at poll, 327–28; lateral,
    305ff.; taught on foot, 327n.
Forehand, turns on: 170
Forward Seat: see Balanced Seat
Fullmer, R.: 46

Gaits: definition of, 301; stabiliz-
    ing the, 302; characteristics of

good, 304; correcting traversed,
    308ff.
Galvayne, "Professor": 17, 18
German breeds: 358
Glad Polly: 69
Goodenough, R. A.: 14
Grand Slam: 57, 58
Gravity, horse's center of: 196ff.
Grip: 199ff.
Grisone, Frederico: 235
Ground driving: 147ff., 170ff.

Hackamores: 86
Haines, Francis B.: 30
Halliday, Dick: 238, 355, 367, 369
Halterbreaking: 122ff.
Hands, coming back to the: 296ff.
Harper, J. D. ("Monty"): 219
Hayes, Captain M. Horace: 8, 10,
    14ff., 113
Head-set: fetish of low, 42n.; as re-
    sult, not cause, of collection, 324
Hidalgo: 51
Hock, turns on: 331ff.
Hopkins, Frank T.: 50, 51, 189
Horse: improving the clumsy,
    261–62; the school, 261; the
    spoiled, 337ff.
Horsemen: bigotry of, 12; myth of
    "born," 71; traits of skilled,
    72ff.; clannishness of, 77
Horse-tamers, old-time: 8ff.

Institute of the Horse: 81
Irving, Ralph: 366–67

James, Will: 187
Jeffers, Claude: 187
Joe Reed: 360
Joker B.: 361
Jones, Mrs. K. W.: 66
Justin Morgan: 27, 46, 47

Kicking, cure of: 107
King Cortez: 24

La Broue: 235
Leads: taking correct, 311ff.; teaching change of, 313ff.
Leg pressure: *see* grip
Legs: obedience to, 94, 170, 289, 292ff.; use of, in halting, 285
Leon, "Professor": 17ff.
Little Joe: 360
Longeing: 125ff.
Longe line: 86

McTaggart, Lieutenant Colonel M. F.: 75, 76, 103
Magner, Dennis: 6, 10, 14, 15
Martingales: running, 240; *see also* tiedowns
"Mastery": 99
Memory, excellence of horses': 106
Millerick Circle M Ranch: 66
Morgans: 43ff.
Mouth: common misconceptions about a good, 250ff.; reactions of a poor, 251–52; the educated, 256ff.
Müseler, Wilhelm: 351
Mustangs: 48ff., 361

Neckreining: 317–18
Newcastle, Duke of: 235

Offutt, Denton: 14
Old Fred: 360
Olympic Three-Day Event: 260
Osborne, Charles E., Jr.: 248n.
Osburn, Sydney: 17
Owners, unscrupulous: 79, 80

Pace: definition of, 301–302; stabilizing, 302
Palominos: 355–56
Parks, Dr. C. D.: 47, 48
Pat W.: 69
Peckinpah, Robert L.: 30
Pignatelli: 235
Pike, Zebulon: 52
"Plowlining": *see* rein effects
Points of the Horse: 14
Ponies: *see* children, suitable ponies for
Post Exchange: 68
Powers, Charles: 62
Privett, "Booger Red": 187

Quarter Horses: types of, 49, 54, 360; improving, 359

Raffles: 39
Ranck, Colonel William A.: 356, 360
Rarey, John S.: 14, 15
Raswan, Carl R.: 43
Reames, Wallace: 364
Rearing, causes of: 341ff.
Red Eagle: 30
Red Fox 370, 371n.
Rein effects: 39ff.
Reining back, first lesson in: 173–74
Reins: side, 174–75; holding double, 246ff.
Riders: one-horse, 75; timid, 345
Rockwell, "Professor": 10, 16
Ross, J. King: 14

Saddlebreds: *see* American Saddle Horse
Saddles: suitable training, 90, 91; faults of stock, 90, 209ff.
Saddling colts: 145ff.

Sample, "Professor": 10, 15ff.
Schooling: common errors in,
    97ff.; opposing concepts of,
    101ff.
Set and turn: *see* turns on hocks
Sharik: 371
Shelibe: 42
Side-step: 330
Sky Tot: 68
Smith, Erwin: 209
Smith, Mark: 42
Spanish Riding School: 132, 237
Spurs: 91ff.
Stable management: 160ff.
Stanley, King: 51
Stevens, Montague: 12, 13
Stirrups,riding without: 353
Stryker, John A.: 42n.

Tail-rope: 122
Taylor, Louis: 45, 357
Thoroughbreds: as stock horses,
    25; bad temper in, 109; modern
    and earlier types of, 358–59; im-
    proving modern, 359
Thompson, Claude J.: 30
Thompson, James R.: 34

Tidbits, feeding: 272n.
Tiedowns: 229ff.
Transitions: 300–301
Trip-rope, running W: 338ff.
Turns on the hocks: 331

United States Morgan Horse
    Farm: 45
United States Mounted Cup en-
    durance rides: 180–81

War Dictator: 64
War Instigator: 64
Wells, Ward W.: 371
Western horses, modern: 22ff.
Weymouth bridle: 90, 240ff.
Whip: use and types of, 286ff.,
    290; for longeing, 88, 131ff.;
    children's use of, 353
"Whoa," importance of command:
    117
Williamson, Charles O.: 369–70
Wing Commander: 56

Xenophon: 8, 72